AN ANNUAL AFFAIR

First published in the United Kingdom in 2024 by

Dewi Lewis Publishing
8, Broomfield Road, Heaton Moor
Stockport SK4 4ND, England
www.dewilewis.com

ISBN: 978-1-9169915-08-4

Design: Dewi Lewis Publishing
Print: EBS, Verona, Italy

www.homersykes.com

AN ANNUAL AFFAIR

Some Traditional British Calendar Customs

Homer Sykes

dewi lewis publishing

For my grandchildren
Margot Juliet Clark
Kenny Homer Clark
Dorothy Putler Sykes

INTRODUCTION

Late one evening in the early 1970s I was driving back from Somerset and needed a break. I turned off the 'A' road to look for a village pub and after a couple of miles I came across one. Back in the bar, I was the only customer, I ordered half a pint. While making small talk to the publican I looked at the framed old black and white photographs on the wall and one caught my eye – it was a group of men, one man standing at the head of the table wearing a strange looking tall hat. I asked him about the photograph. Mournful and sucking on his cigarette, he responded "it's the Duck Feast… it takes place once a year."

As I drove away, I made a mental note of the name of the pub and the village, intending to phone them in the morning. Within five minutes I had completely forgotten what I had hoped to remember and over the years I often wondered where I was that night.

Thirty years later I was driving back from Somerset after a long day and, for reasons best known to itself, my satnav decided to take me off the main road and across country. I wanted a break and stopped at The Charlton Cat in Charlton St Peter. As I pulled into the car park I was sure I had been there before. The pub interior was brand spanking new and the publican said he had only been running it for a couple of weeks and was obviously very proud of the new polished pine bar and fittings. As I stood there it dawned on me that this might be the pub I had visited all those years ago. Back in the bar I asked if there was a feast, a special meal, a gathering of local farmers from the village or anything similar that happened in the pub. He looked at me, surprised, and said " Well yes, one of the farmers had phoned only a few days ago and said they would be up as usual on the first Monday in June for the Duck Feast." I asked what it was all about, he didn't know, but said it was an annual affair; local farmers would be getting together for a meal. I asked for the farmer's contact details and this time I wrote it all down. Two weeks later I may well have been the only photographer to make photographs of that annual celebration since the 1940s photograph I had noticed on the wall over thirty years previously.

In 1968 I was at college in London studying photography and the first year's Easter holiday project was to go and take some photographs. I always spent my lunch hour walking the streets of the Elephant and Castle learning how to make street photography, or in the library looking through magazines and working out why some photographs worked and others didn't. In one magazine I came across a photograph of the Bacup Coconut Dancers that took place every Easter Saturday and thought it would be interesting to visit and photograph. I was curious. I had never been up north and that Easter I photographed the Bacup Coconut Dancers in colour.

In that first year at college, I became enamoured of the work by the Swiss American photographer Robert Frank. I read *Creative Camera* magazine in which the editor, Bill Jay, had introduced readers to Frank's book *The Americans*. During the summer holidays of 1969, I worked as a janitor in New Jersey and on July 9th I visited the Museum of Modern Art in New York. For the first time I saw photography as art hanging on the walls – Henri Cartier-Bresson, Garry Winogrand, Burk Uzzle, Robert Frank, Bruce Davidson. It was an epiphany. I thought, I can do that. I would restart the project that I had begun on traditional folklore customs that took place once a year. But as serious photographers worked in monochrome not colour in those days, I would reshoot in black and white. When I returned home, and back at college I made the change.

The Photography Study Centre at the Institute of Contemporary Arts in London was newly opened and in 1971, Bill Jay exhibited my work along with that of Sir Benjamin Stone (1838-1914). This was Bill's first show at the gallery and my first exhibition, it was entitled Festival Customs and Pageants. My photographs were in black and white. A year later I was the youngest photographer included in *Personal Views 1850-1970*, a British Council touring exhibition. Other British photographers included Sir Cecil Beaton, Ian Berry, Bill Brandt, George Davidson, Roger Fenton, Bert Hardy, Thurston Hopkins, David Hurn, Paul Martin, Tony Ray-Jones, George Roger, Sir Benjamin Stone, John Thomson and Patrick Ward. That same year, Sue Davies gave me a show at the recently opened Photographers Gallery in London: *Four Young Photographers*. We were Dinah, Chris Killip, Stephen Shore and myself. *Once A Year, Some Traditional British Customs* was published in 1977. It was one of the first photography books by a young British photographer to be published in Britain.

Through the mid 1970s, 80s and early 1990s, I was a busy editorial photographer shooting for the weekend colour supplements and also shooting news features covering the politics of the day for *Newsweek* magazine in America. I worked with Viva, my agents in Paris, and Woody Camp, an agent in New York. In England I looked after my own business interests for the most part. The work from *Once A Year* was put on the back burner, forgotten by all apart from myself and the curator, writer and photographic historian, Val Williams. A major photographic exhibition, *How We Are: Photographing Britain*, curated by Val and Susan Bright opened at Tate Britain in 2007. *Once A Year, Some Traditional British Customs* was beginning to be rediscovered.

When the digital era arrived in the late 1990s, the independent editorial photography business was turned upside down almost overnight. The freelance landscape completely changed and those first years of the new millennium were bleak. Wanting to start work on a new project, I decided that I would revisit the annual traditional folk customs I had photographed in the early 1970s to see what had changed — perhaps do a 'then and now'. I photographed several and knew almost immediately that it wasn't going to work. Firstly because too often I was repeating myself and to make matters worse there were now so many other photographers, amateur photographers and phone camera users. If I wanted to start a new project about traditional annual events I realised that I would have to find subjects that I had not documented in the past.

While researching *An Annual Affair*, I came across mentions of various Friendly Society Club Walk Days. I made contact with the organisers of one in South Harting in West Sussex, sixty miles south of London. As I made arrangements to attend and buy a ticket for the men-only lunch, I asked if anything else happened in addition to the parade and church service that day. Hesitantly I was told "Well, we go out at dawn and cut green beech tree boughs from the Warren and drag them into the village to decorate the church and some old houses. We also plant one at the bottom of the village which we later parade around." Surely this couldn't be a throwback to some pre Christian pagan tree worship ritual? Perhaps inherited from the days when the Harting Old Club Friendly Society was formed in the early 1800s.

In Somerset I came across a Harvest Home celebration started by Archdeacon George Denison and the church warden John Higgs in 1857. They decided that after the harvest had been gathered in, September 3rd should be a holiday for all the agricultural workers in their community. The villagers still keep that tradition alive, although now it is held in late August, when as many as 500 people attend a marquee luncheon. Women take part in a Parade of Christmas Puddings through the village, while a group of men carry a 100lb block of Cheddar cheese and a six foot loaf of bread to the marquee. The Vicar blesses the cheese, speeches are made, and below the top table it appears that enough bread is provided for the feeding of 5,000.

I was giving a talk about my work in Aberystwyth, afterwards while chatting over a drink or two a member of the audience asked if I had photographed the event that took place in his village. He wasn't sure of the details but I was able to find a contact and that December, on St Thomas' Day, I photographed the William Rogers bequest, which I don't think, had ever been photographed professionally before.

Hendred House has been continually occupied since 1265 and many generations of the Eyston family have lived there. On St Thomas' Day they used to distribute 'The Flour' to all eligible pensioners in the village but in 2016 it was replaced by a tin of biscuits and-distributed to the pensioners gathered together for a Christmas Drink in the Great Hall. At Sherborne Castle, the ancestral home of the Wingfield Digby family, they distribute 'The Penny' to all who gather in the estate yard before Christmas Day lunch. The Oddfellows Caledonian Friendly Lodge parade through the village of Newburgh, Fife on New Year's Eve with an Oddfellow apprentice riding a horse, sitting back to front wearing a double faced mask to drive away the evil spirits. At Laymore in Dorset on Old New Year's Eve, they burn a fifteen foot long Ashen Fagot in the fireplace of the village pub. According to legend, if a woman straddles it she will fall pregnant within a year.

The events documented in *An Annual Affair* for the most part have a very rich history; they relate directly with the past, with the place, with the community's life and spirit. As I developed *An Annual Affair* I came to realise that food and drink in some form played an absolutely vital role in so many of these events. It could be a beer, mashed potato, a biscuit or a simple meal. In the gathering together of the community an essential part of the celebration, the final act, was the sustenance.

The British countryside is of course changing. Almost everywhere I travelled new estates are rising up across our green and rural landscape, and Britain's traditional villages and small town communities are adapting. It's heartening that many of the events in this book are revivals of a cherished past.

An Annual Affair illustrates a community's wish to preserve its history, changed a little with time, now moulded for the 21st century, and passed with pride from one generation to another. Collectively they are testament to our rich heritage, our unique British culture.

Homer Sykes
July 2024

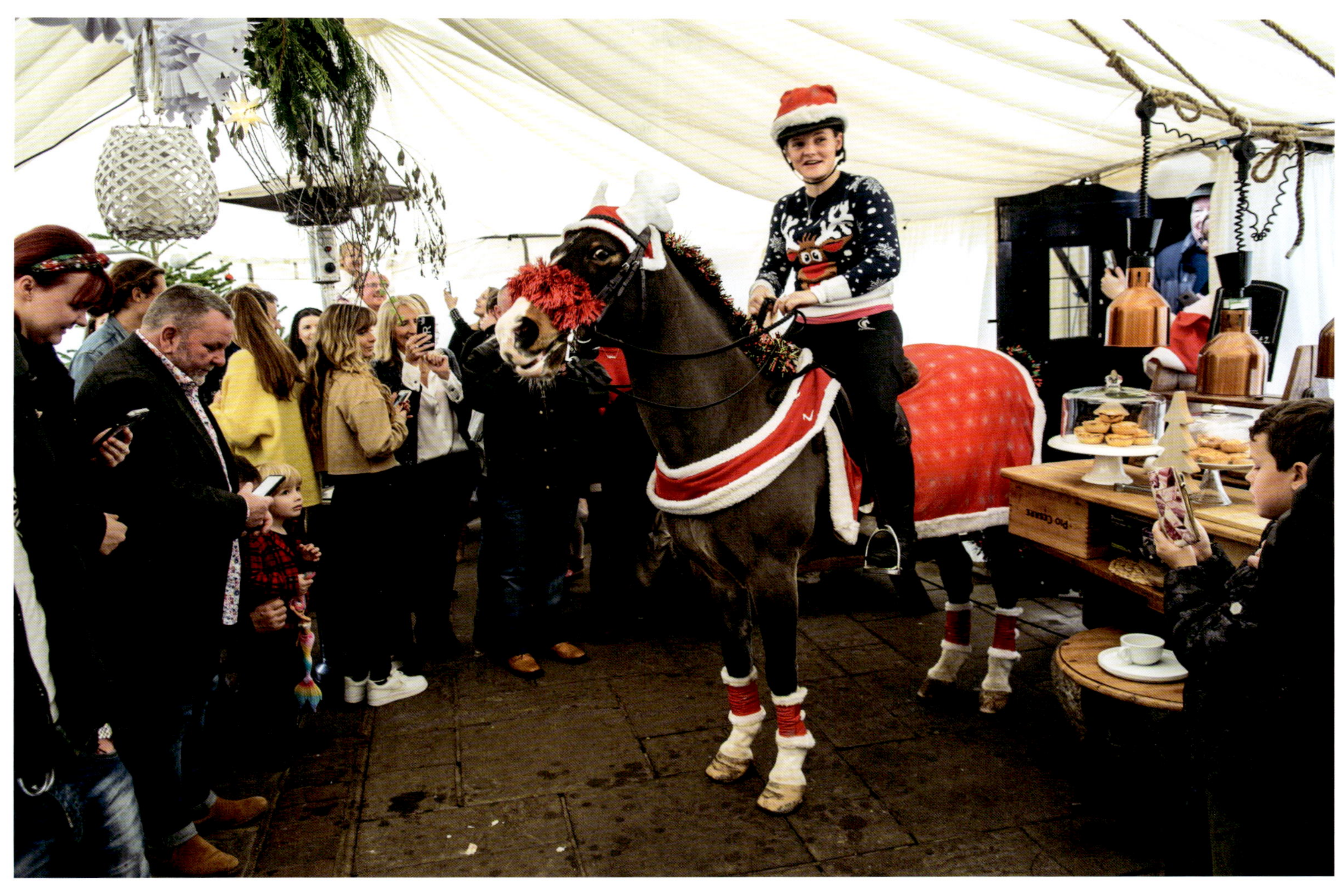

KEEPING OPEN AN ANCIENT RIGHT OF WAY
Bucks Green, Sussex
2022

On Christmas Day a horse is ridden through the Fox Inn from the front garden to the back along a bricked path to keep open an ancient right of way.

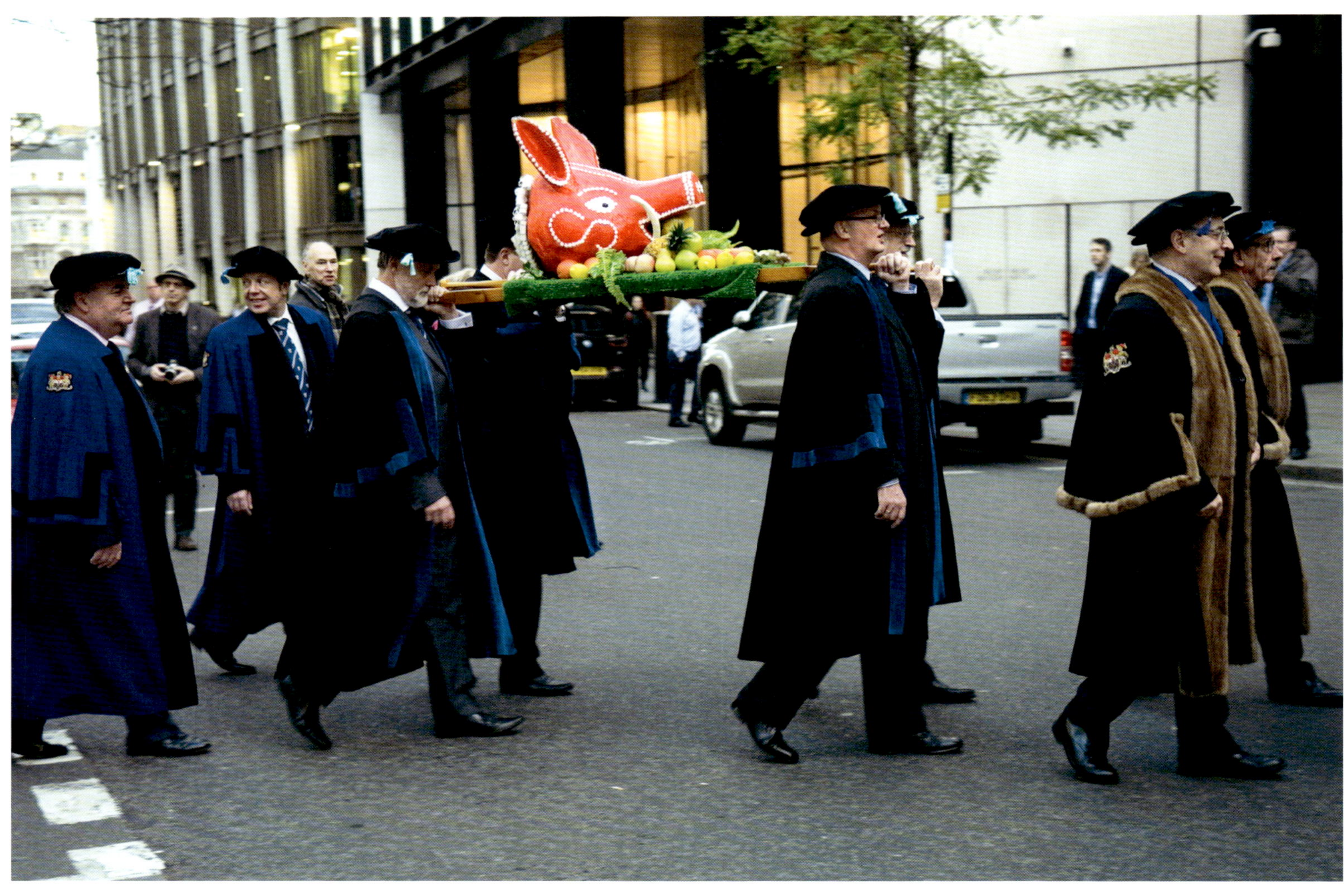

BOARS HEAD CEREMONY
The City of London
2015

The Worshipful Company of Butchers carry a papier-mâché model of a boar's head in procession. It will be presented to the Lord Mayor.

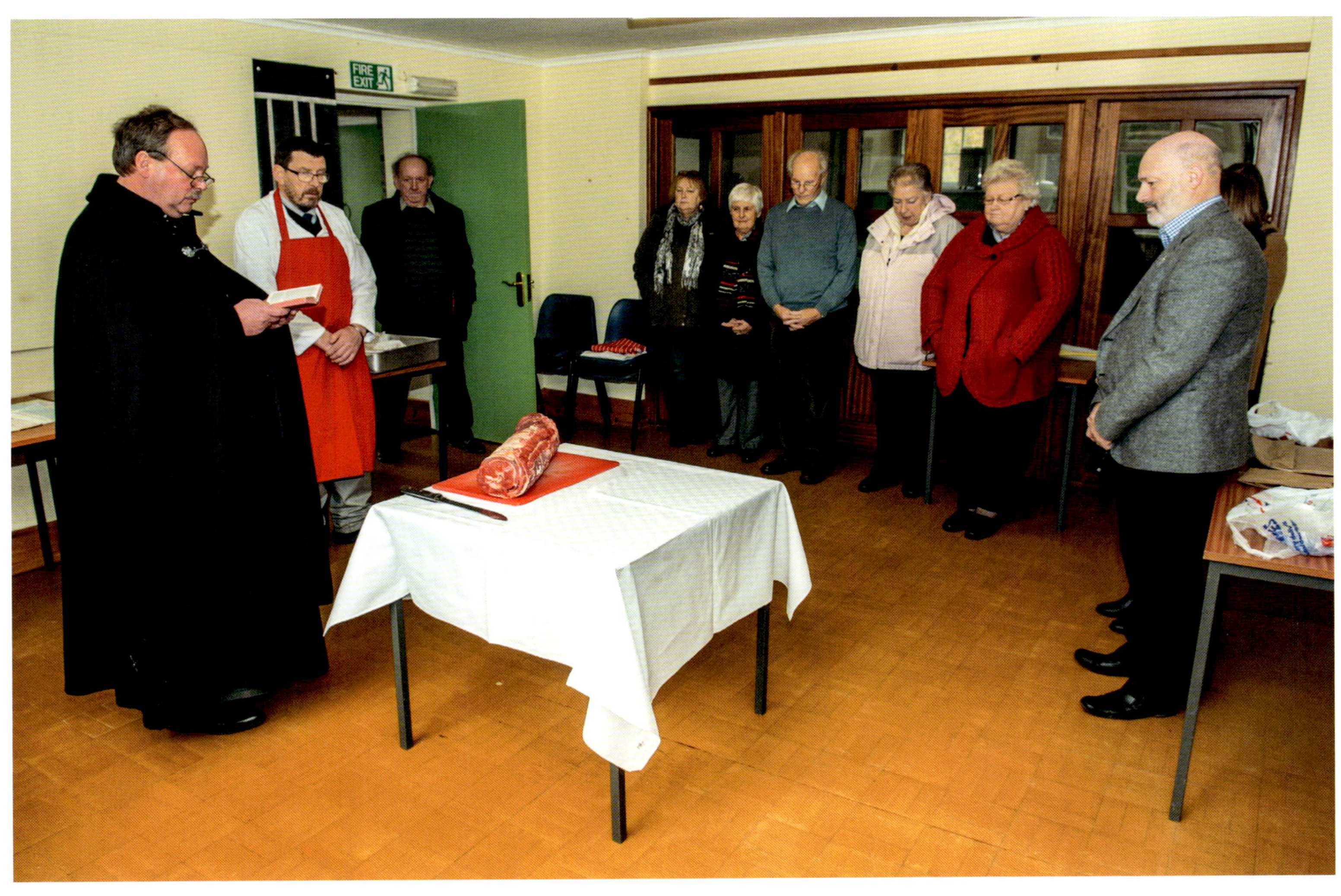

WILLIAM ROGERS BEQUEST
Nevern, Pembrokeshire
2014

A bible reading in the village hall by the Revd. Neil Llwellyn before the distribution of beef and barley on St Thomas' Day to all eligible pensioners.

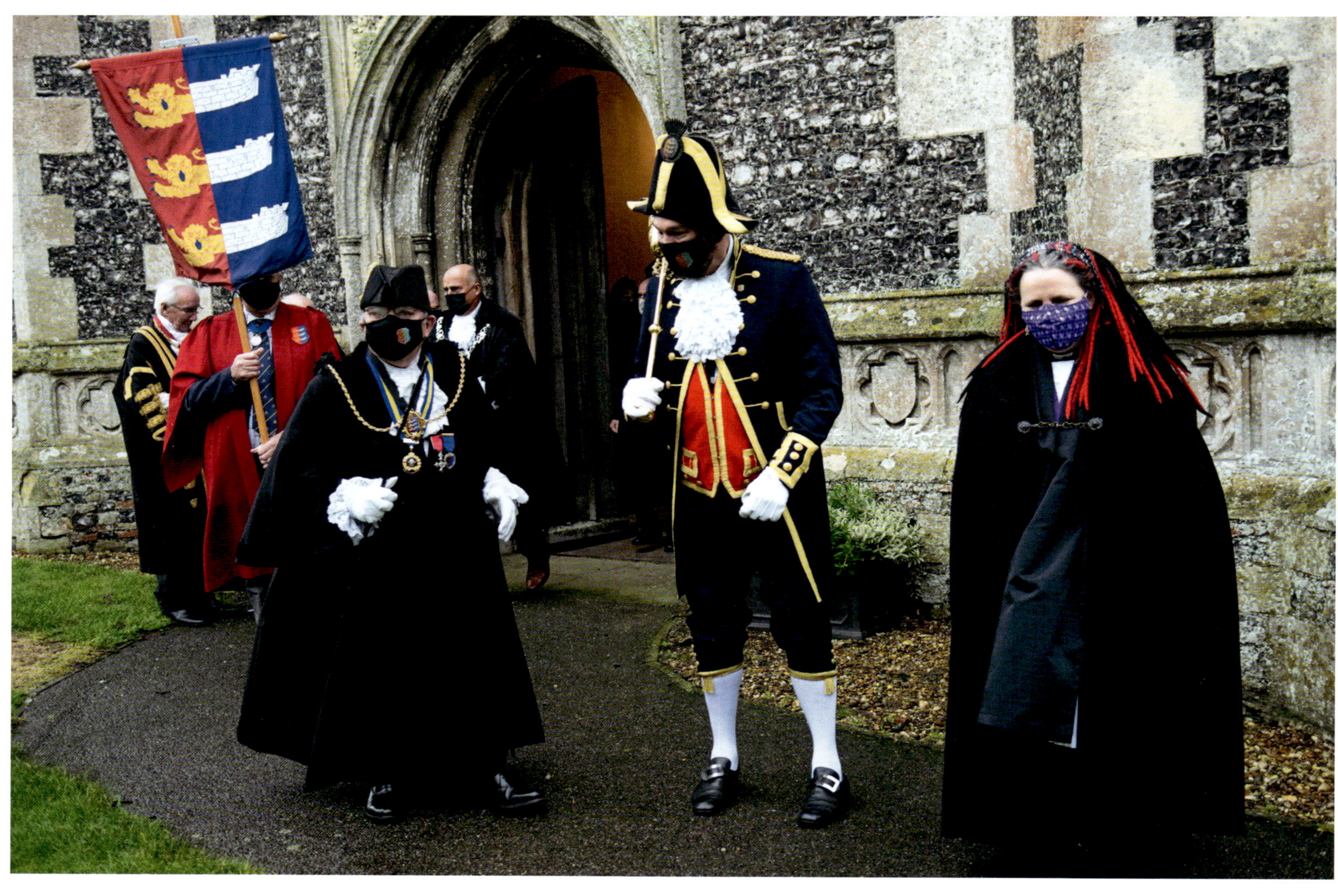

CHOOSING DAY
Brightlingsea, Essex
2021

Choosing Day takes place at All Saints Church on the first Monday following St Andrew's Day. The Mayor of Sandwich and the Town Serjeant leave church with the Revd. Caroline Beckett for the Liberty Hall Community Centre and lunch.

Top table guests, the Mayor Cllr. Robert Davidson gives a round of applause to Liz the Lady Mayoress.

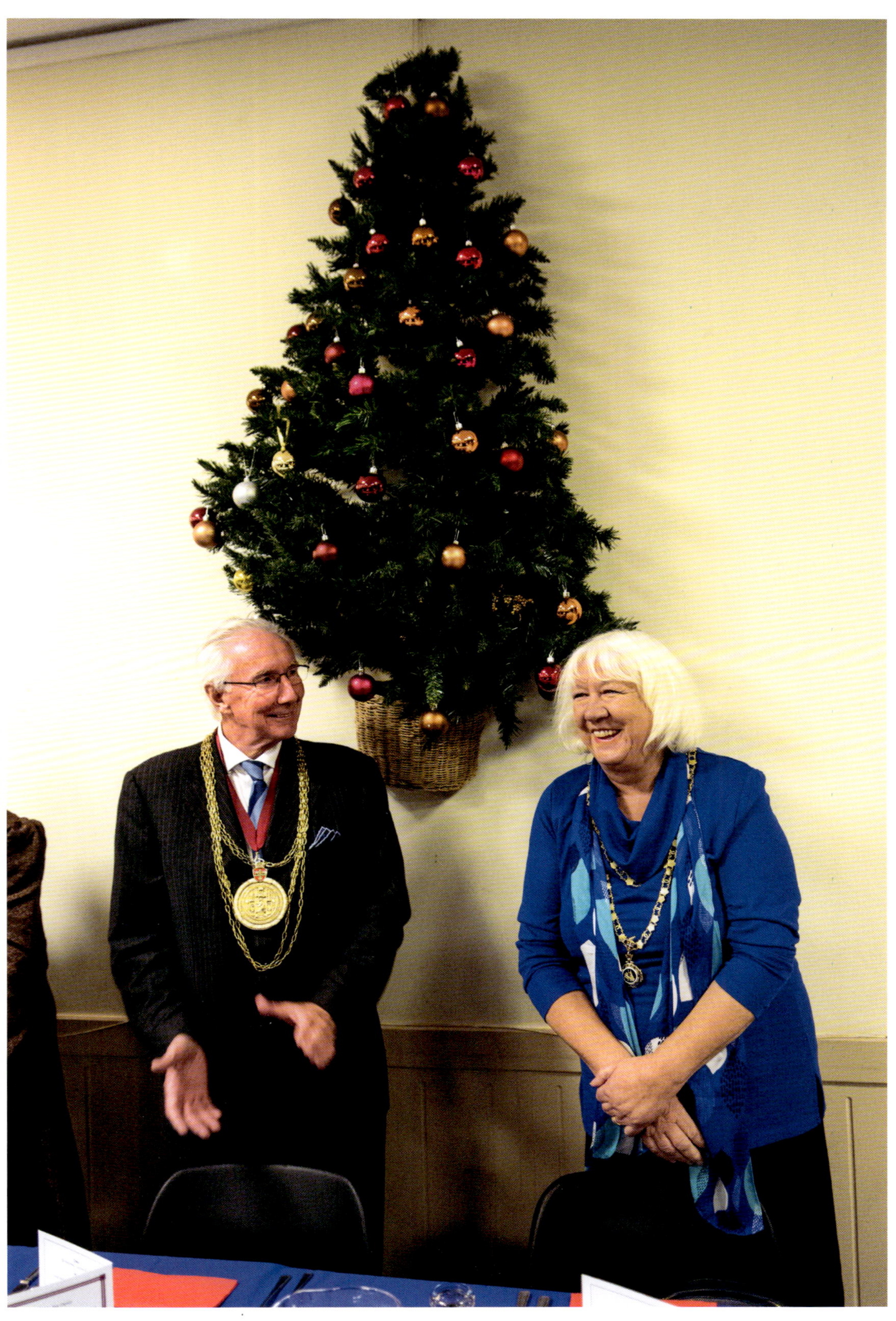

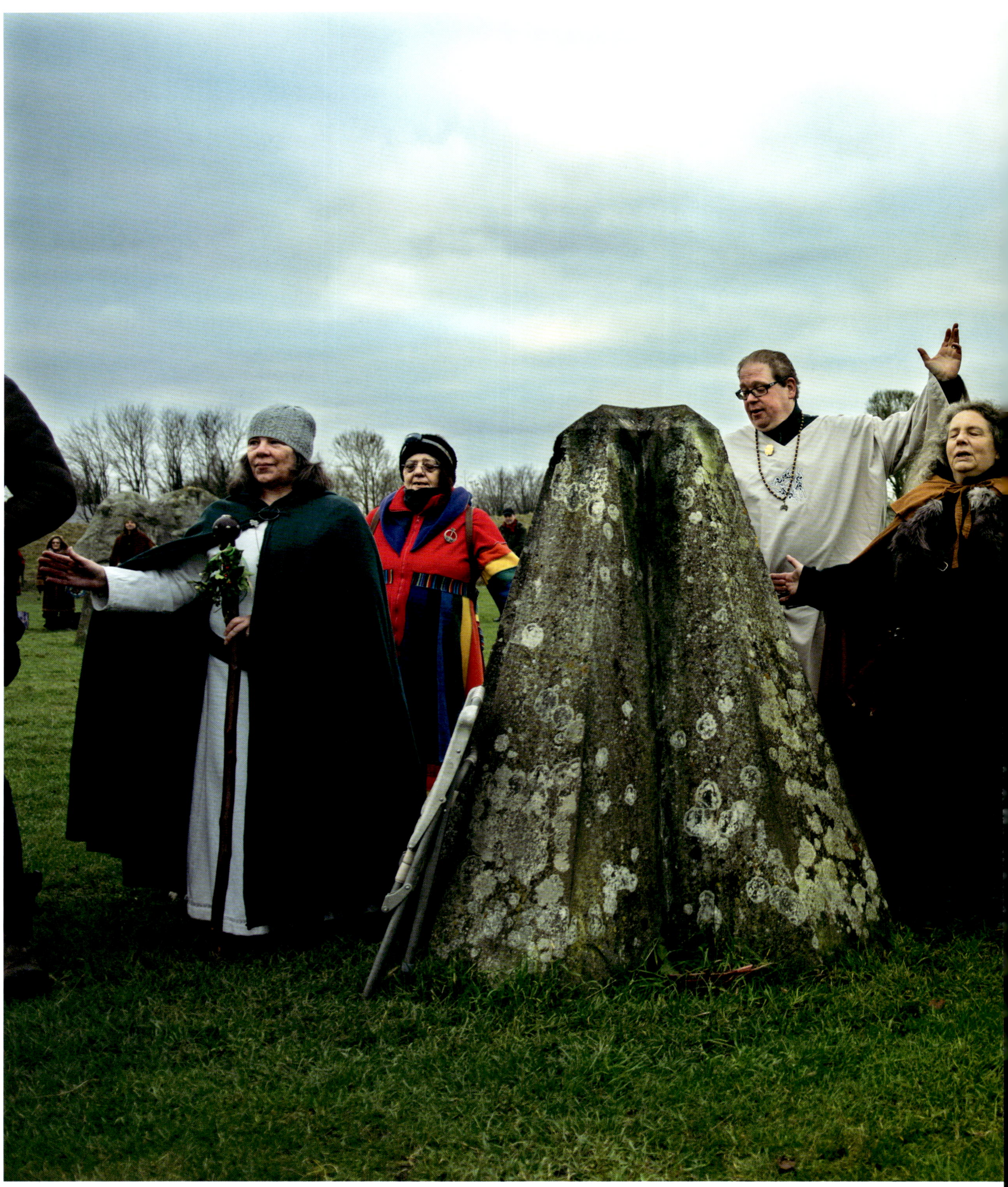

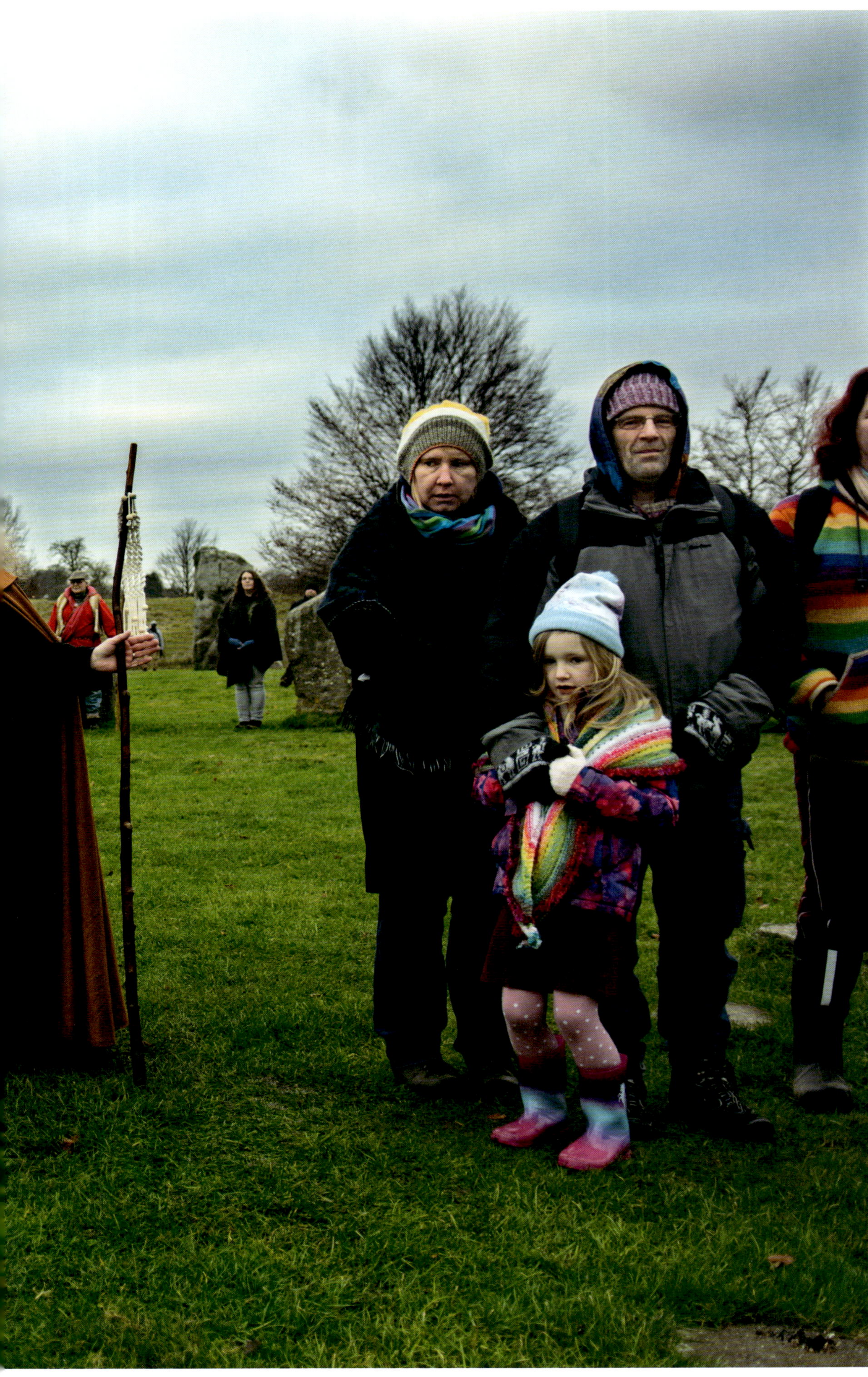

WINTER SOLSTICE
Avebury, Wiltshire
2021

Celebrating the Winter Solstice the Archdruid of Avebury, Henk Vis, forms a circle at the Obelisk; as part of the druidic ritual he calls the Cardinal Directions of East, South, West and North.

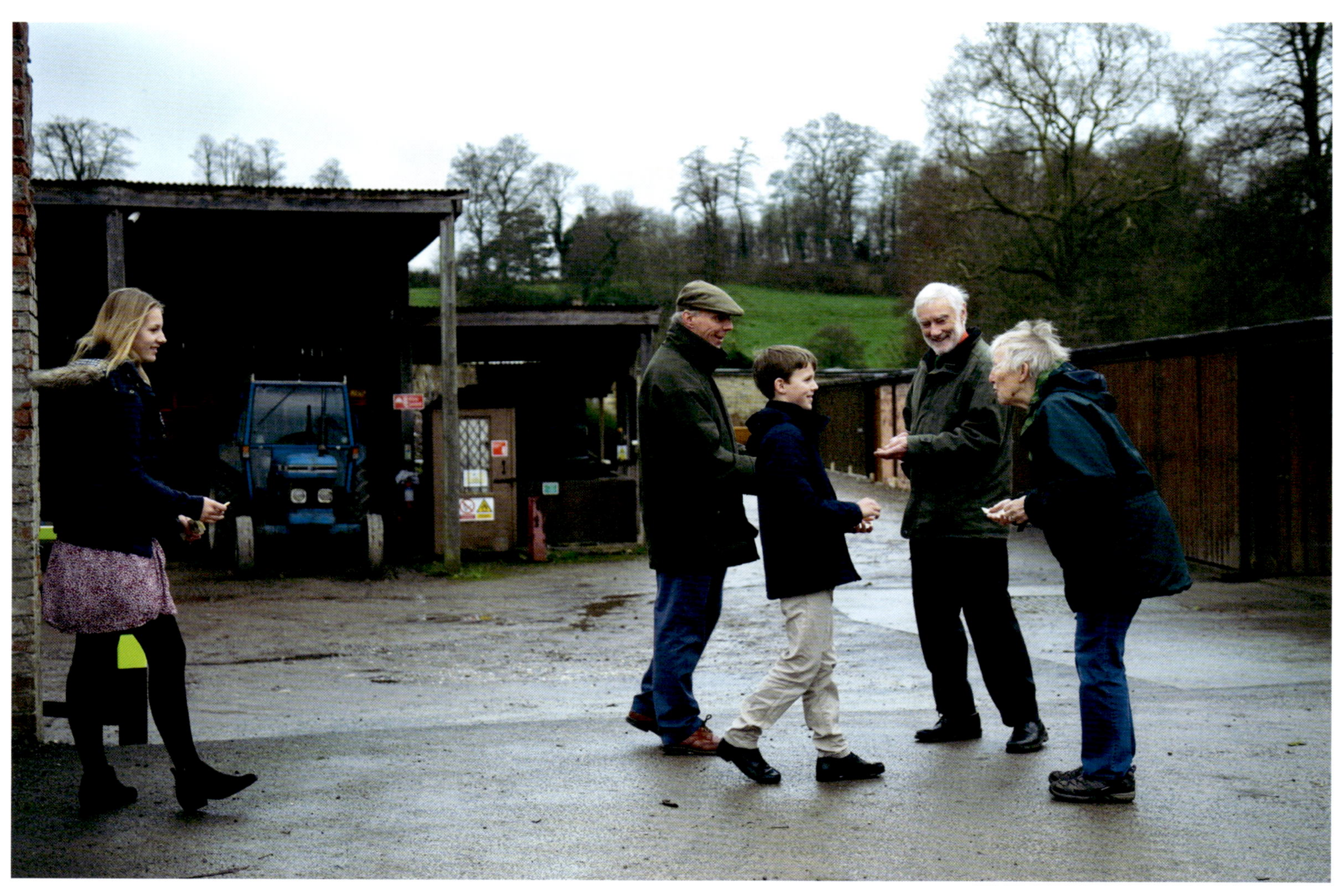

THE PENNY
Sherborne, Dorset
2015

The Wingfield Digby family distribute The Penny on Christmas Day to all who attend at the Estate Yard at Sherborne Castle.

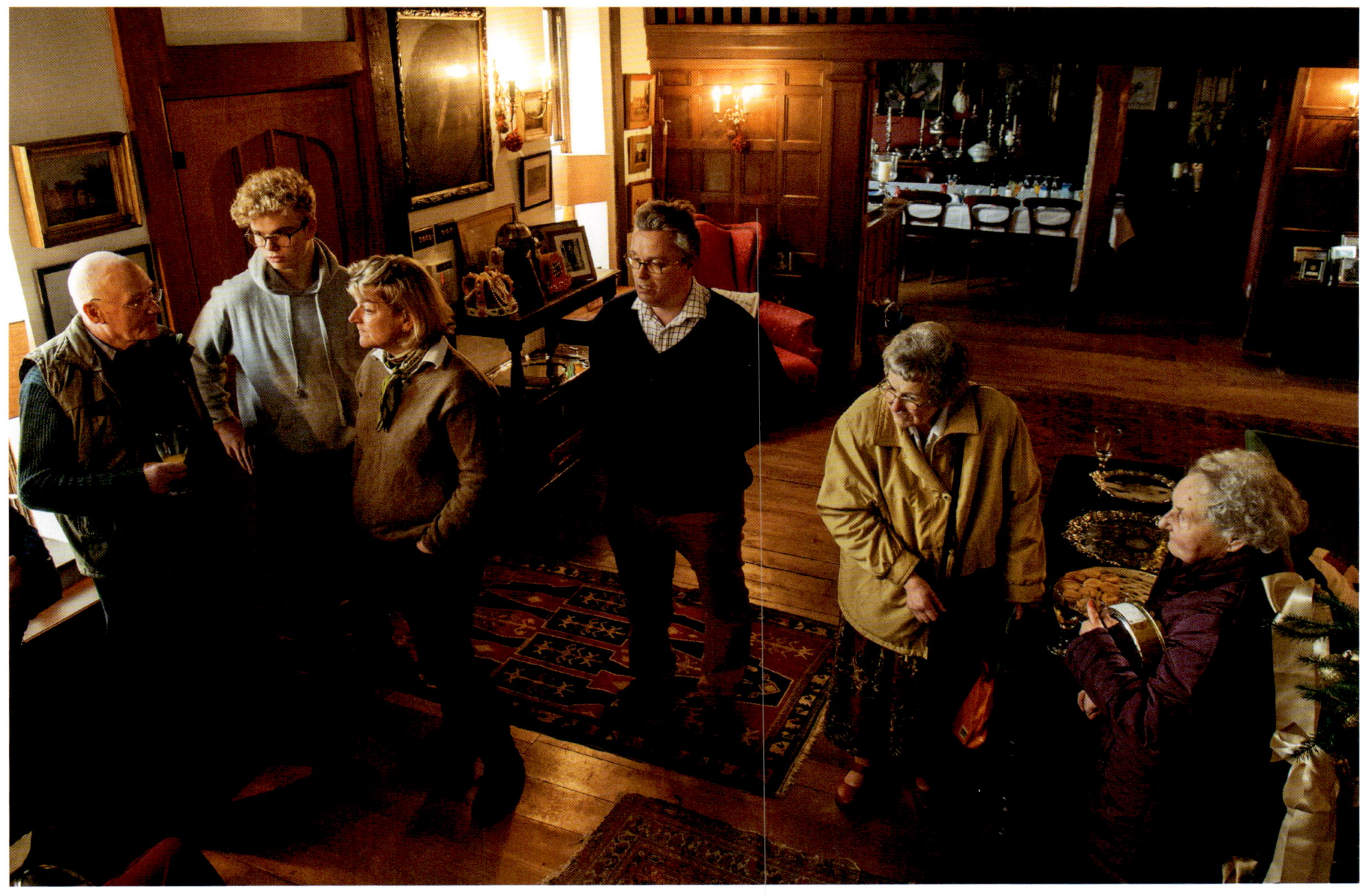

FLOUR
East Hendred, Oxfordshire
2016

Flour takes place on St Thomas' Day, the 21st December, in the Great Hall of Hendred House and is given to qualifying pensioners living in the village.

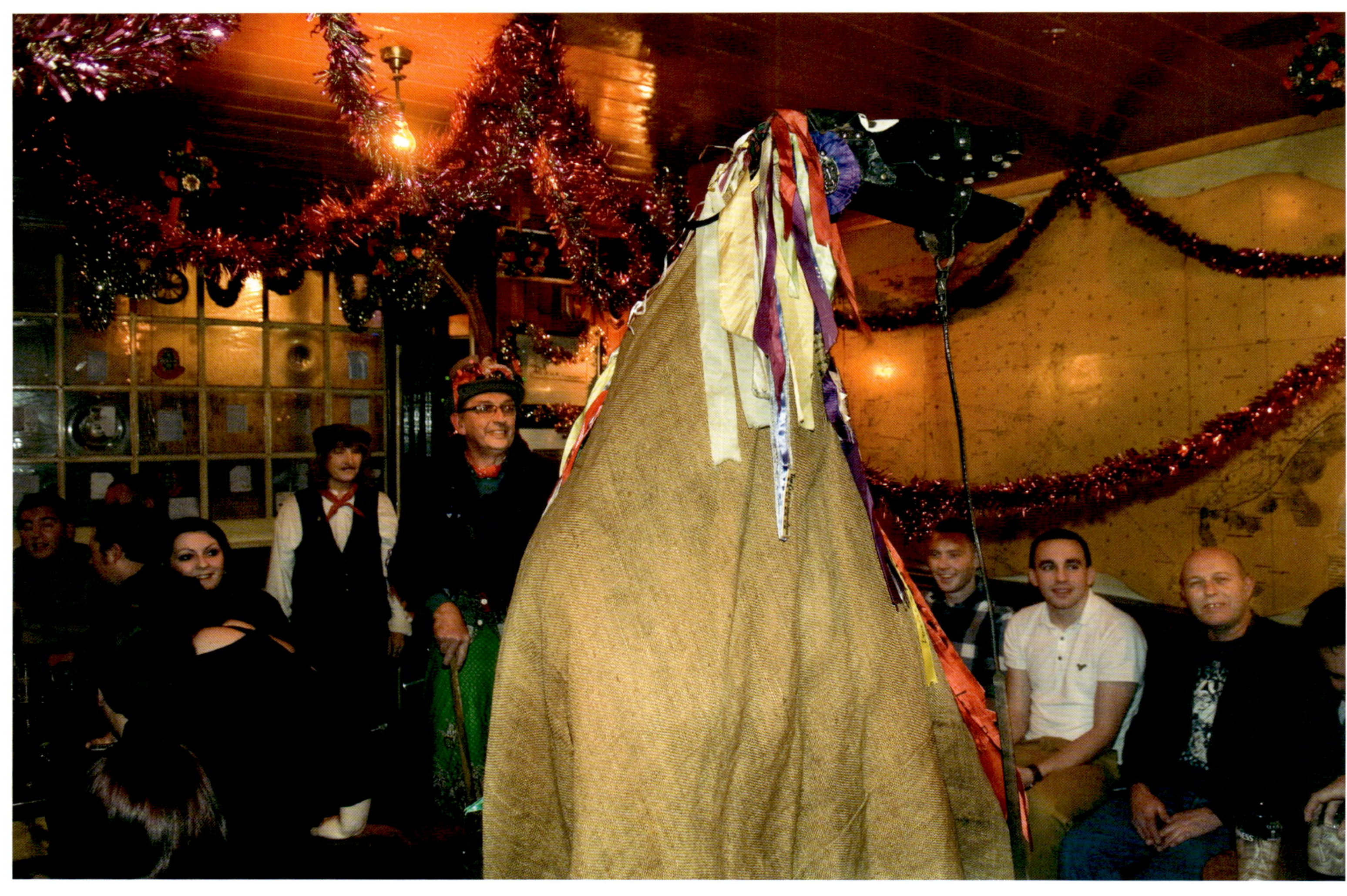

SANGATE HOODENERS
Sandgate, Kent
2012

The Hoodeners, the hooden horse, Mollie and the Lad surprised and entertained Christmas drinkers in the Ship Inn.

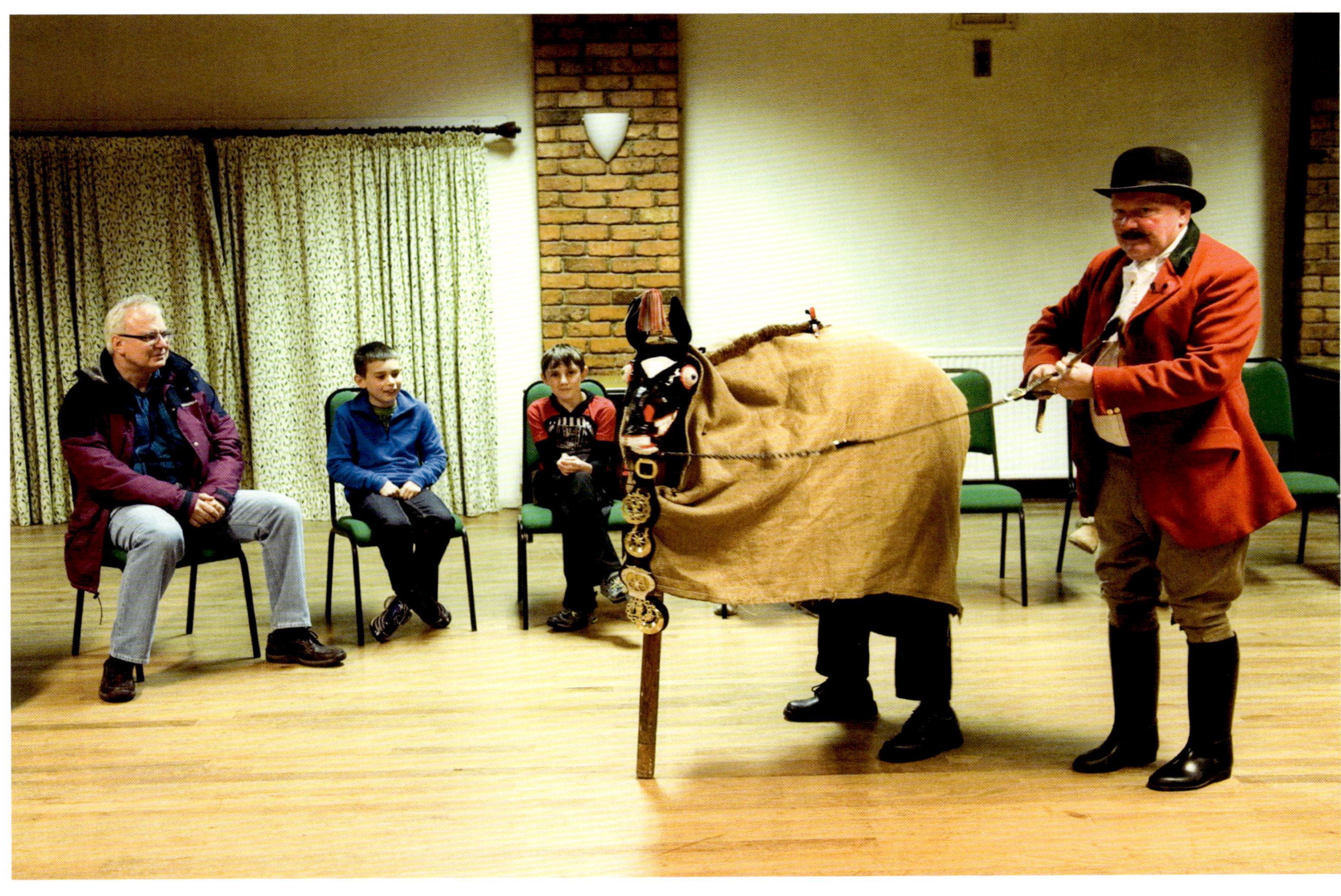

SOUL CAKING
Antrobus, Cheshire
2012

The Soul Caking play is performed on All Souls' Day evening in the new village hall. Trevor Collins, in Cheshire Hunt livery, entertains a very small crowd.

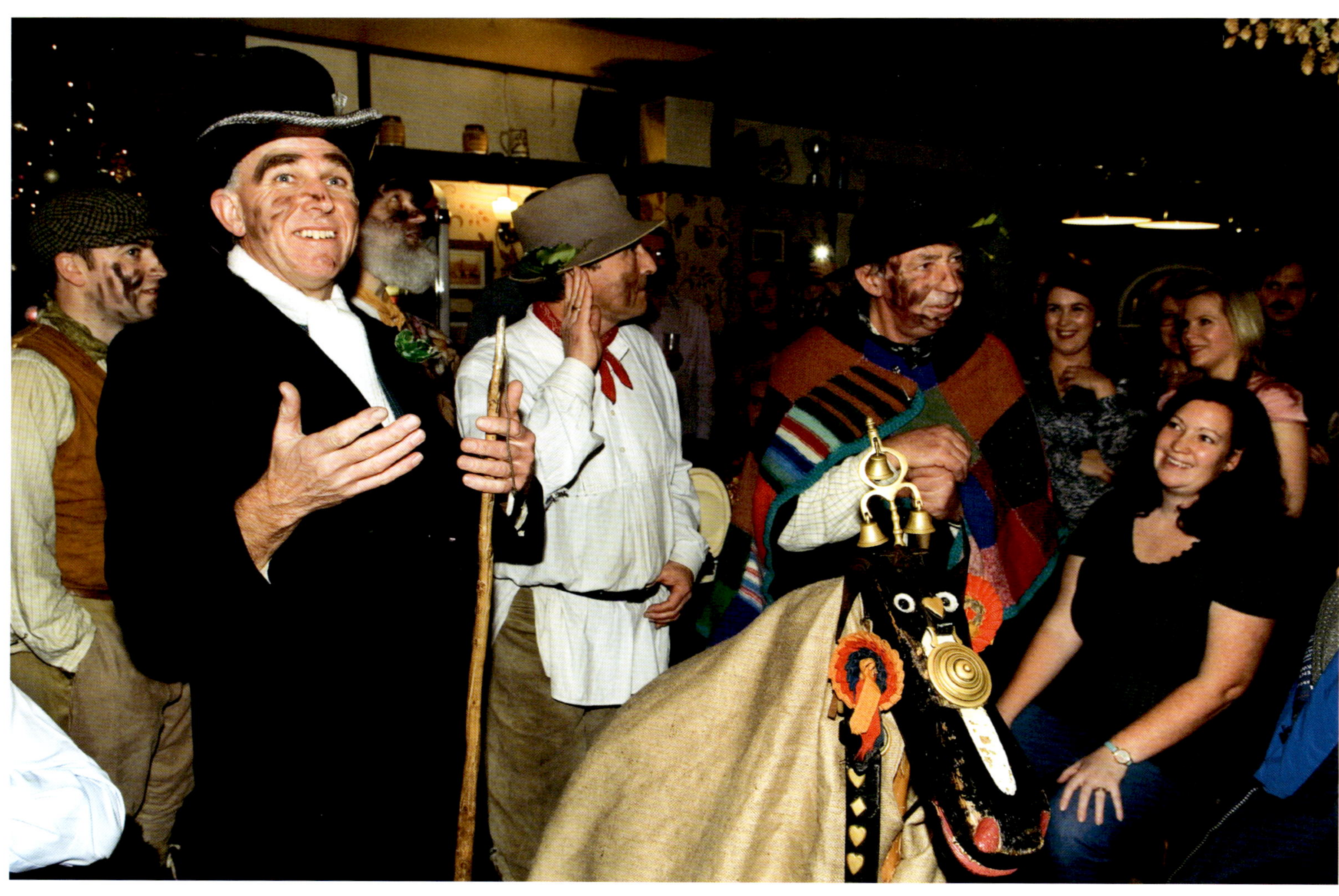

HOODENERS
St Nicholas-at-Wade, Kent
2014

The Hoodeners perform the village traditional mid-winter folk play to a packed house in the Bell Inn.

Following a performance by the Hoodeners the audience joins them singing Christmas carols at Street Acre, a private house in the village.

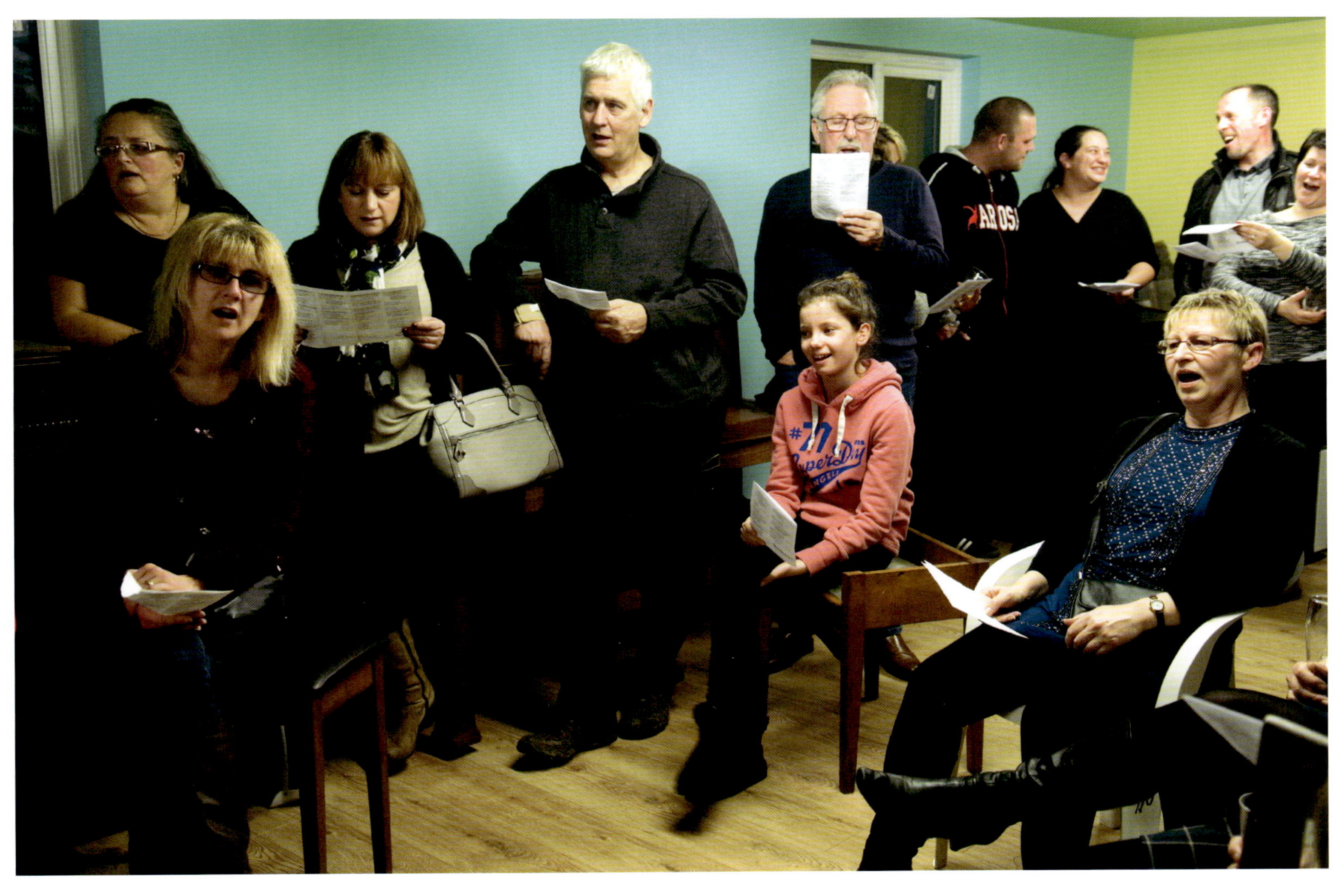

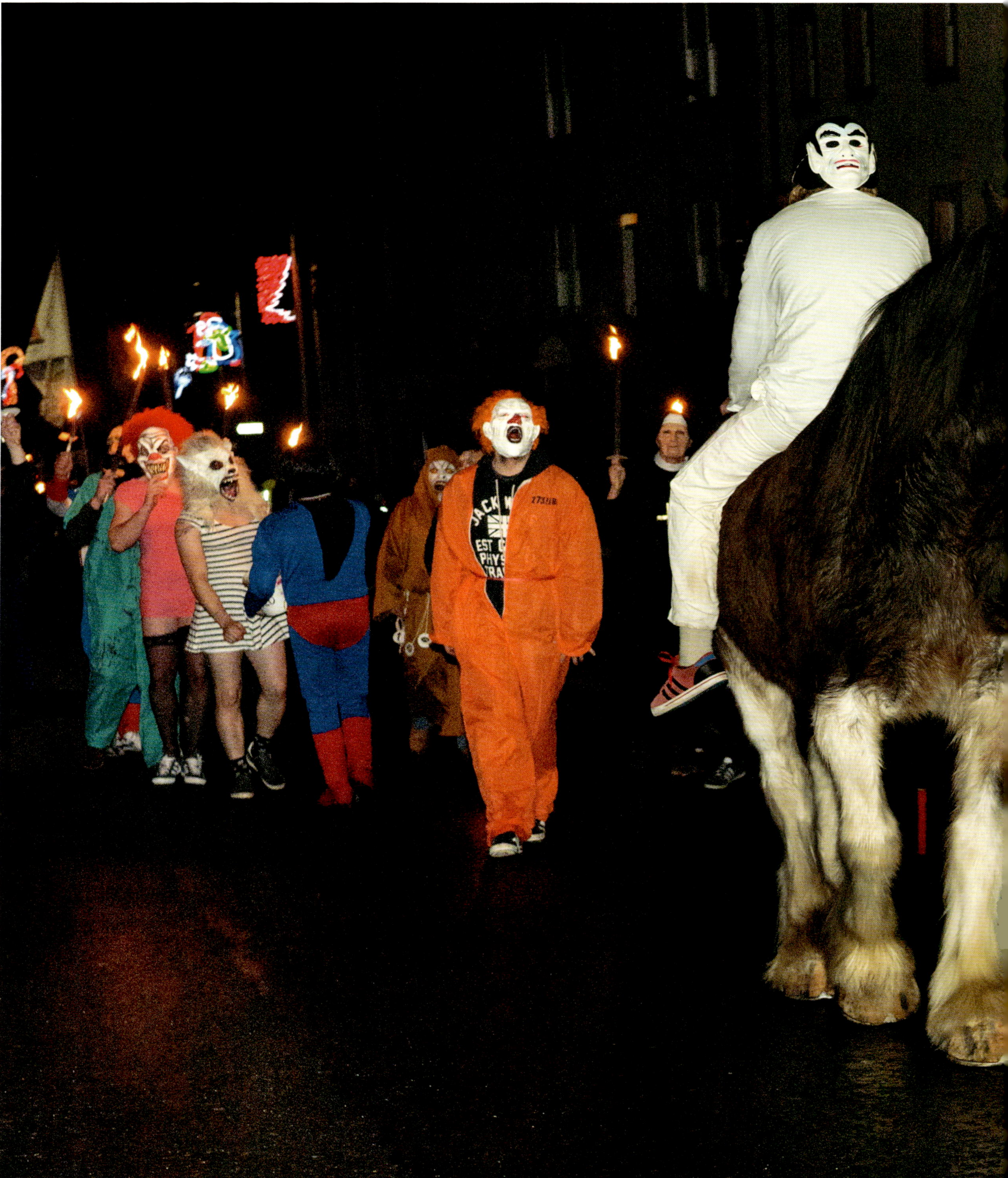

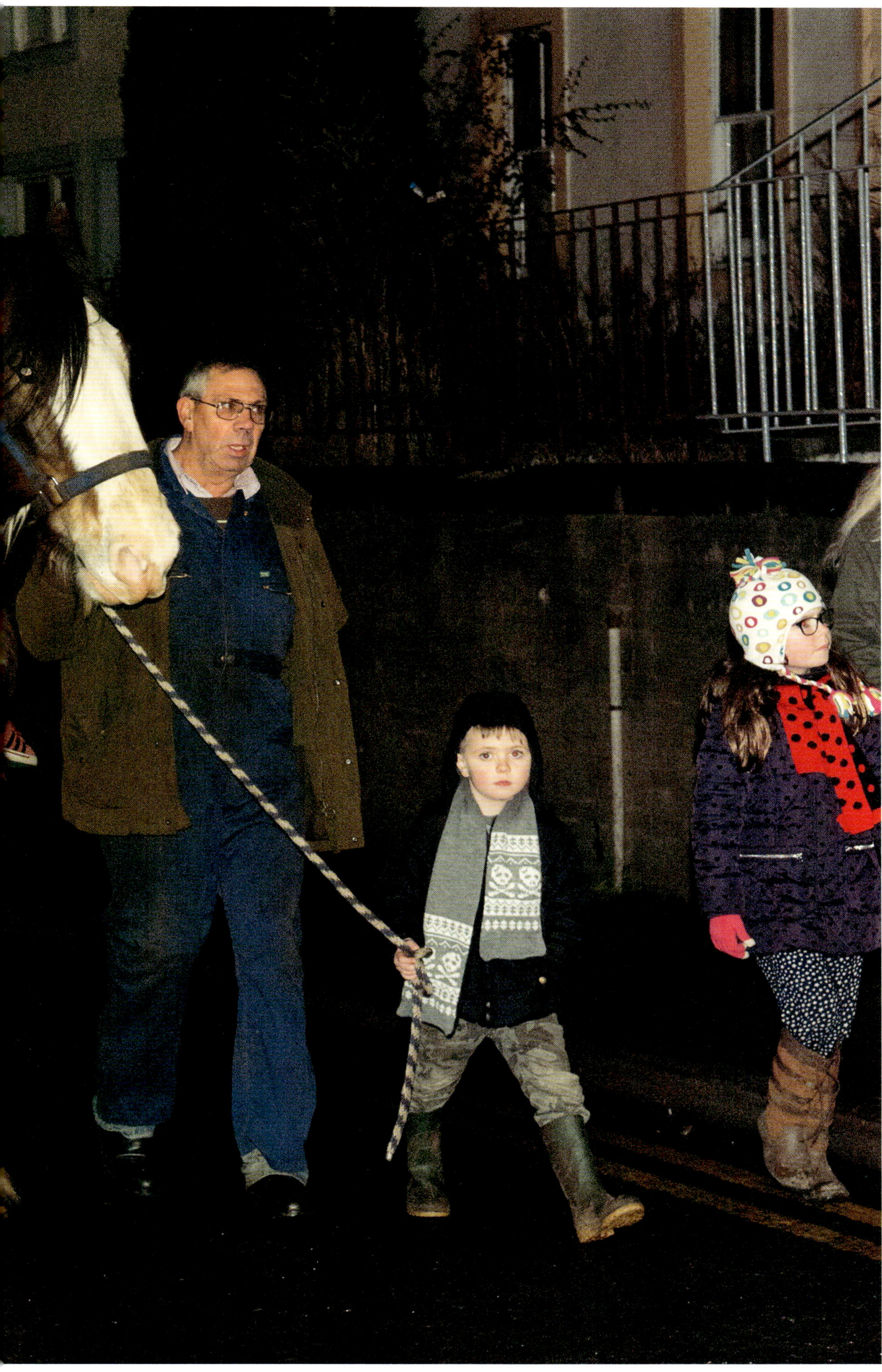

CALEDONIAN FRIENDLY LODGE OF ODDFELLOWS
Newburgh, Fife
2016

The Caledonian Friendly Lodge of Oddfellows is the last remaining Oddfellows Lodge in Scotland. On New Year's Eve an Apprentice rides a horse sitting back to front wearing a double faced mask, the All Seeing Eyes.

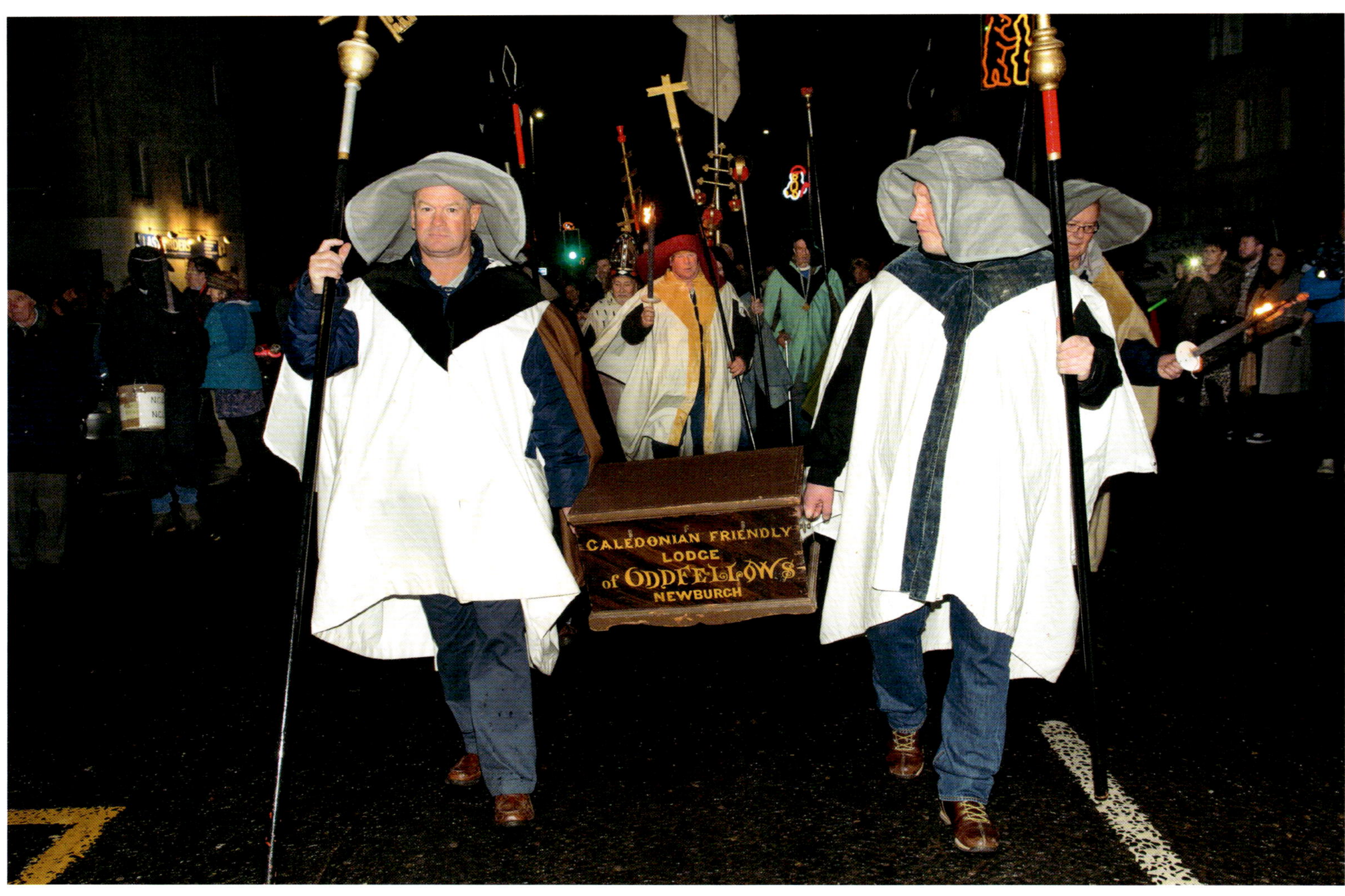

CALEDONIAN FRIENDLY LODGE OF ODDFELLOWS
Newburgh, Fife
2016

The Keepers of the Keys carrying the Lodge Box that contains the Lodge Keys. Behind is the Grand Steward carrying the golden cross.

The Most Noble Grand Oddfellow accompanied by the Left Hand Supporter to the Most Noble Grand contemplates a dram as the procession stops outside Lodge Lindores 106.

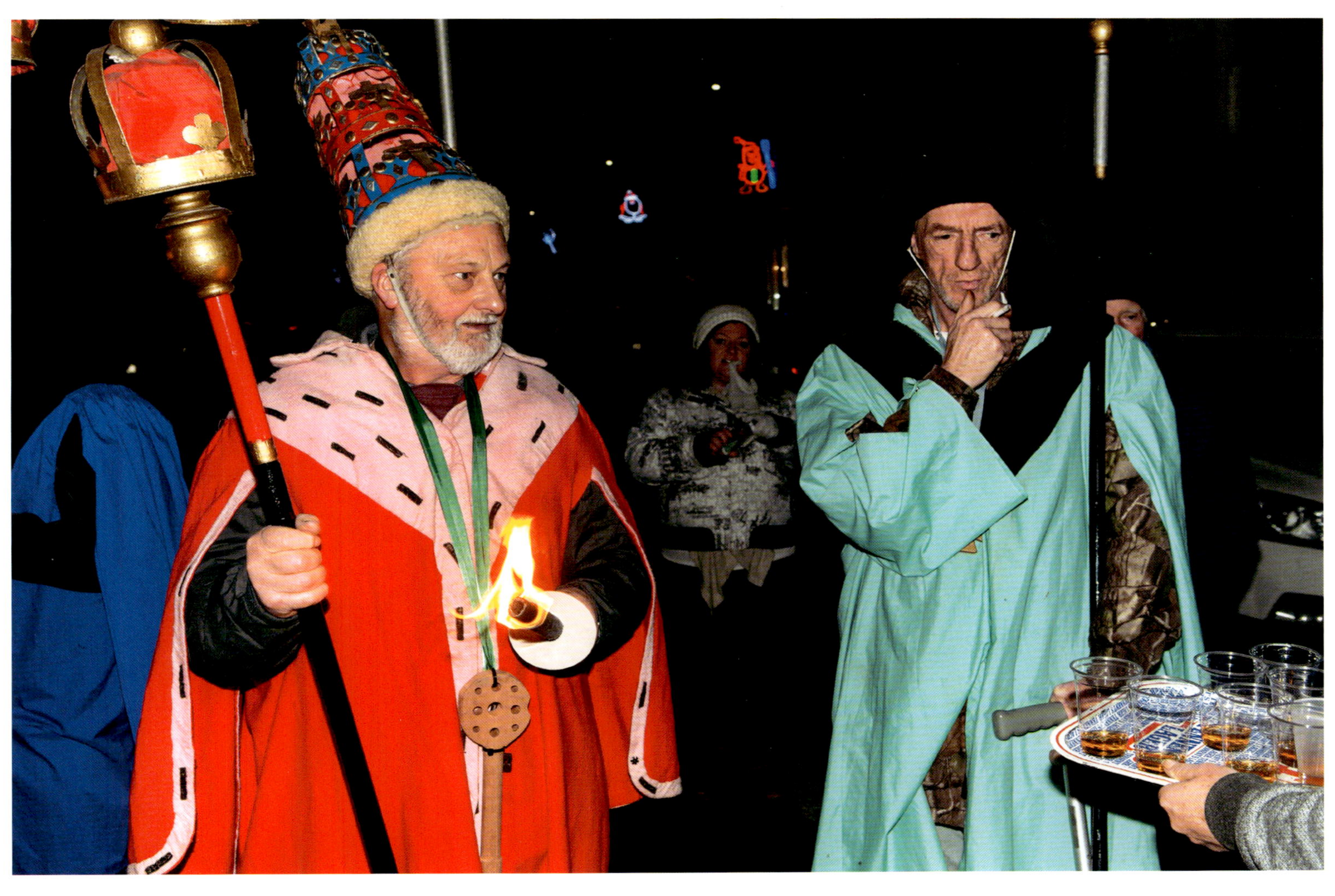

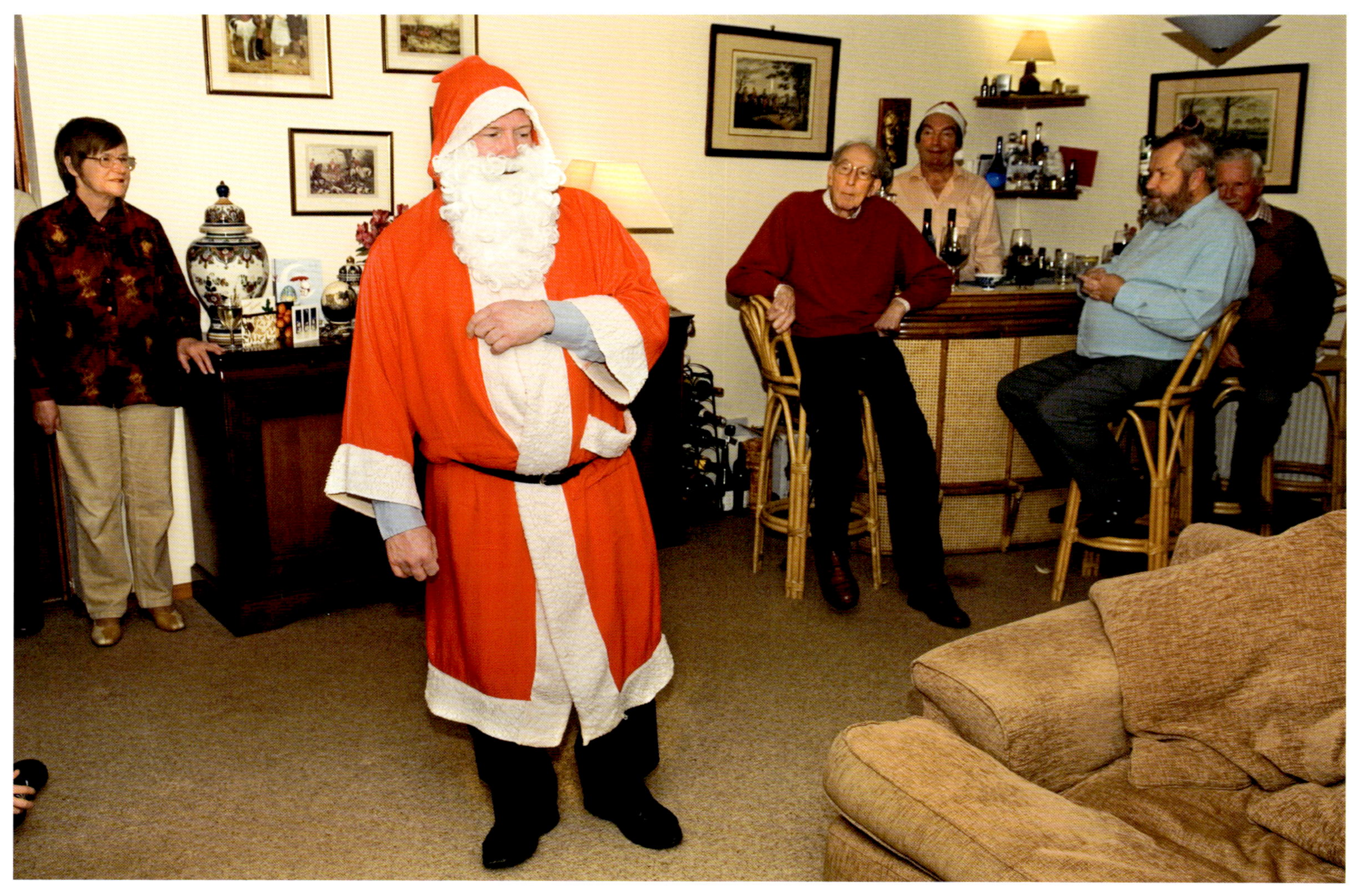

BAMPTON MUMMERS
Bampton, Oxfordshire
2008

Father Christmas, played by Jeff Dando, introduces the Bampton Mummers play to the audience while the householder, wearing a Christmas hat, stands behind his own living room bar serving drinks to friends.

Don Rouse, who has been playing Doctor Good for over sixty years, enters to rapturous applause from Christmas guests at a private home in the village, while Soldier Bold warms by the fire.

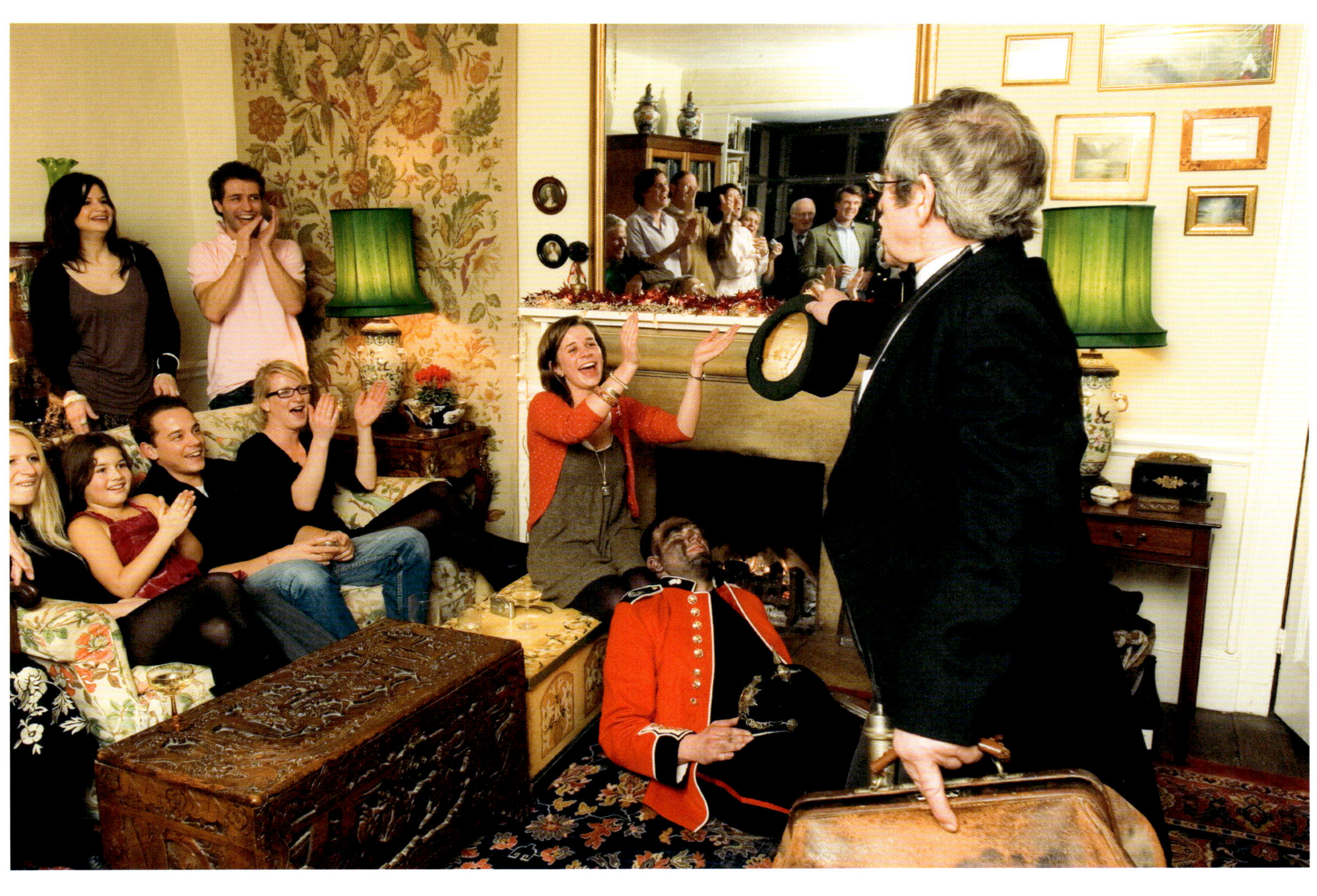

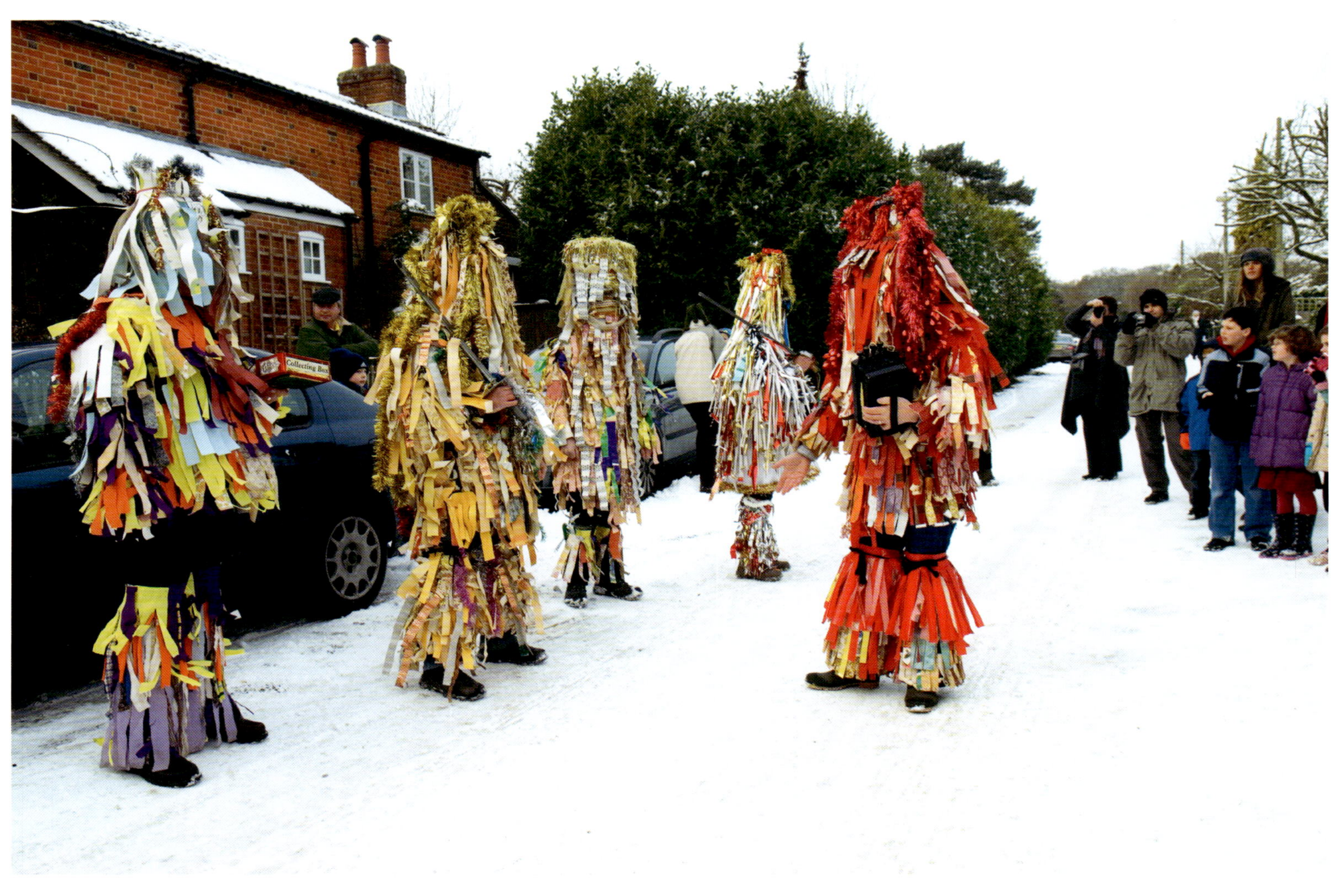

OTTERBOURNE MUMMERS
Otterbourne, Hampshire
2010

The Otterbourne Mummers play was traditionally performed on the last Sunday before Christmas.

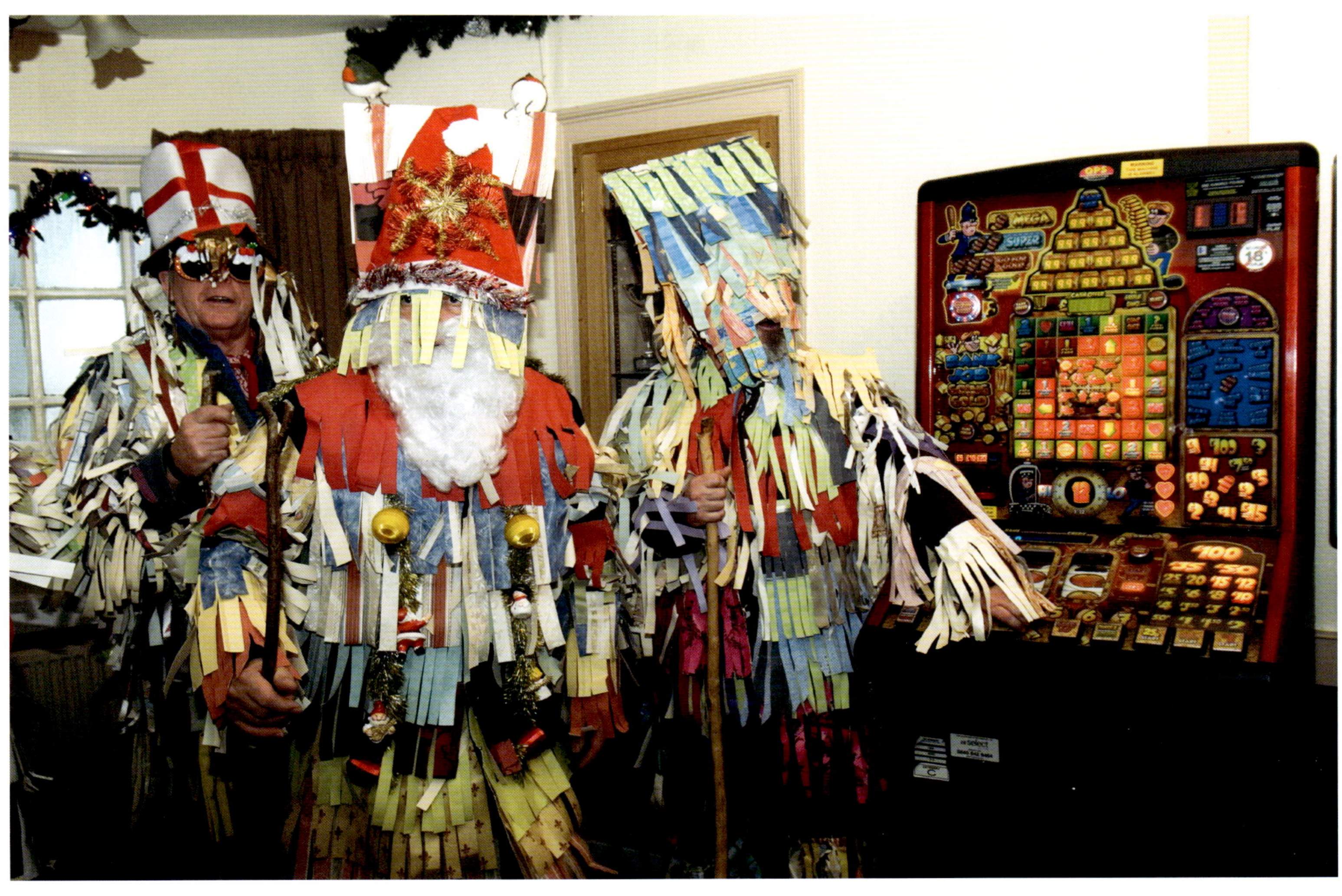

OVERTON MUMMERS
Overton, Hampshire
2014

The Overton Mummers, King George, Father Christmas and the Turkish Knight, perform in the Greyhound village pub on Boxing Day, rather than outside as is traditional due to extremely inclement weather.

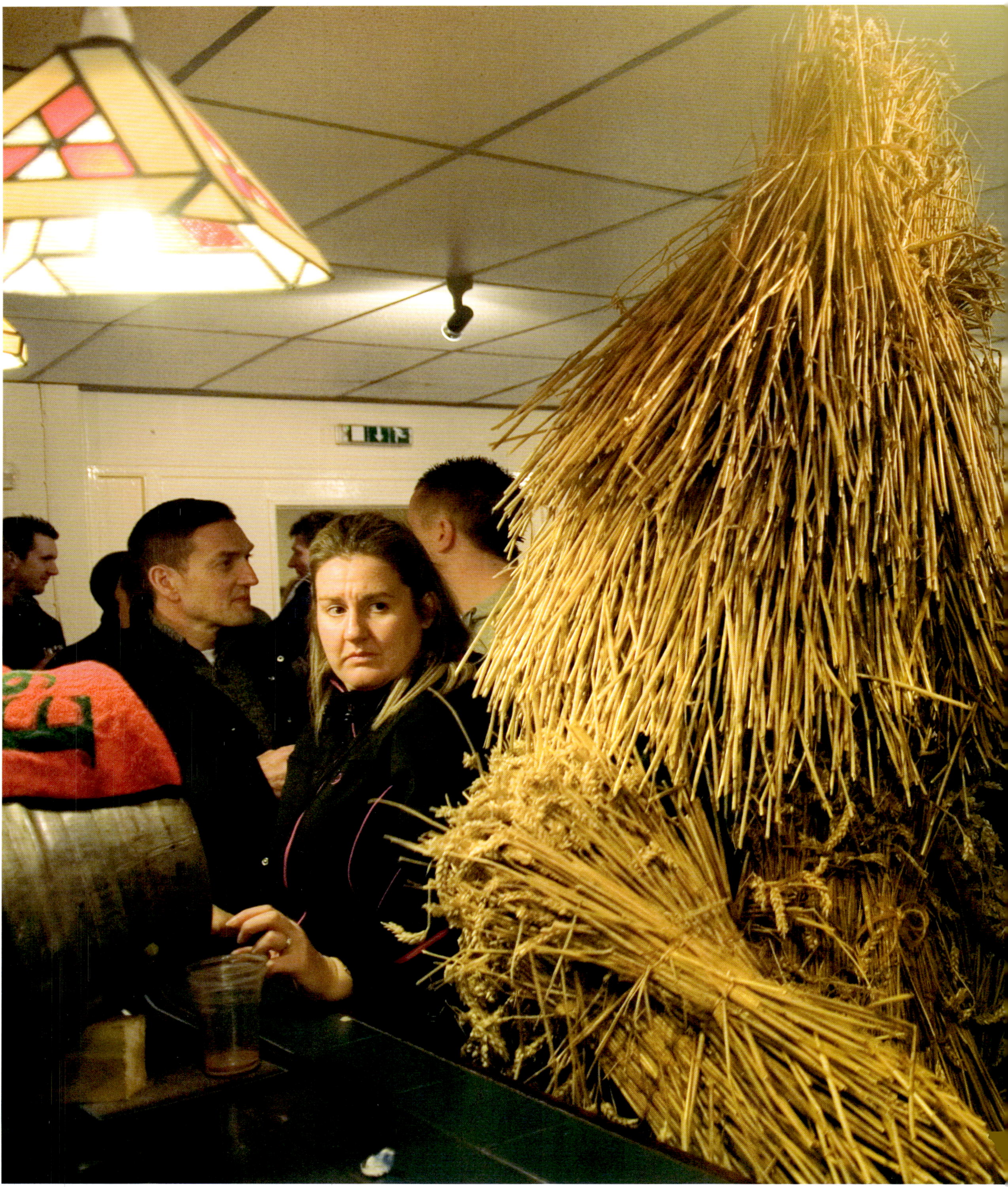

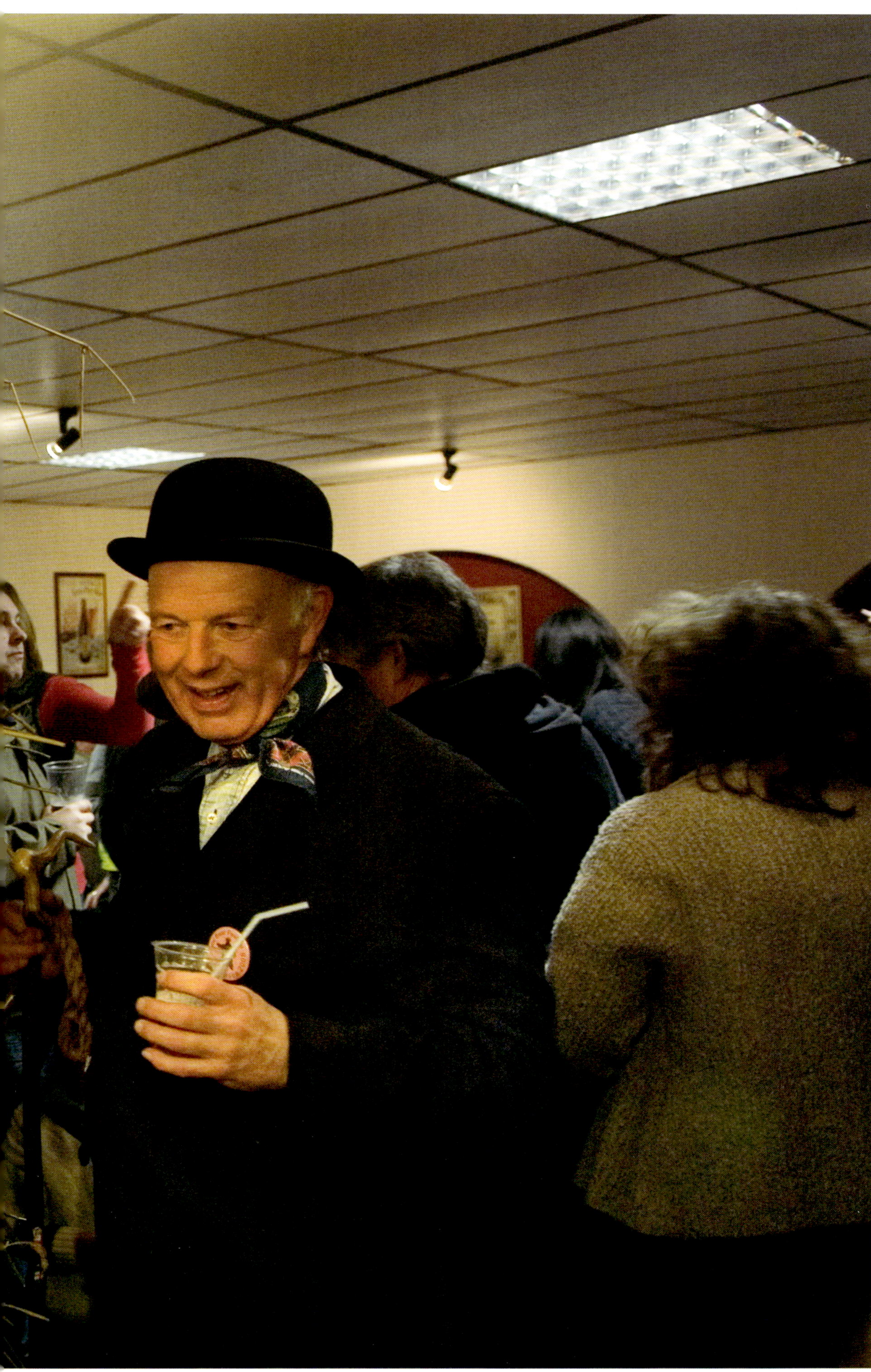

STRAW BEAR FESTIVAL
Whittlesea, Cambridgeshire
2008

The Straw Bear with the Big Bear Keeper, Rob Taylor, holding a plastic cup and straw so that Straw Bear can more easily wet his whistle in the bar of the Childers Social Club.

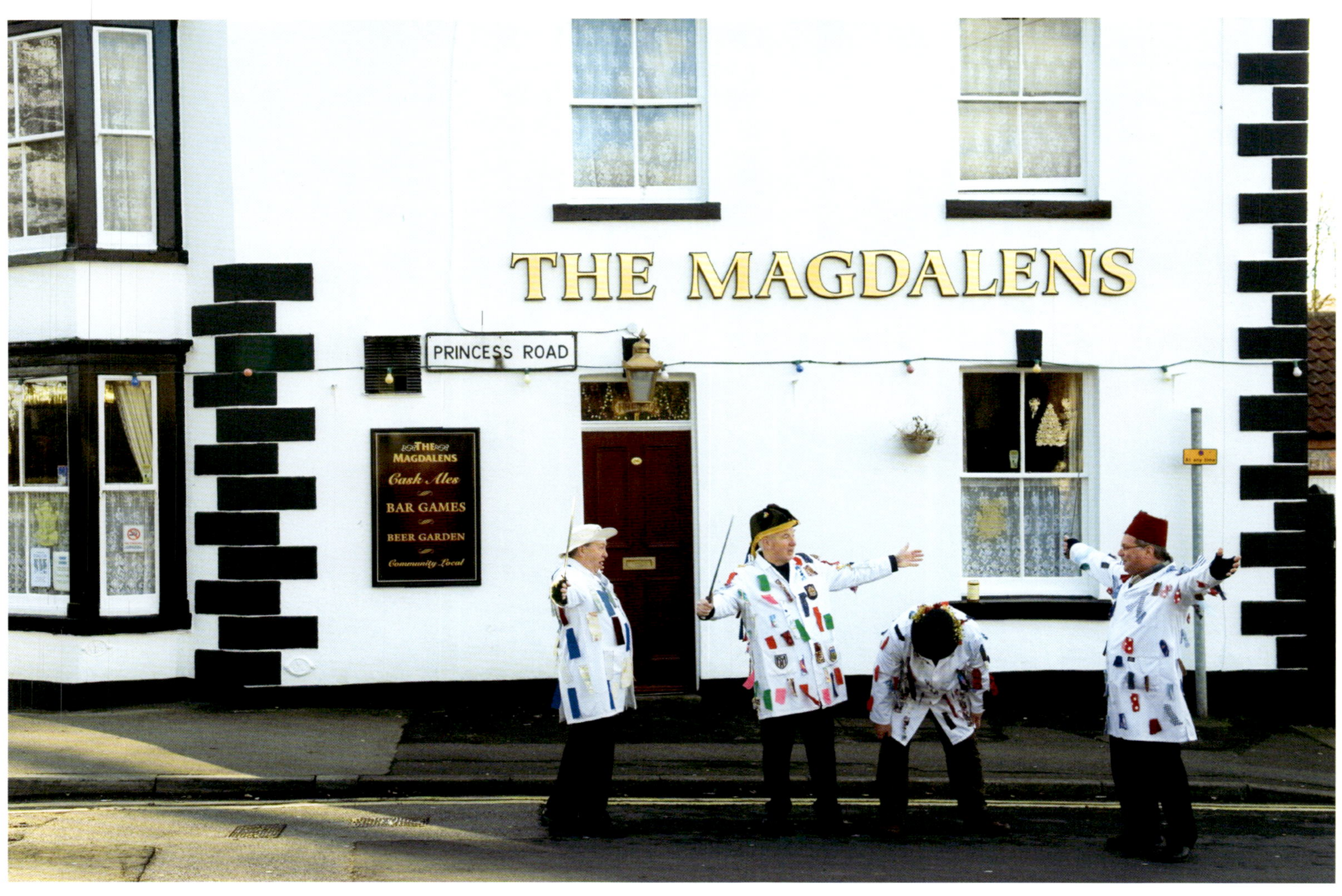

RIPON SWORD DANCE PLAY
Ripon, North Yorkshire
2008

The Boxing Day plays starts from the Market Square; there are just four team members, who perform during the morning, often to no audience at all. Outside The Magdalens, the Doctor calls out, "I cured Sir Harry of a nags nail almost fifty yards long."

Later that morning Simon McCudden's wife, Sheila, serves cake and drinks in their kitchen after a private performance. Simon plays Slasher & Little Wit.

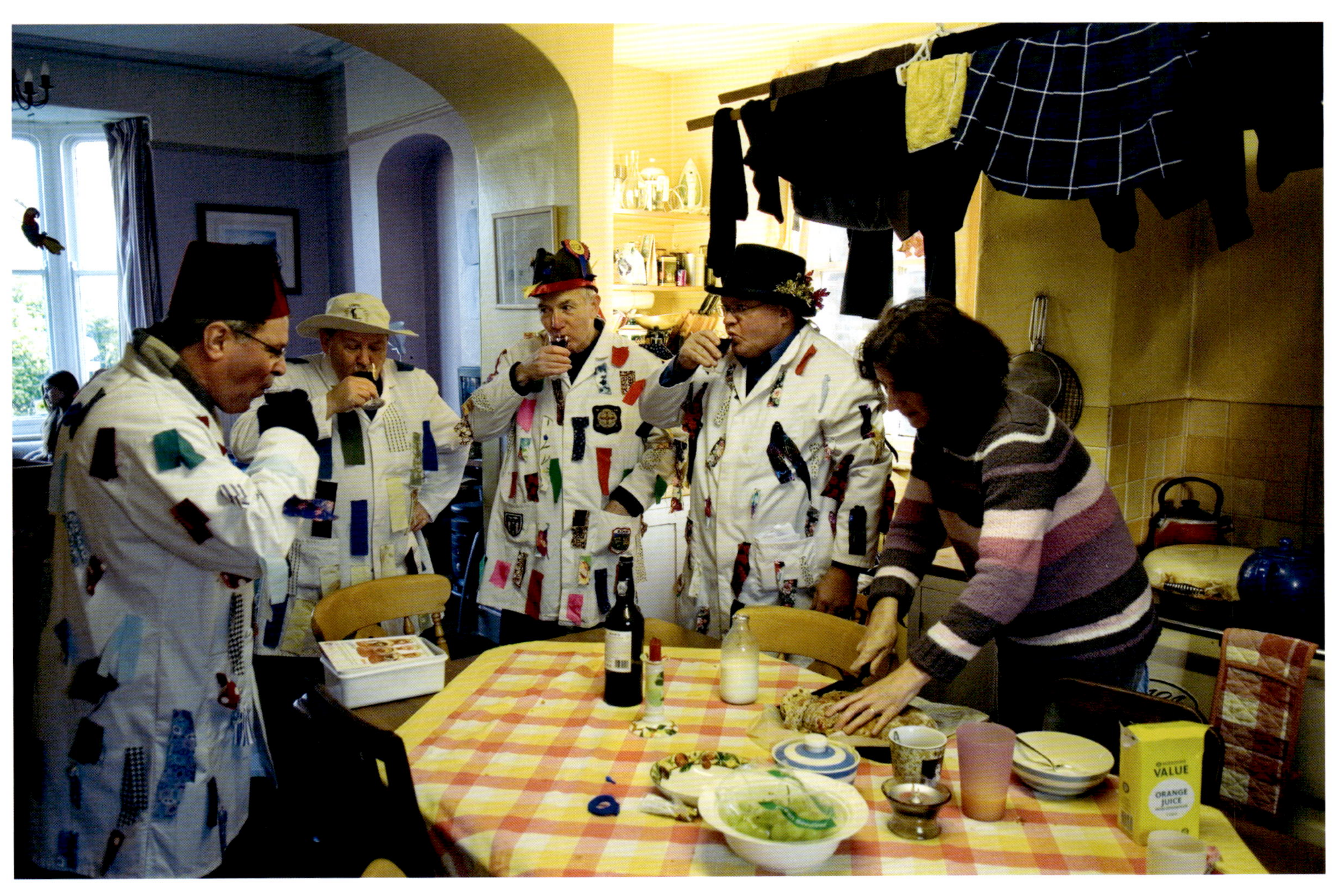
VALUE
ORANGE
JUICE

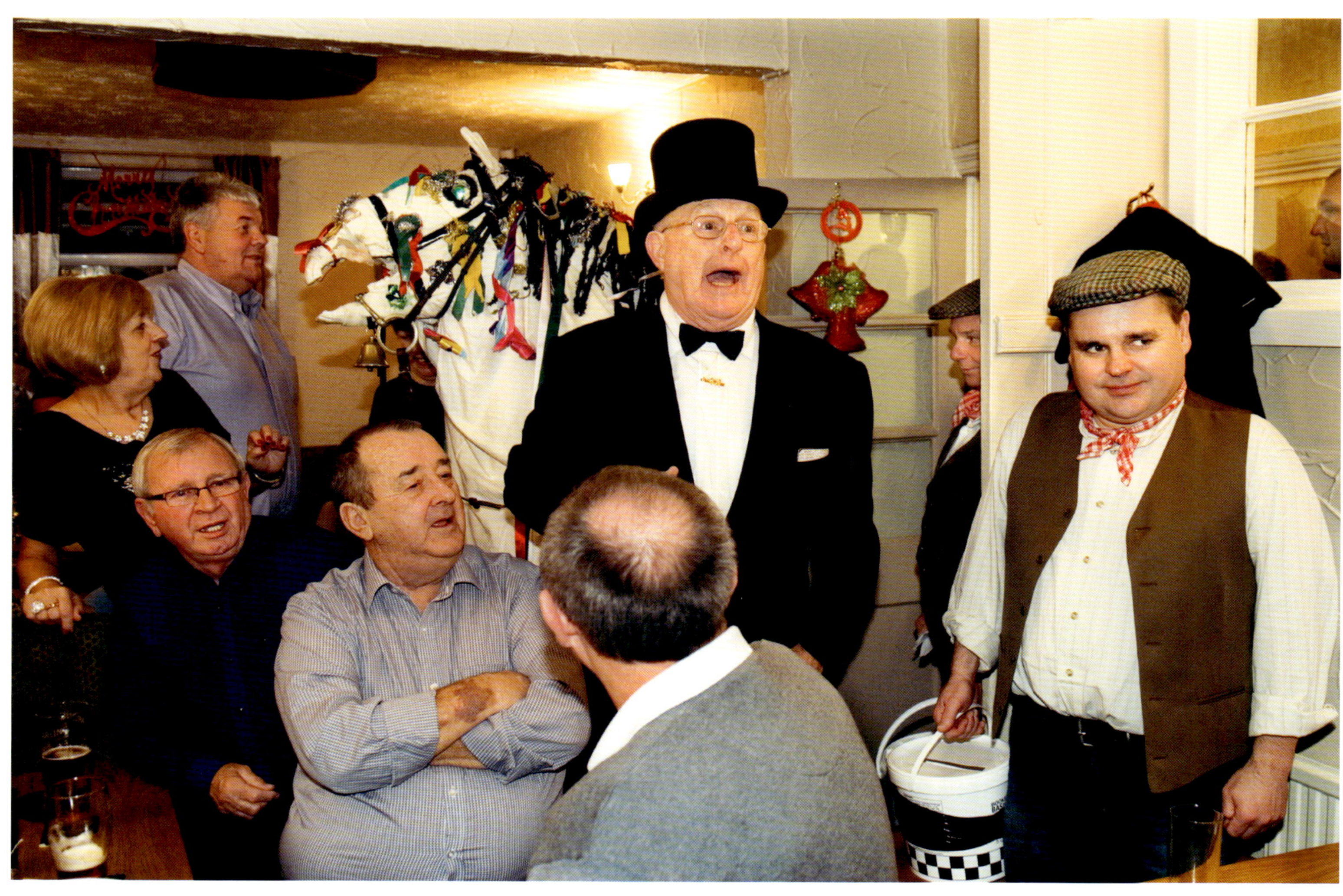

MARI LWYD
Llangynwyd, Bridgend, Glamorgan
2012

The Railway Inn is packed with New Year's Eve customers; Gwyn Evans the ostler carries on the Mari Lwyd tradition passed down from his father Cynwyd.

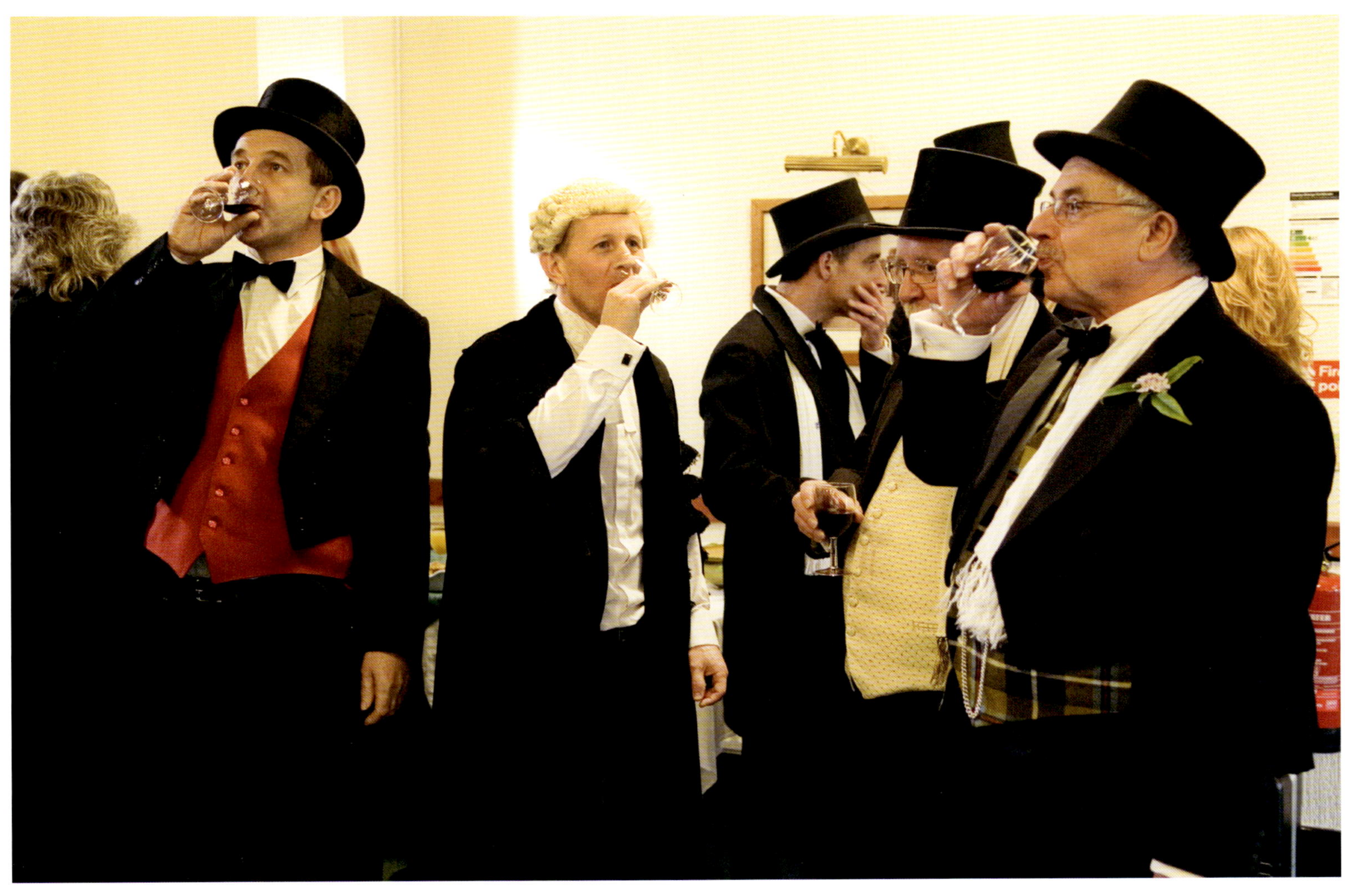

BODMIN WASSAILERS
Bodmin, Cornwall
2016

The Town Clerk, Stephen Facer entertains the Bodmin Wassailers on Old New Year's Day. They drink a toast to the former Town Clerk, Nicholas Sprey who left in his will of 1624, 13 shillings and 4 pence to provide an annual Wassailing Cup.

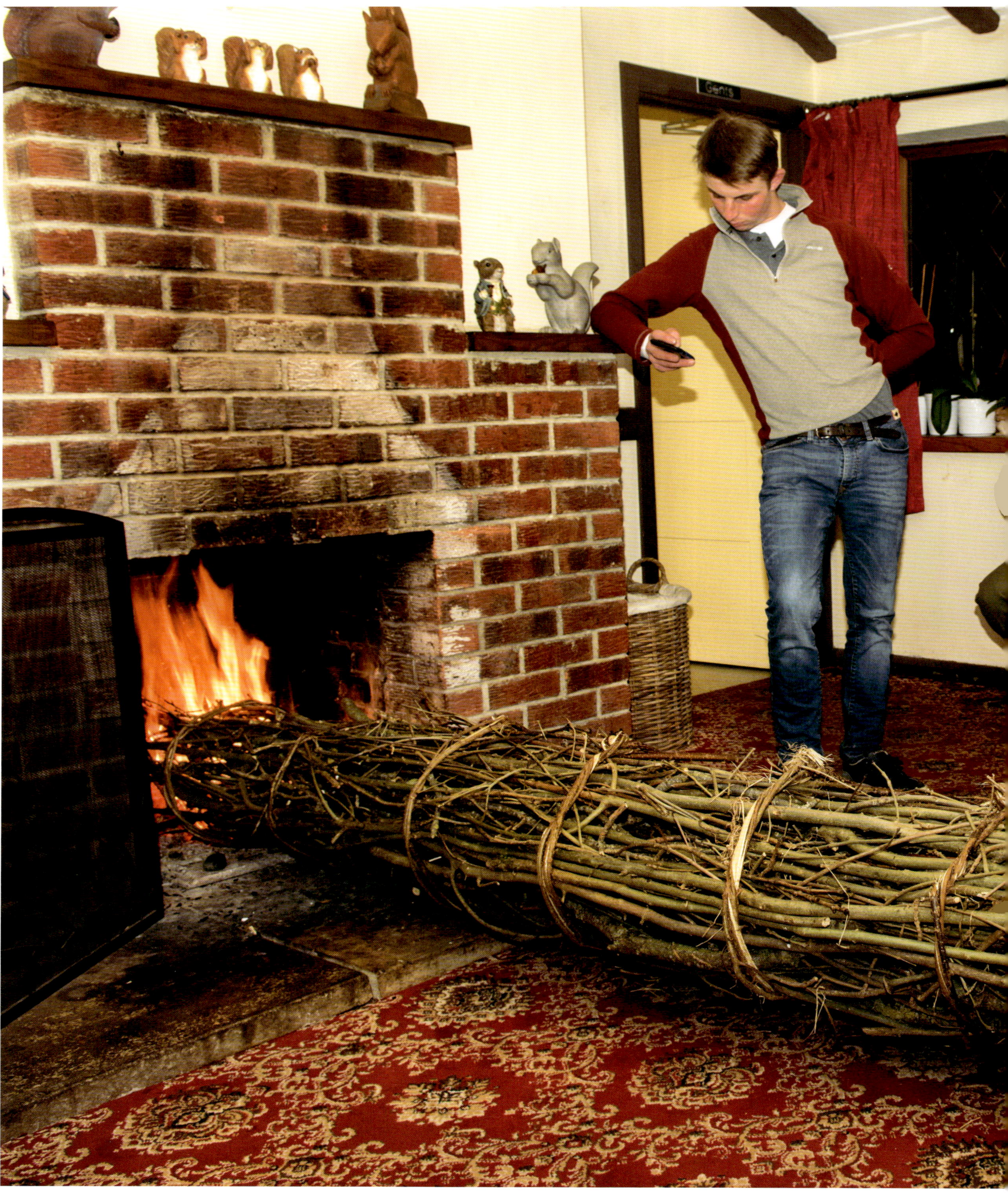
Gents

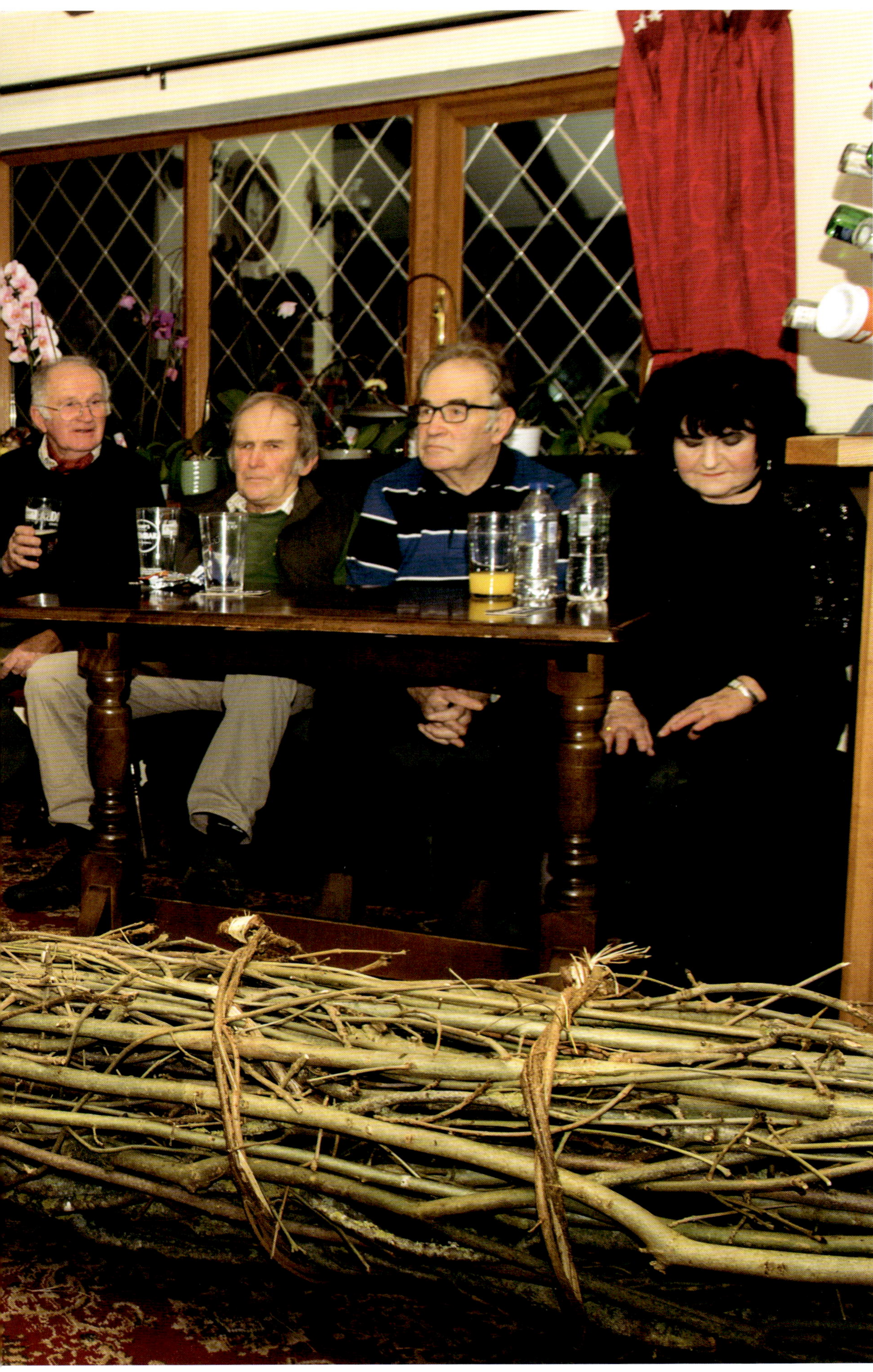

BURNING THE ASHEN FAGGOT
Laymore, Dorset
2020

On Old New Year's Eve at The Squirrel Inn regulars sup their pints as the pub fire slowly consumes the 15 foot long Ashen Faggot.

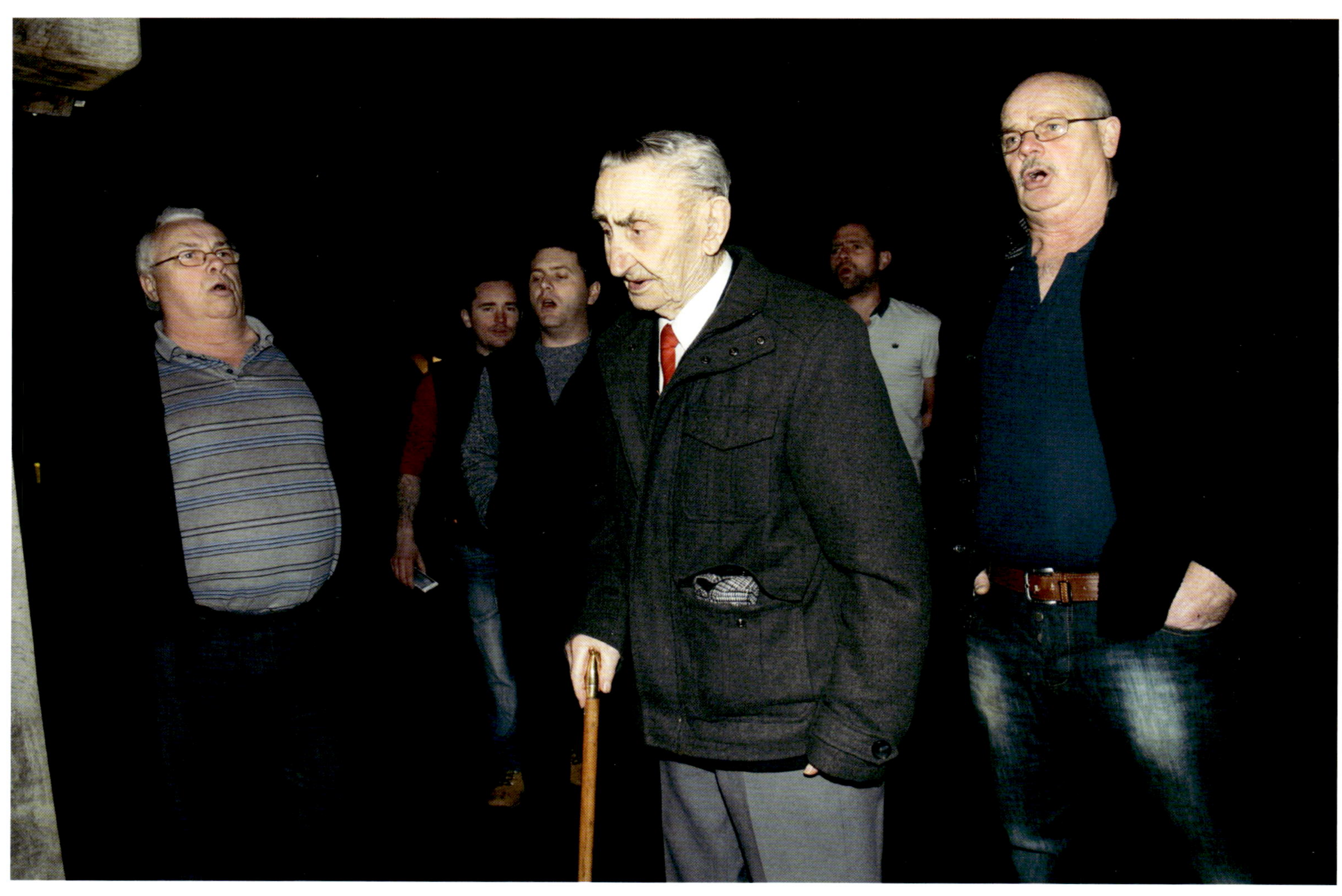

WASSAILING
Curry Rivel, Somerset
2016

Bill Richards leads the village Wassailers on Old New Year's Eve, singing the village traditional wassailing song and bidding the house holders, "... and a happy New Year," before being invited in to enjoy some well deserved party food.

Bill Richards makes a short speech before placing the Ashen Faggot onto the fire in the King William IV pub.

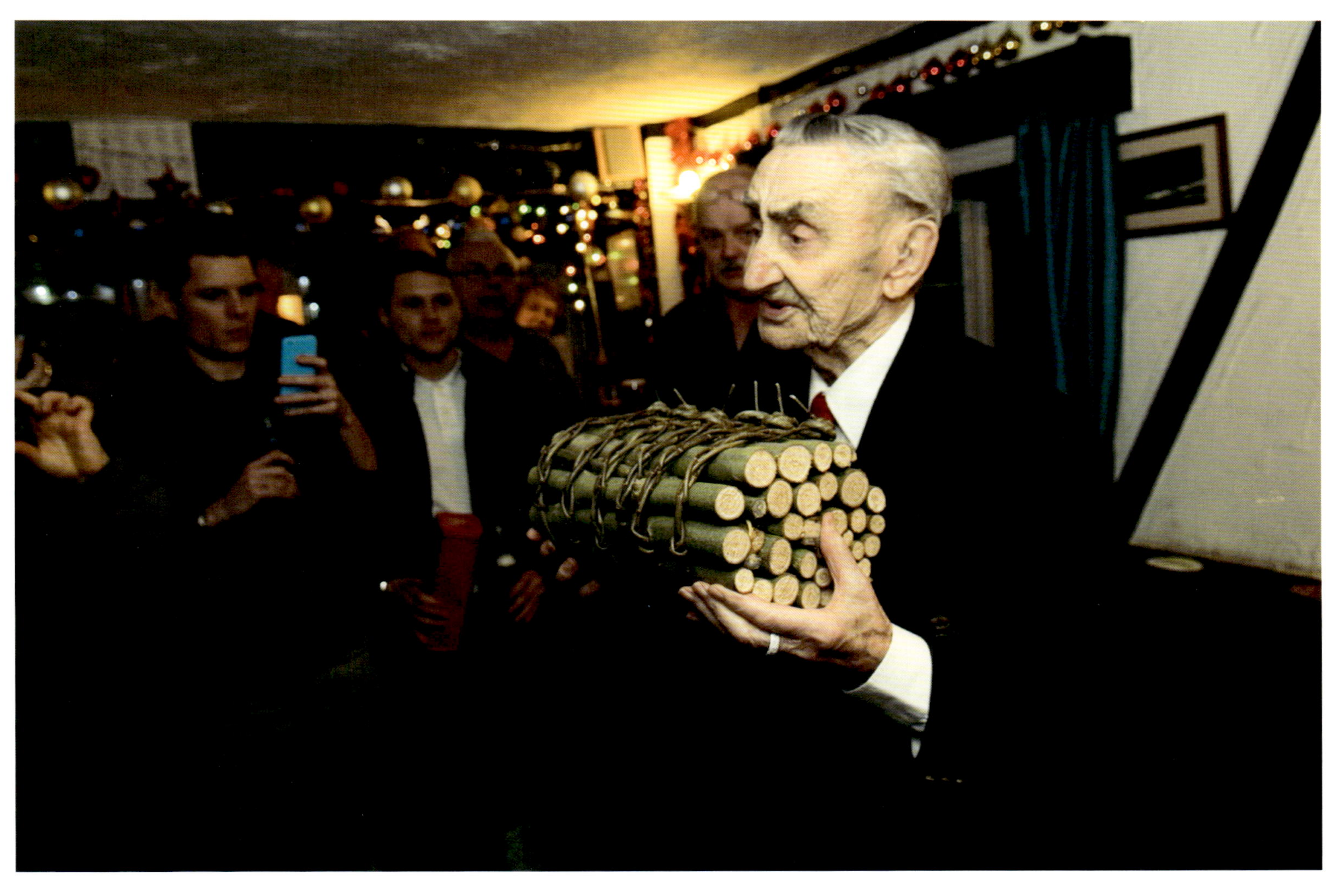

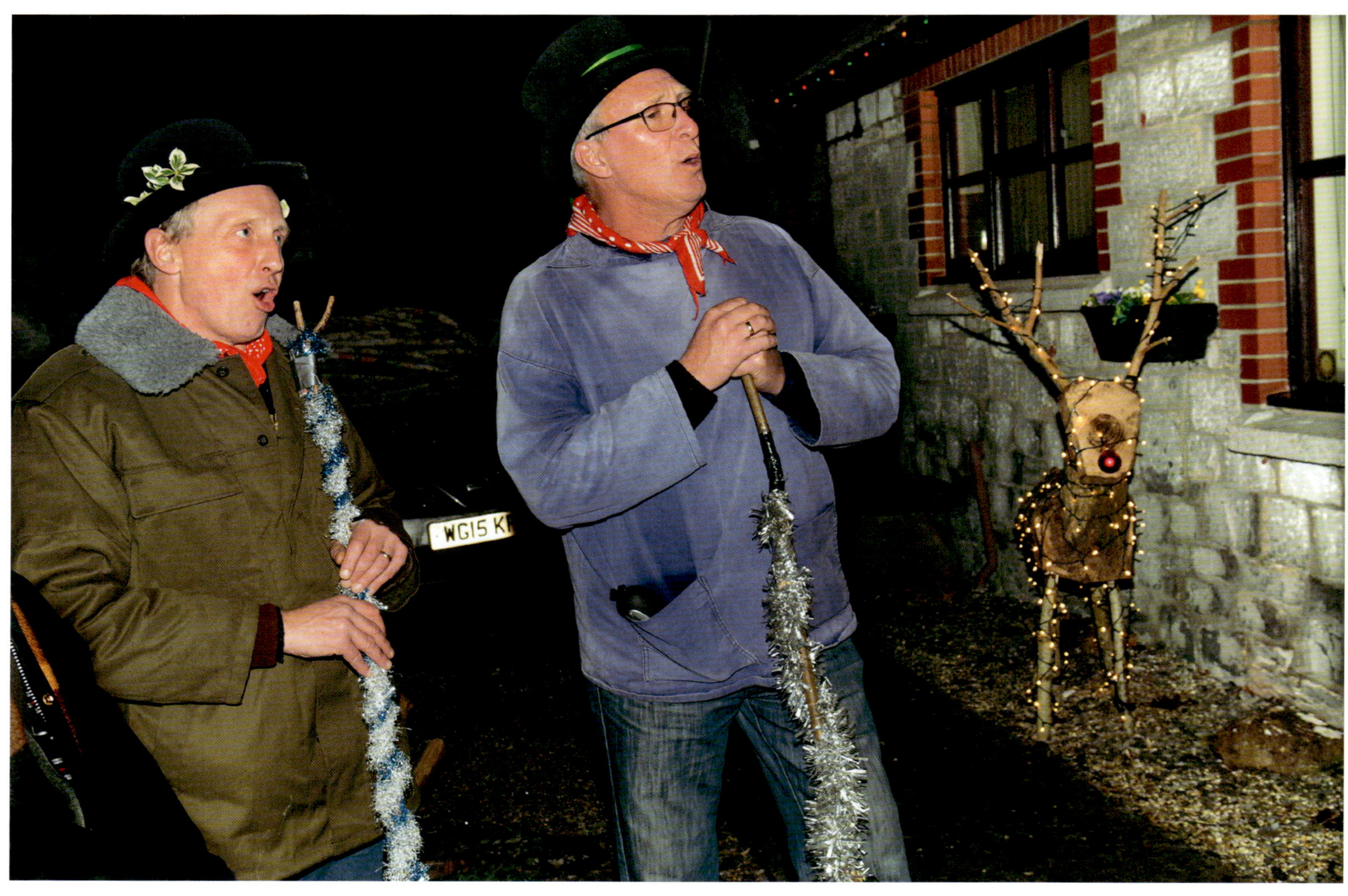

DRAYTON WASSAIL
Drayton, Somerset
2017

Dave Adams and Steven Burrows two members of the Wassail party on Old Christmas Eve visiting houses in the village singing the wassailing song, and bidding the householders, “a happy Christmas and New Year.”

Patricia Robinson, Chair of the Parish Council and her neighbour Morris Munn, a retired livestock farmer, are being wassailed at Northover Farm.

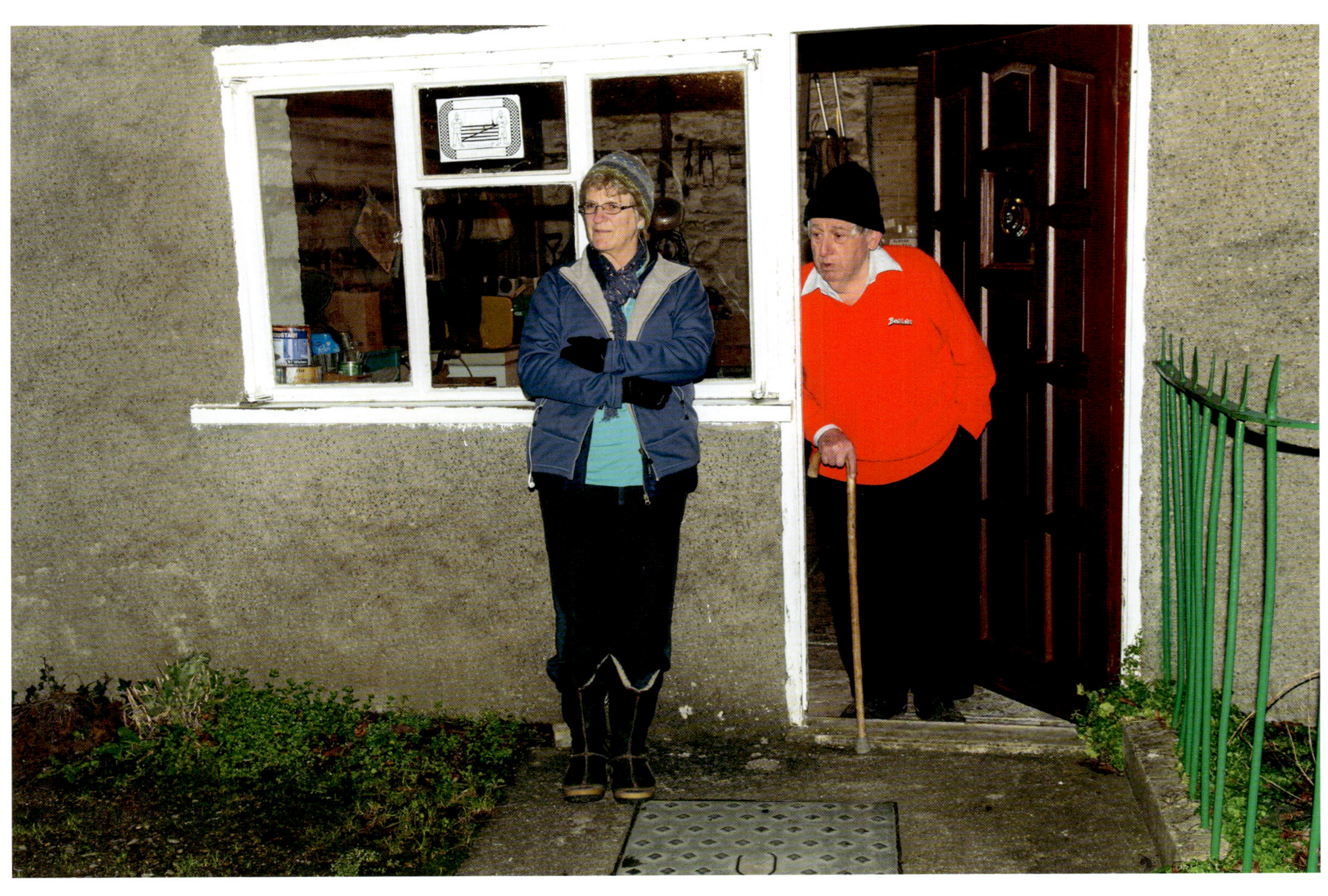

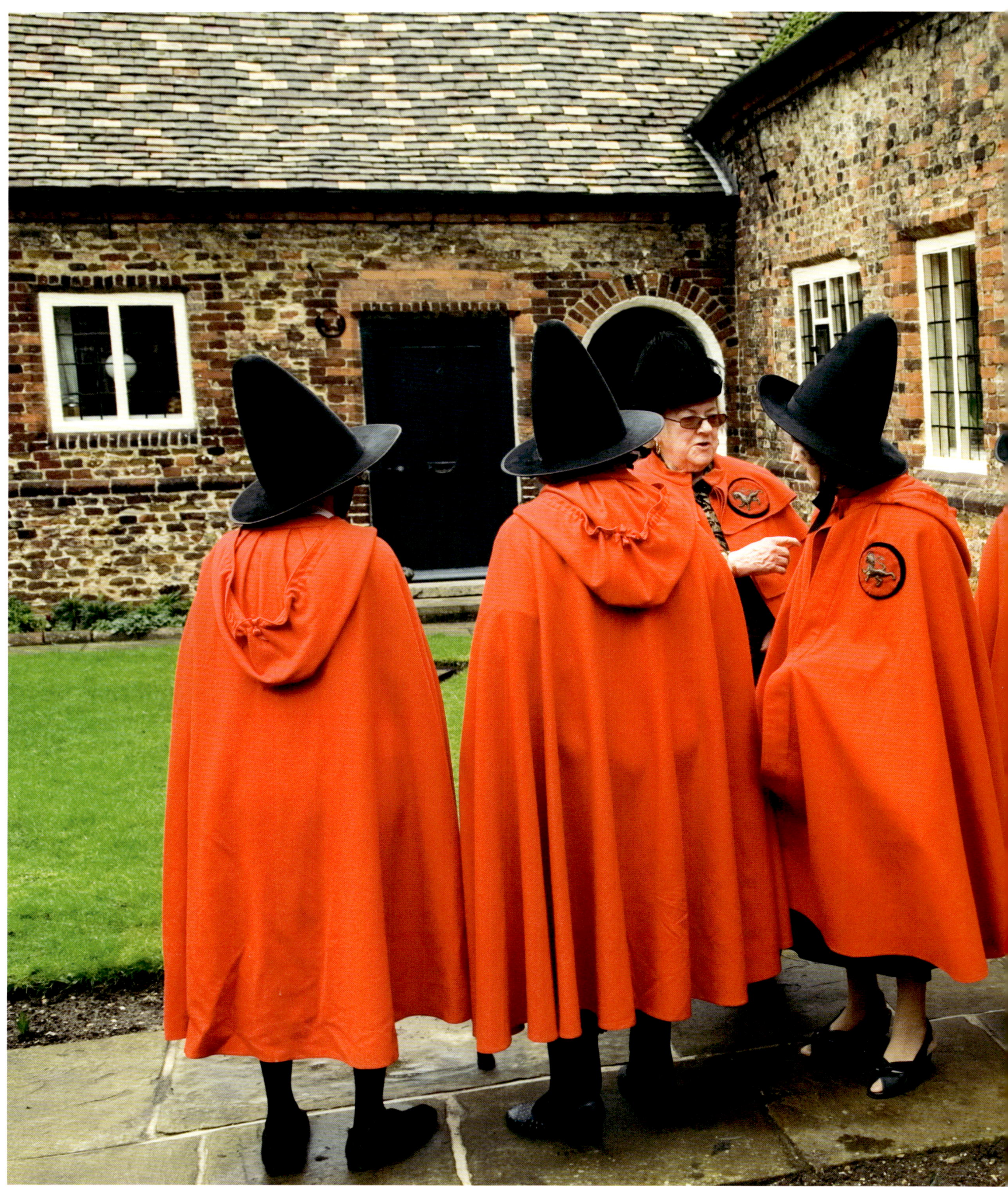

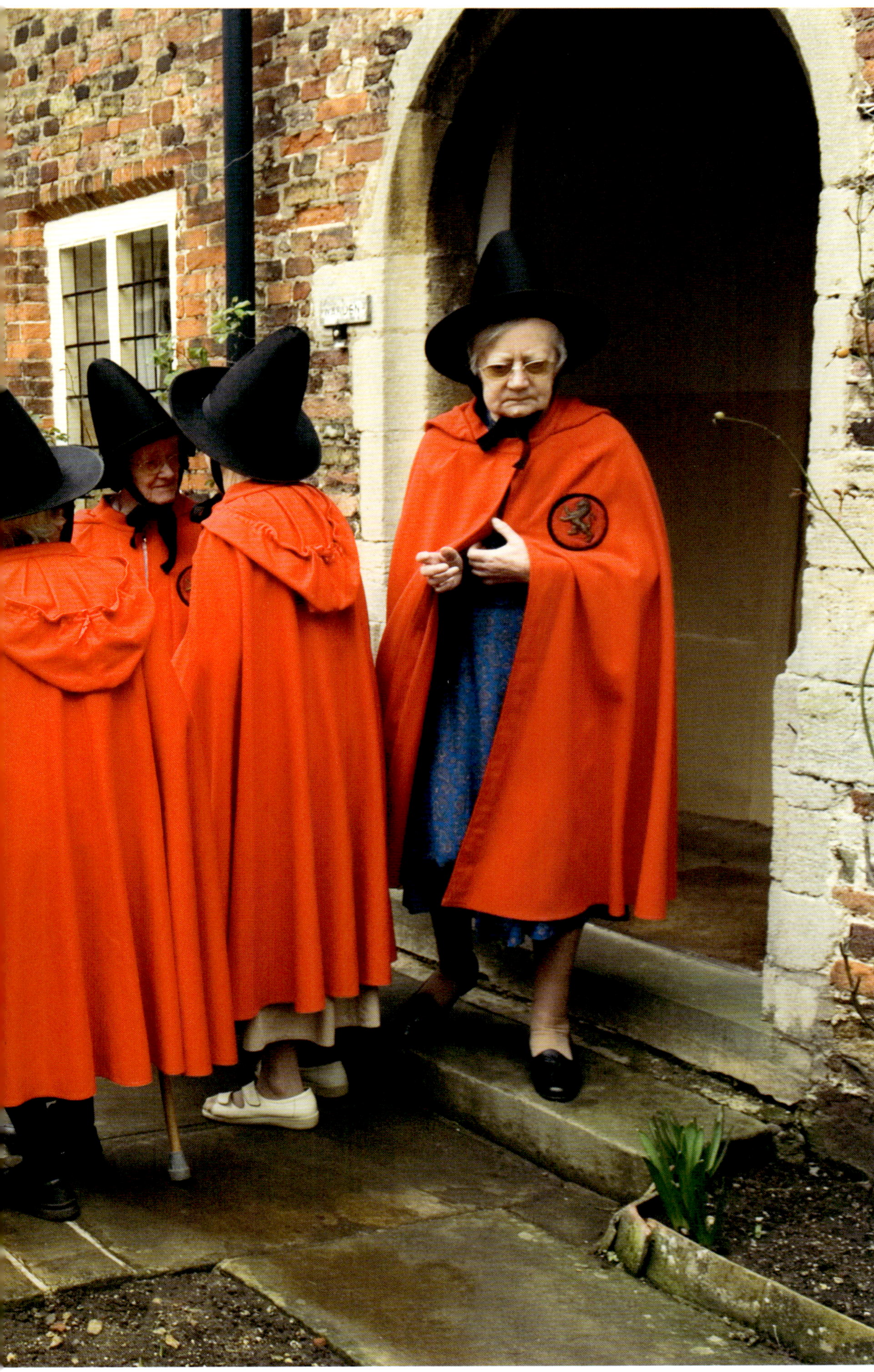

OLD LADIES OF CASTLE RISING
Castle Rising, Norfolk
2007

On Founders Day residents of The Hospital of the Holy and Undivided Trinity wear their traditional scarlet cloaks and pointed black hats to attend a memorial service in the 'Hospital' chapel.

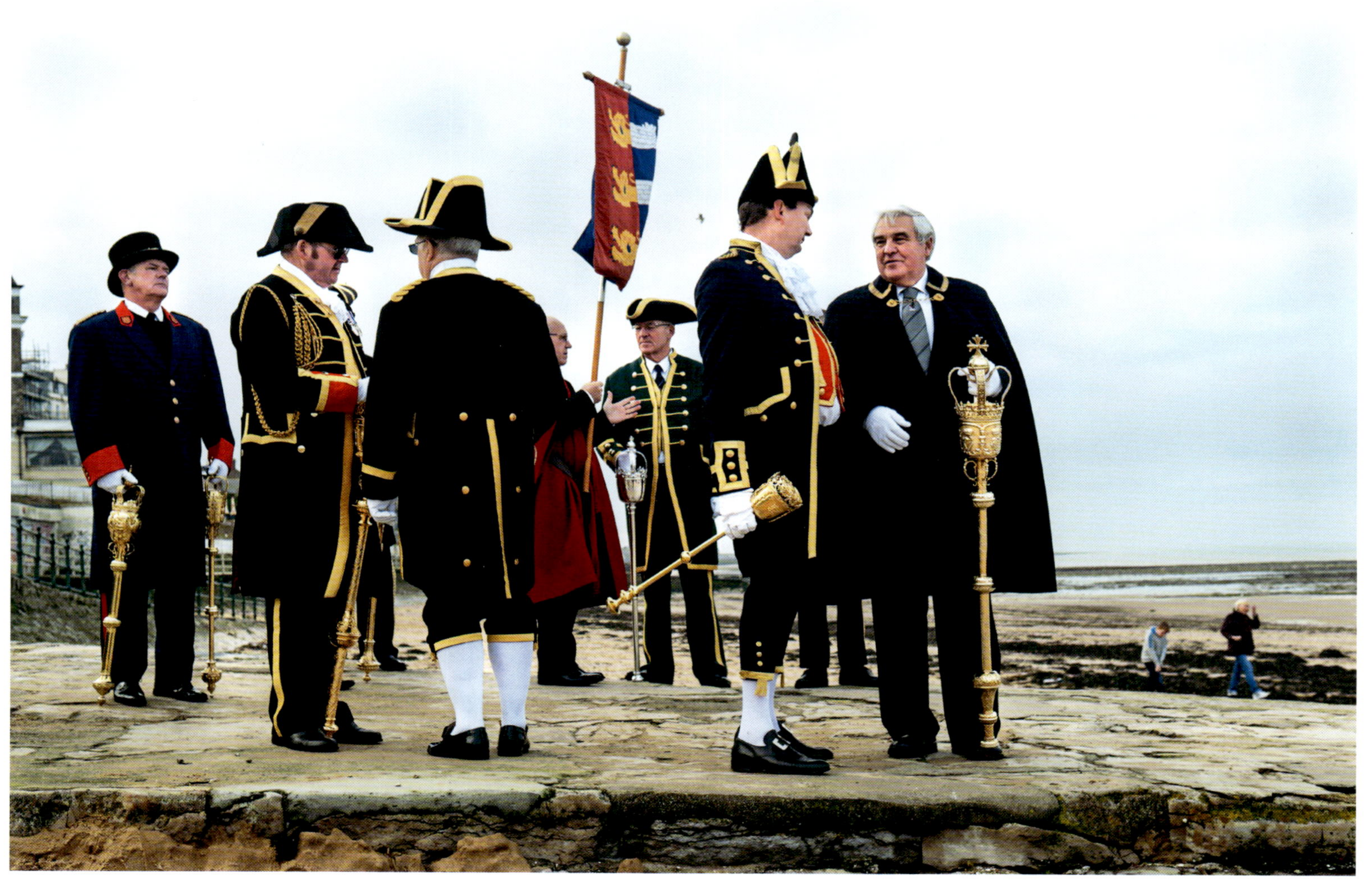

BLESSING OF THE SEA
Margate, Kent
2017

Local Kentish town hall dignitaries and religious leaders gather in their regalia along with members of the Greek Orthodox church for the Blessing of the Sea, which takes place on Epiphany, 6th January, marking the baptism of Christ. Prayers and blessings are intoned and a white dove, a symbol of peace is released.

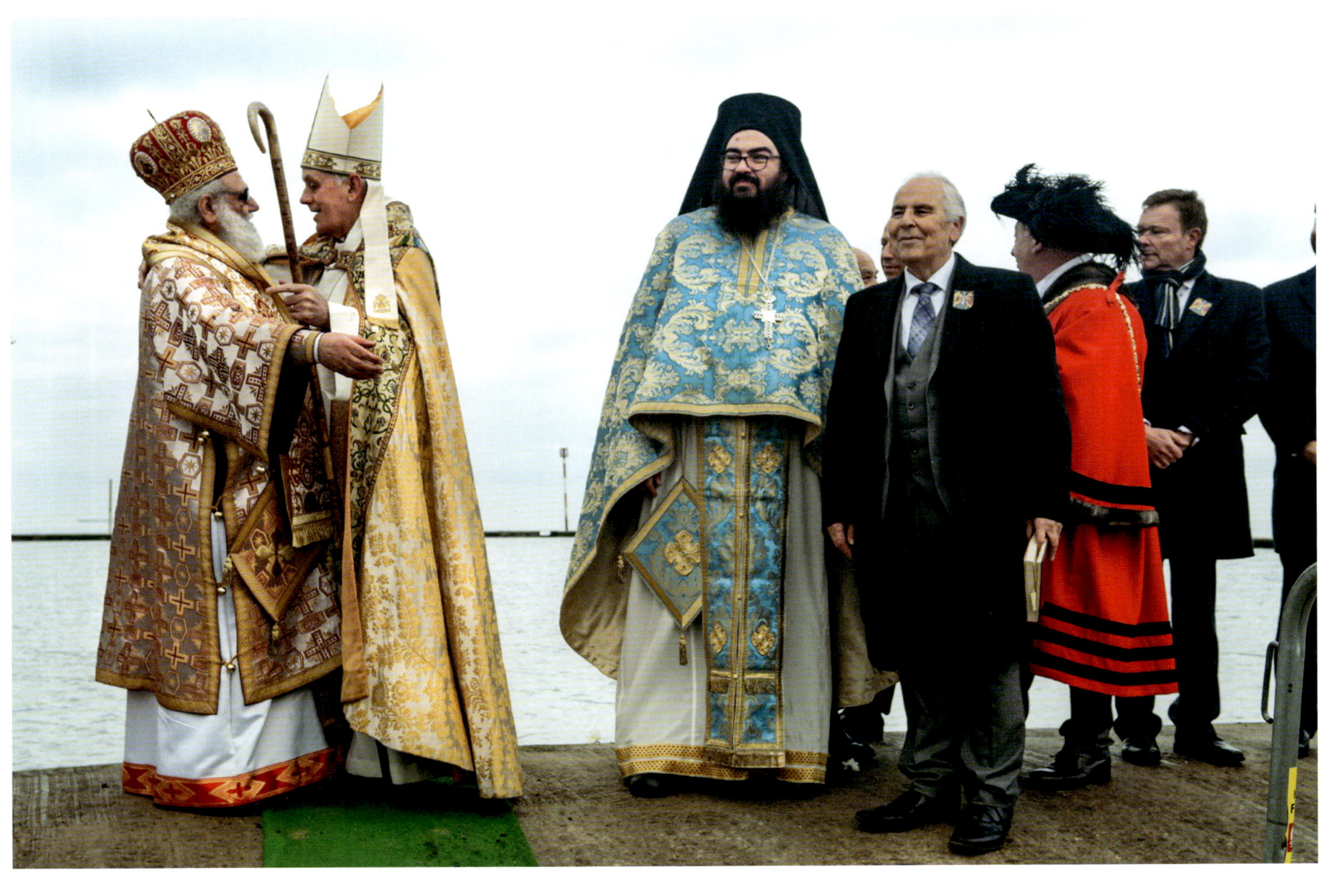

BLESSING OF THE SEA
Margate, Kent
2017

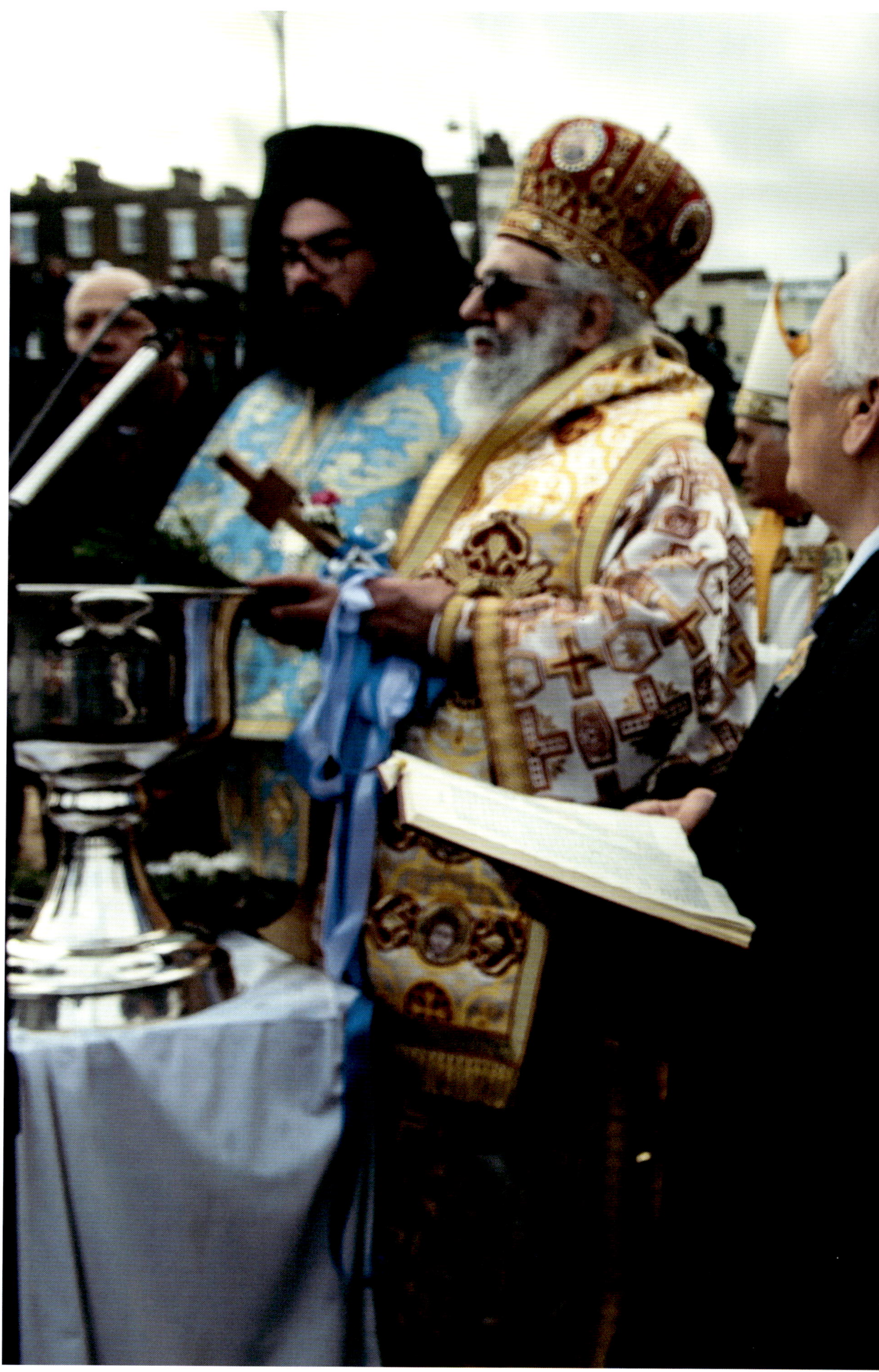

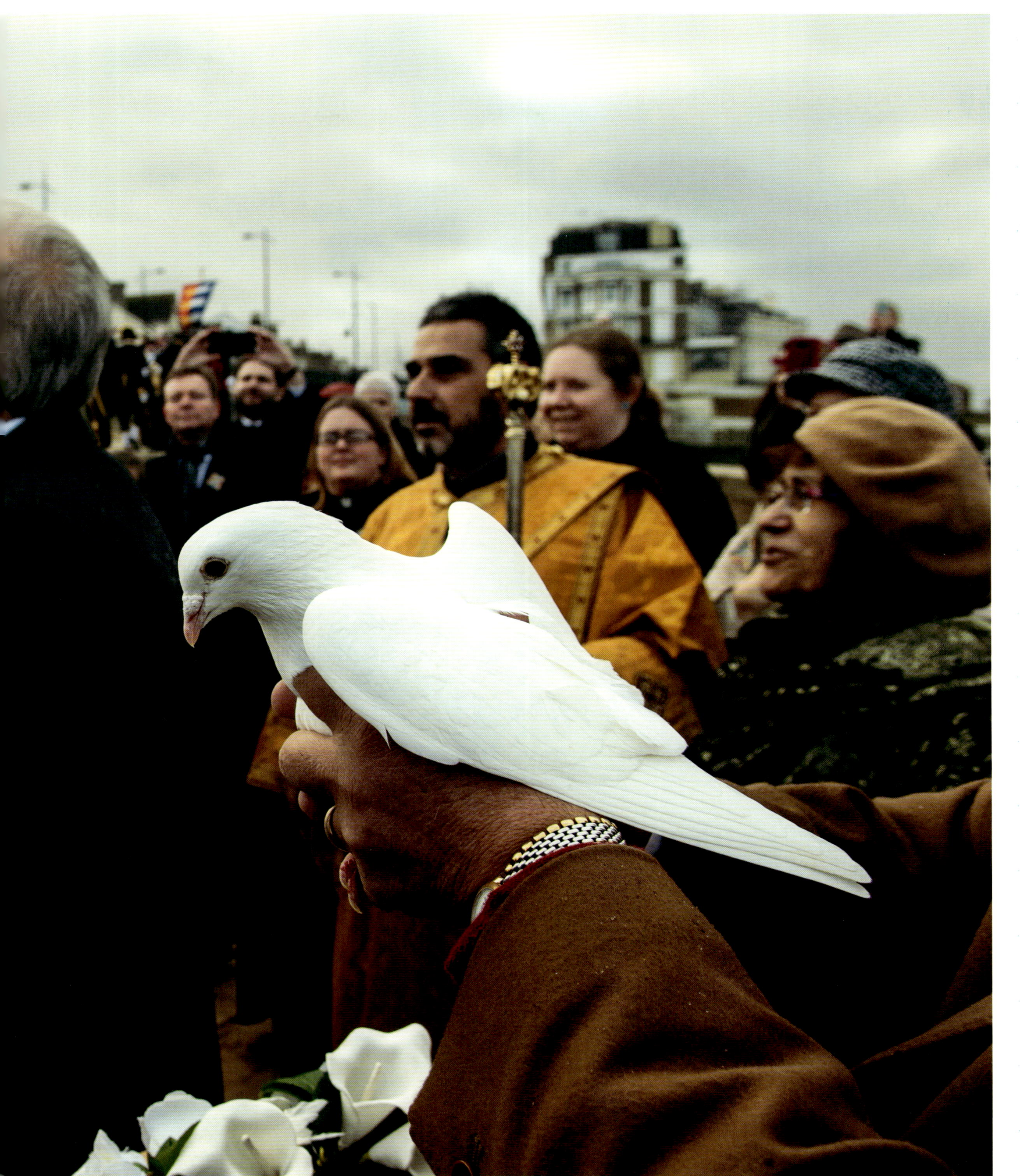

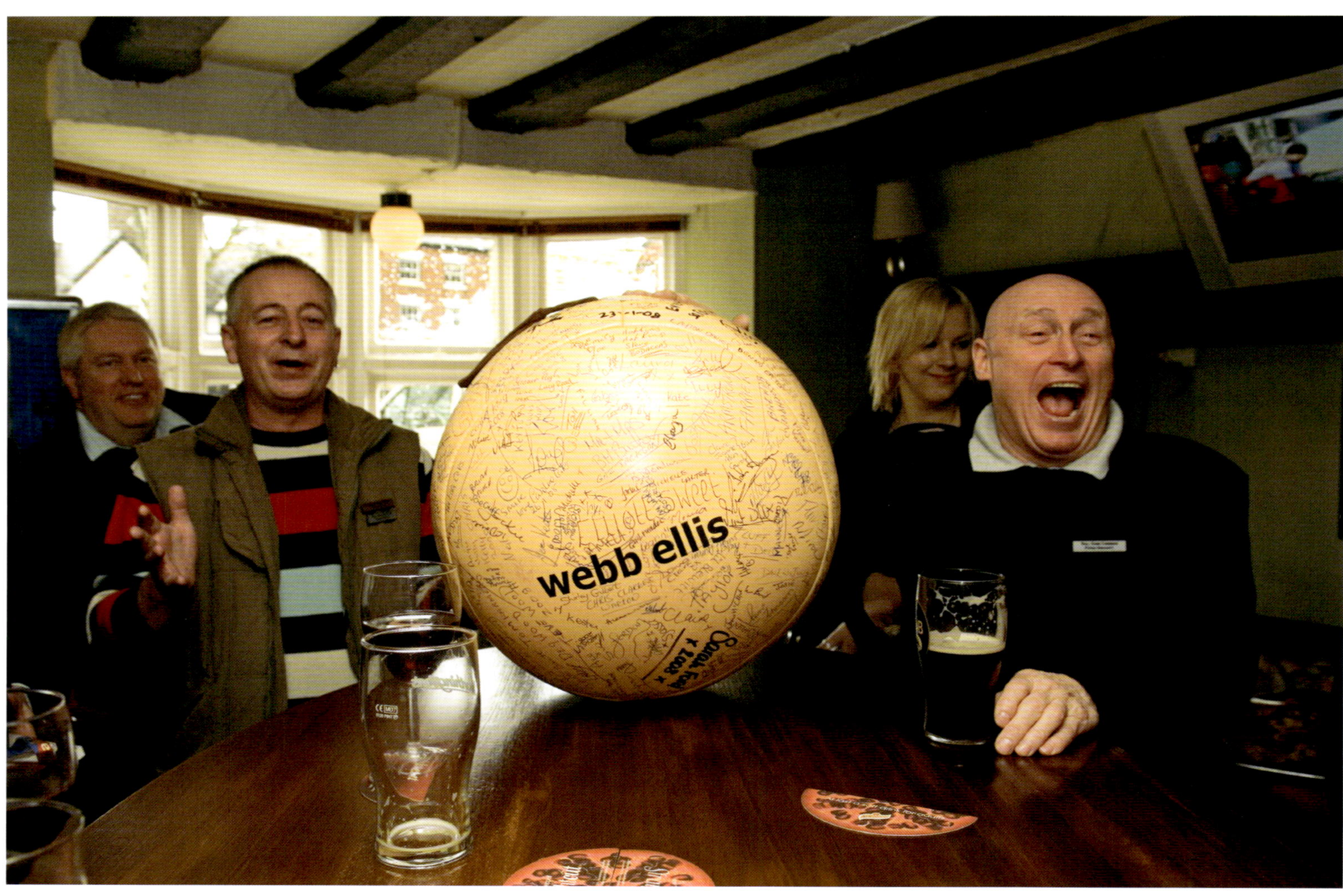

SHROVE TUESDAY FOOTBALL
Atherstone, Warwickshire
2008

Committee members gather at the Angel Inn with the signed football before the start of the annual game. There are few rules; two being that the game must be played in Long Street and no one is to be killed.

A young man is carried aloft out of the scrummage soon after the start of the game, when the ball is thrown to the waiting crowd.

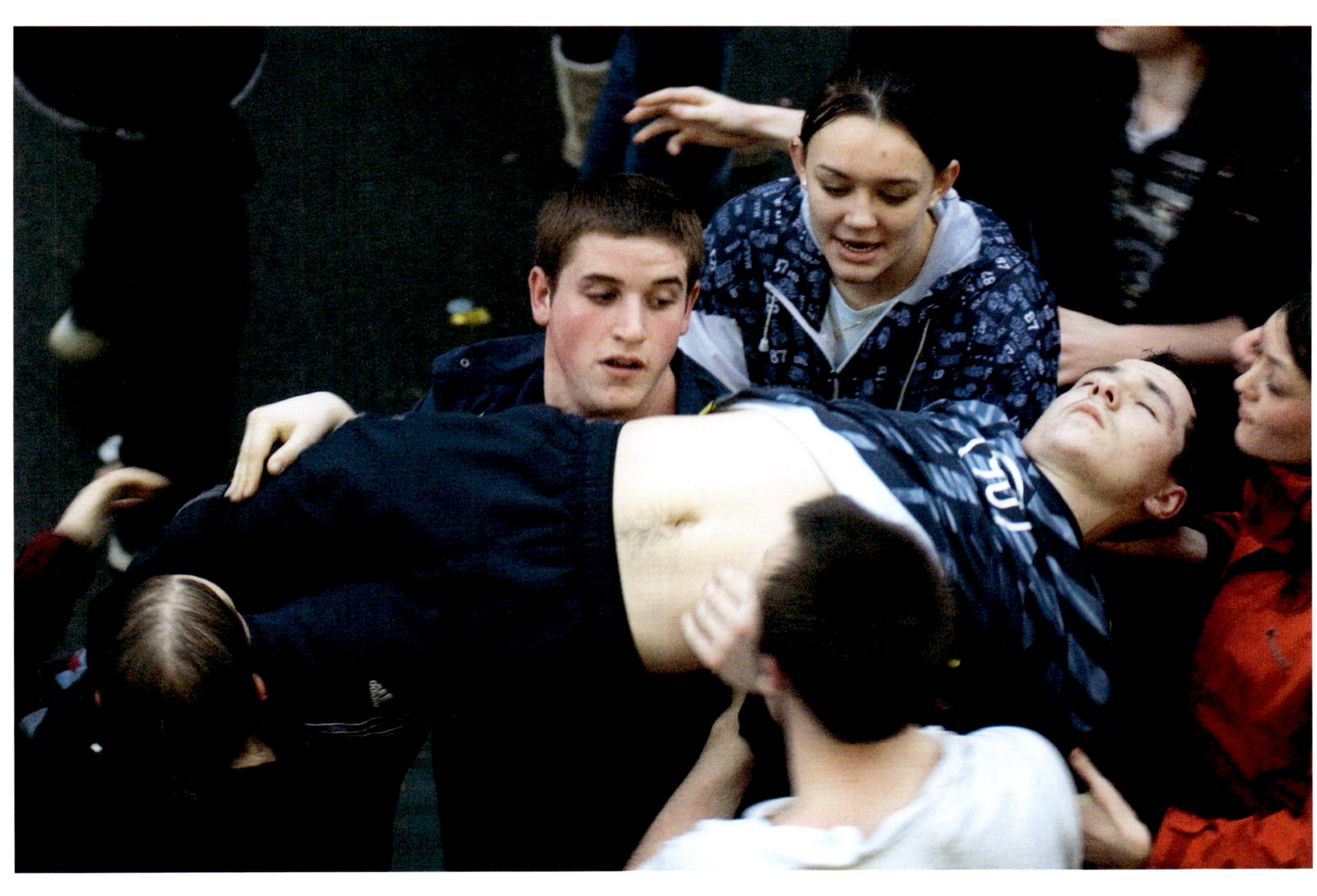

SHROVE TUESDAY FOOTBALL
Atherstone, Warwickshire
2008

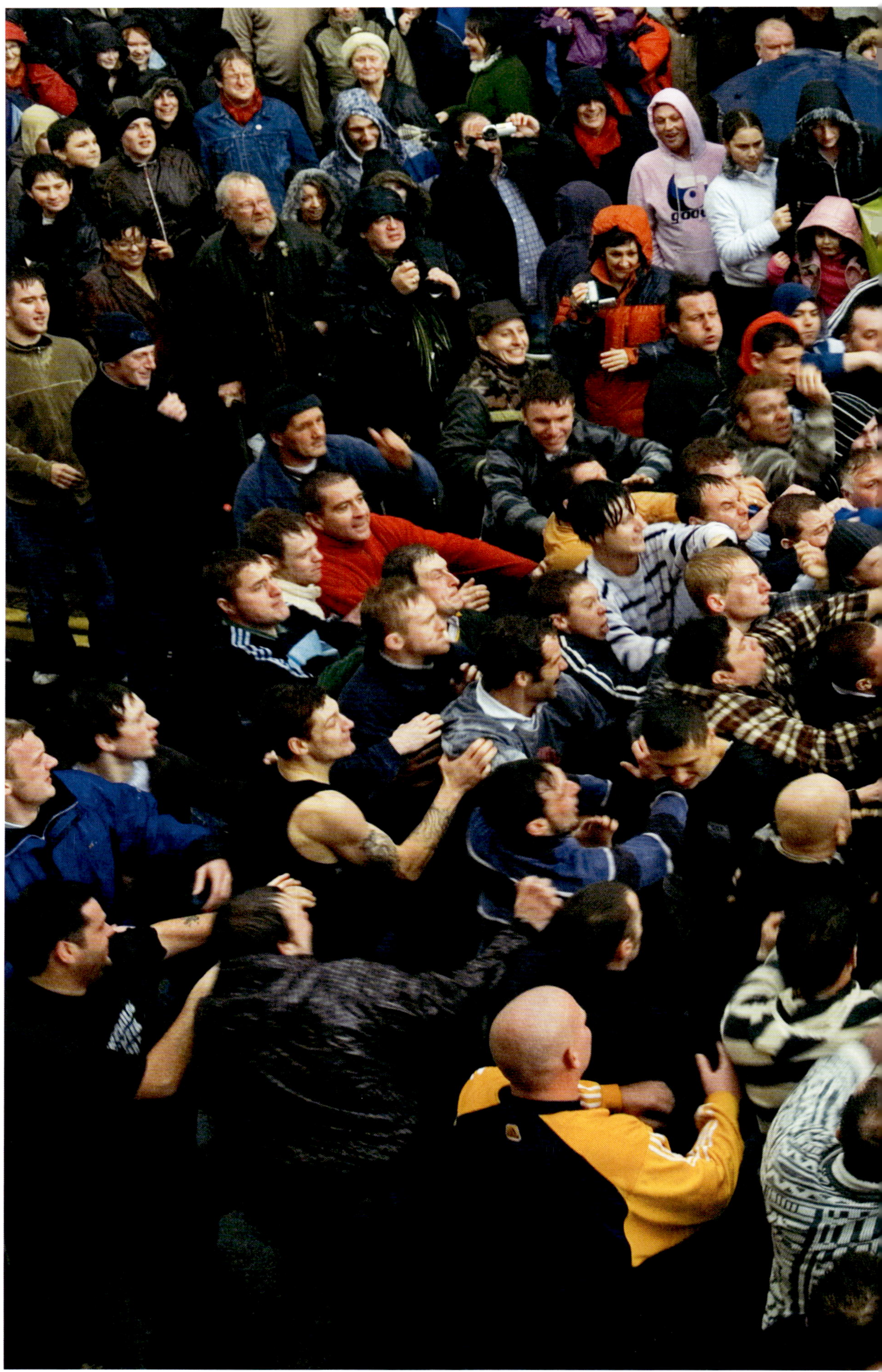

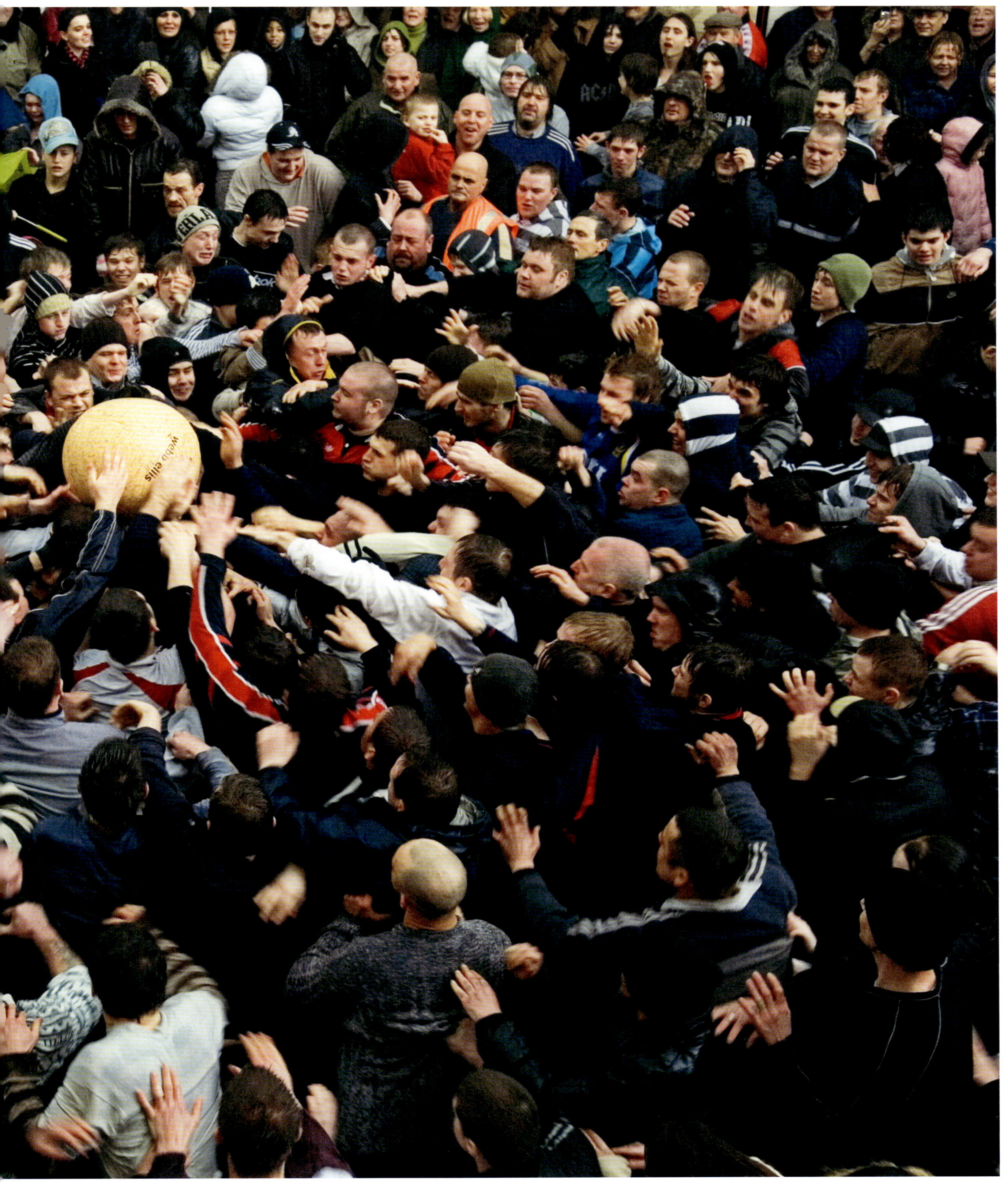
webb ellis

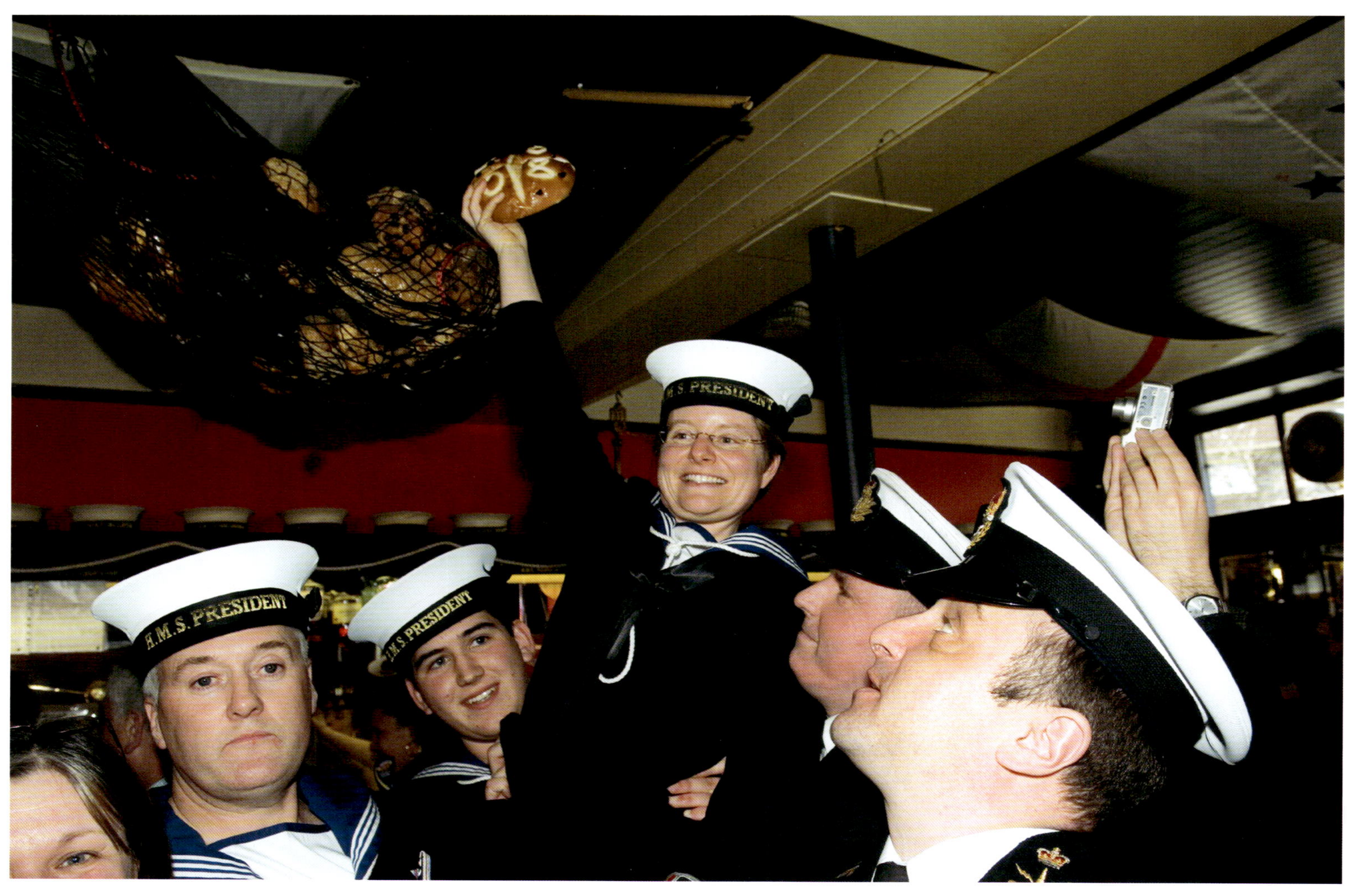

WIDOWS BUN
Bromley-by-Bow, London
2008

On Good Friday at the Widows Son Inn a young sailor from the Royal Navy places a new hot cross bun in a net hanging above the bar.

Afterwards there is disco dancing, karaoke and the Good Friday Hot Cross Bun feast provided free for the locals.

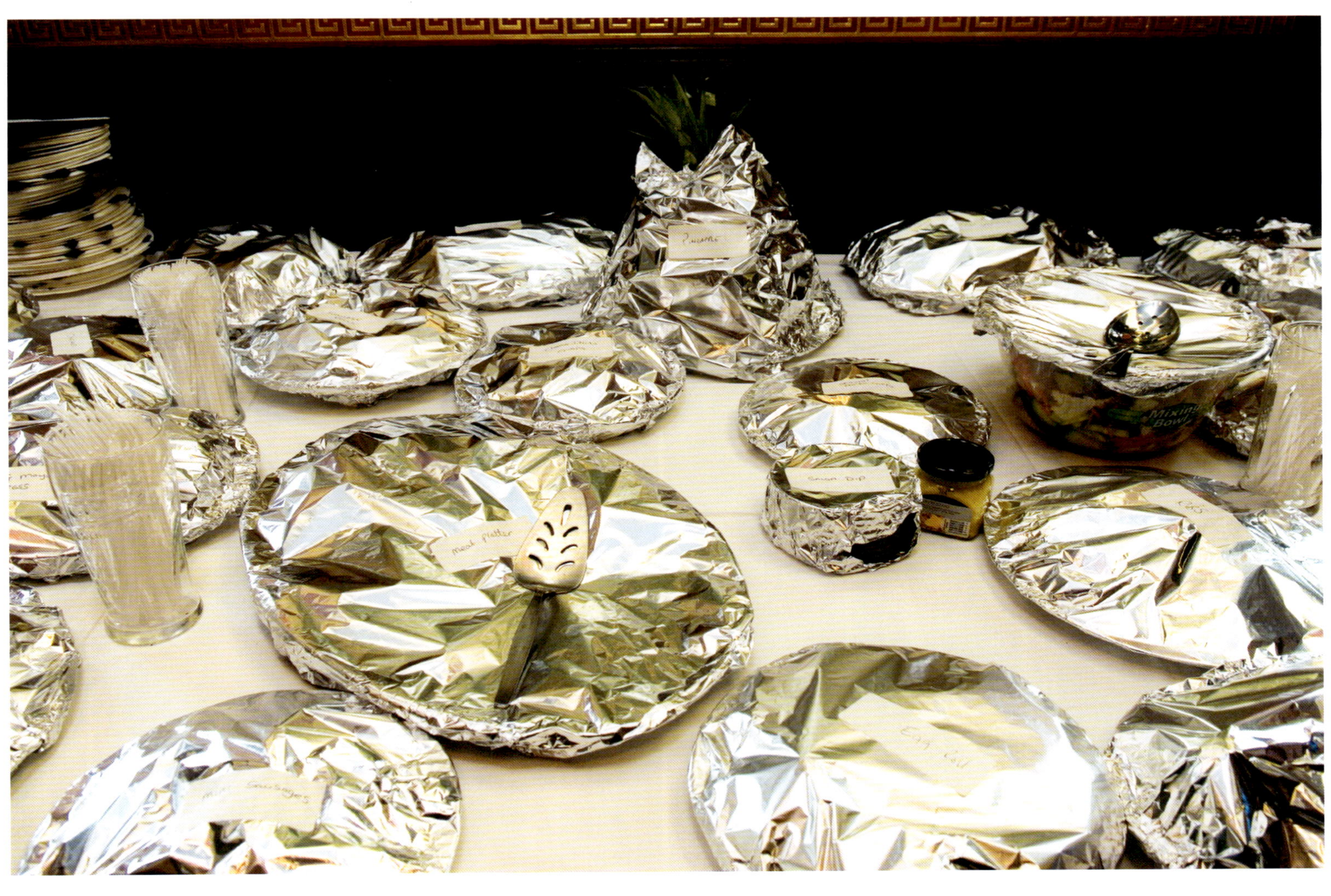
Meat platter

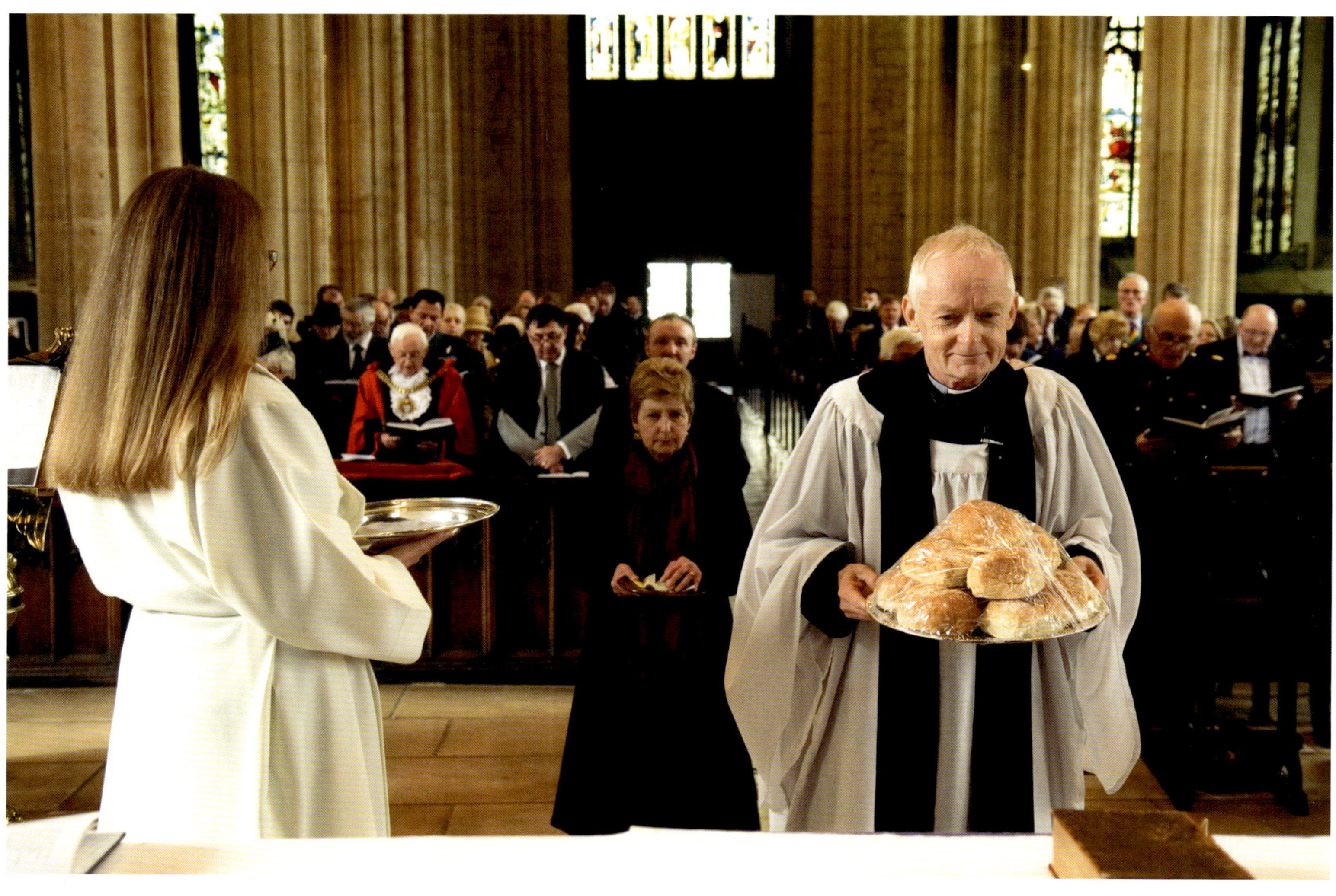

HERCULES CLAY PENNY LOAF DAY
Newark-on-Trent, Nottinghamshire
2015

Stephen Morris the Rector of St Mary Magdalene Church with twelve Penny Loafs on a silver platter as requested by Hercules Clay in his will dated 1645.

The Mayor of Newark, Tom Bickley, and the Lady Mayoress, Ondra Bickley, along with other town hall officials wait in line to receive guests at the start of the Penny Loaf reception in the town hall.

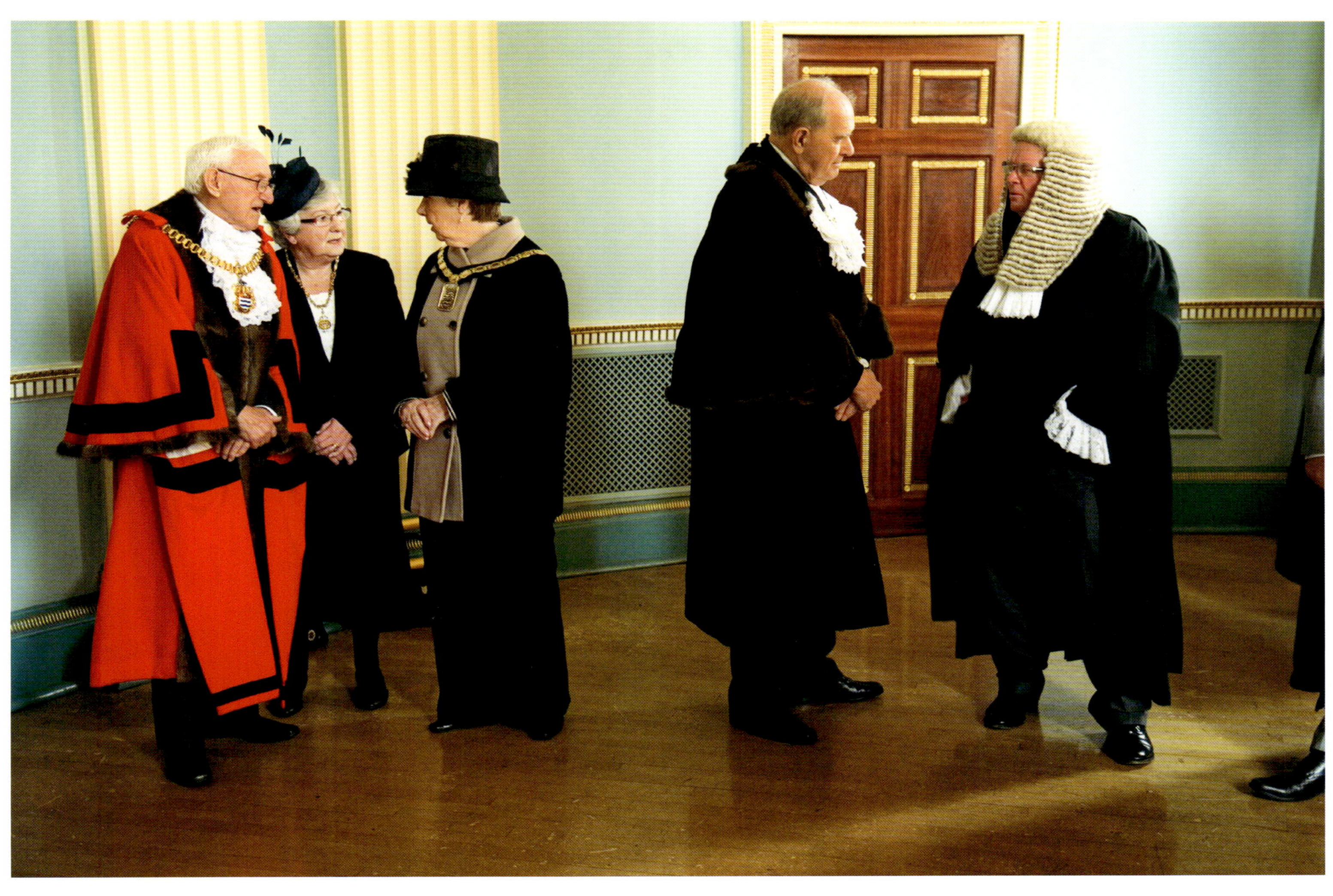

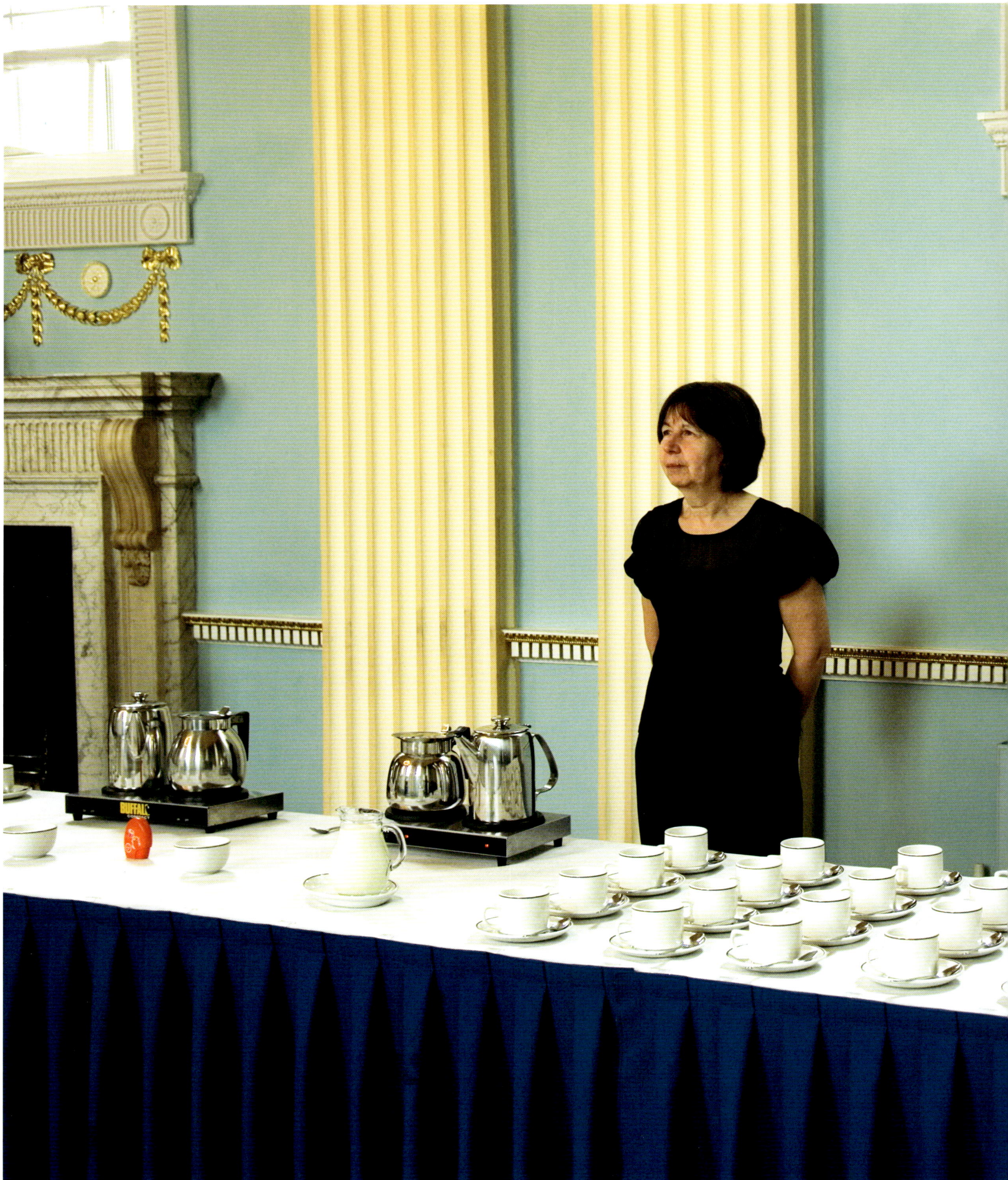
BUFFAL

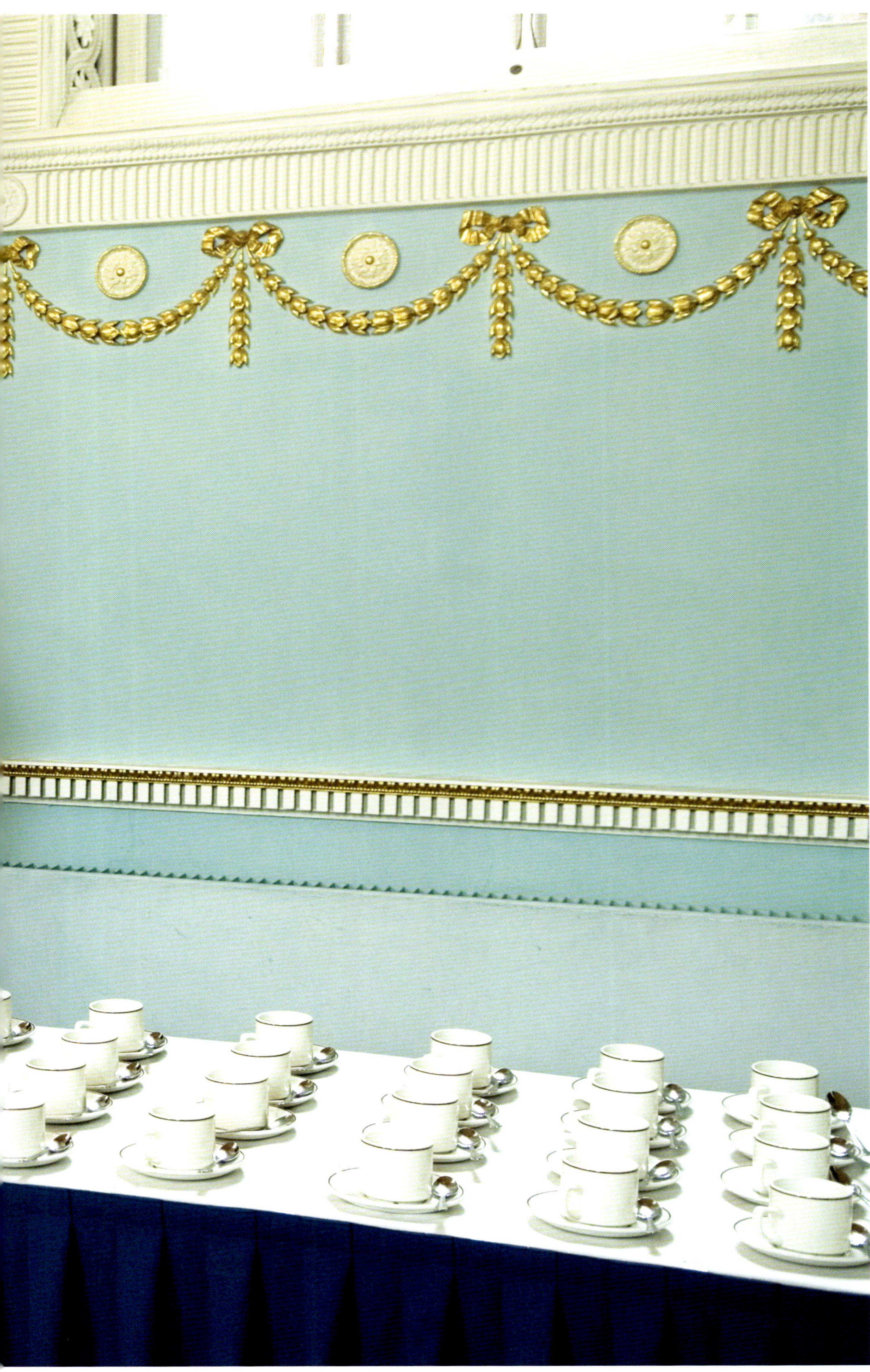

HERCULES CLAY PENNY LOAF DAY
Newark-on-Trent, Nottinghamshire
2015

A town hall employee waits to serve tea and coffee at the Penny Loaf reception.

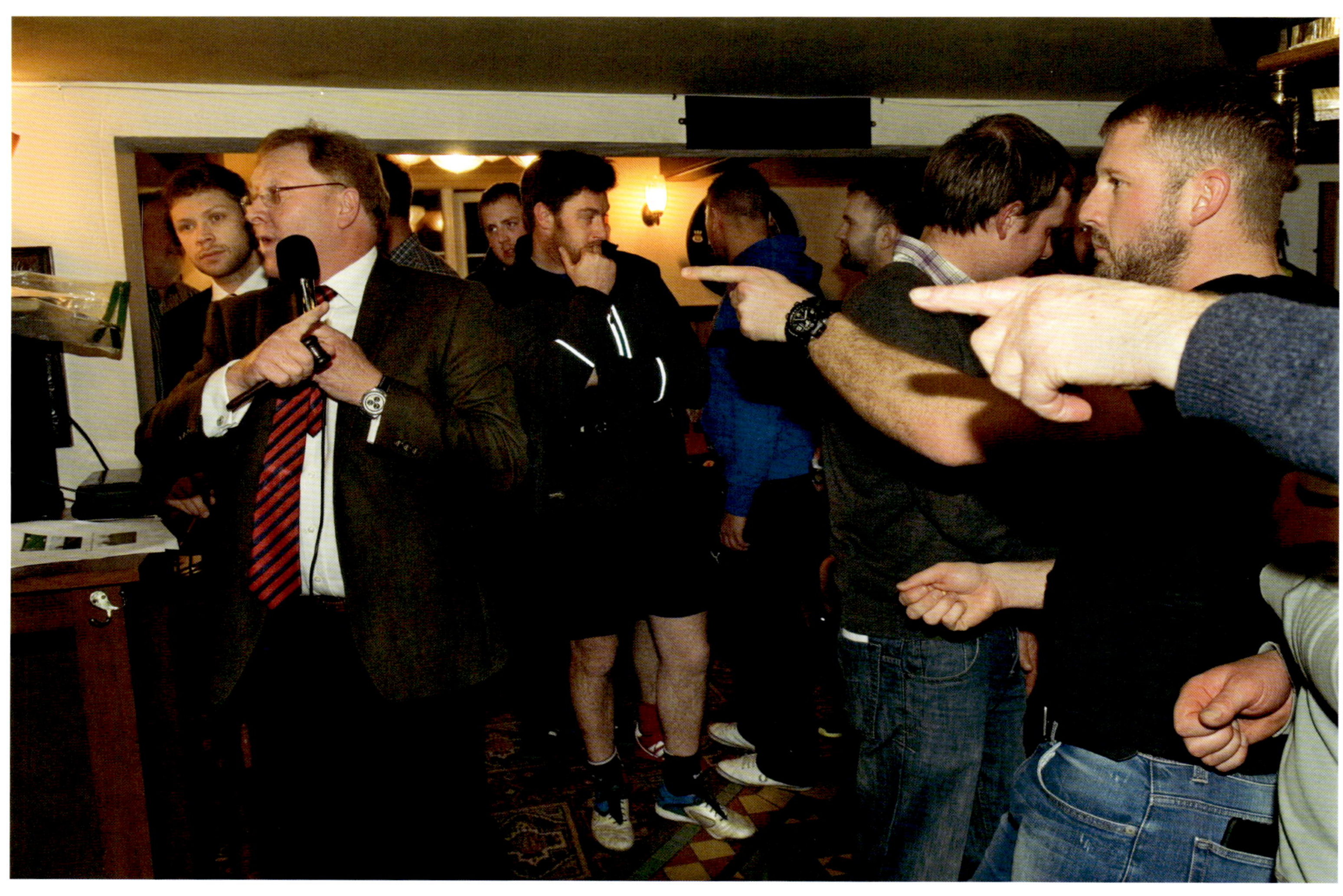

LANE SETTING GRAZING RIGHTS
Ratcliffe Culey, Leicestershire
2016

The Lane Setting Grazing Rights hold their auction at the Gate Inn, as they have been doing since 1786.

Afterwards those present traditionally sing the *Little Yellow Bird* song along with other music hall favourites followed by a buffet supper for all.

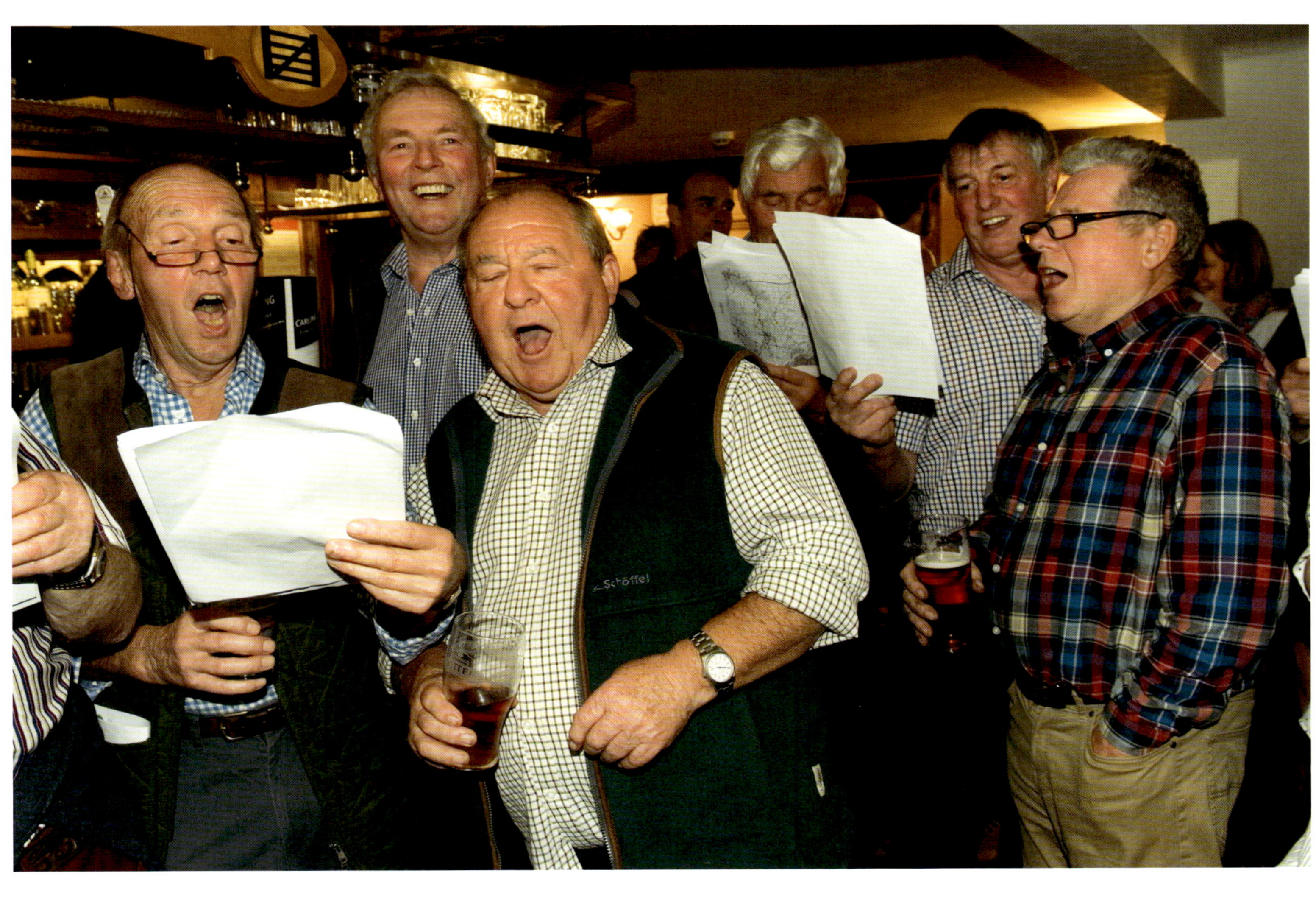
Schöffel

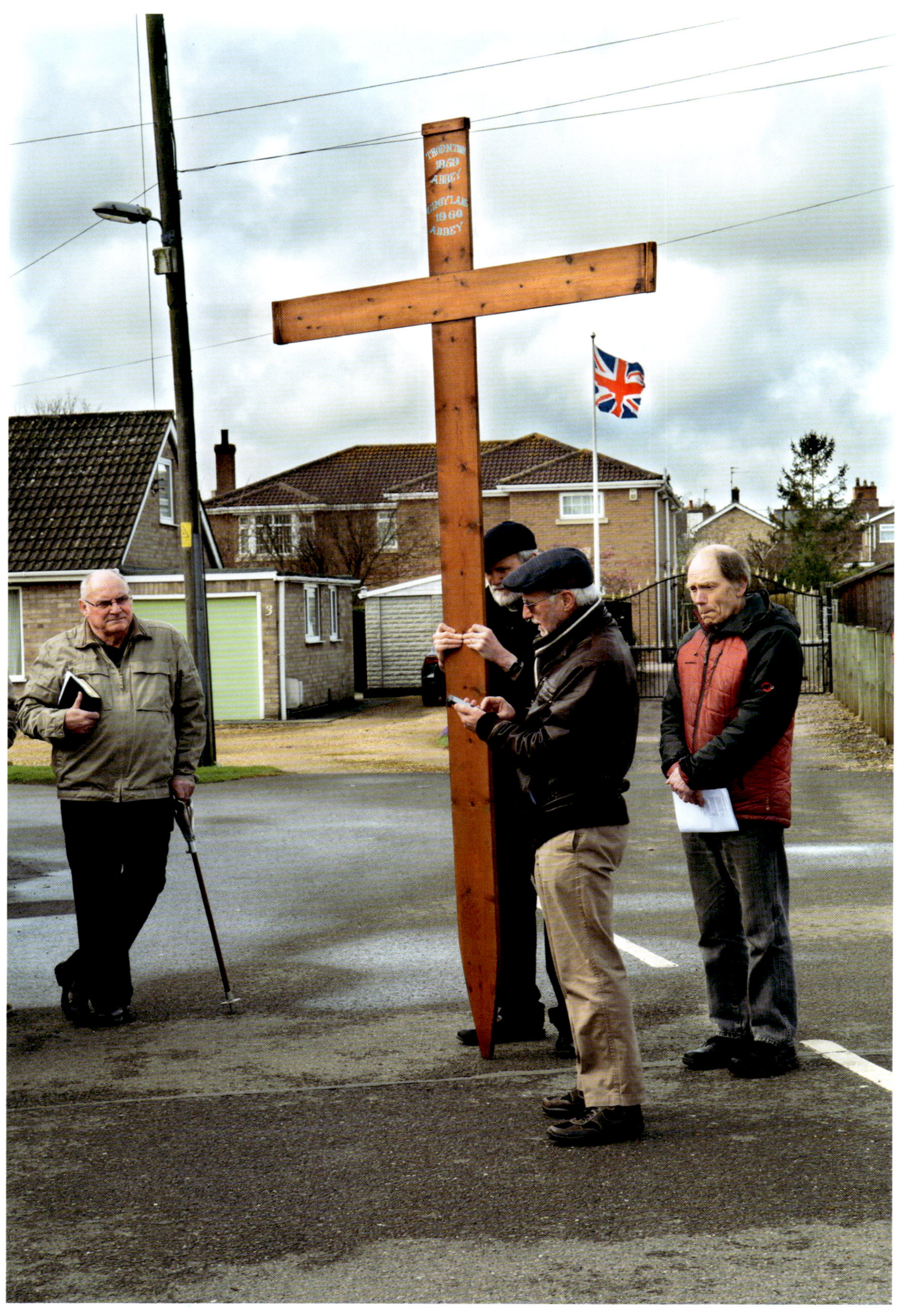

GOOD FRIDAY WALK OF WITNESS
Crowland, Lincolnshire
2018

In Crowland an interdenominational Walk of Witness imitates the journey that Jesus Christ took carrying his cross through the streets of Jerusalem. A Union Jack flag flutters as a member of the congregation reads a passage from the bible on his smartphone. At the end of the walk, hot cross buns and tea are served in the Methodist Chapel.

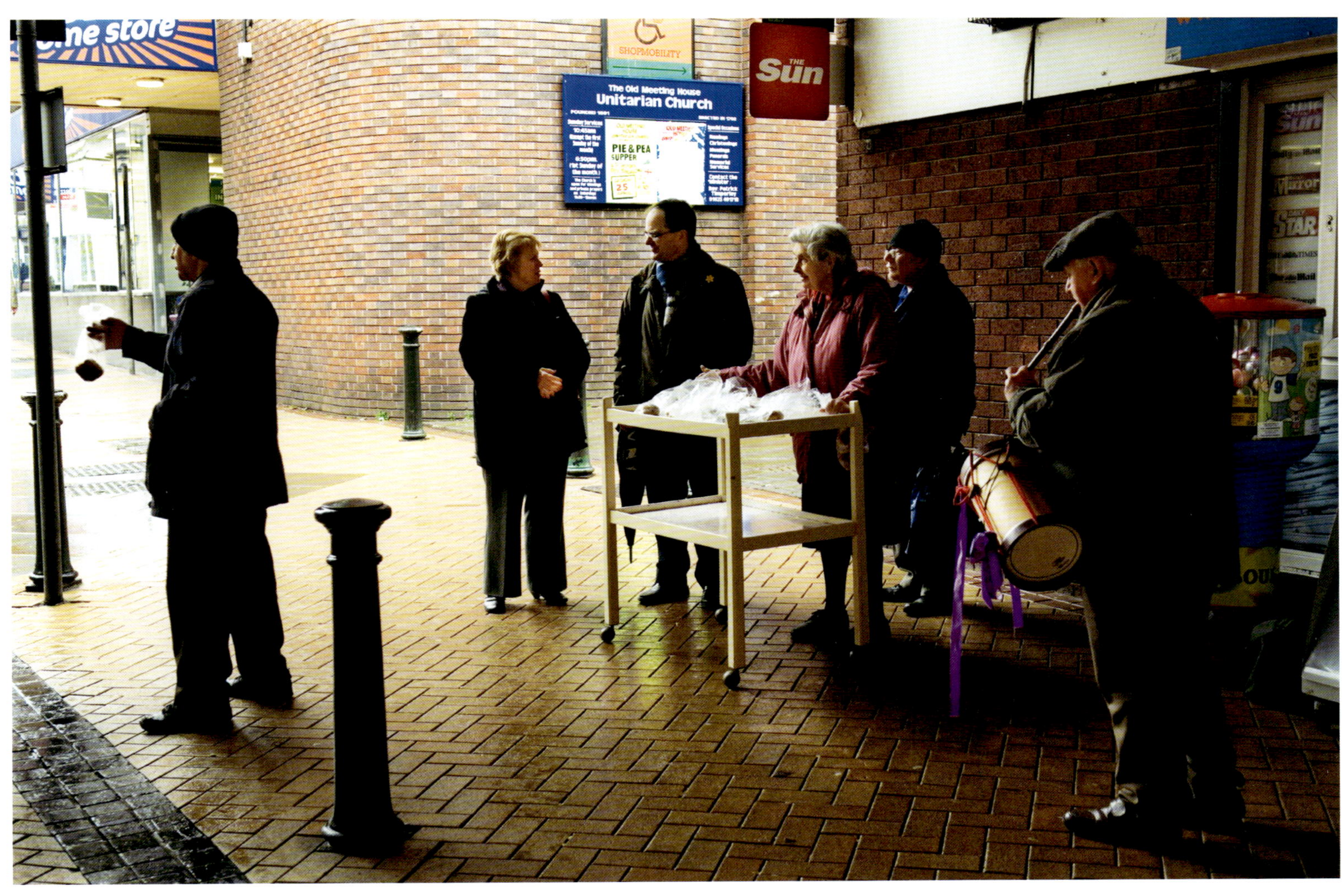

MARY MALLATRATT
HOT CROSS BUN LEGACY
Mansfield, Nottinghamshire
2015

Unitarian Church members distribute Hot Cross Buns to children on Good Friday in clear plastic bags in the Four Seasons shopping centre close to their church, as provided for by Mary Mallatratt in her will of 1876.

GOOD FRIDAY HOT CROSS BUNS
Horndon on the Hill, Essex
2016

In 1906 Jack Turnell took over the 15th century pubic house, the Bell Inn, on Easter Good Friday and hung a celebratory Hot Cross Bun from a rafter to mark the occasion. The tradition has continued.

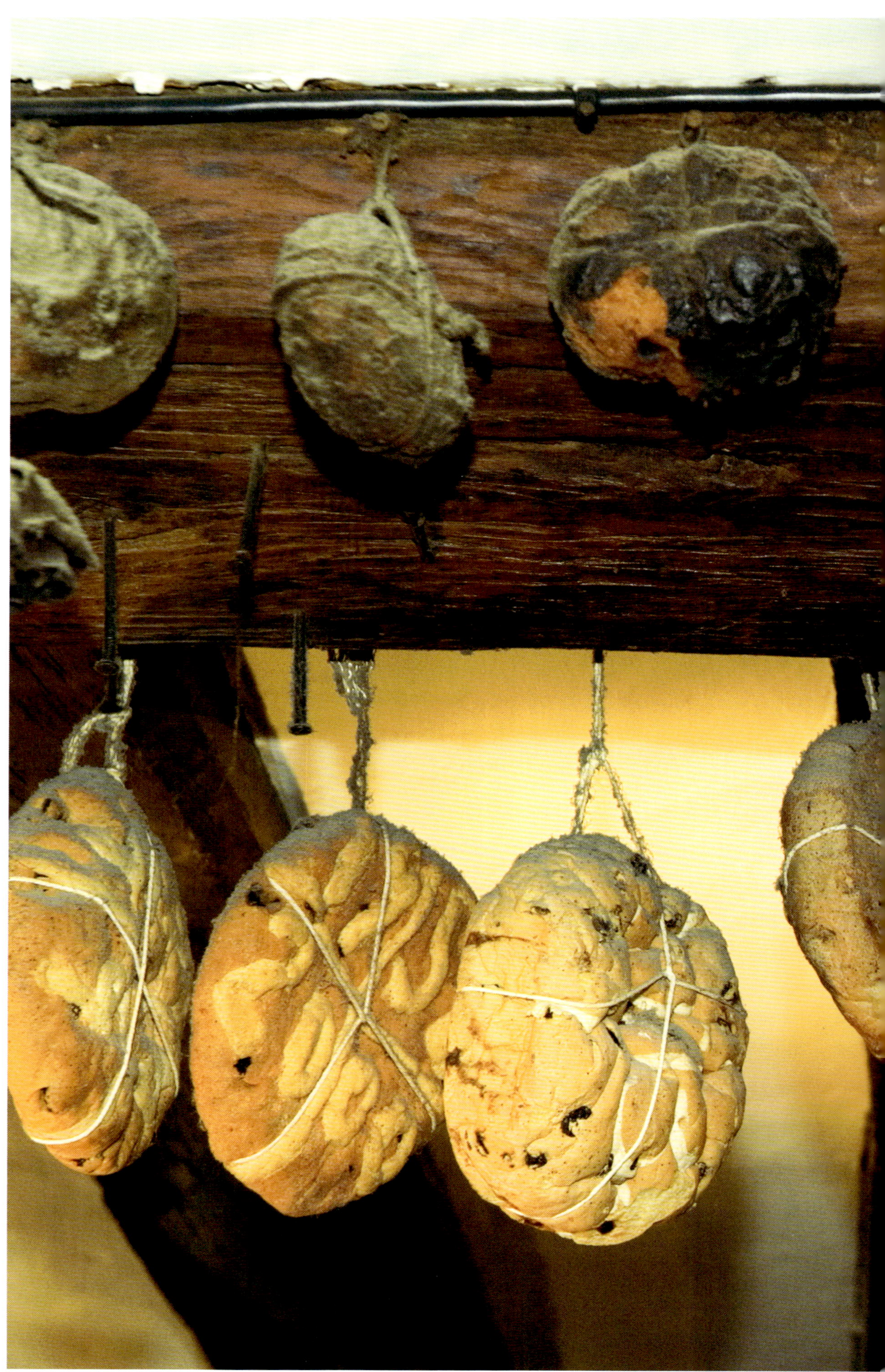

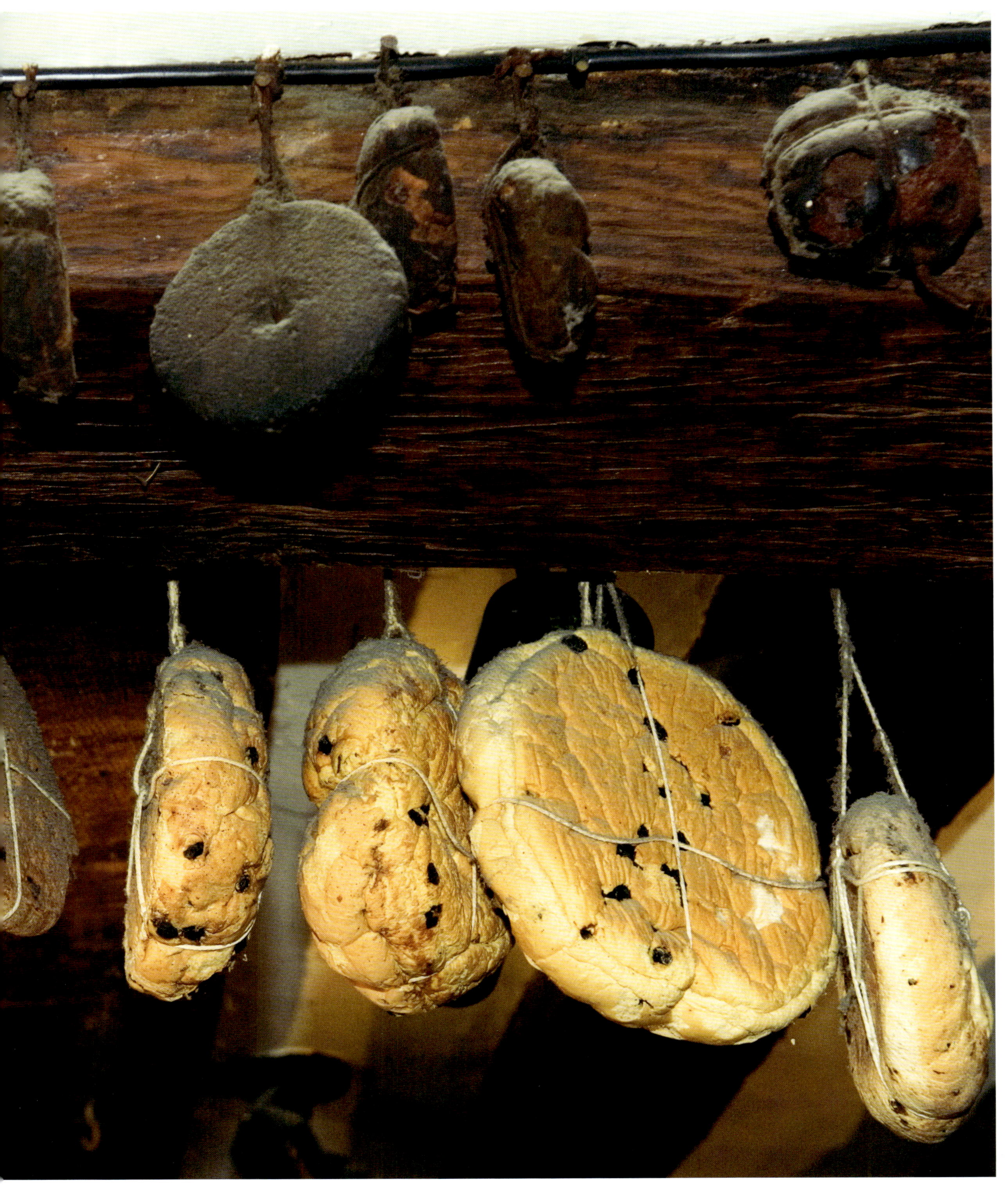

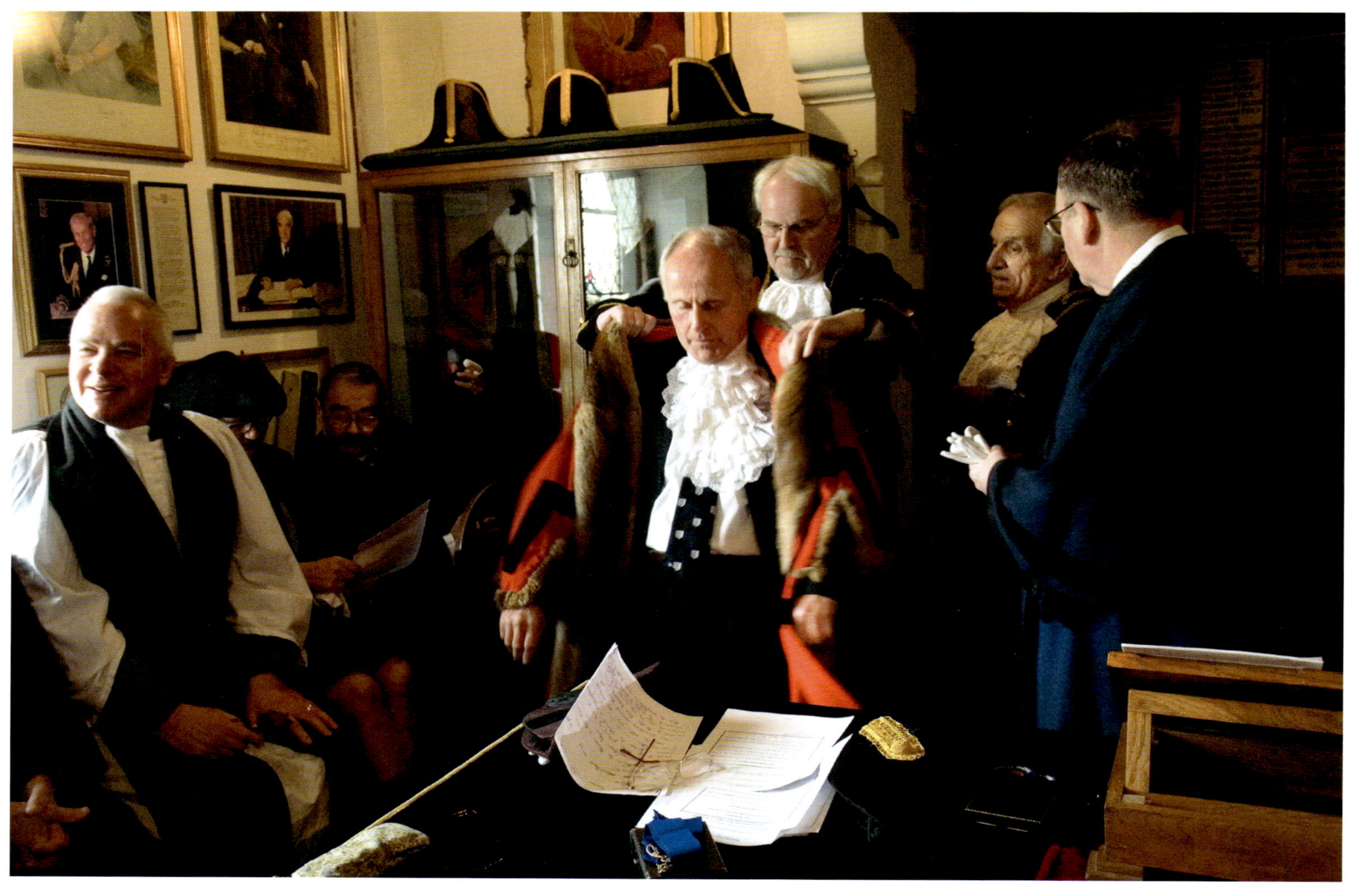

MAYORING CEREMONY
Winchelsea, East Sussex
2015

In the Upper Court Hall the newly elected Mayor, Dr John Spencer is helped into his robes. The ceremony recognises the continuing existence of one of the last surviving unreformed Corporations of England and Wales, which comprises of an Assembly of the Freemen of Winchelsea.

Afterwards, in the New Hall, the incoming Mayor provides the traditional lunch.

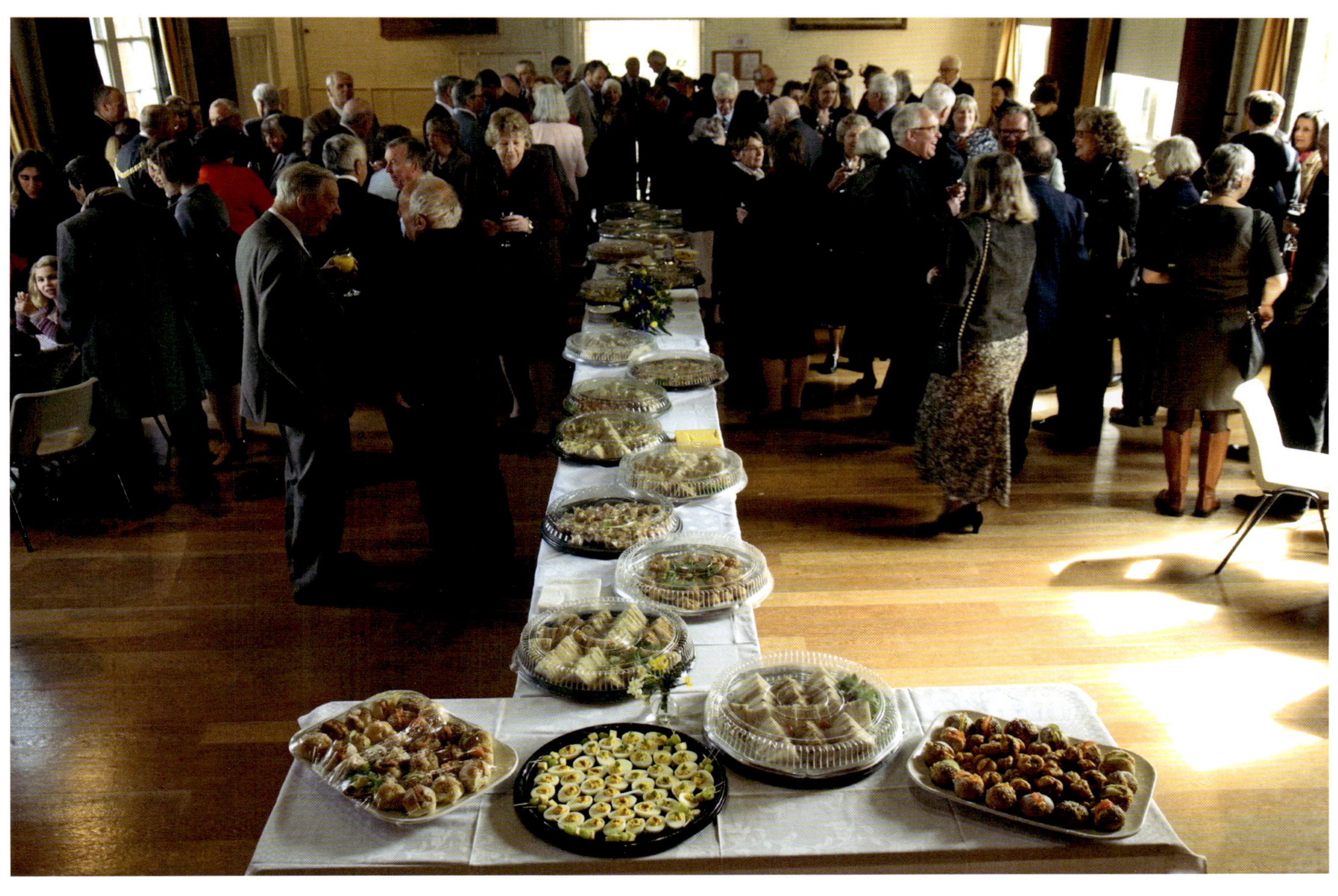

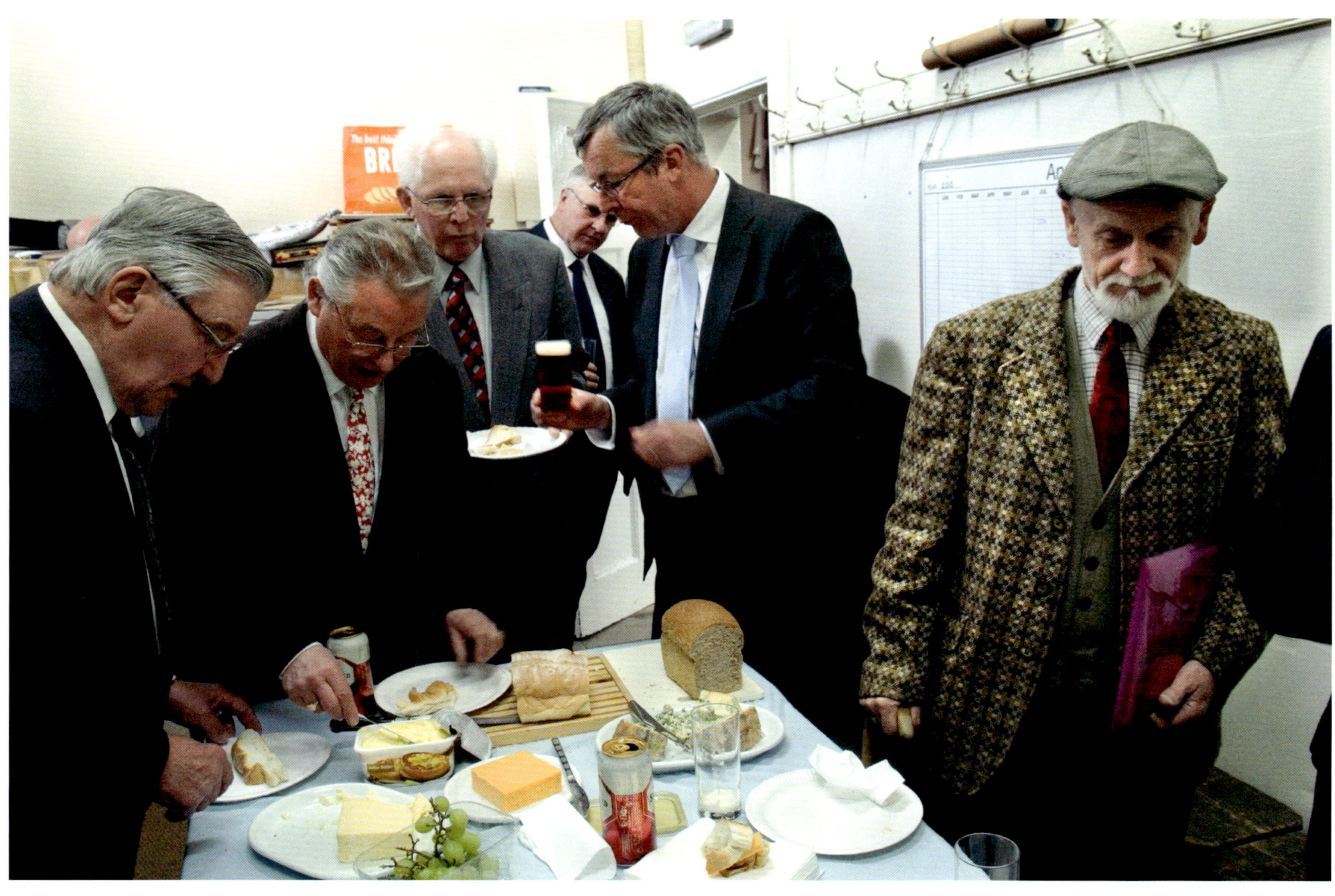

THE GREAT BARMOTE COURT
Wirksworth, Derbyshire
2015

The traditional bread, beer and cheese lunch is served in the Moot Hall before the start of the Great Barmote Court, which exists to uphold the laws relating to lead mining in the Derbyshire ore field.

Presiding over the day's business is Mr Michael Cockerton the Steward, a solicitor appointed by the Sovereign under Seal of the Duchy.

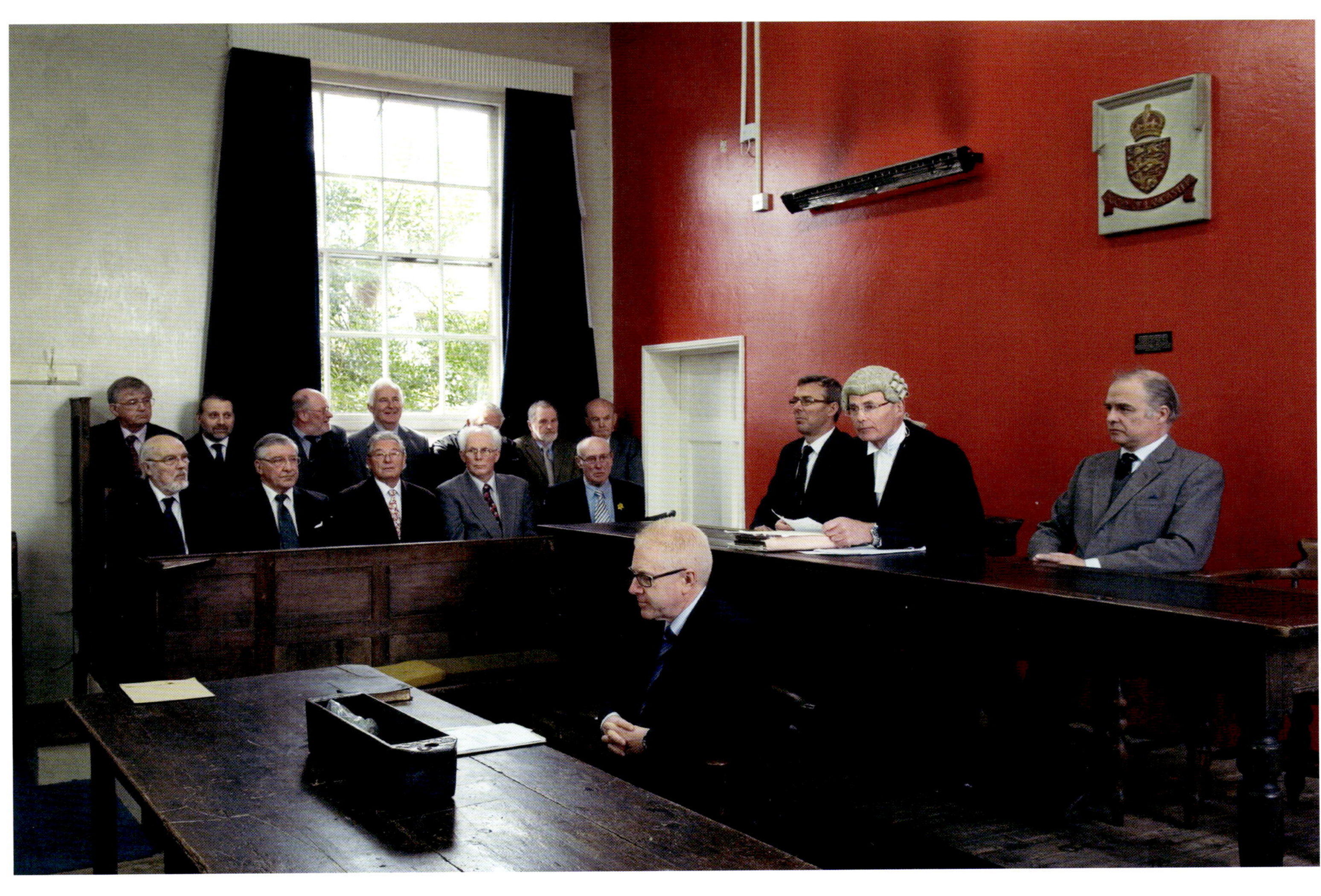

IDDESLEIGH MEN'S FRIENDLY SOCIETY
Iddesleigh, Devon
2022

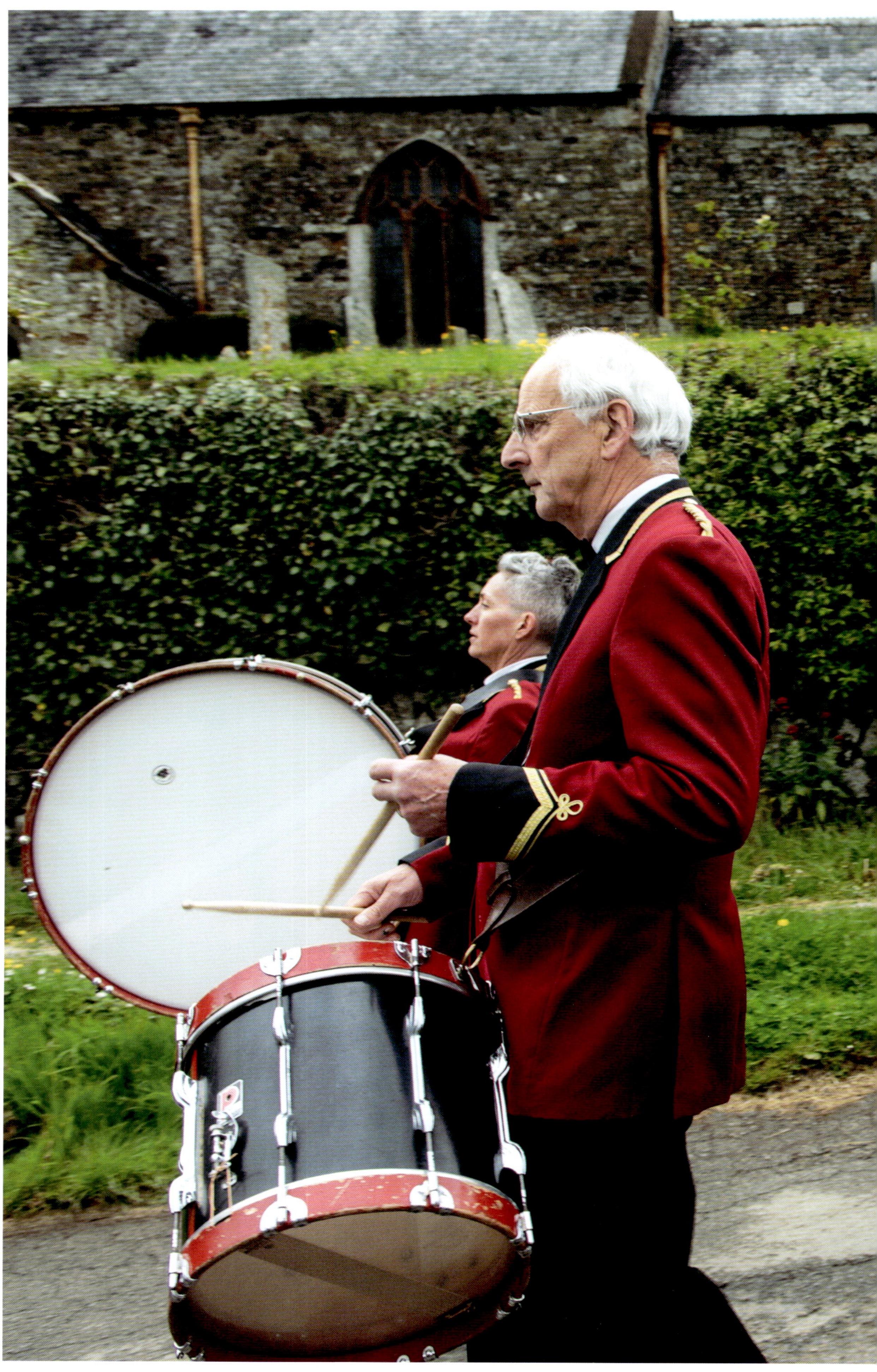

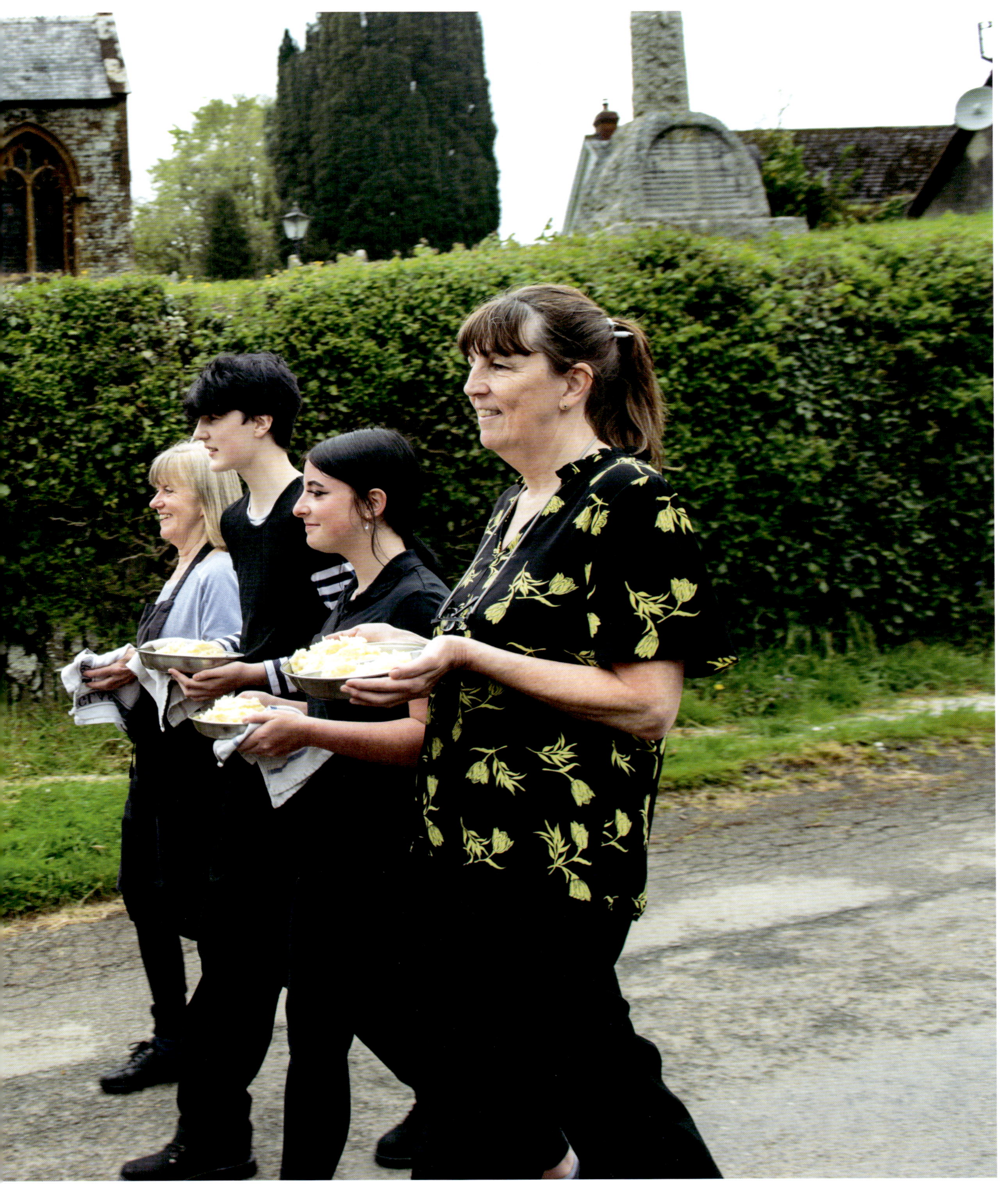

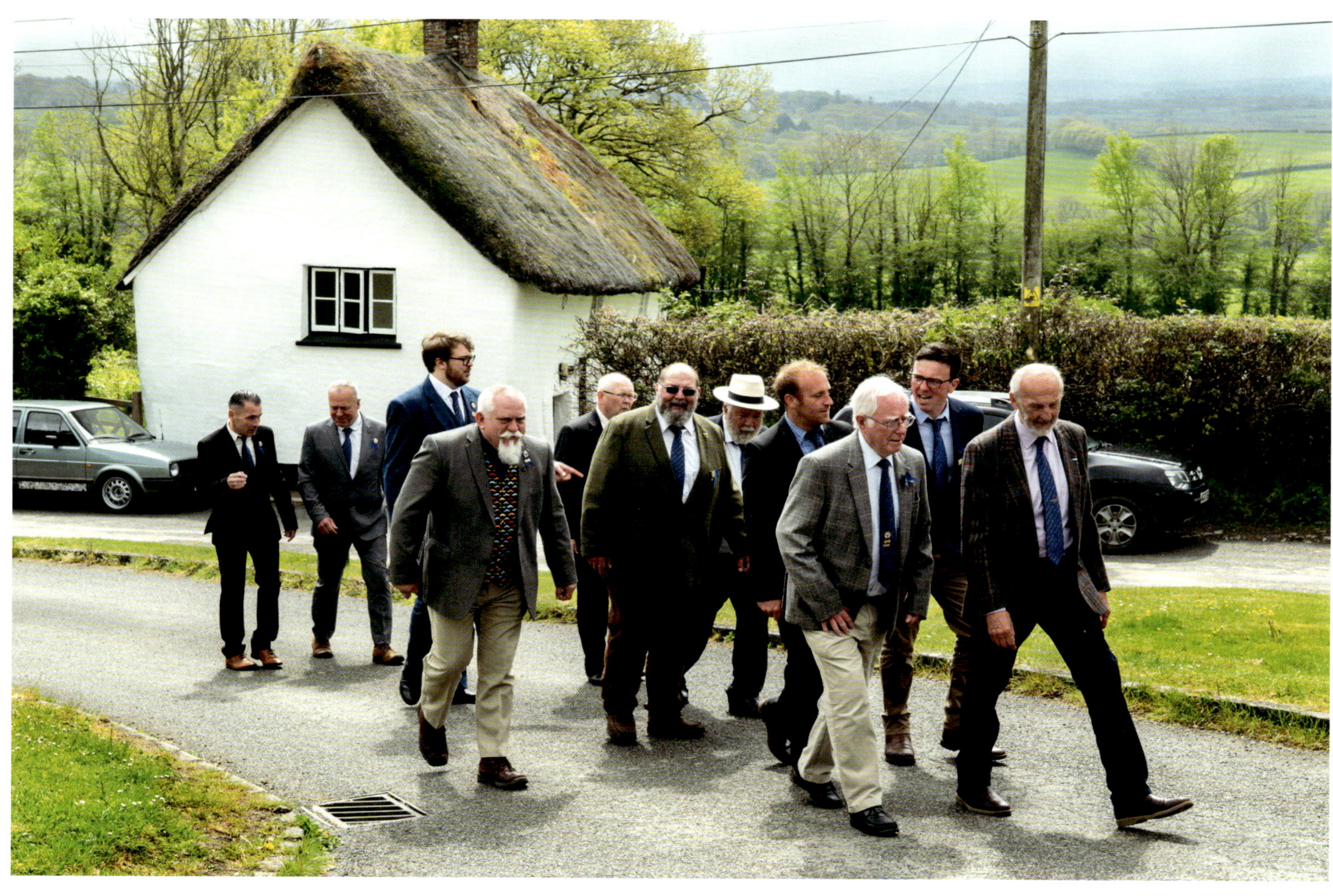

IDDESLEIGH MEN'S FRIENDLY SOCIETY
Iddesleigh, Devon
2022

Members walk back to the village pub, The Duke of York Inn, after the annual church service. Plates of hot mashed potatoes are carried at the front of the procession behind the Hatherleigh Silver Band from the Duke of York Inn to the Northcote village hall where members enjoy the annual Club Day Feast.

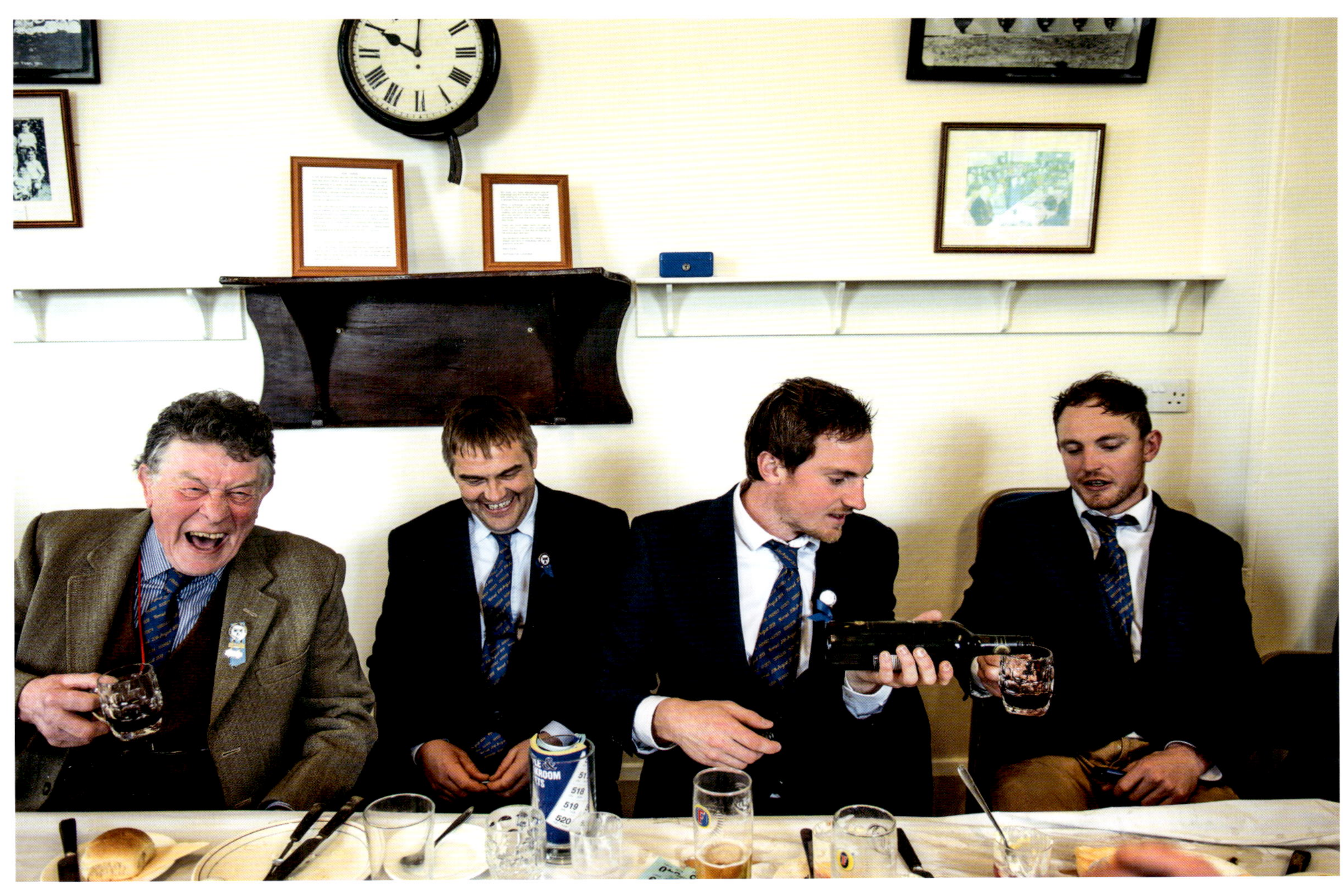

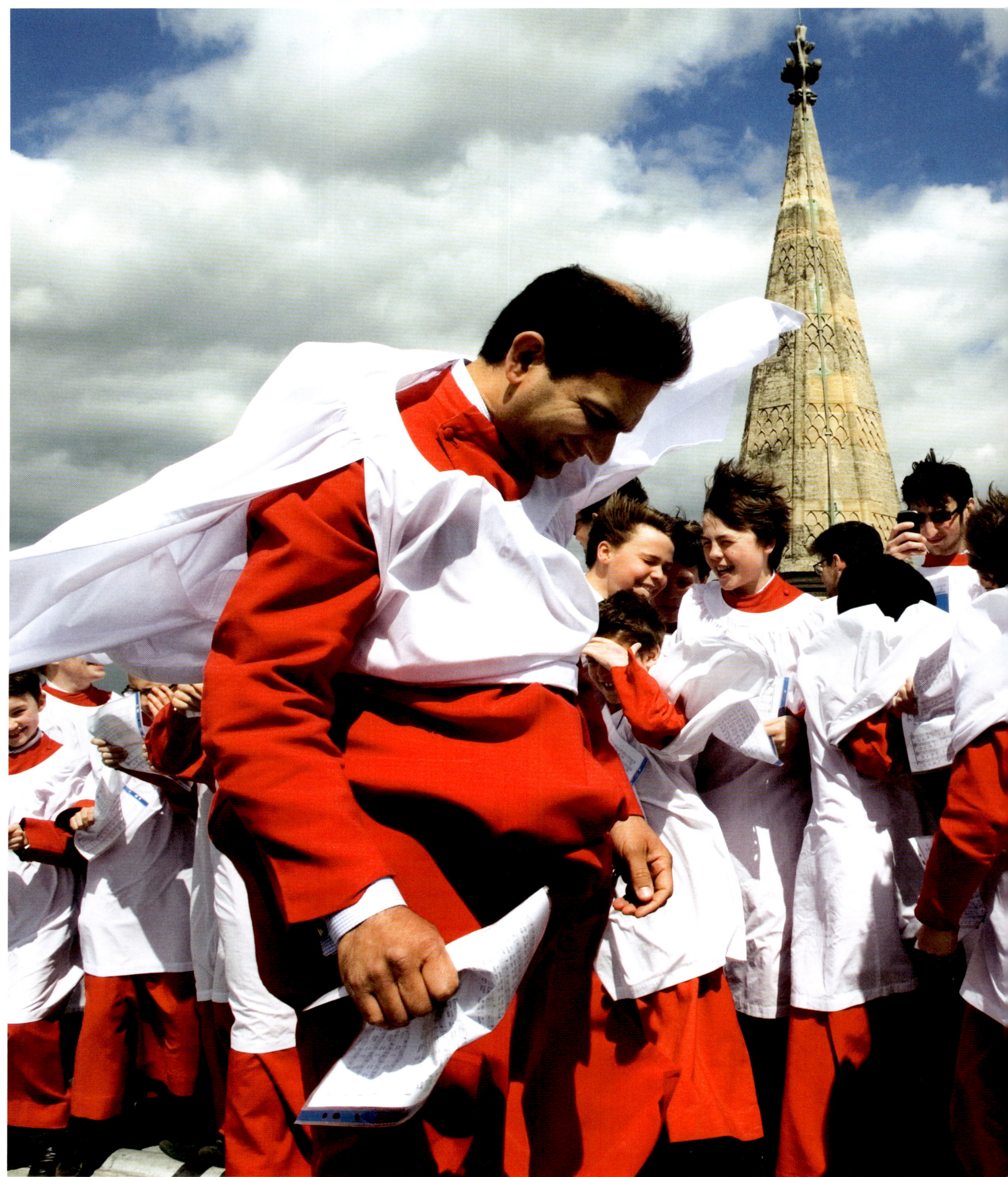

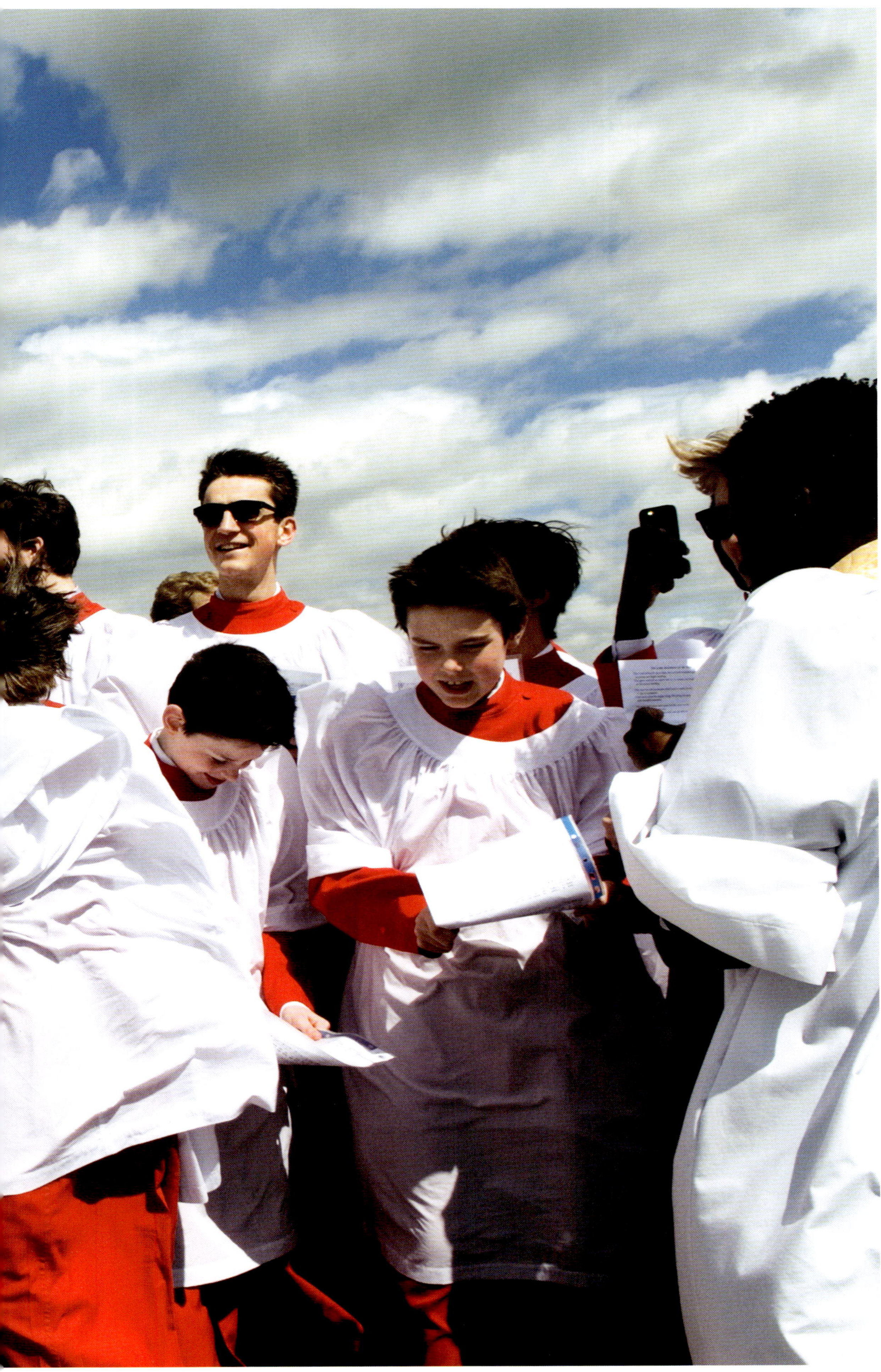

ASCENSION DAY CAROL
Cambridge, Cambridgeshire
2013

On a very windy day Mr Andrew Nethsingha, the Director of Music and members of the St John's College choir sing the Ascension Day Carol at 12 noon from the rooftop of the College Chapel.

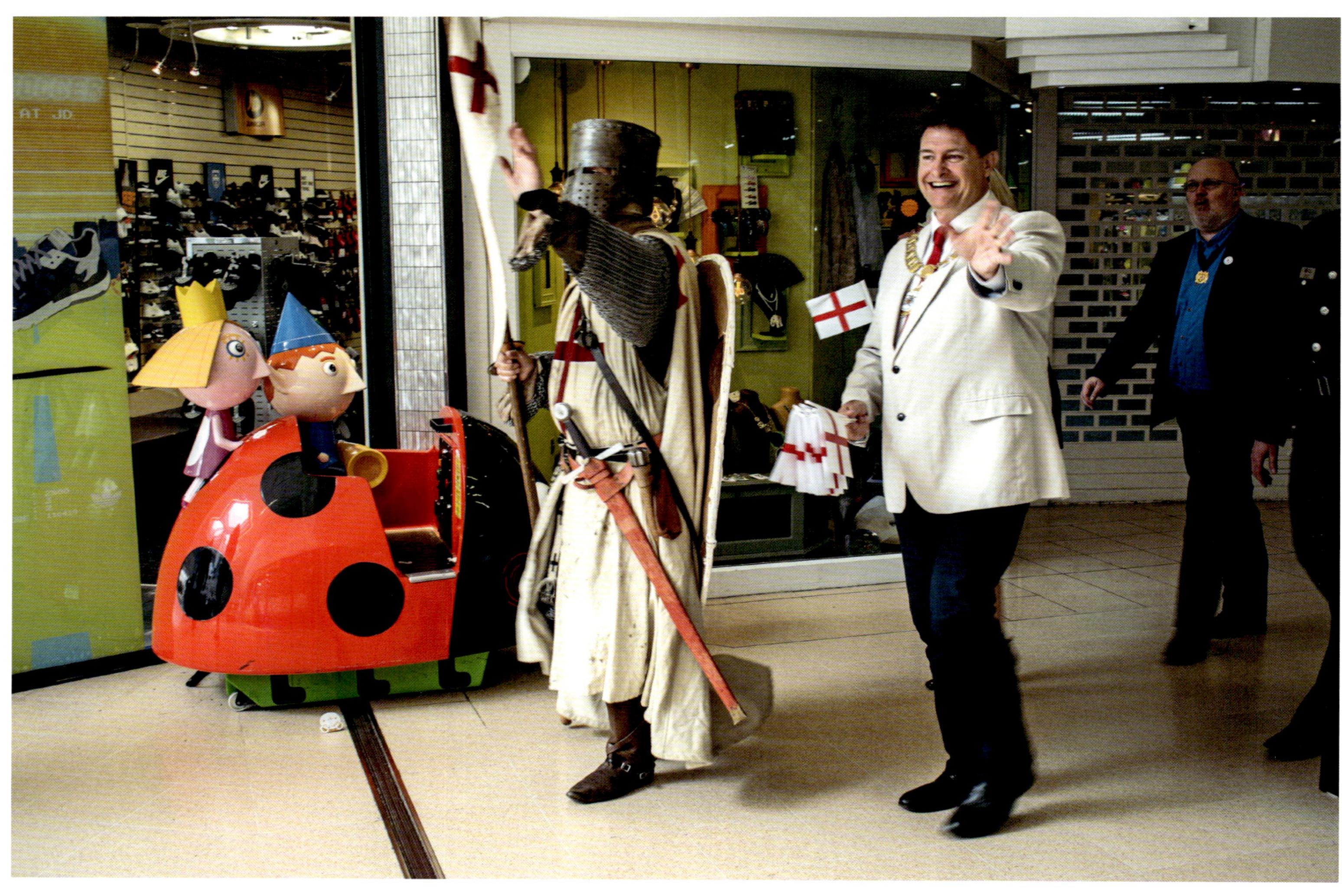

SAINT GEORGE'S DAY
Dartford, Kent
2019

Councillor Mayor David Mote and Saint George the crusader Knight walk through the nearly empty Priory shopping centre promoting being English. Sitting in a Car Kiddie Ride, Princess Holly and her best friend Ben Elf from the magical Kingdom of Elves and Fairies look on, they are surprised.

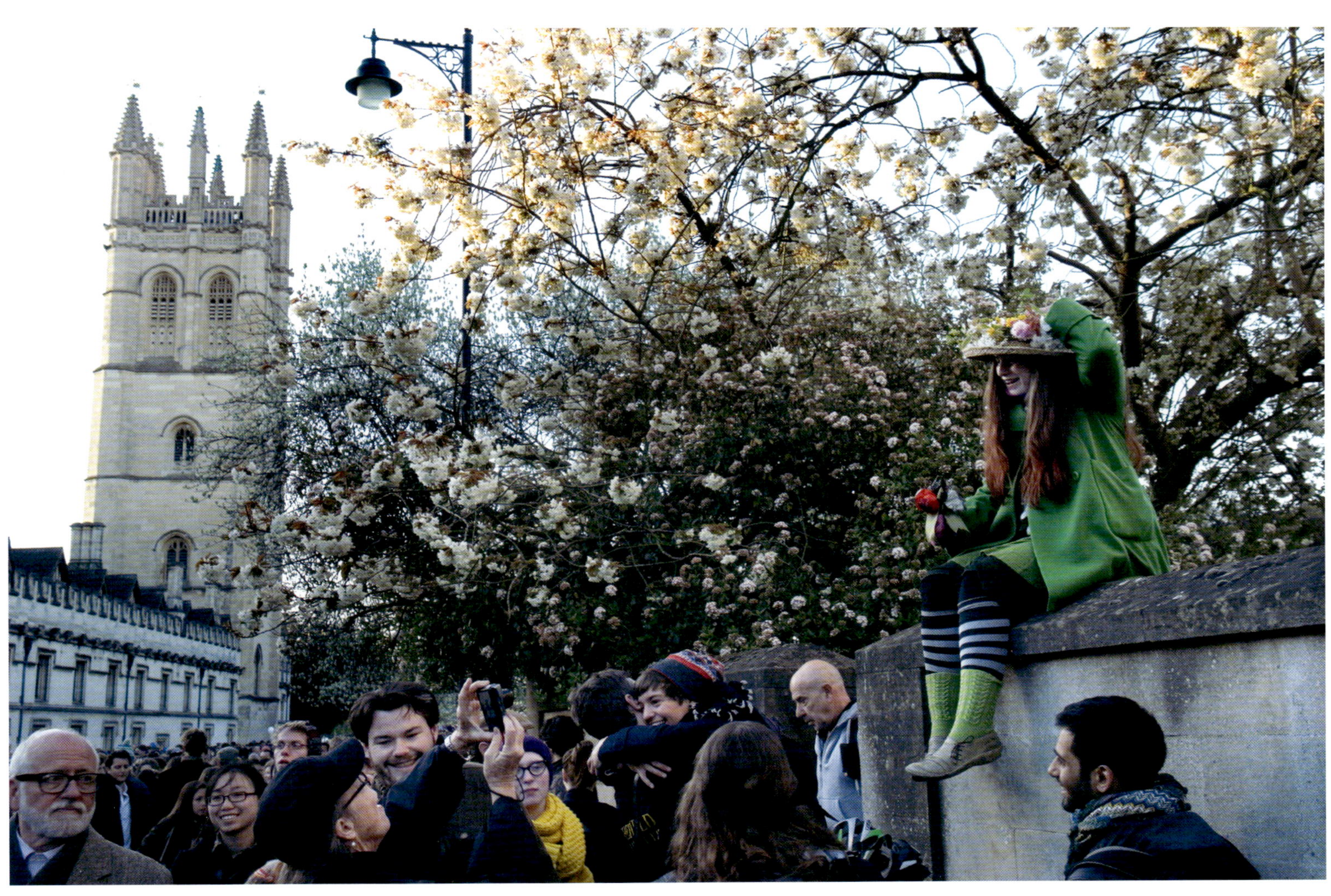

MAY DAY
Oxford, Oxfordshire
2013

University students and May Day revellers celebrate the coming of spring and the end to winter at dawn as Magdalen College Choir sing from the top of the College Great Tower. The party is over by 9 am

MAY DAY
Oxford, Oxfordshire
2013

An exhausted Morris Man and his wilting Green Man companion slowly make their way home.

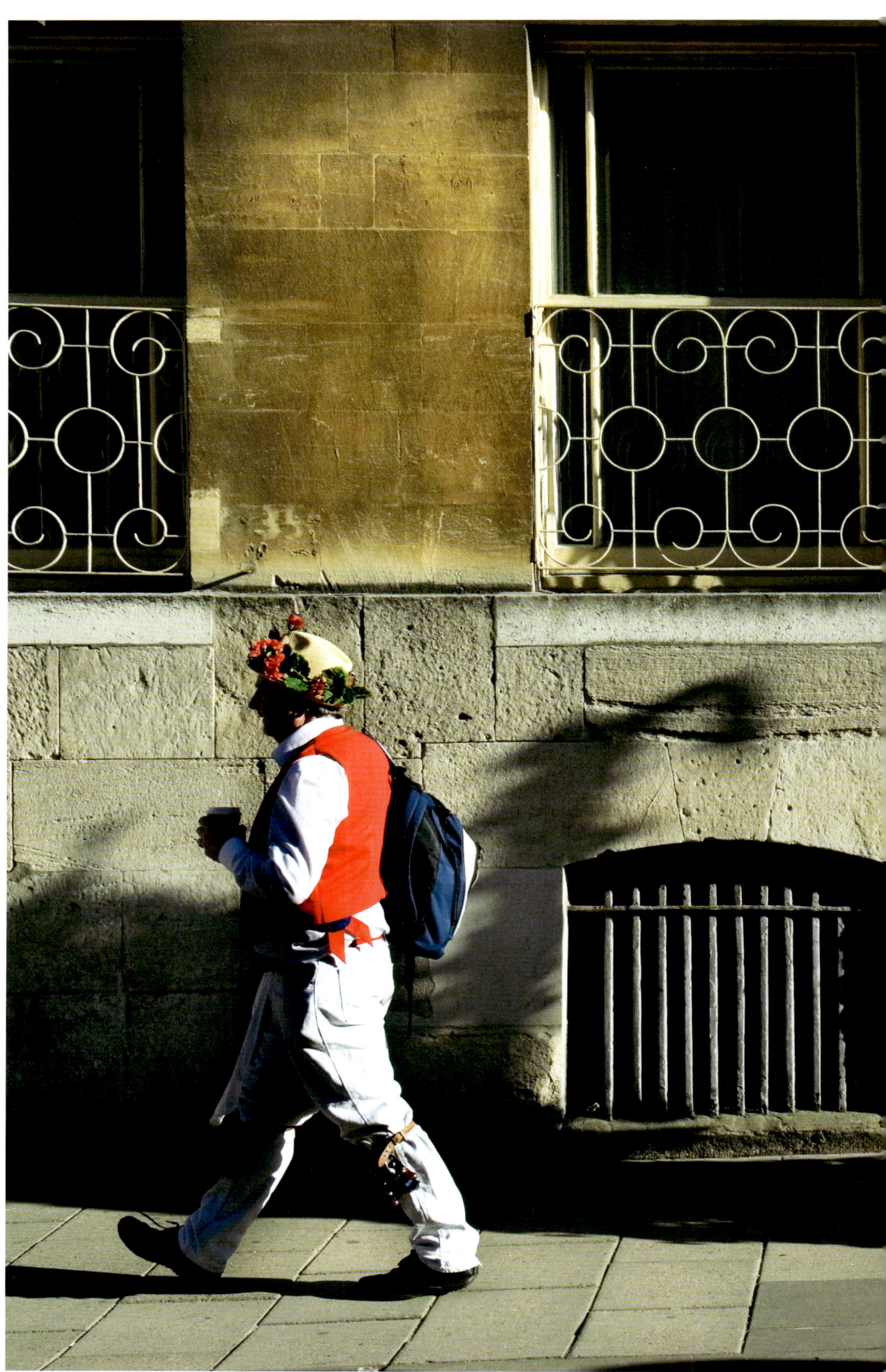

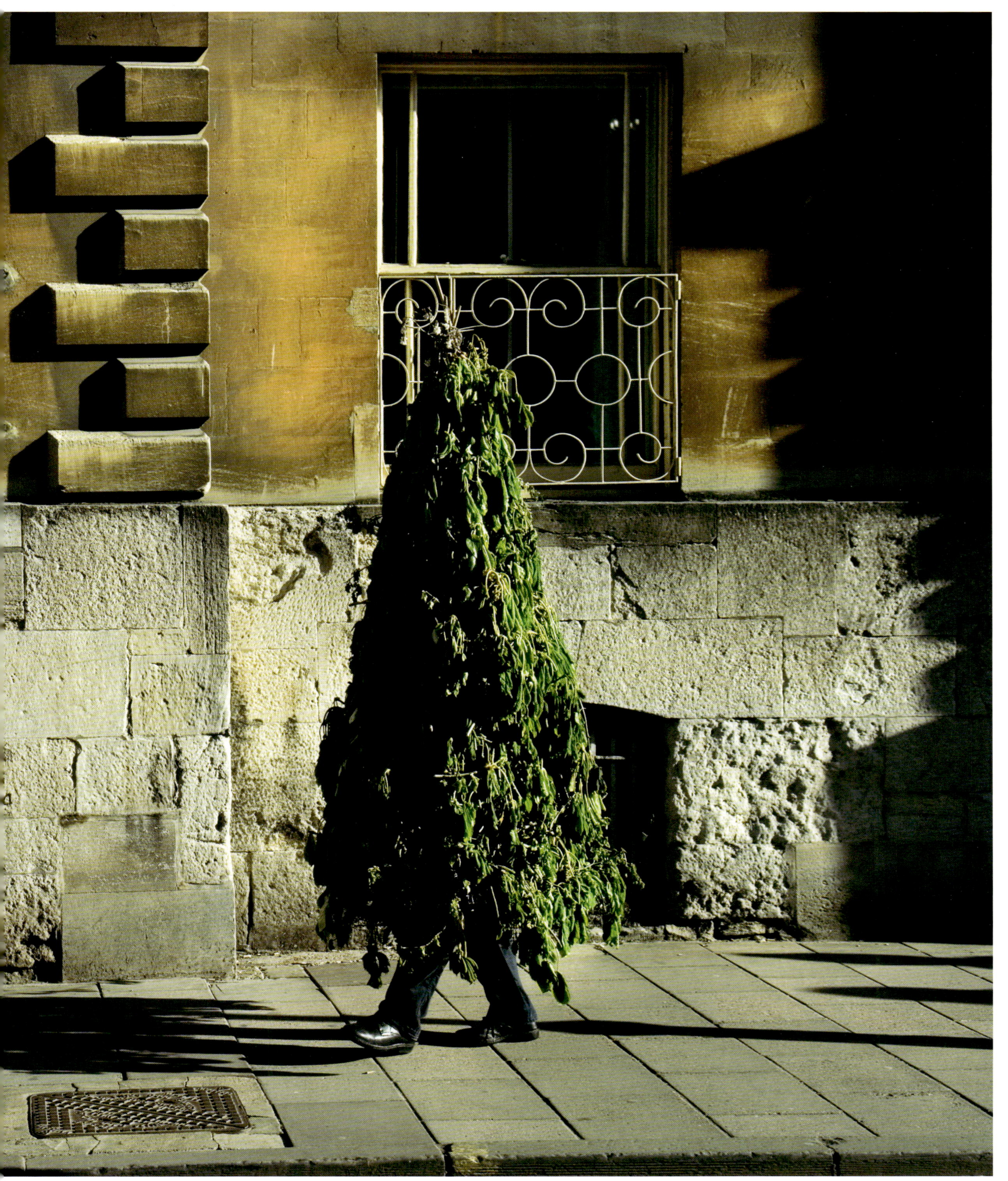

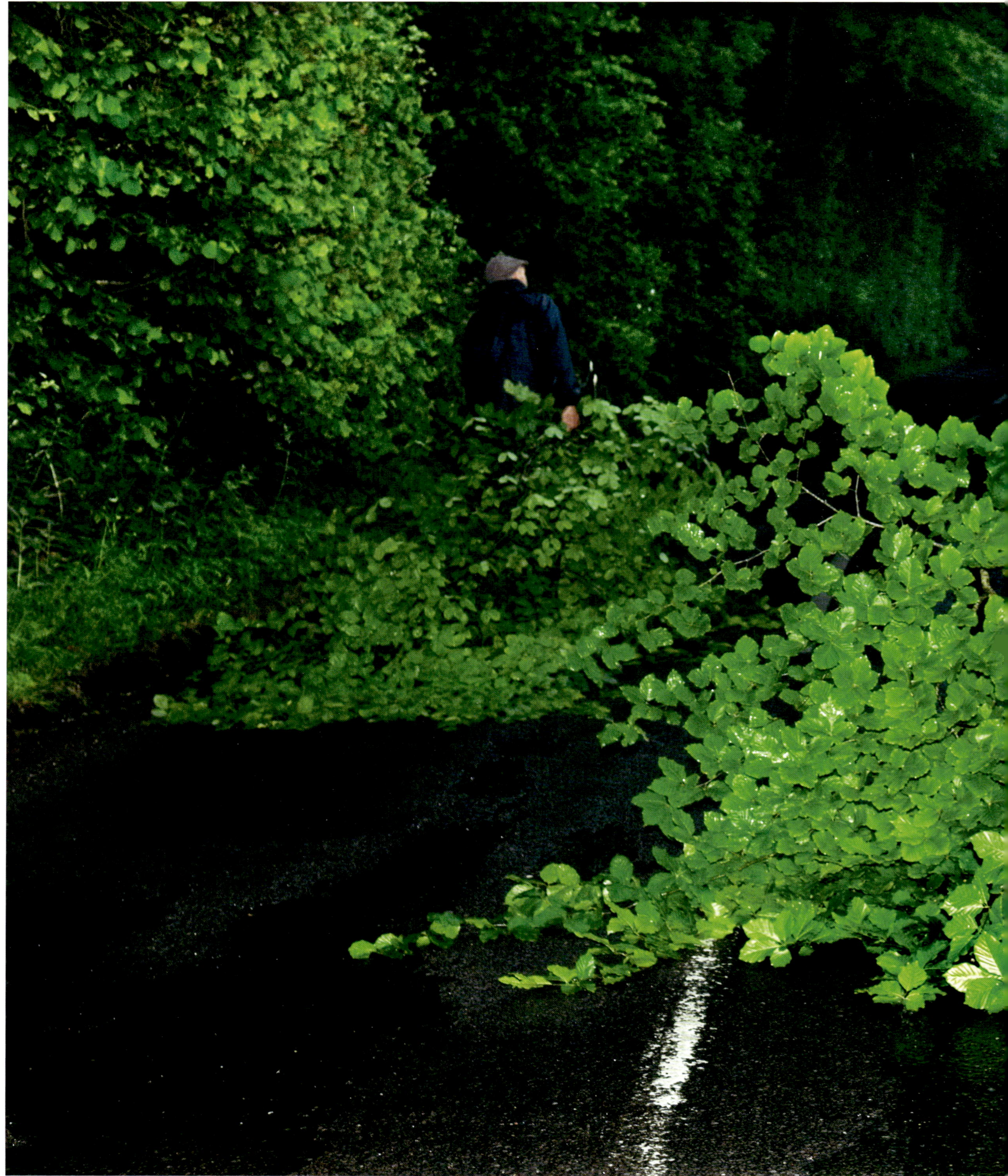

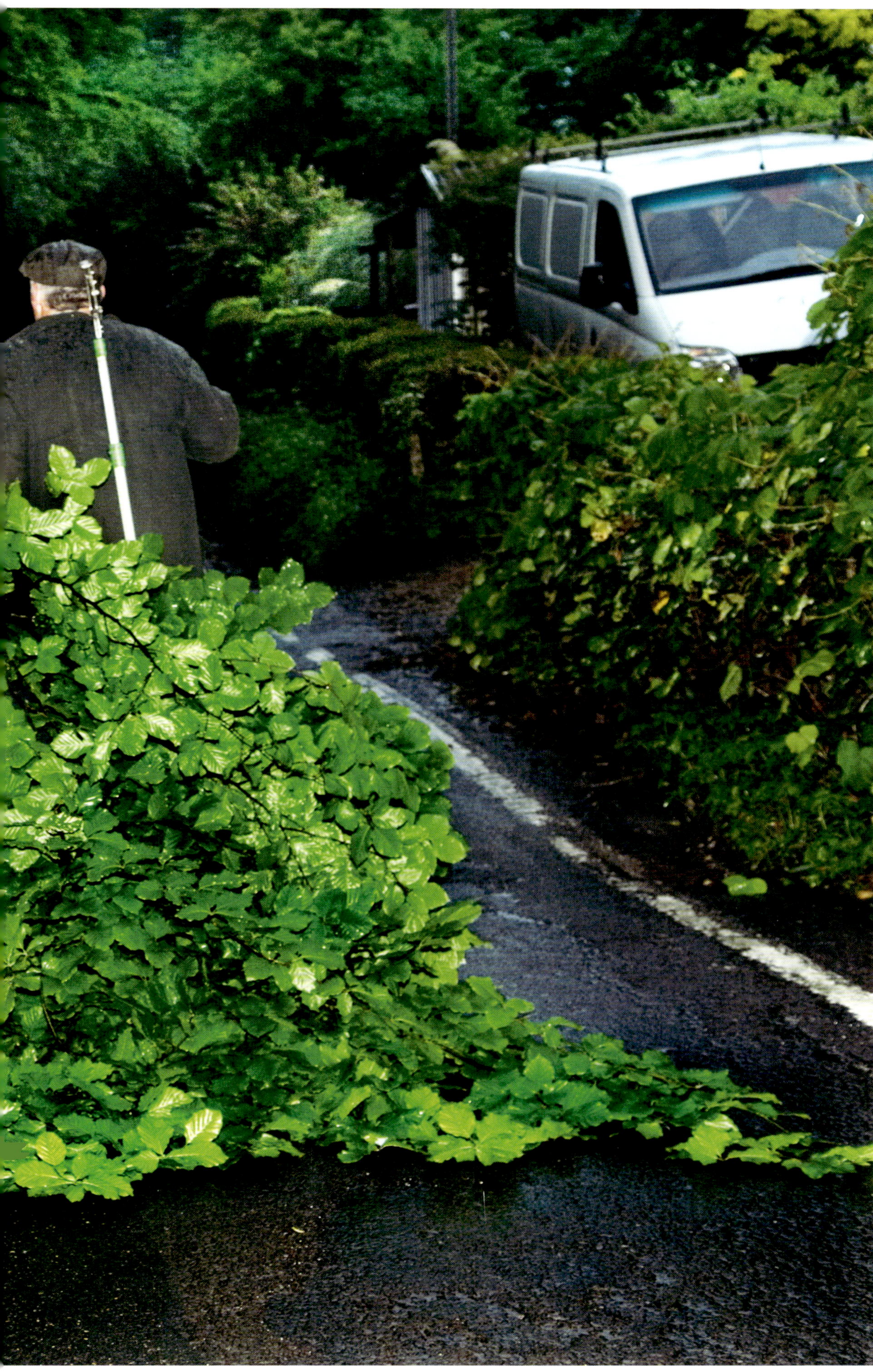

THE HARTING OLD CLUB
South Harting, West Sussex
2014

Committee members collect green beech tree boughs from Warren Wood at dawn and drag them back into the village. They are used to decorate the church steps and the White Hart pub.

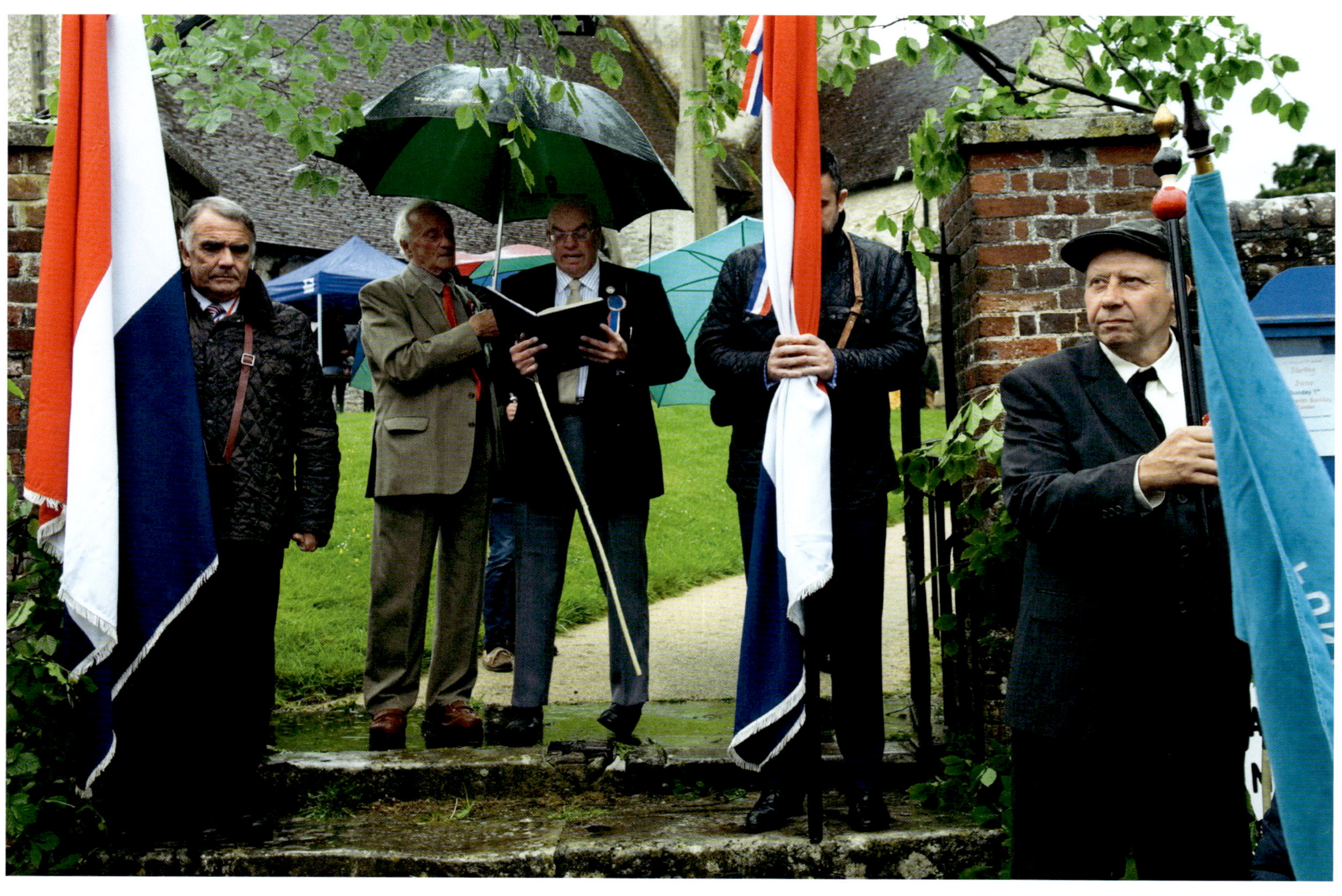

THE HARTING OLD CLUB
South Harting, West Sussex
2014

At 11 am The Old Club roll call and members notices are read from the steps of St Mary's and St Gabriel Church.

An annual lunch is held for club members and their male guests in Hartington Community Hall.

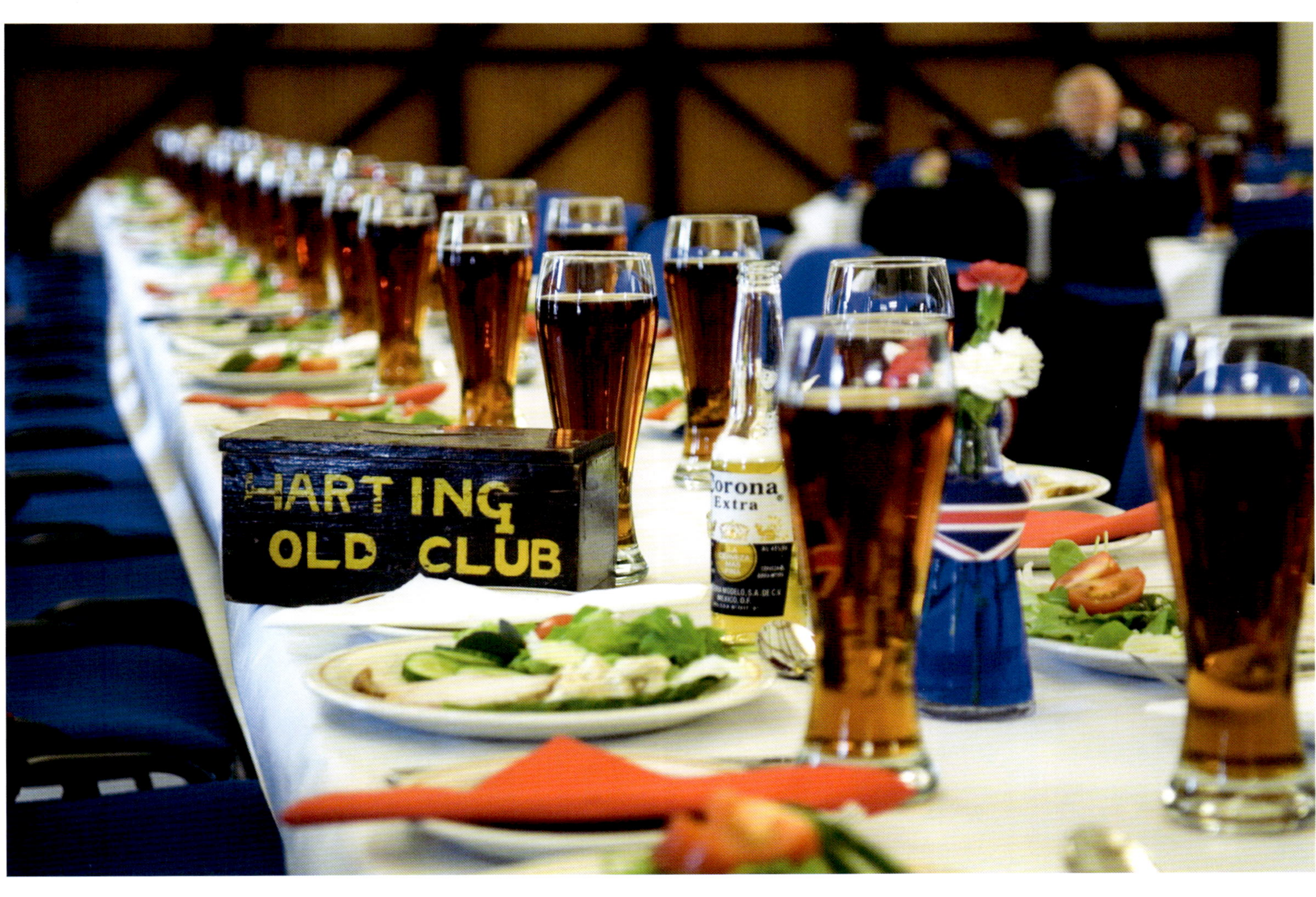
HARTING
OLD CLUB
Corona
Extra

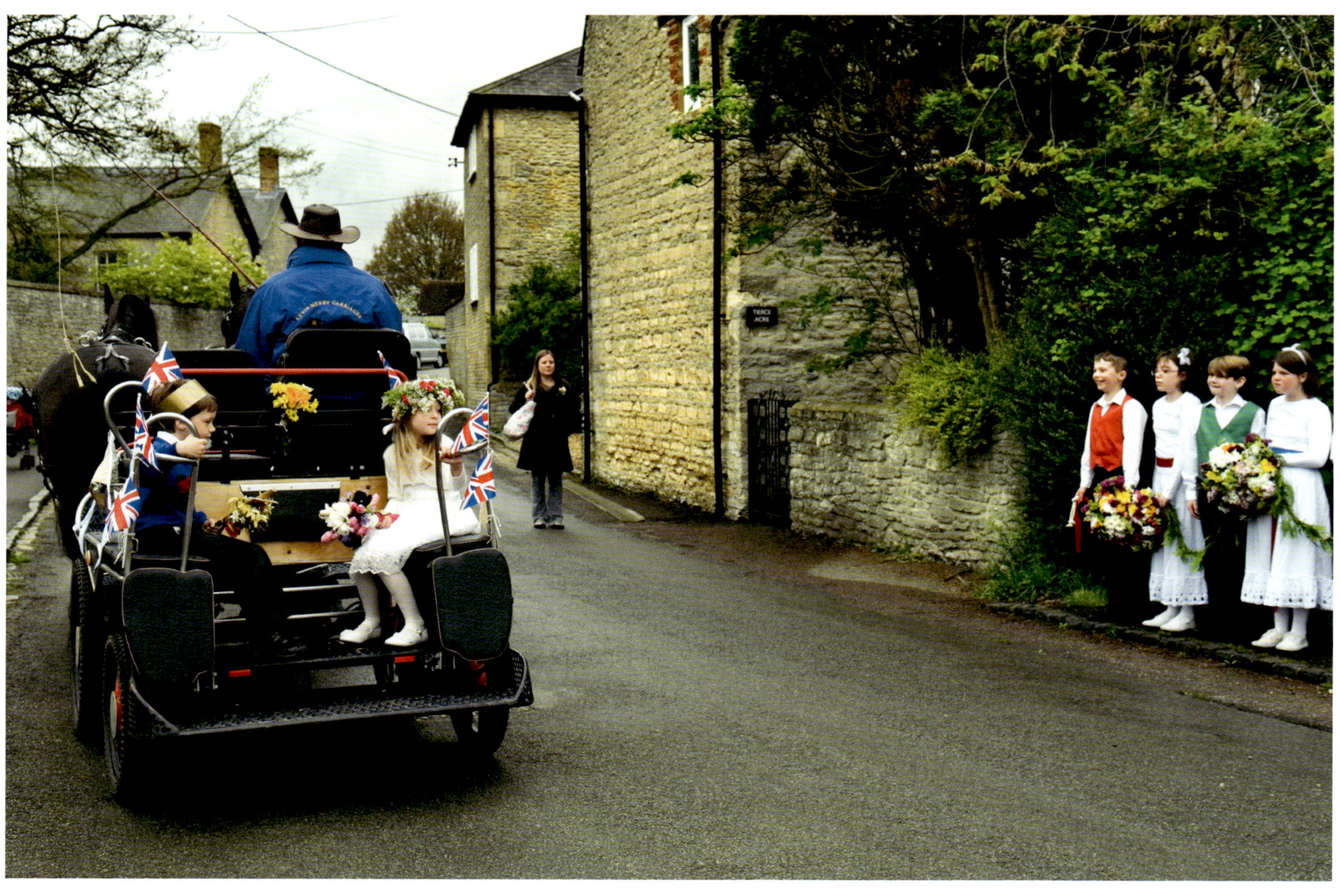

GARLAND DAY
Charlton-on-Otmoor, Oxfordshire
2014

Children from the Church of England St Mary the Virgin Primary School with their May Queen and King – riding in a horse drawn cart – process to the village church where May Garlands are hung on the 16th century Rood Screen.

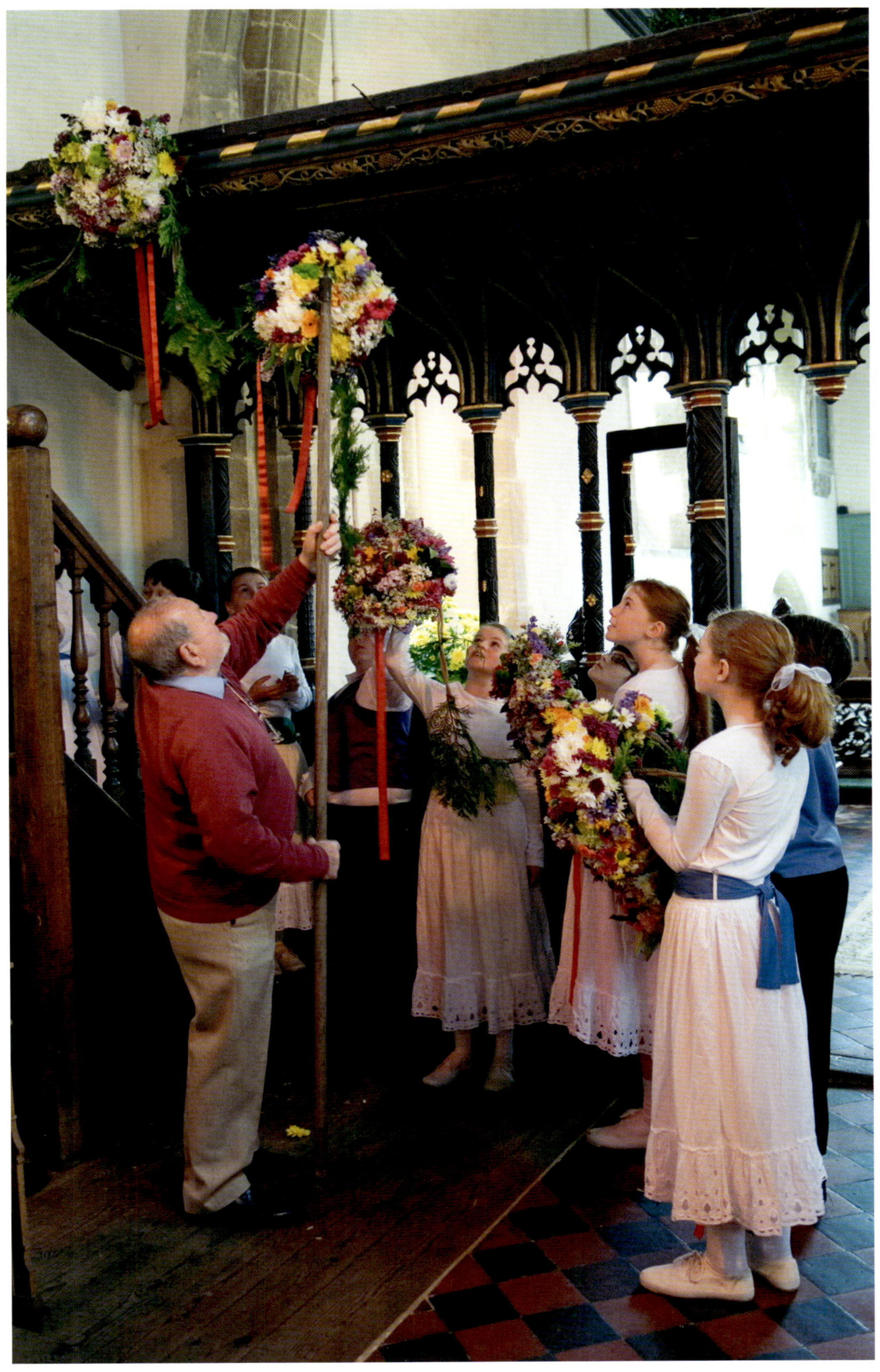

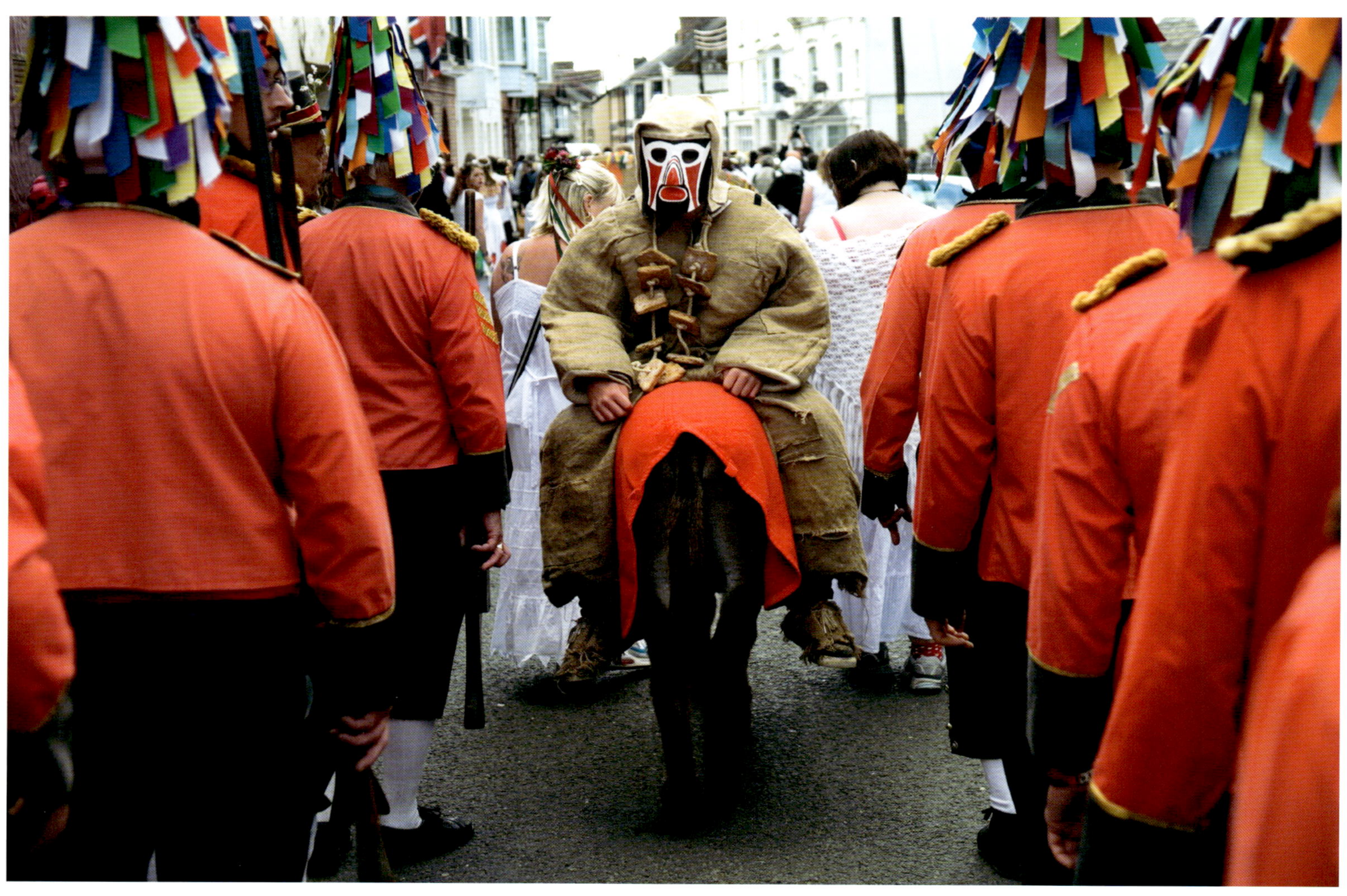

HUNTING THE EARL OF RONE
Combe Martin, Devon
2011

The Earl of Rone dressed in sackcloth and wearing a fanciful mask; the emblem of the festival rides on a donkey facing backwards through this North Devon seaside town. Shot by the Grenadier guards, he is revived by the Fool and Hobby Horse several times, before being finally dispatched and thrown into the sea.

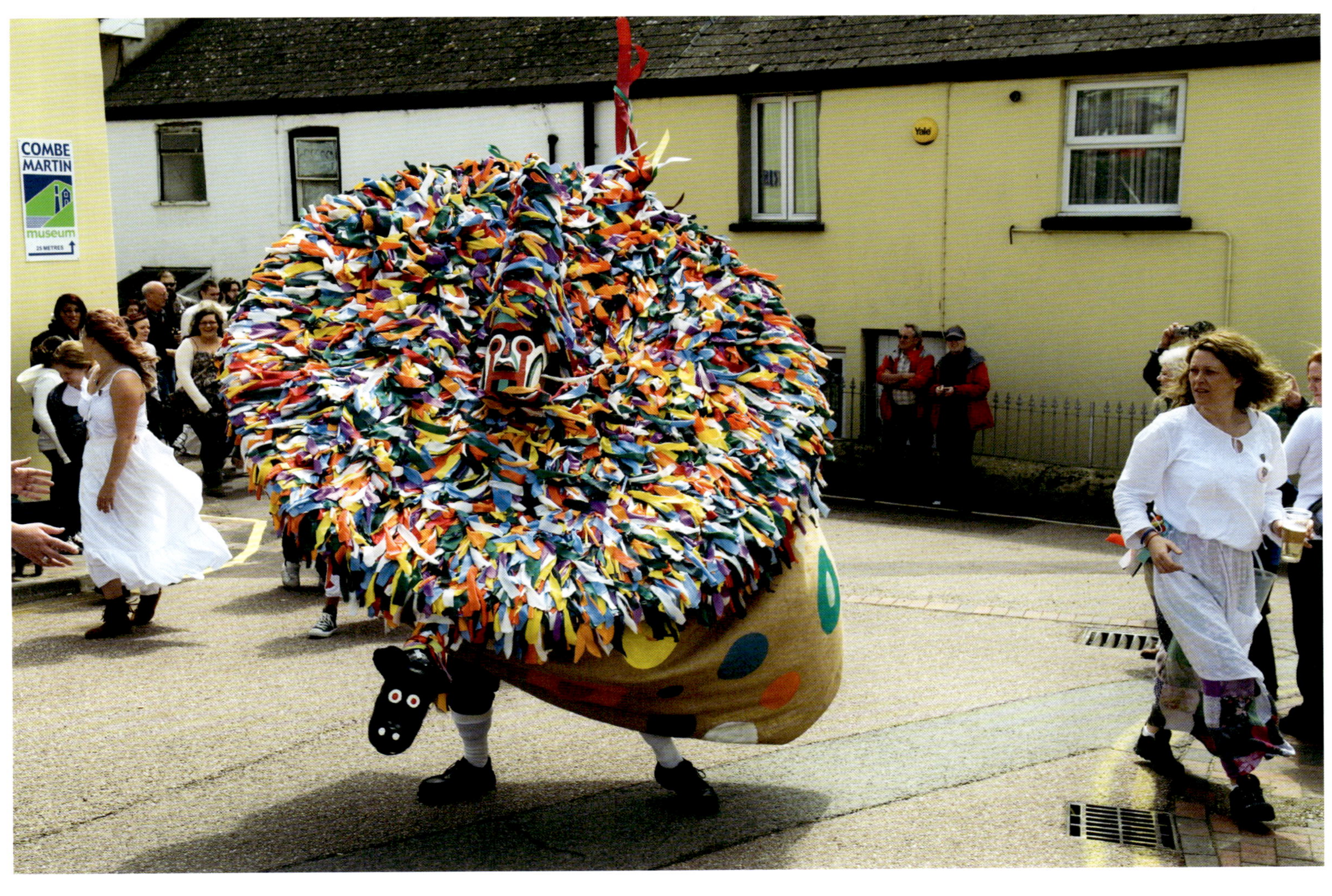
COMBE
MARTIN
museum
25 METRES
Yale

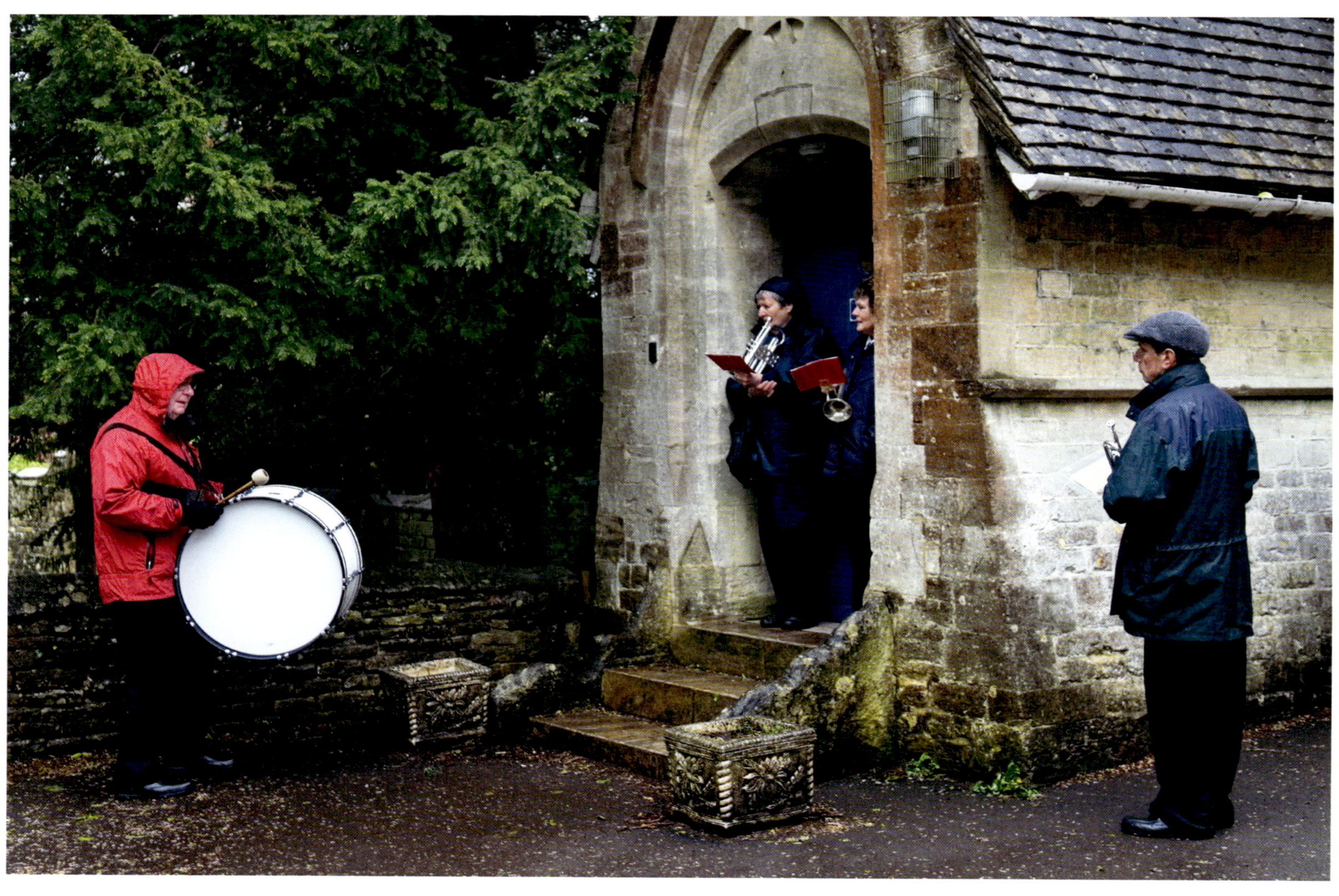

WELL DRESSING
Bisley, Gloucestershire
2015

Well Dressing on a very wet Ascension Day, the local silver band shelter from the storm.

School children wait with their garlands of summer flowers for the short service to begin at the Victorian stone water-head.

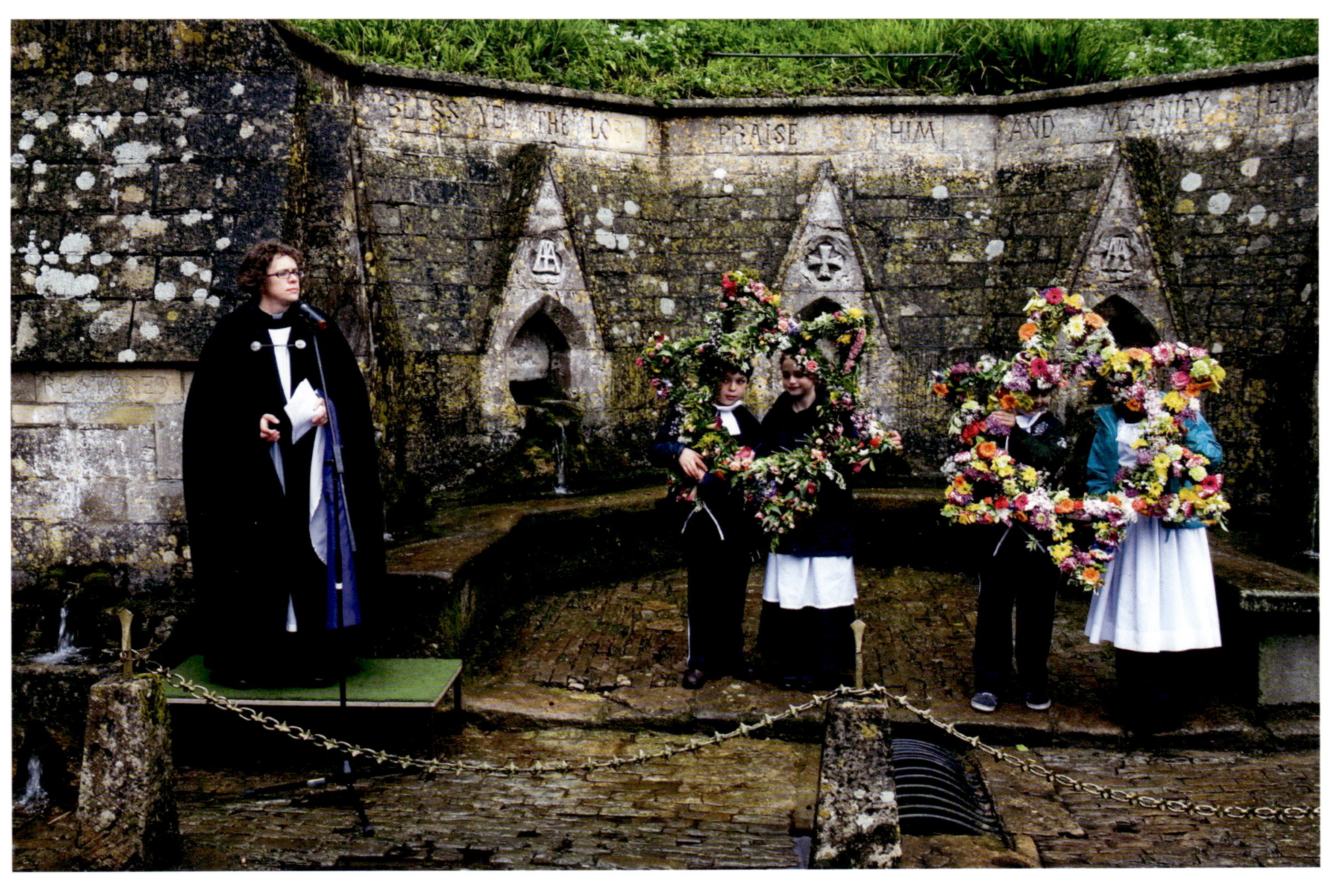
BLESS YE THE
PRAISE HIM
AND MAGNIFY HIM

WELL DRESSING
Bisley, Gloucestershire
2015

Home made cakes and tea are provided for all, courtesy of the Women's Institute, in the village hall.

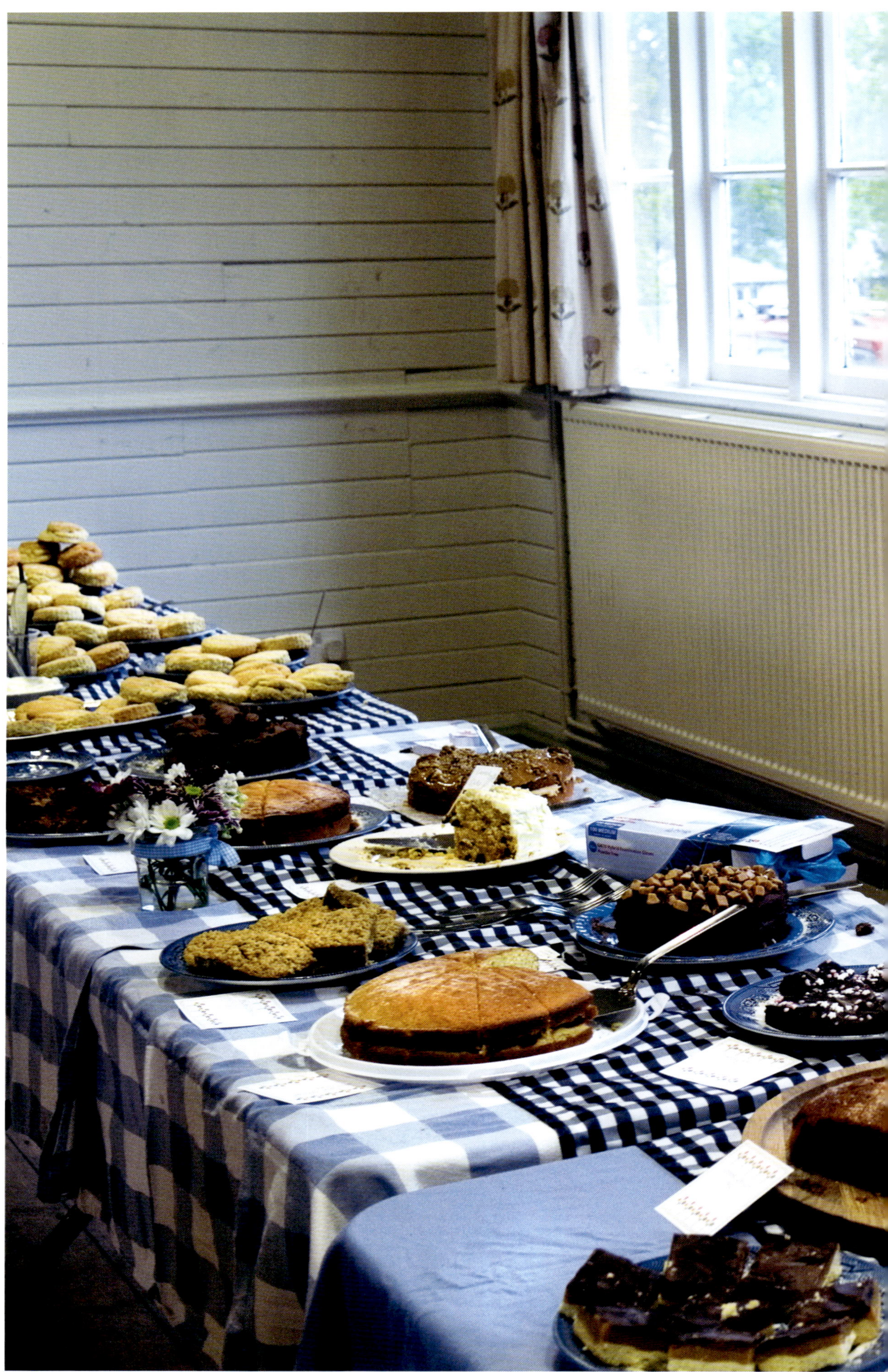

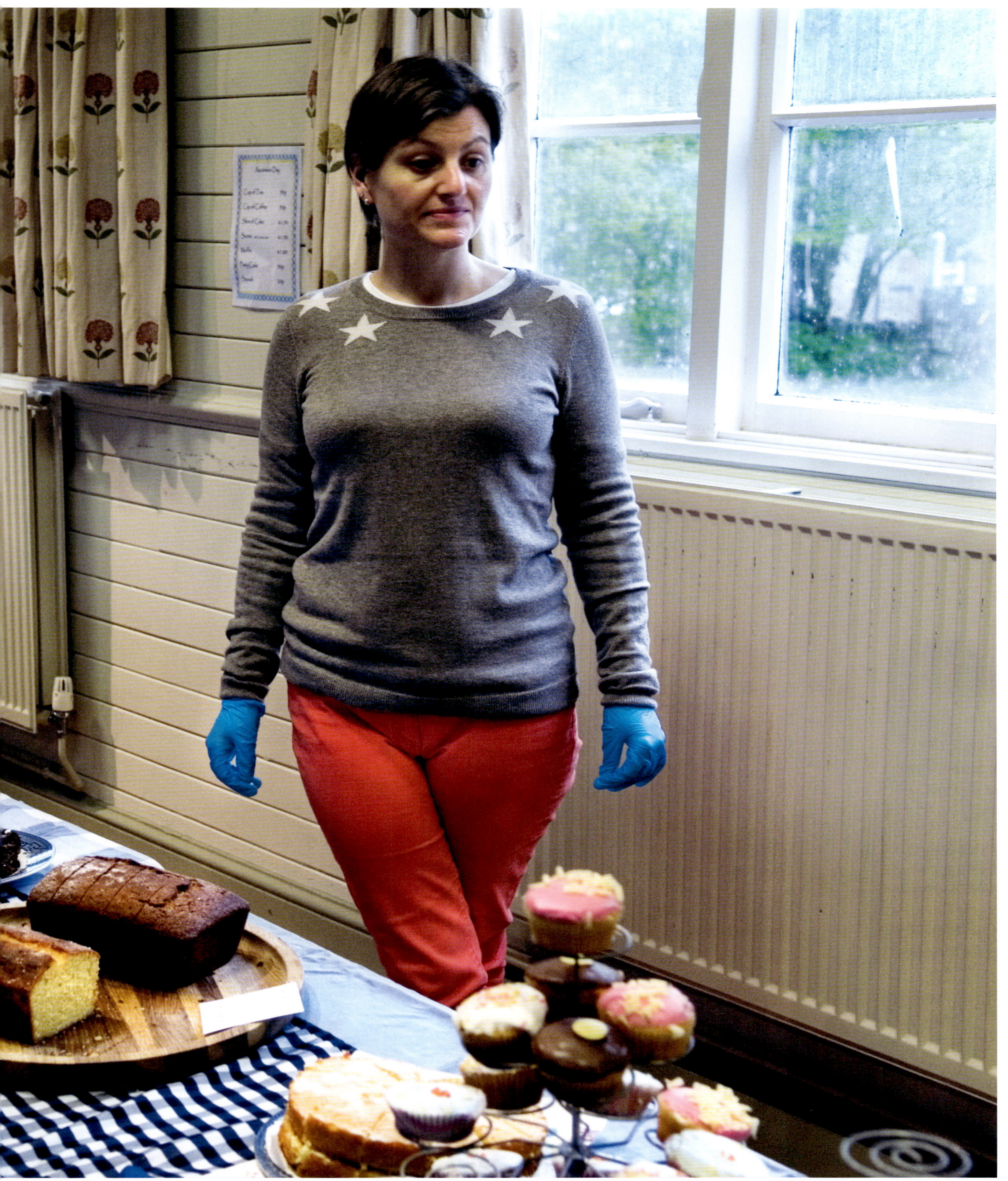

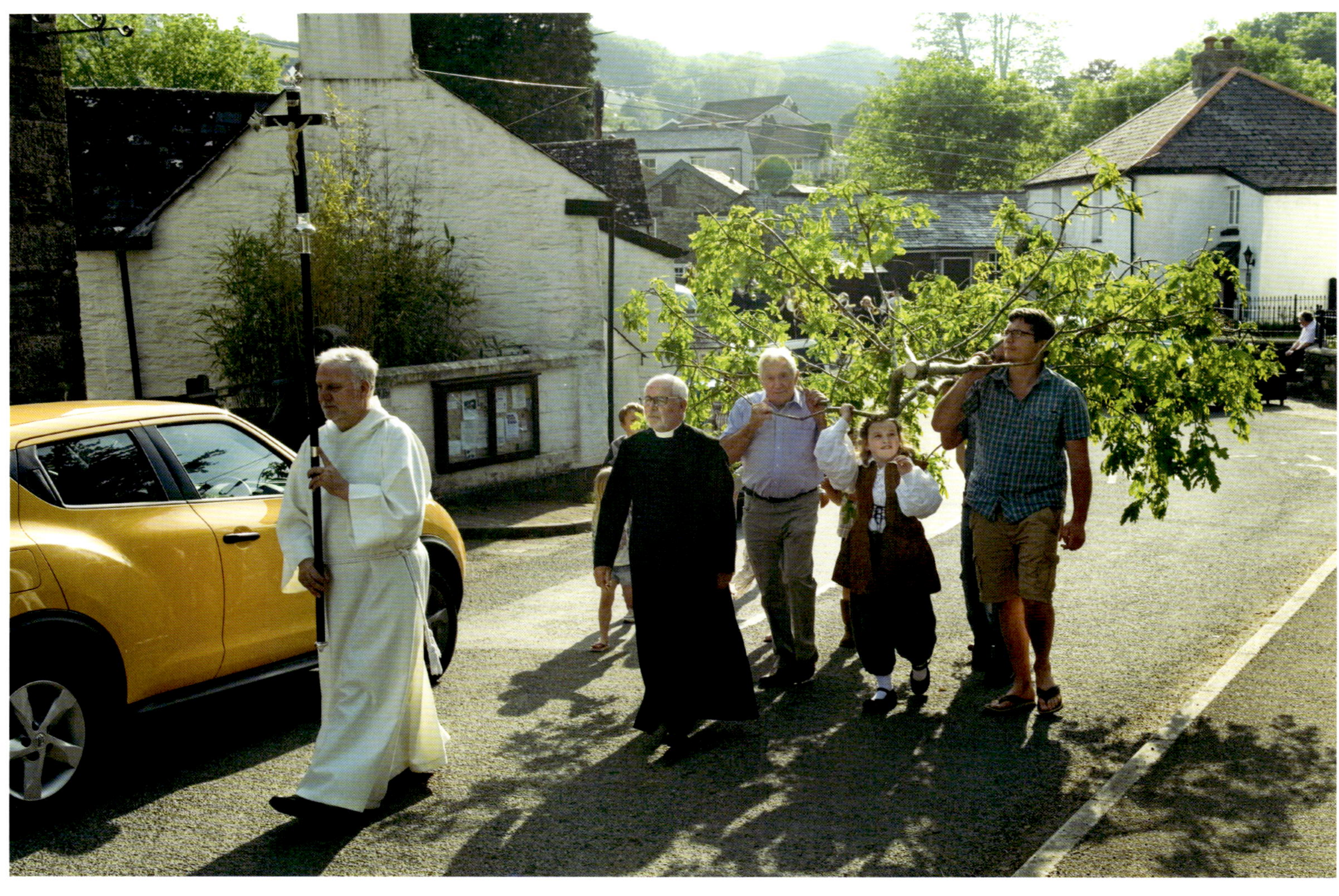

OAK APPLE DAY
St Neot, Cornwall
2016

An oak bough is carried through the village led by the Revd. Phillip Biggs to St. Neot Church where it is hoisted to the top of the church tower.

Afterwards villagers enjoy a barbeque, refreshment and entertainment in the church.

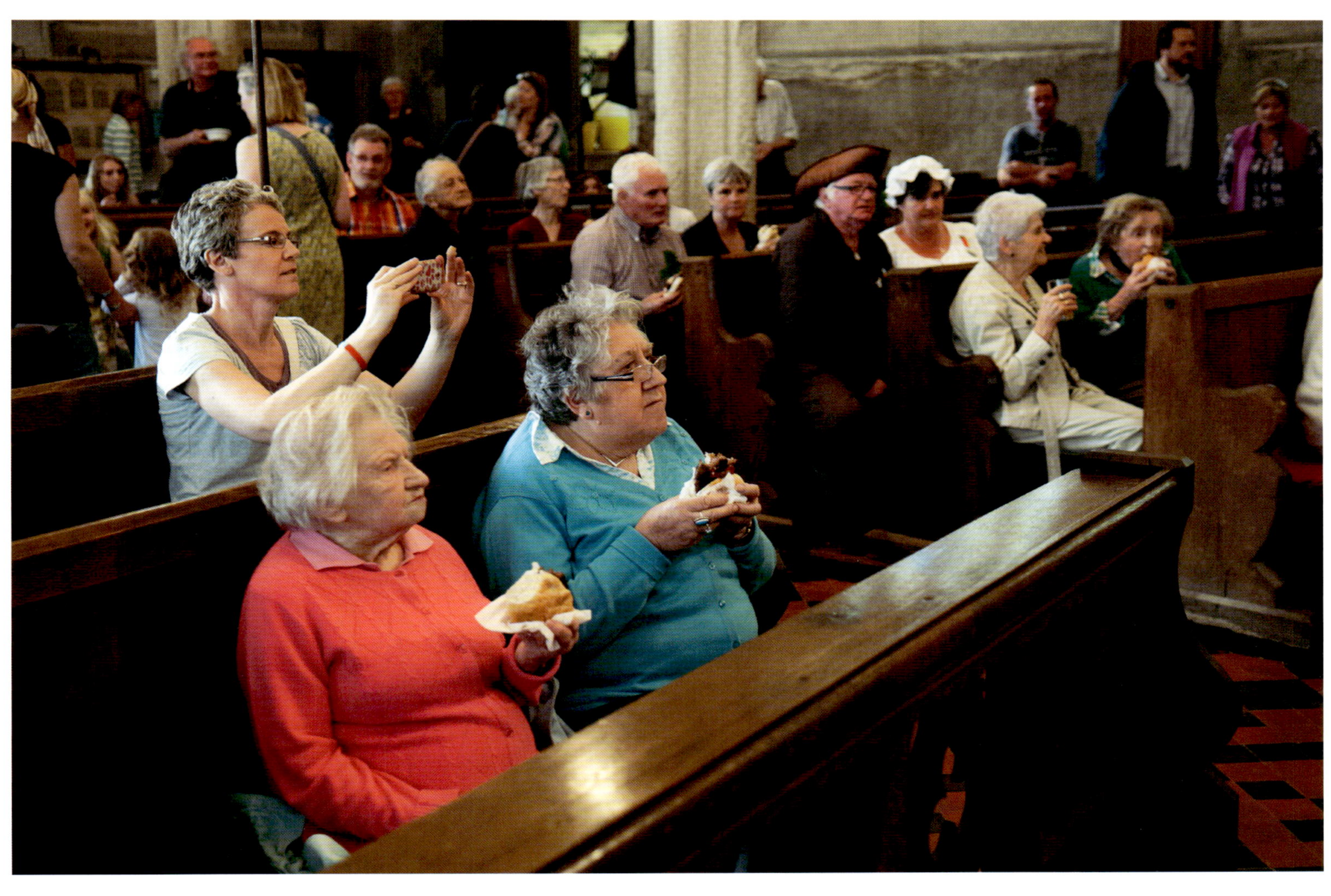

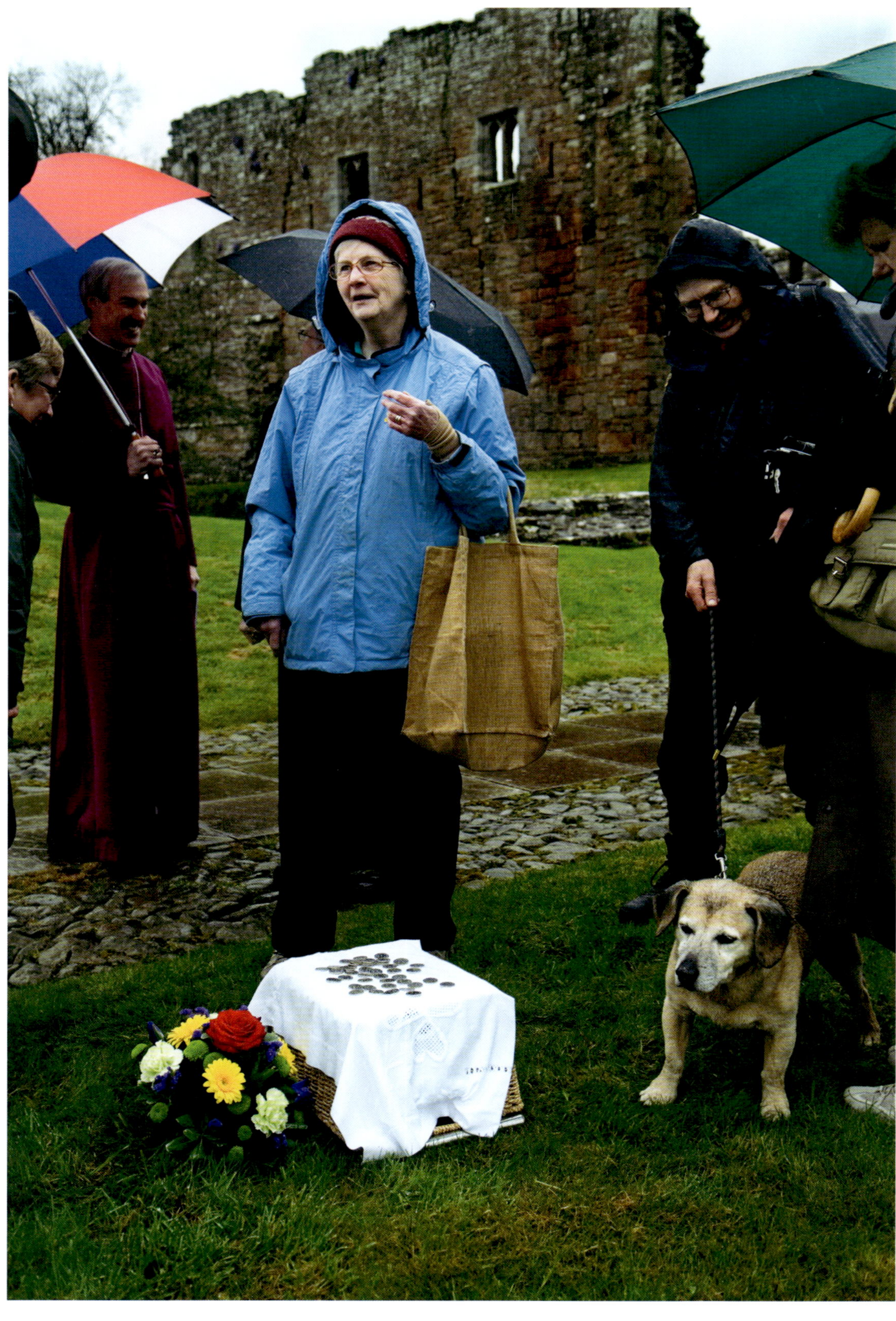

LADY ANNE CLIFFORD DOLE
Brougham, Cumbria
2016

Amongst the ruins of Brougham Castle, Lady Anne Clifford is remembered; a short service took place, hymns were sung, a collection was taken – the proceeds going to the poor of the parish of Brougham in memory of Lady Anne's mother Margaret Clifford, Countess of Cumberland.

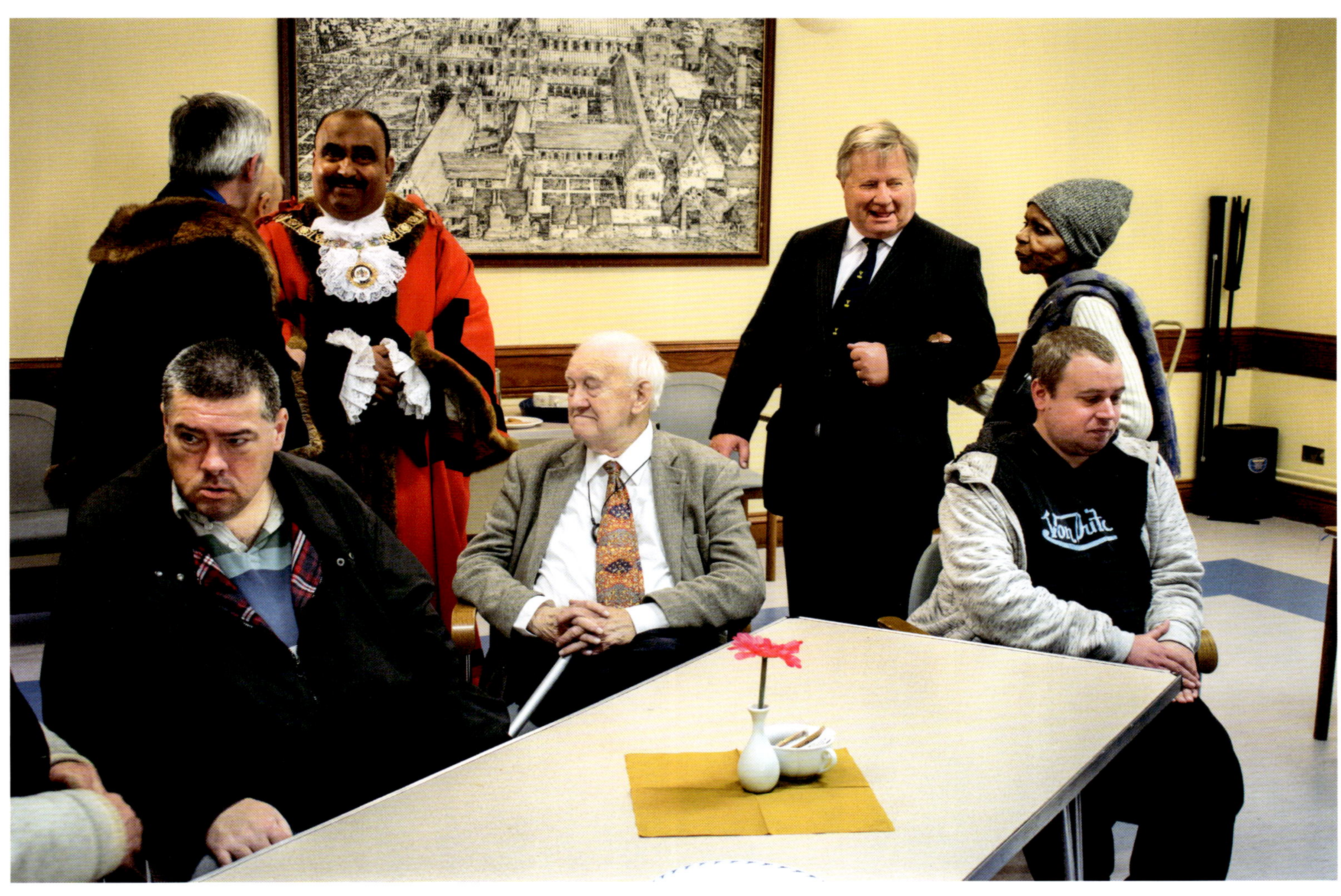

NEPTON DISTRIBUTION
Barking, Essex
2019

Over a tea and biscuit gathering, Members of the Company of Pouters, a London Livery Company, along with the Mayor of Barking and town hall dignitaries make the annual distribution to the "... poor people of Barking in the county of Essex."

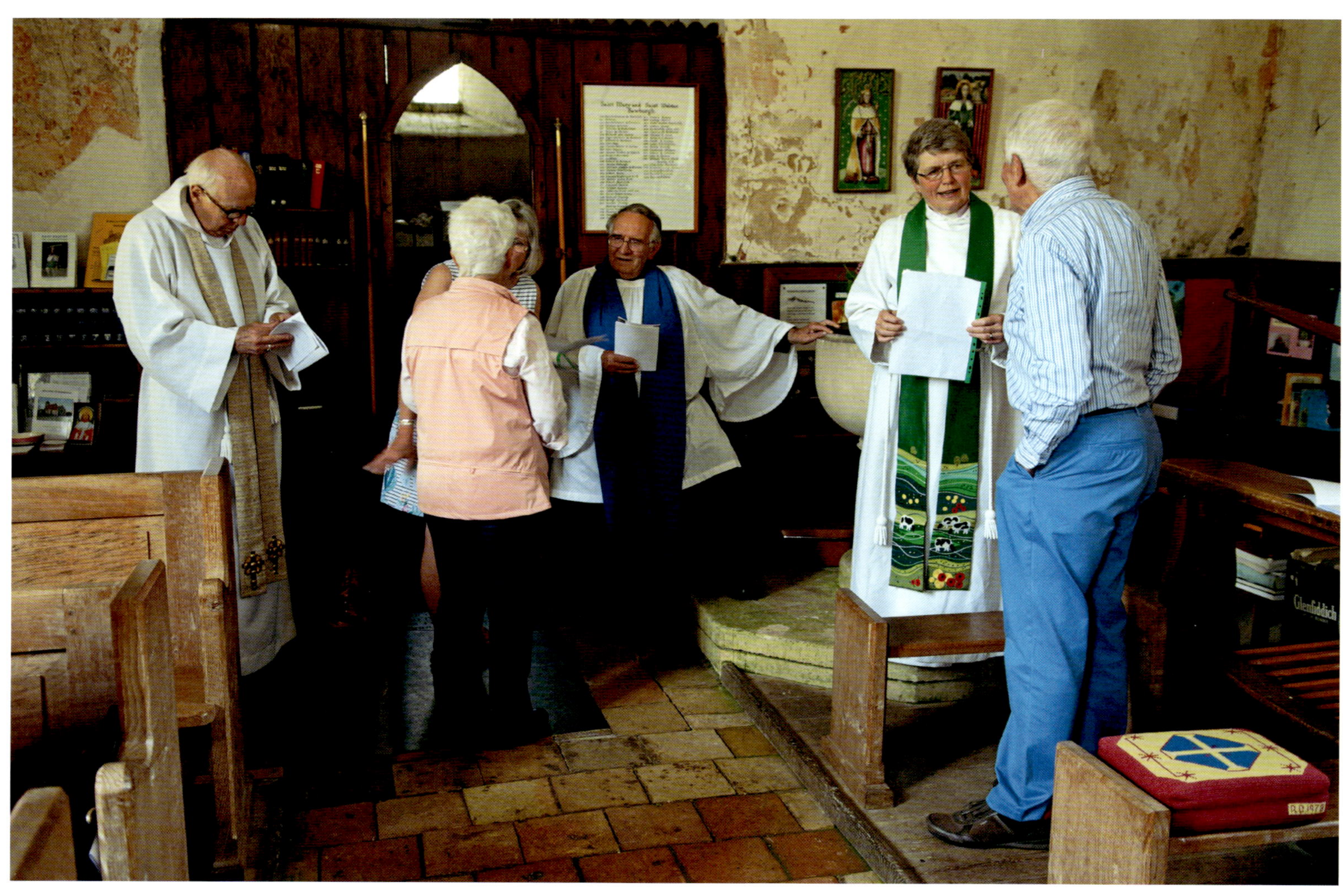

SAINT WALSTAN'S DAY
Bawburgh, Norfolk
2018

The Revd. Penny Goodman chats to a member of the congregation of St Mary and Saint Walstan's Church who have gathered for Sunday service; following which they walk in a procession to the Healing Well where a short Patronal Service takes place.

In the village hall a Ploughman's lunch with homemade cakes is provided for all.

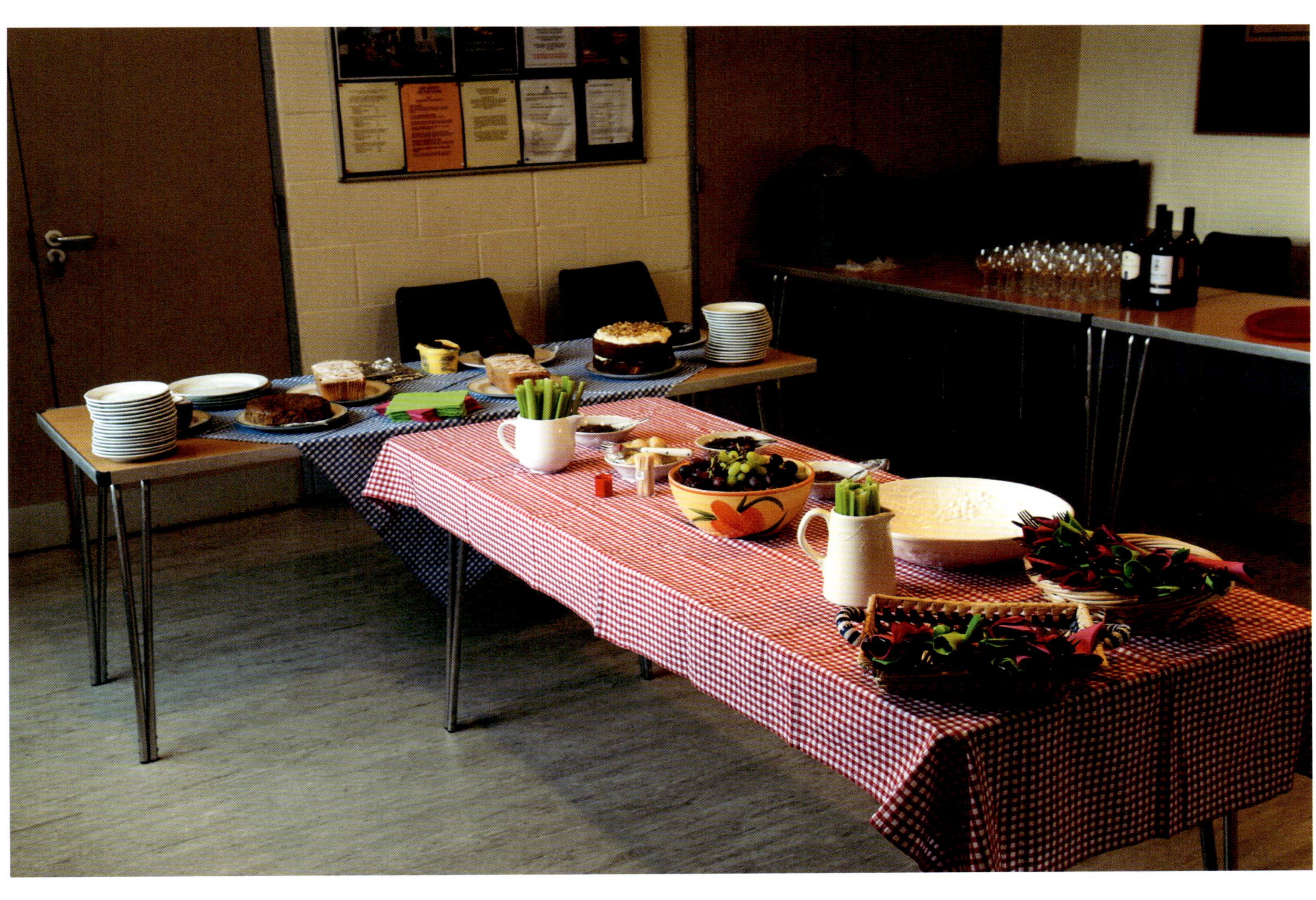

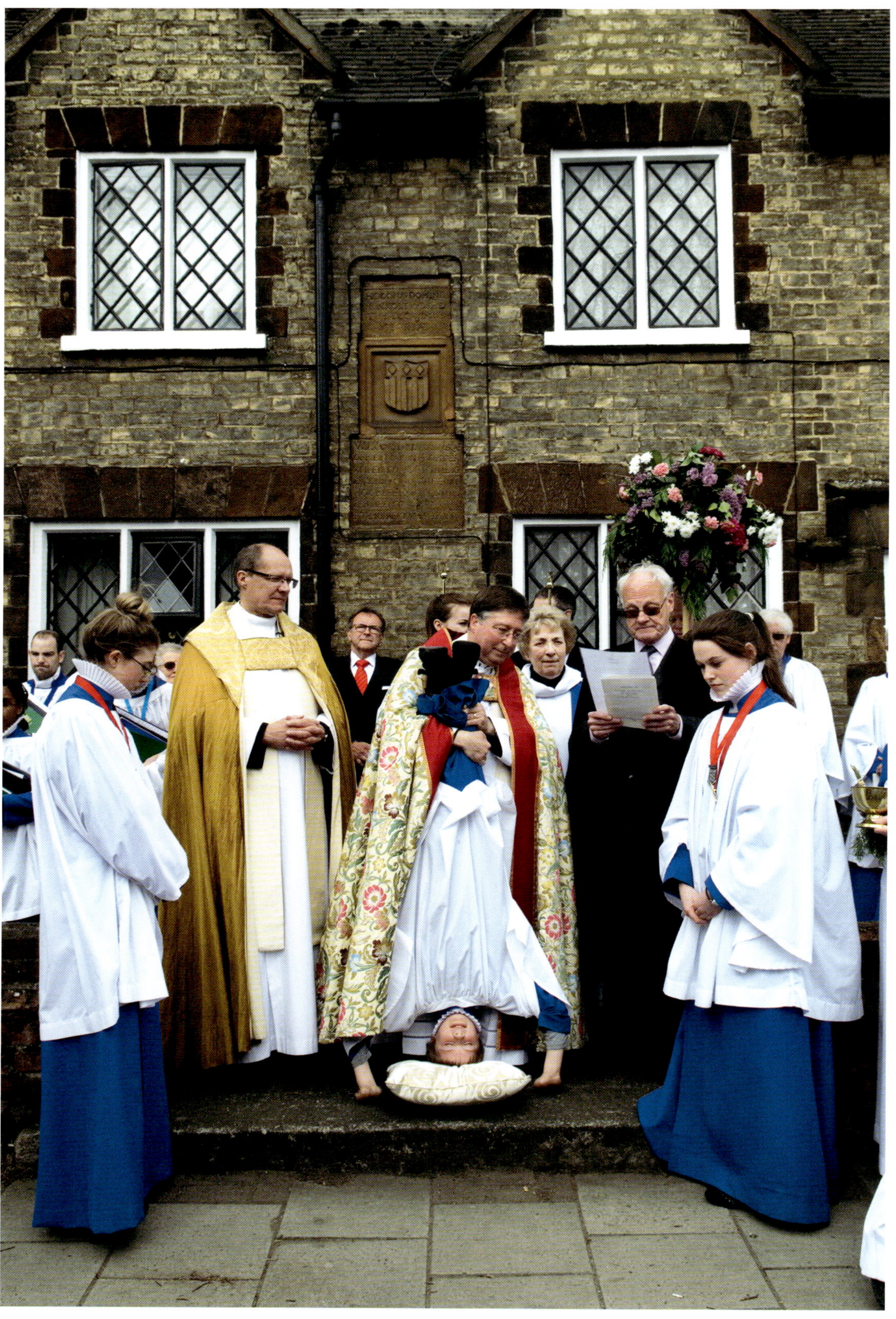

WILKES WALK
Leighton Buzzard, Bedfordshire
2015

Wilkes Walk from All Saints Church on Rogation Sunday is in memory of John Wilkes, father of William Wilkes who founded the Almeshouses that were built in 1630. A choir member must stand on their head during the reading of an extract of the 1646 will of Mathew Wilkes the son of William.

Afterwards refreshments are provided back at the church.

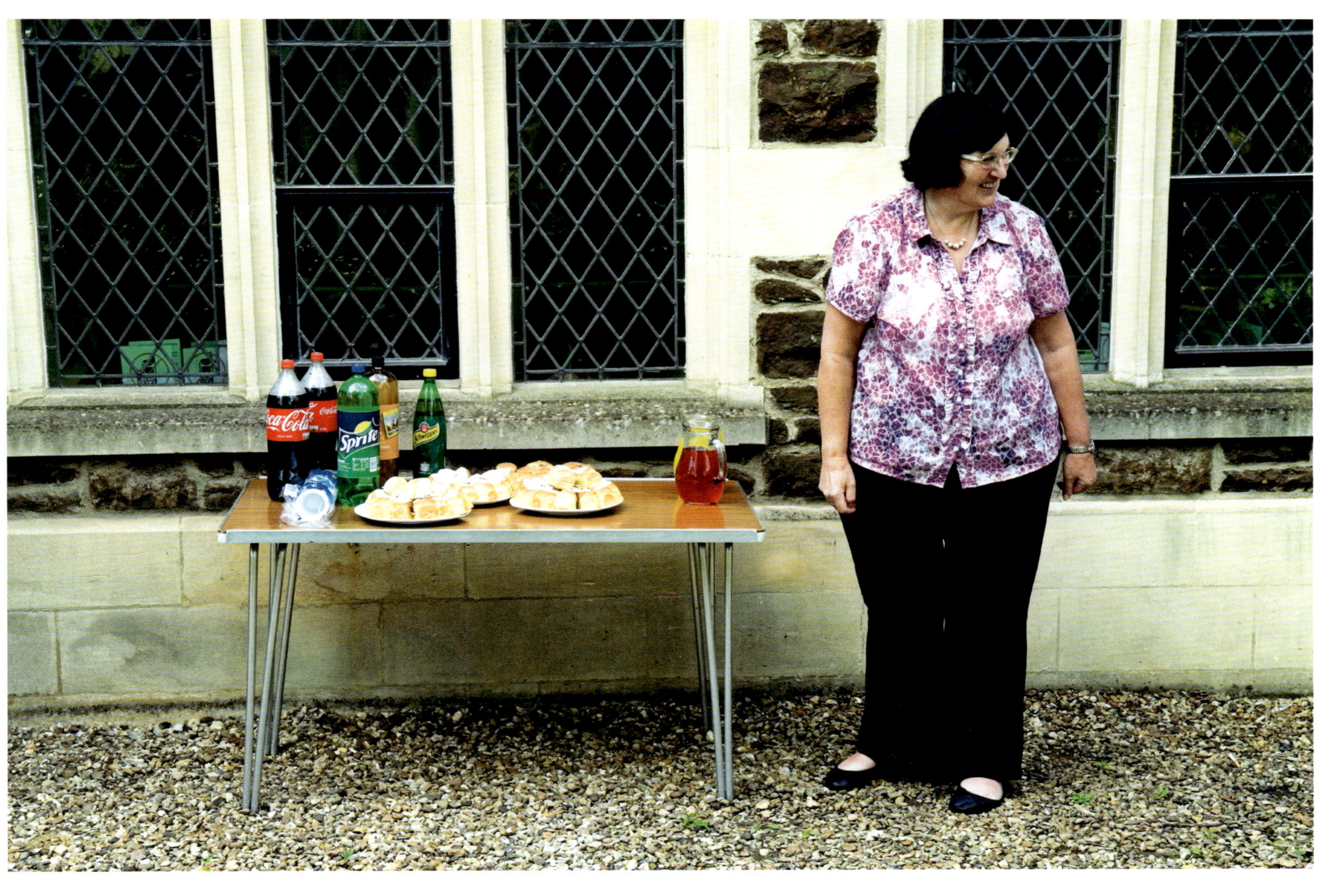
Sprite

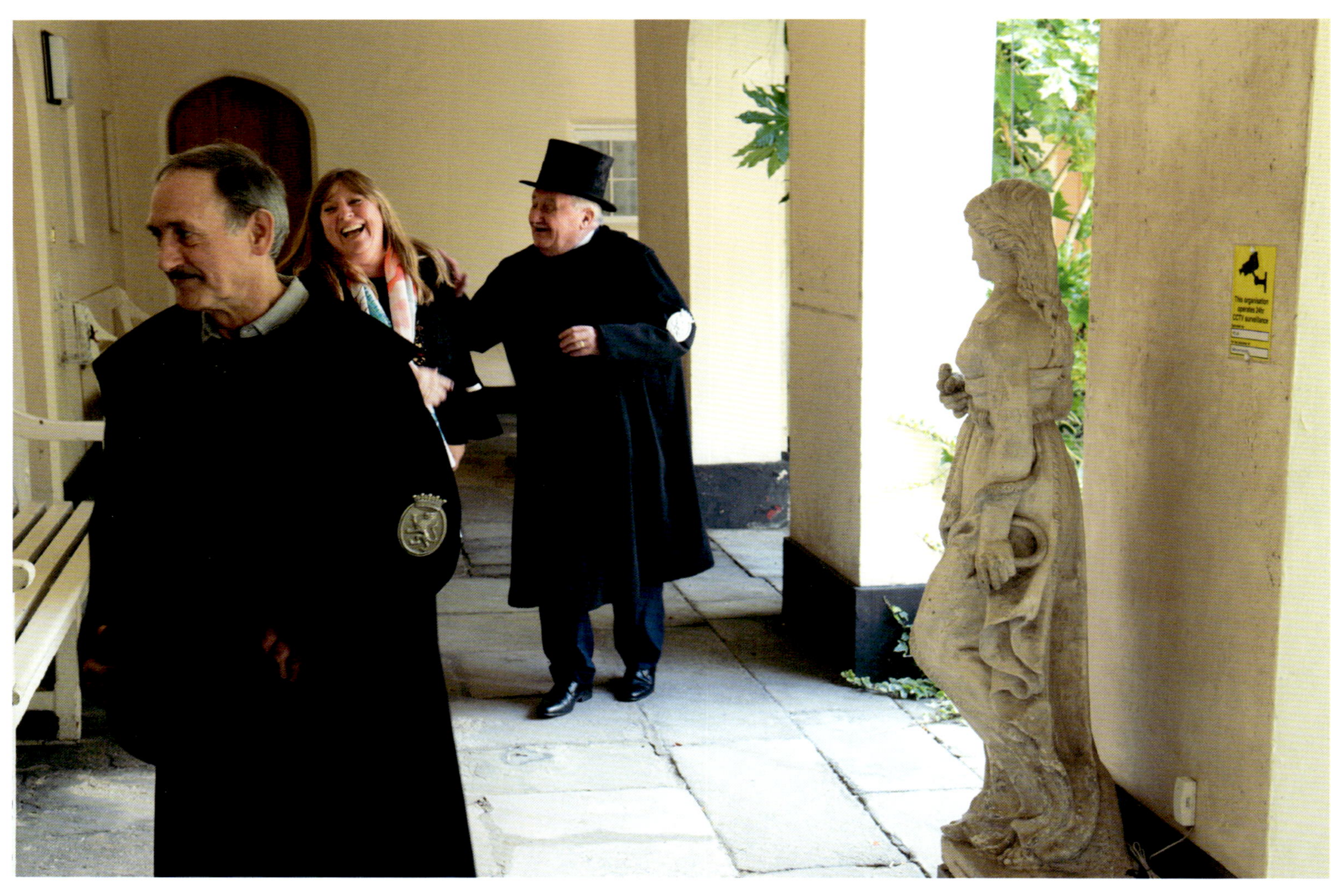

VISITATION COURT DAY
Greenwich, London
2019

The Trinity Hospital almshouses were founded in 1614 by Henry Howard, the Earl of Northampton, for the poor men of Greenwich. On Visitation Day residents may wear their traditional frock coats and top hats to attend a service in the chapel.

JANKYN SMYTH CAKE AND ALE CEREMONY
Bury St Edmunds, Suffolk
2015

The Cake and Ale Ceremony at the Guildhall celebrates the life of Jankyn Smyth an important benefactor to the town who died in 1481, seen here in the portrait.

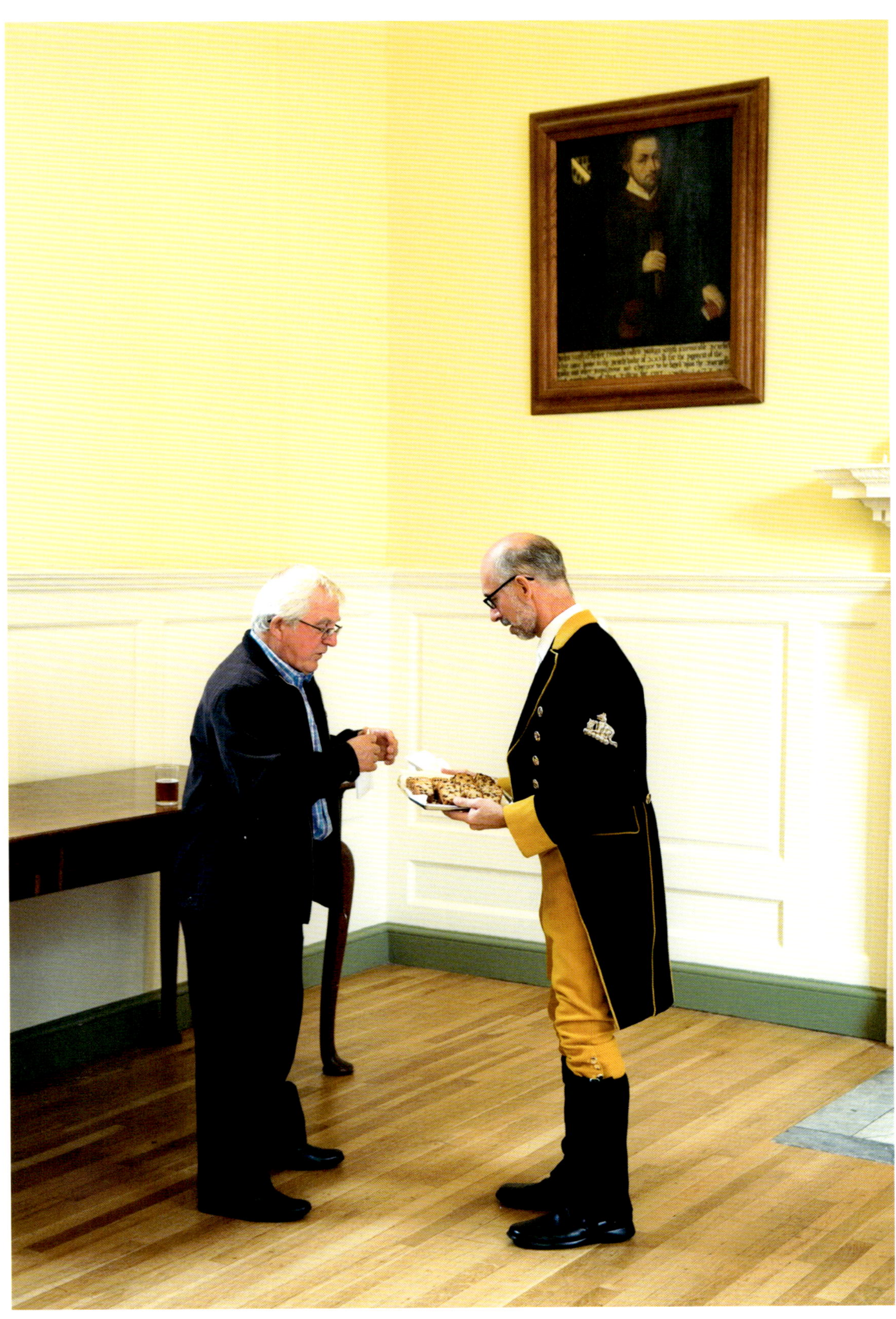

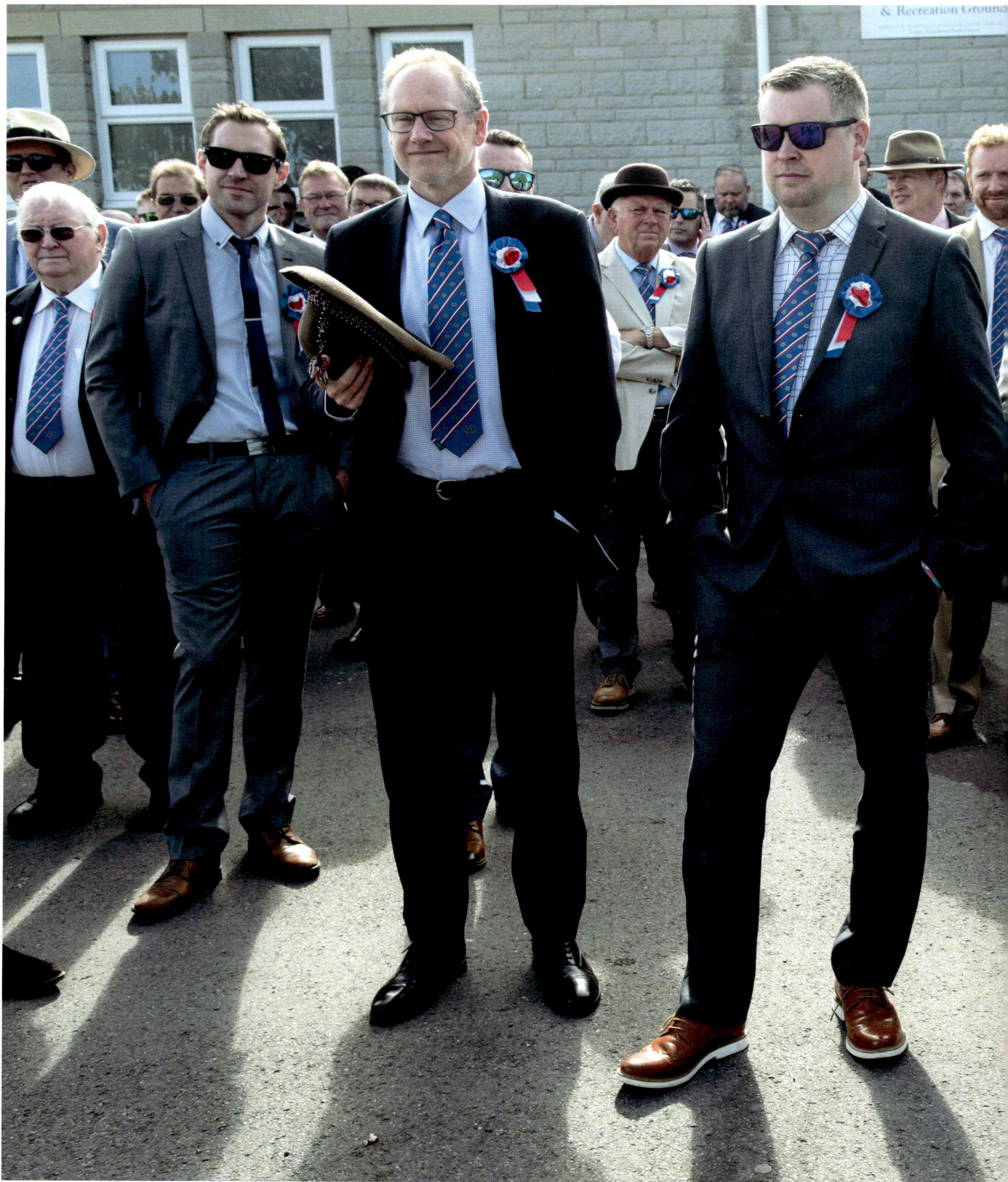
& Recreation Groun

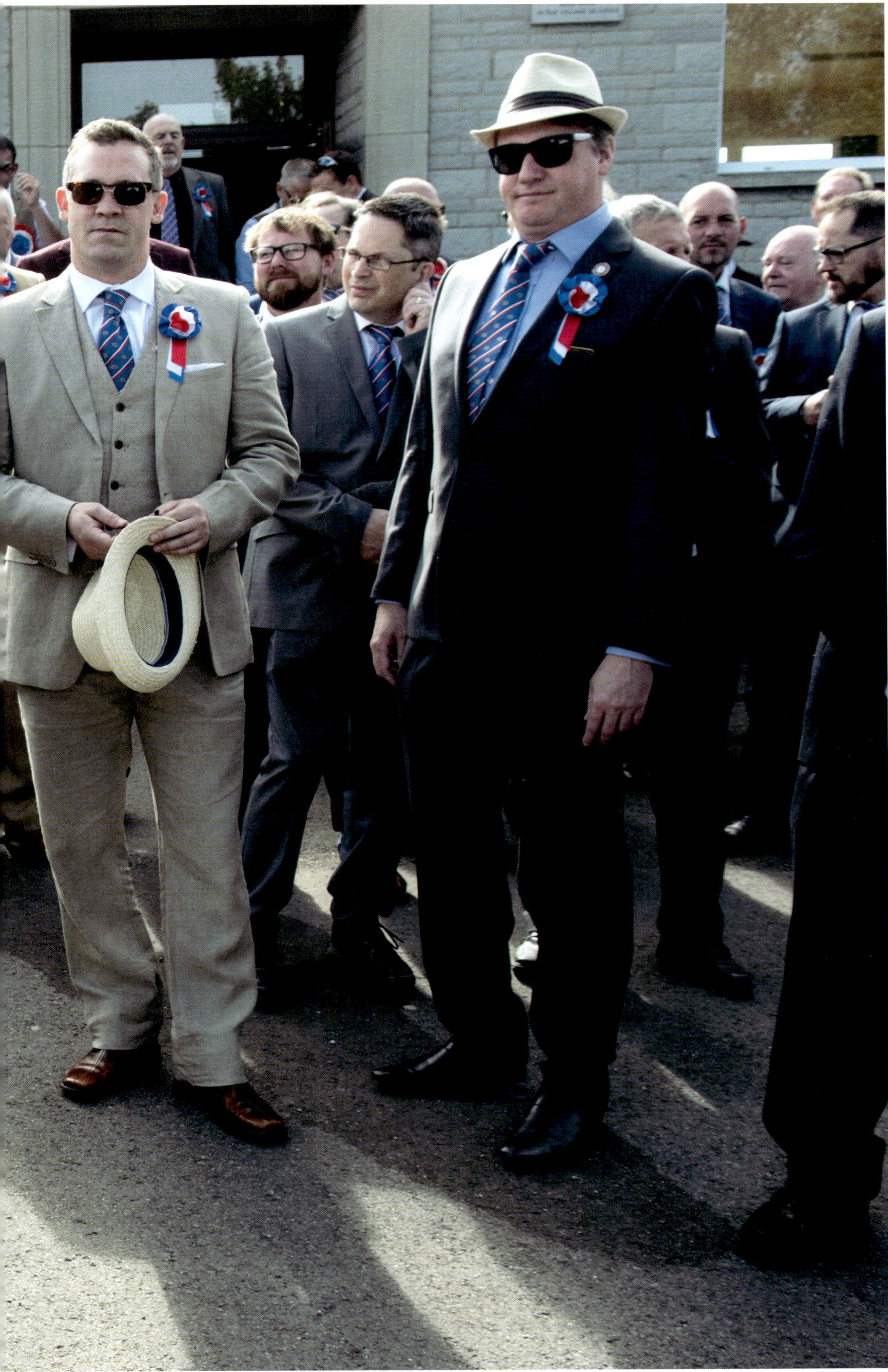

FRIENDLY SOCIETY CLUB WALK DAY
Long Sutton, Somerset
2019

The Roll Call of Members, who gather outside the village hall at the start of the Club Walk Day.

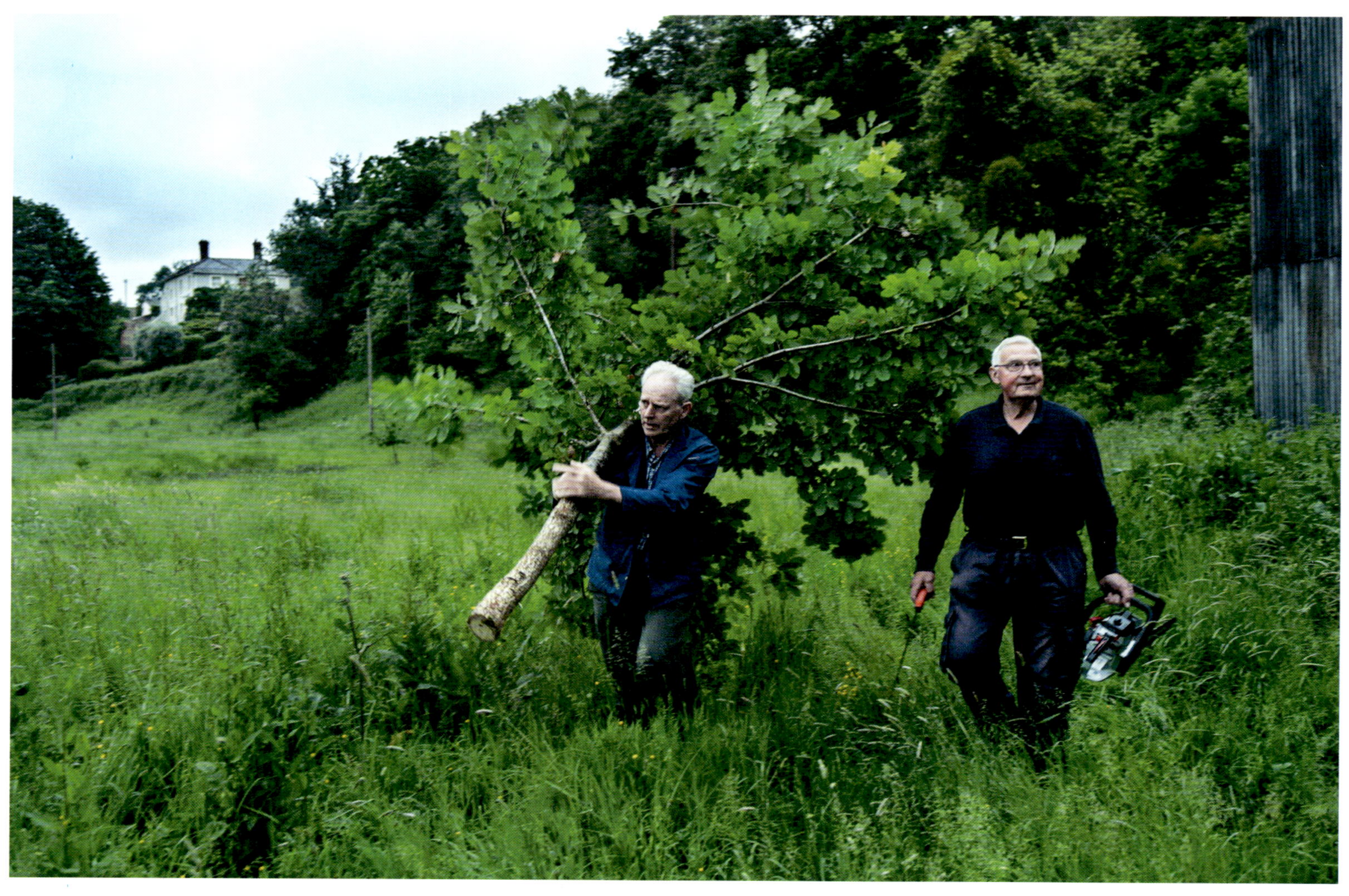

FOWNHOPE HEART OF OAK SOCIETY
Fownhope, Herefordshire
2018

At Lechmere Ley, as dawn breaks, Geoff Hardwick, chairman, and Mike Andrews, president of the Fownhope Heart of Oak Society, cut an oak tree bough that is then decorated and driven back into the village.

The decorated oak bough followed by the society banner is carried to the New Inn for the start of the Club Walk Day parade around the village.

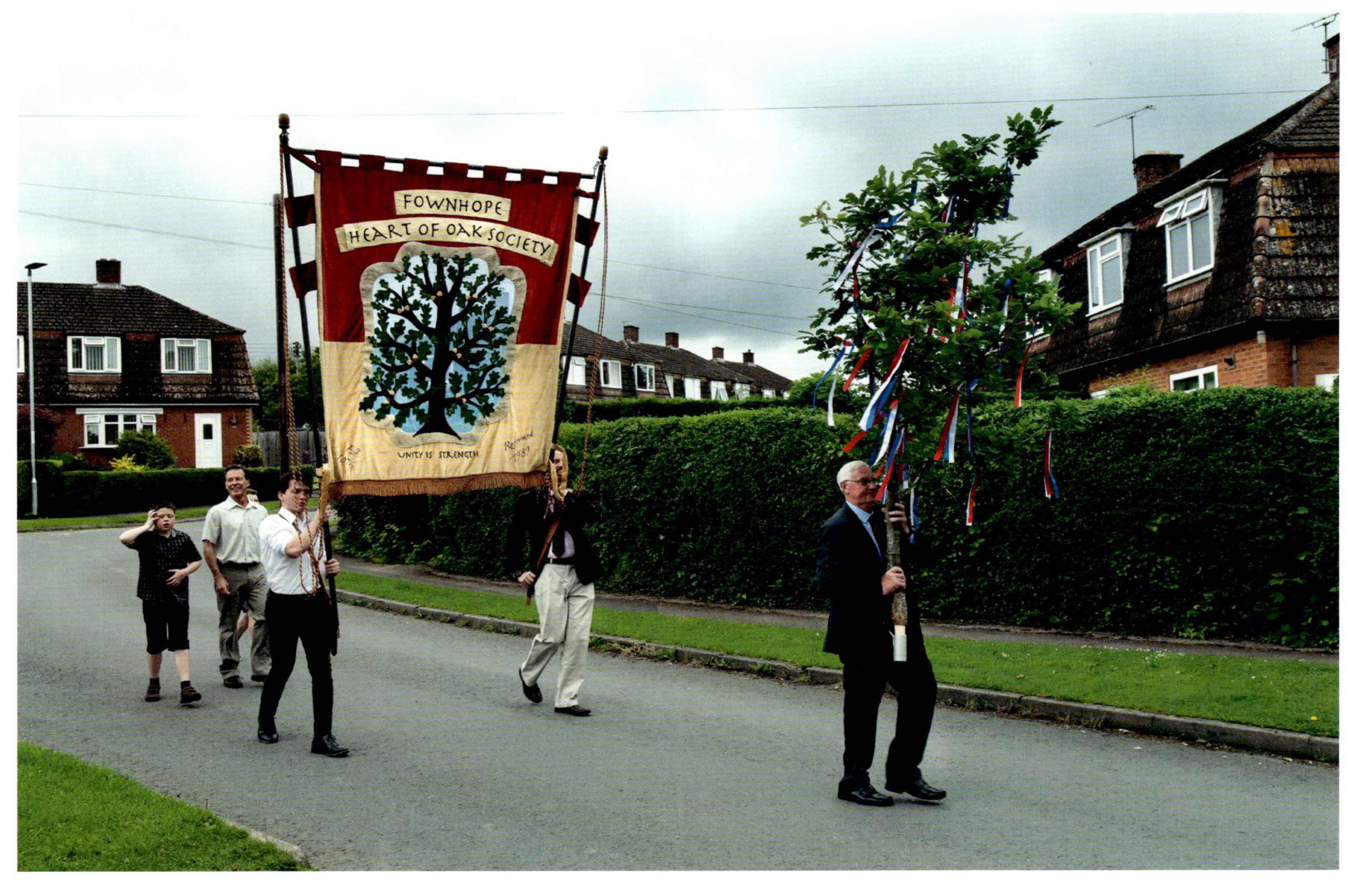
FOWNHOPE
HEART OF OAK SOCIETY
UNITY IS STRENGTH
Reformed

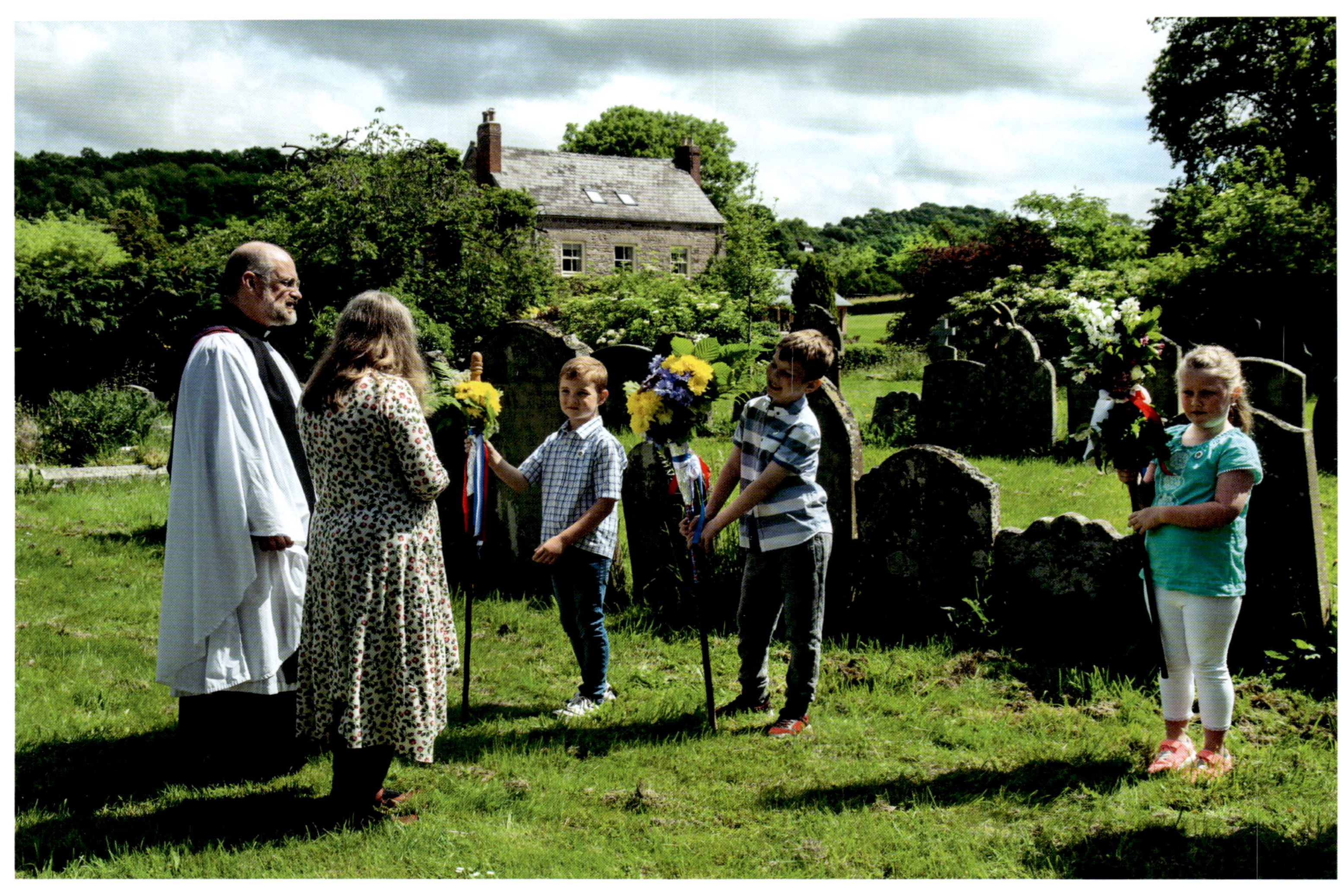

FOWNHOPE HEART OF OAK SOCIETY
Fownhope, Herefordshire
2018

In the grounds of St. Mary's church, Fownhope, the Rector Chris Moore and his wife Mary look for the best flower decorated Junior Club Stick. Standing apart from the two boys, Evie Wilks wonders if her flower stick will win a prize.

Locally brewed cider is provided, a much needed refreshment, during a stop on the Club Walk Day around the village.

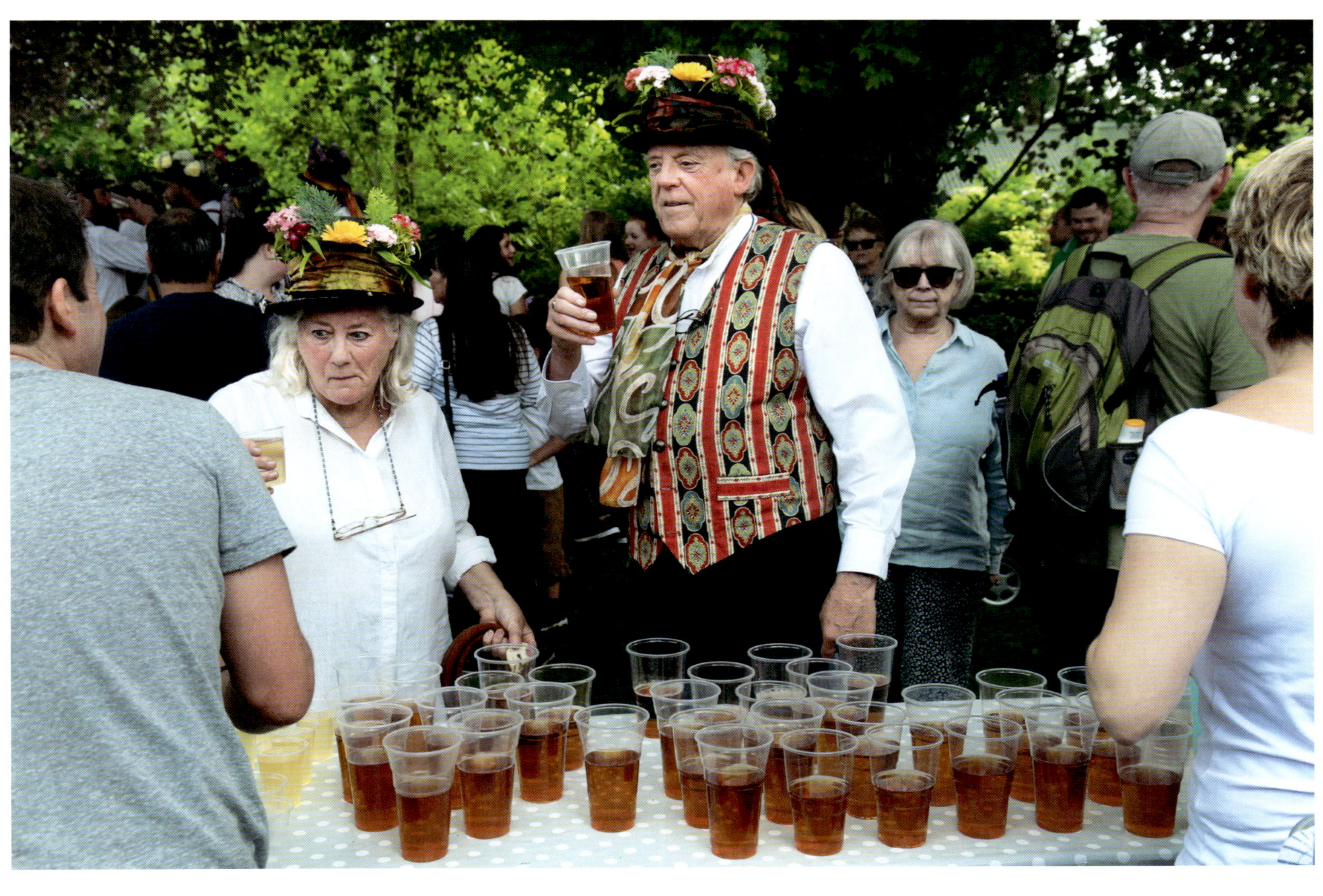

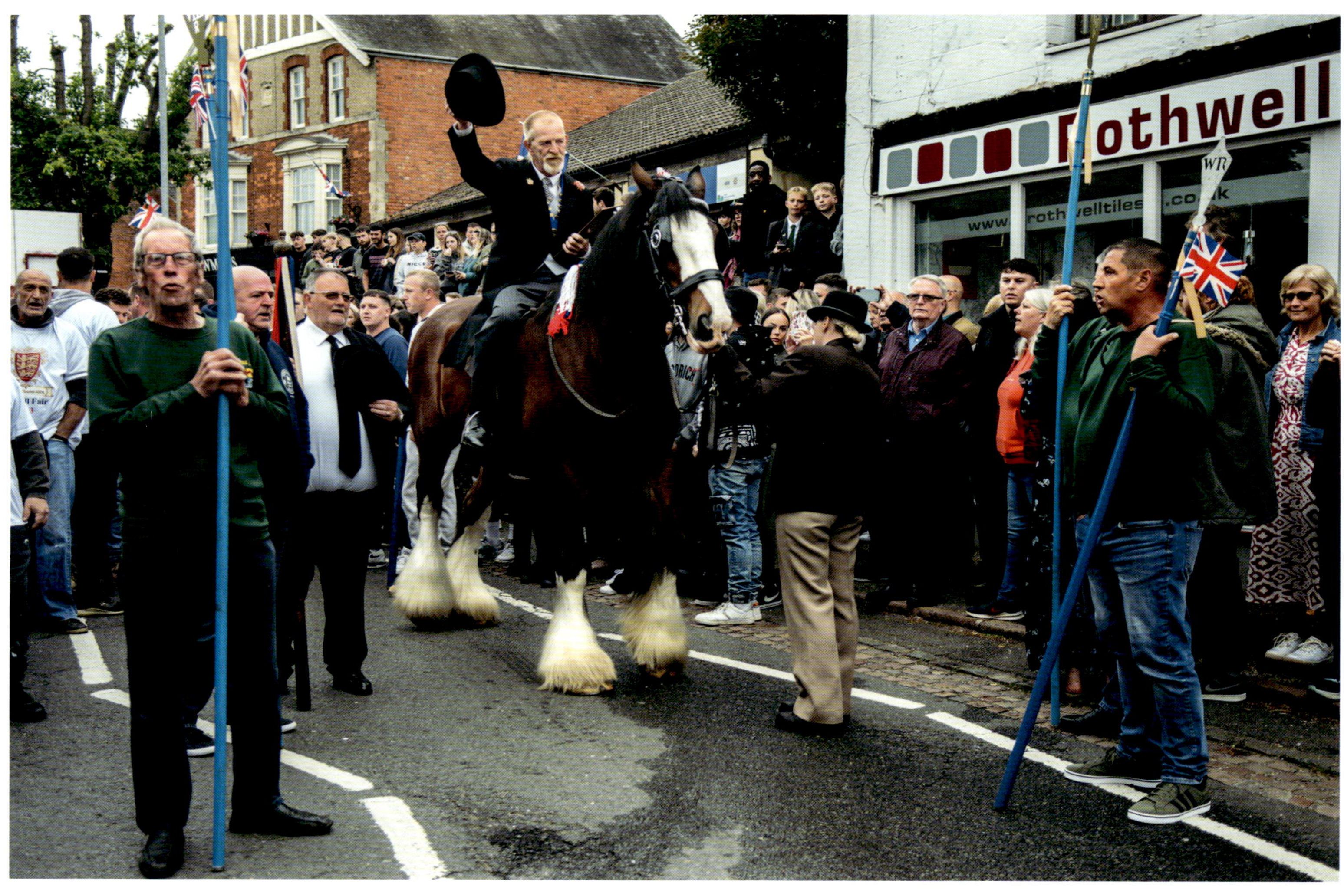

ROWELL CHARTER FAIR
Rothwell, Northamptonshire
2023

Frank York, the Bailiff to the Lord of the Manor, on horseback, accompanied by John Newman, the Chief Halberdier and local civic dignitaries gather as the Charter Fair Proclamation is read and the fair declared open.

The traditional Fair tipple of rum and milk, or a pint of beer if you prefer, is served outside The Blue Bell public house.

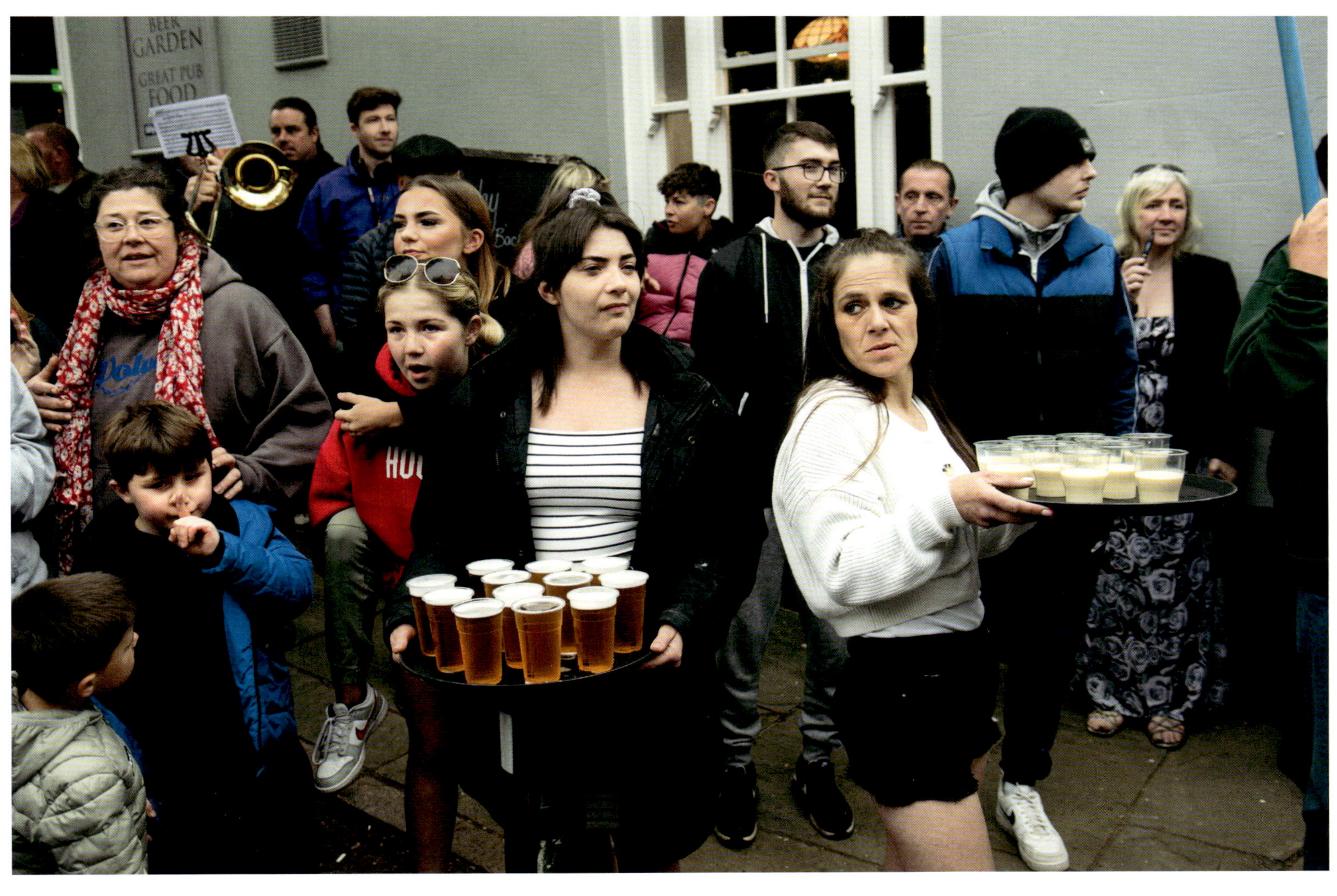
GARDEN
GREAT PUB
FOOD

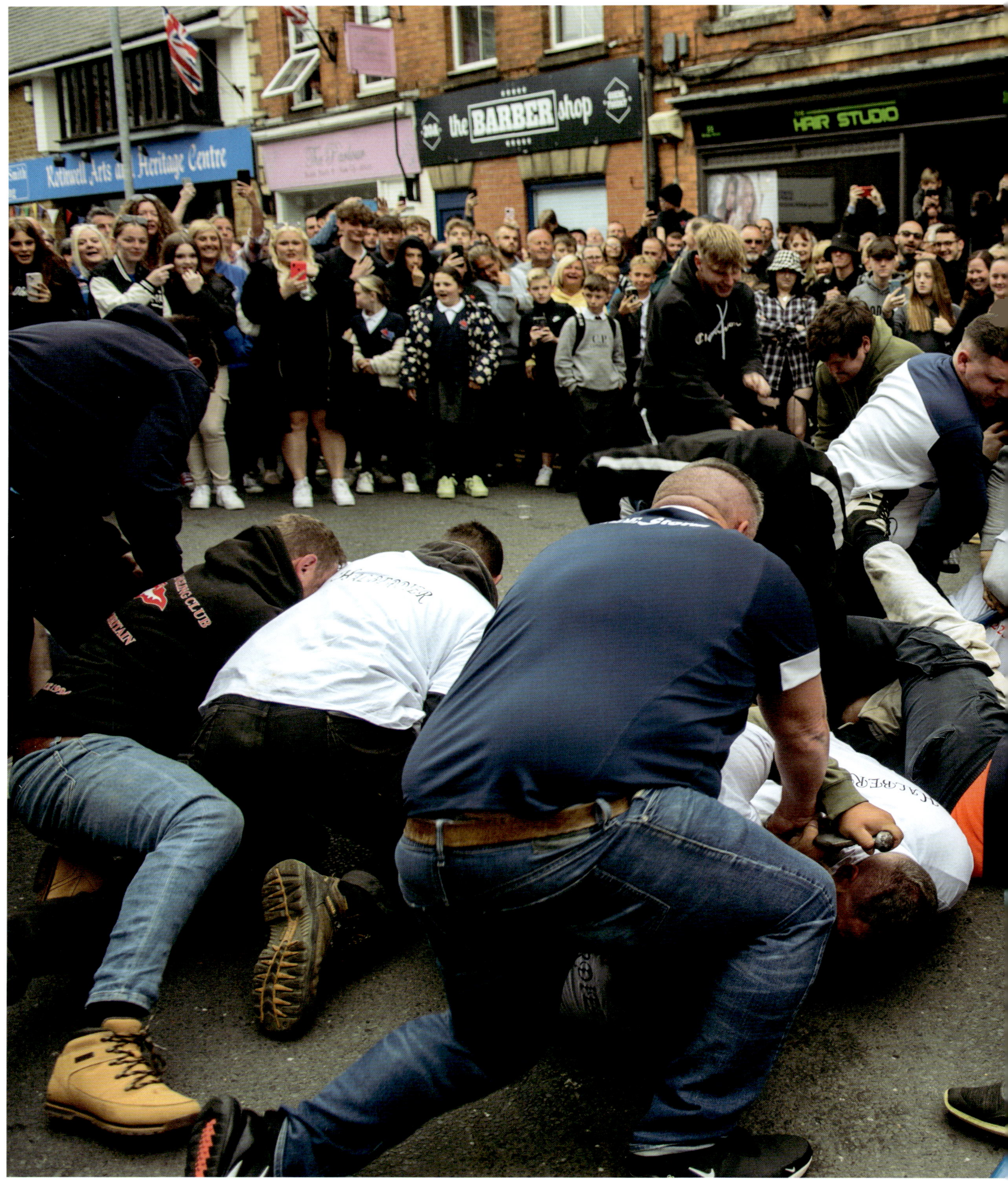
the BARBER shop
HAIR STUDIO

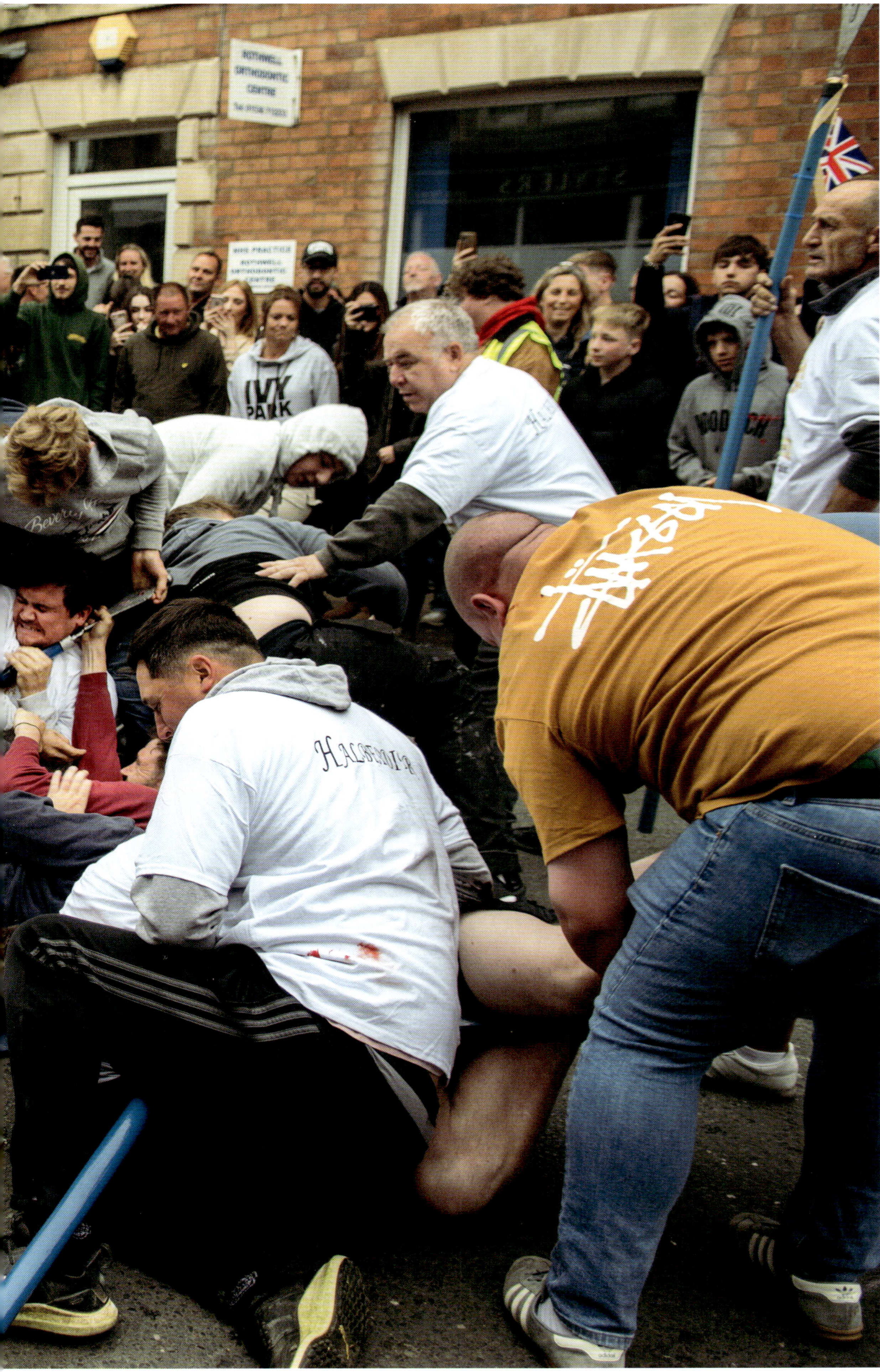

ROWELL CHARTER FAIR
Rothwell, Northamptonshire
2023

Townsfolk vigorously scuffle with the halberdiers, attempting to capture their two-handed polearm.

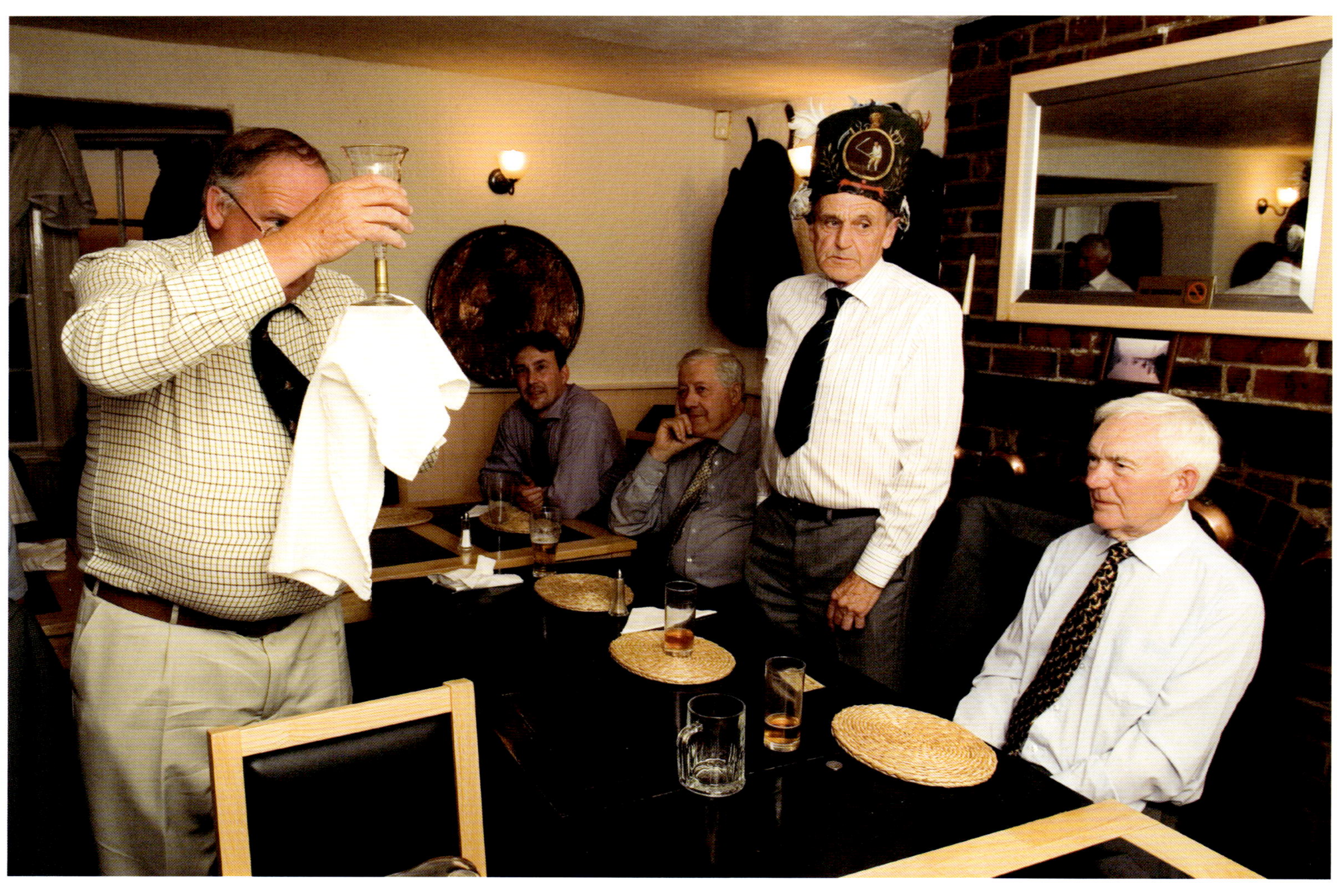

DUCK FEAST
Charlton St Peter, Wiltshire
2009

The feast commemorates the poet Stephen Duck (1705-1756). A toast of 2/3 of a pint of ale is drunk from a special glass and downed in one.

After the feast, there is a reading from Duck's epic poem *The Thresher's Labour*.

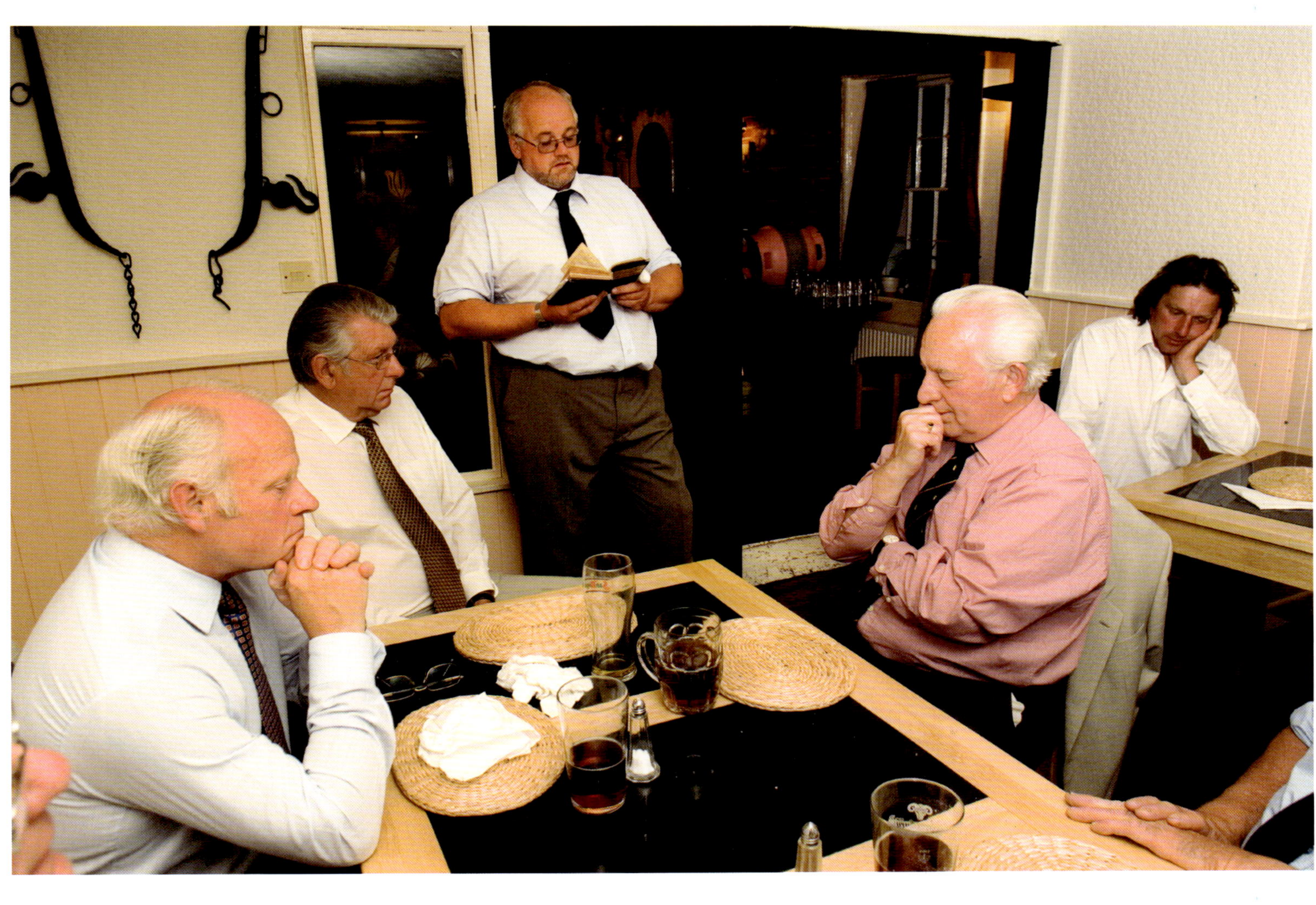

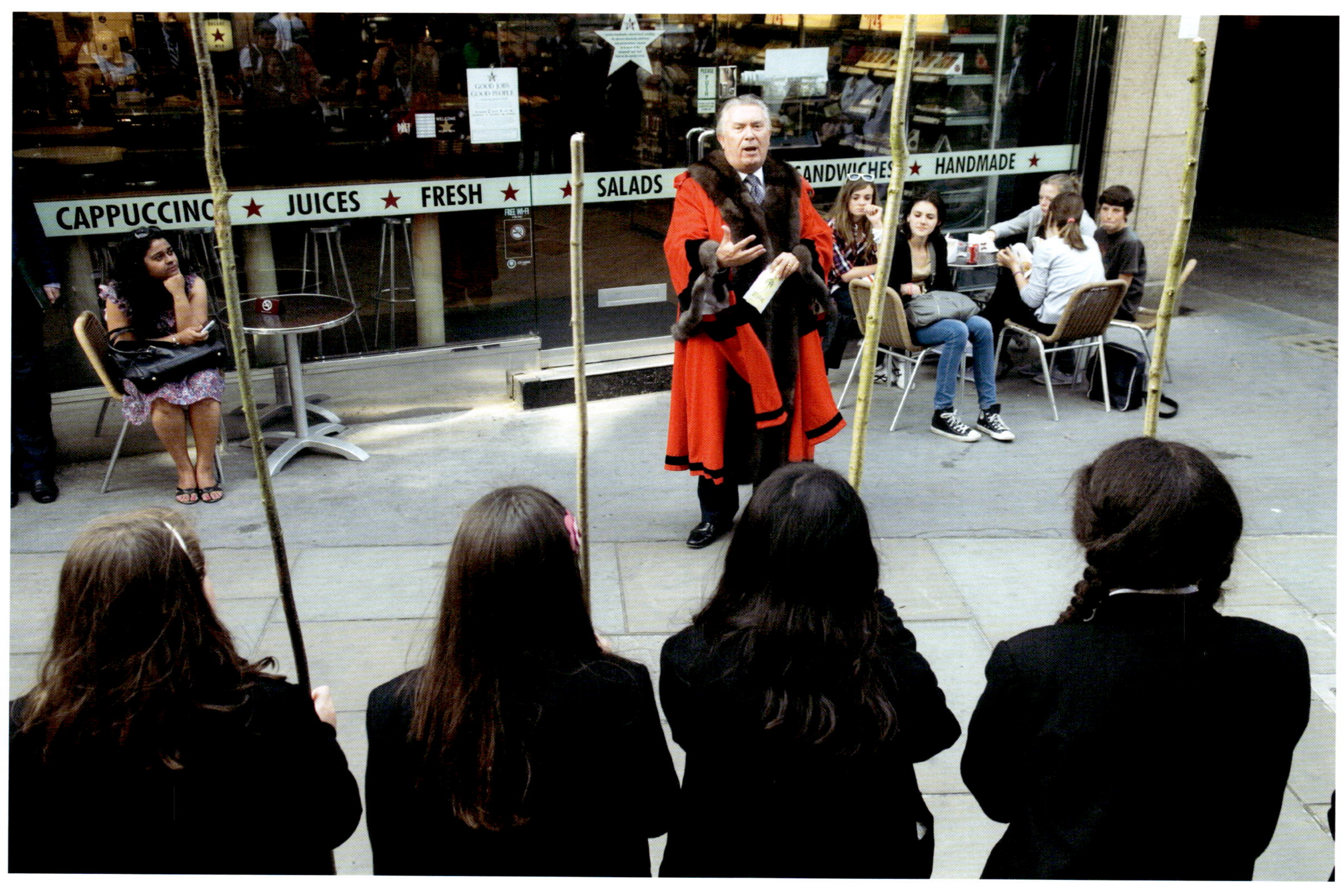

BEATING THE BOUNDS
All-Hallows-by-the-Tower
City of London, 2011

Outside a Pret A Manger café Sir Paul Judge, explains the meaning of Beating the Bounds to St Dunstan's College students.

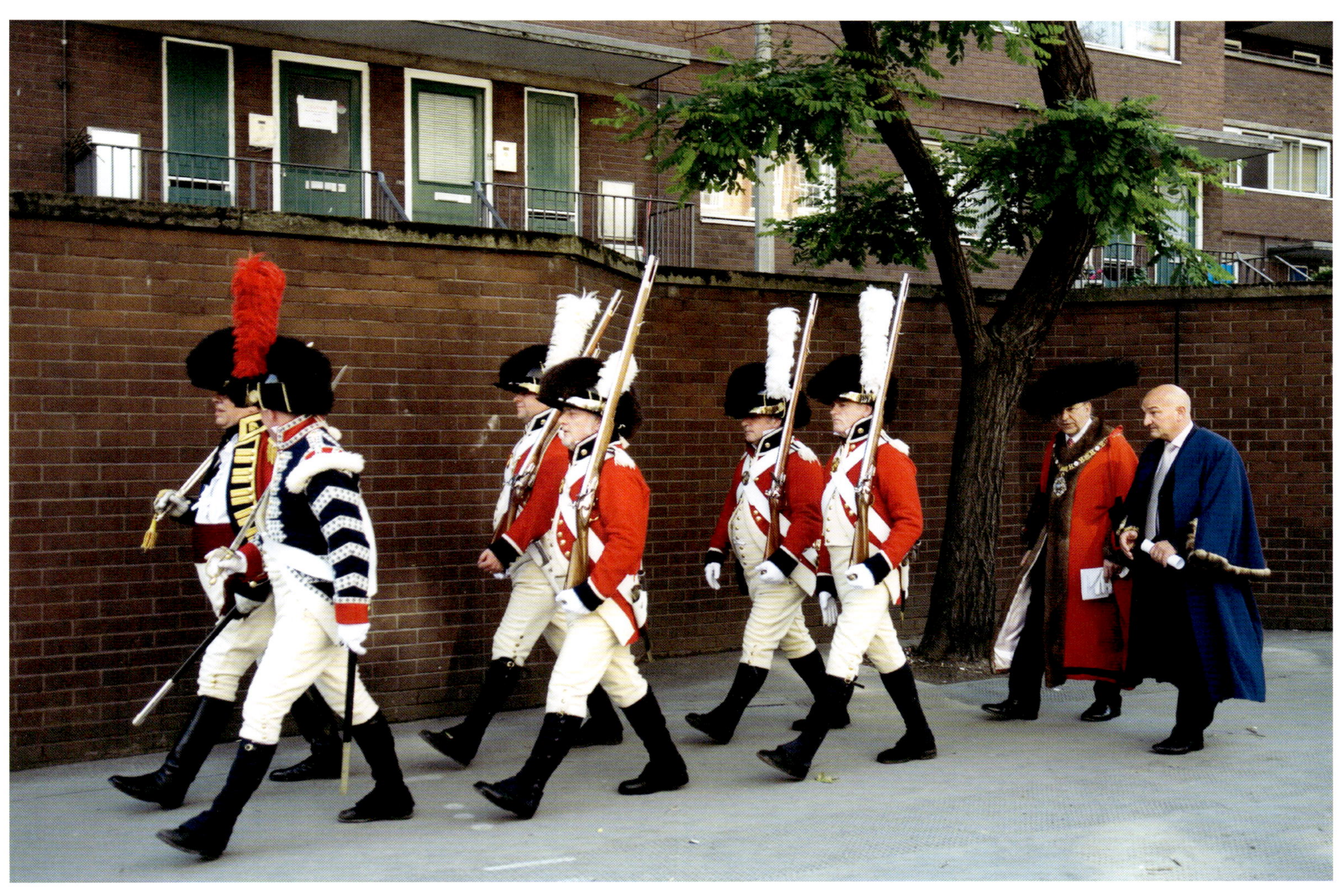

BEATING THE BOUNDS
St Botolph without Aldgate
City of London, 2011

The Portsoken Volunteers and Alderman Michael Bear, the Lord Mayor of the City of London, walk the boundaries of the ward of Portsoken, the ancient parish boundaries of St Botolph without Aldgate.

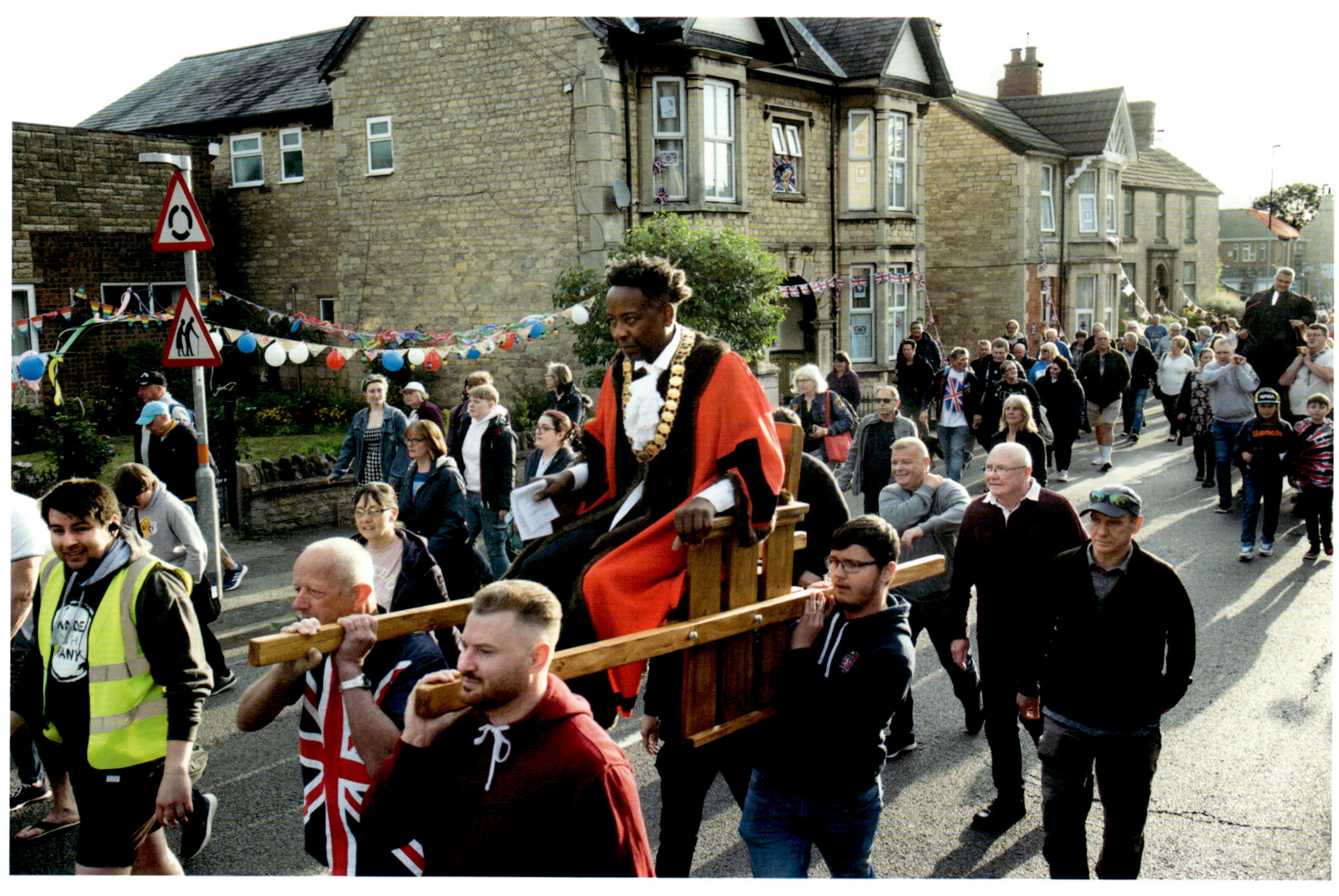

CORBY POLE FAIR
Corby Old Village, Northamptonshire
2022

The Pole Fair takes place in Corby Old Village once every 20 years. Mayor Cllr. Tafadzwa Chikoto and the Revd. Paul Frost are 'chaired' along the High Street to the White Hart pub where a second reading of the Charter takes place.

After the final reading of the Charter in the village centre residents sing *God Save the Queen*.

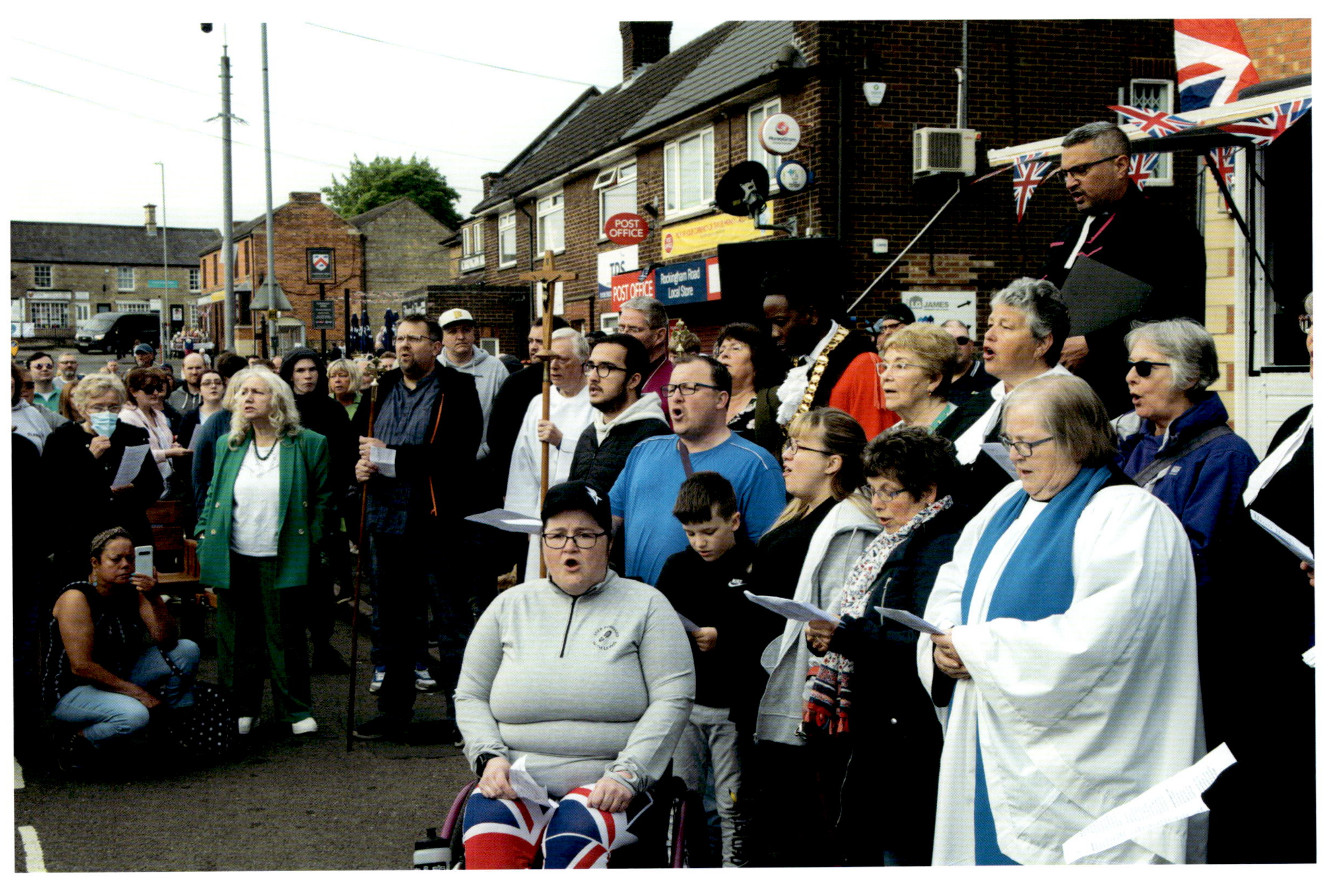
POST OFFICE
POST OFFICE
Rockingham Road
Local Store

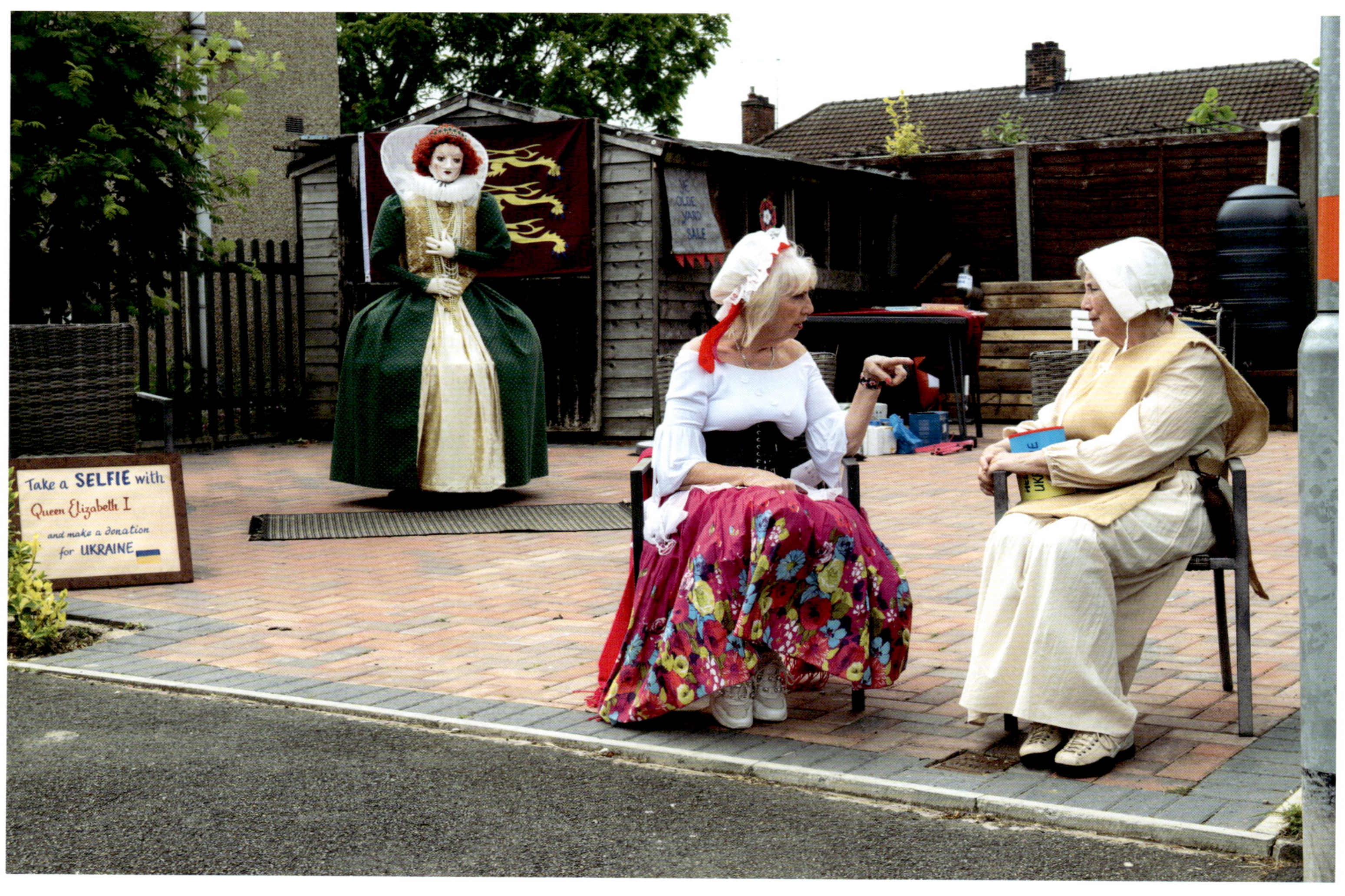

CORBY POLE FAIR
Corby, Northamptonshire
2022

In Elizabethan period costume, friends are in animated conversation. Visitors can take a selfie with Queen Elizabeth I, and donations are collected to support Ukraine against Russian aggression in what is known as 'Putin's War'.

All the shops in the village are closed for the day apart from a Fish and Chips fast food takeaway outlet.

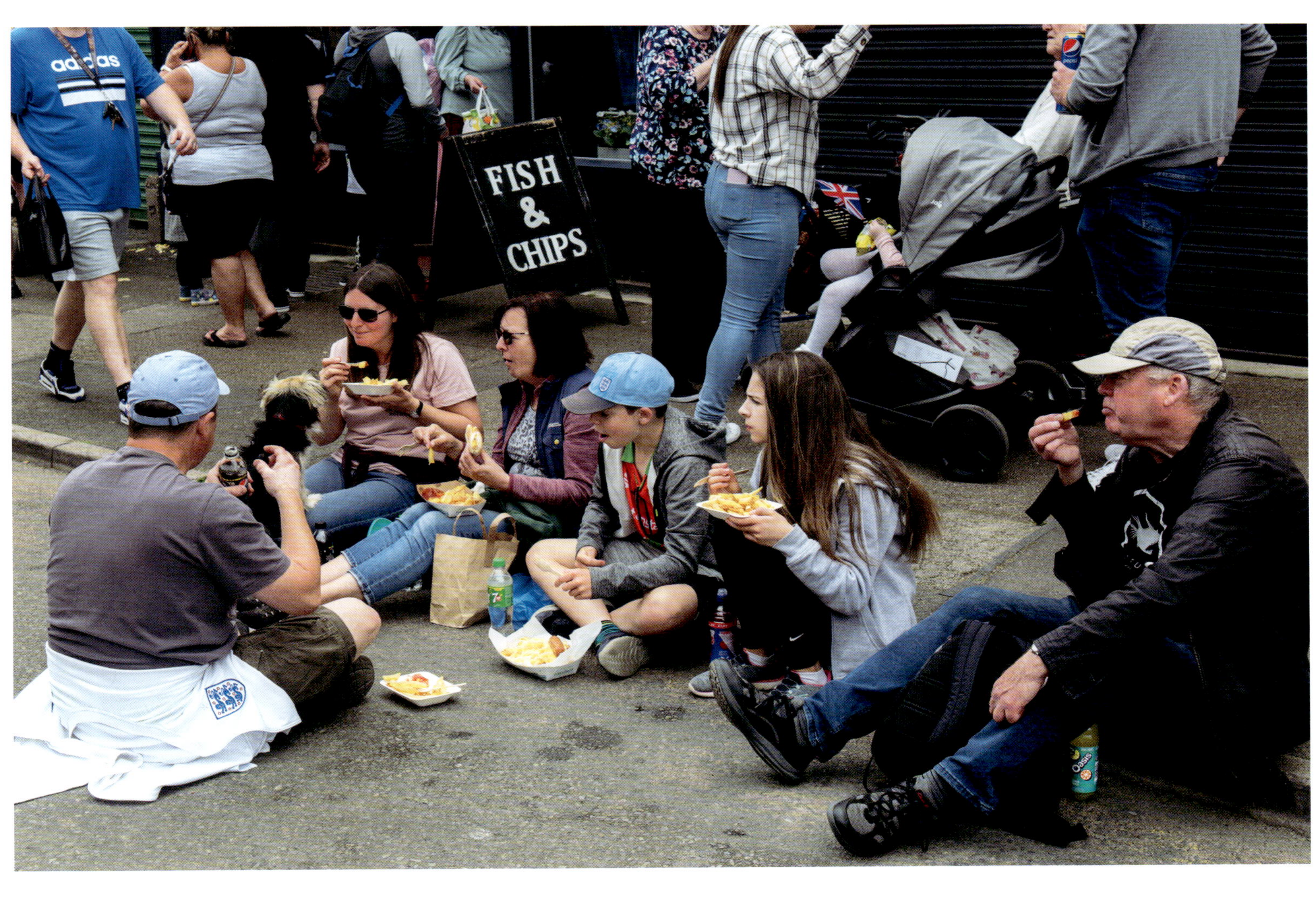
adidas
FISH
&
CHIPS

ODDFELLOWS: THE LOYAL LAUREL AND CROWN LODGE
Parwich, Derbyshire
2023

Mrs Alice Shields greets members of the lodge on the steps of Parwich Hall where refreshments will be taken in the extensive gardens.

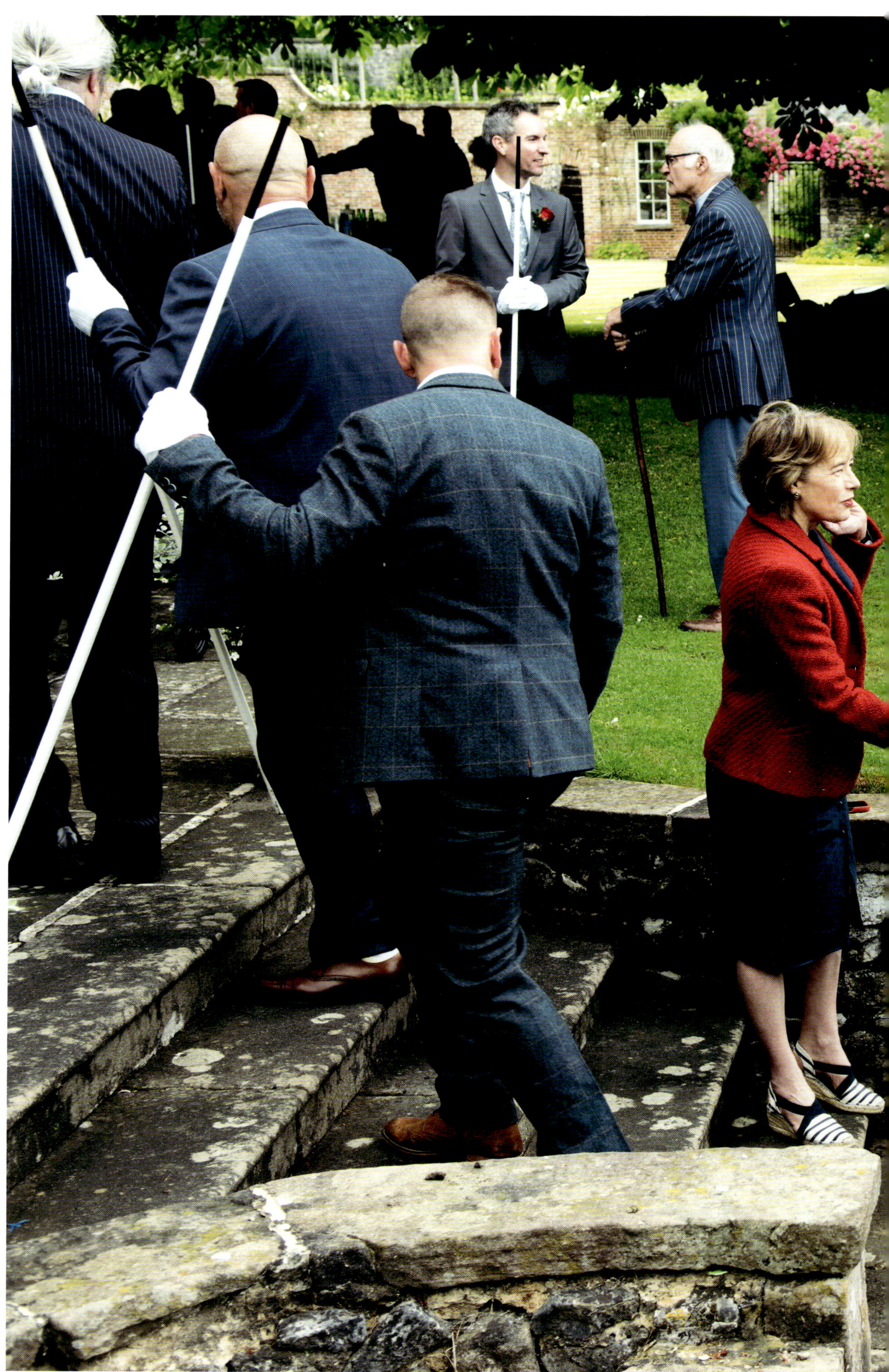

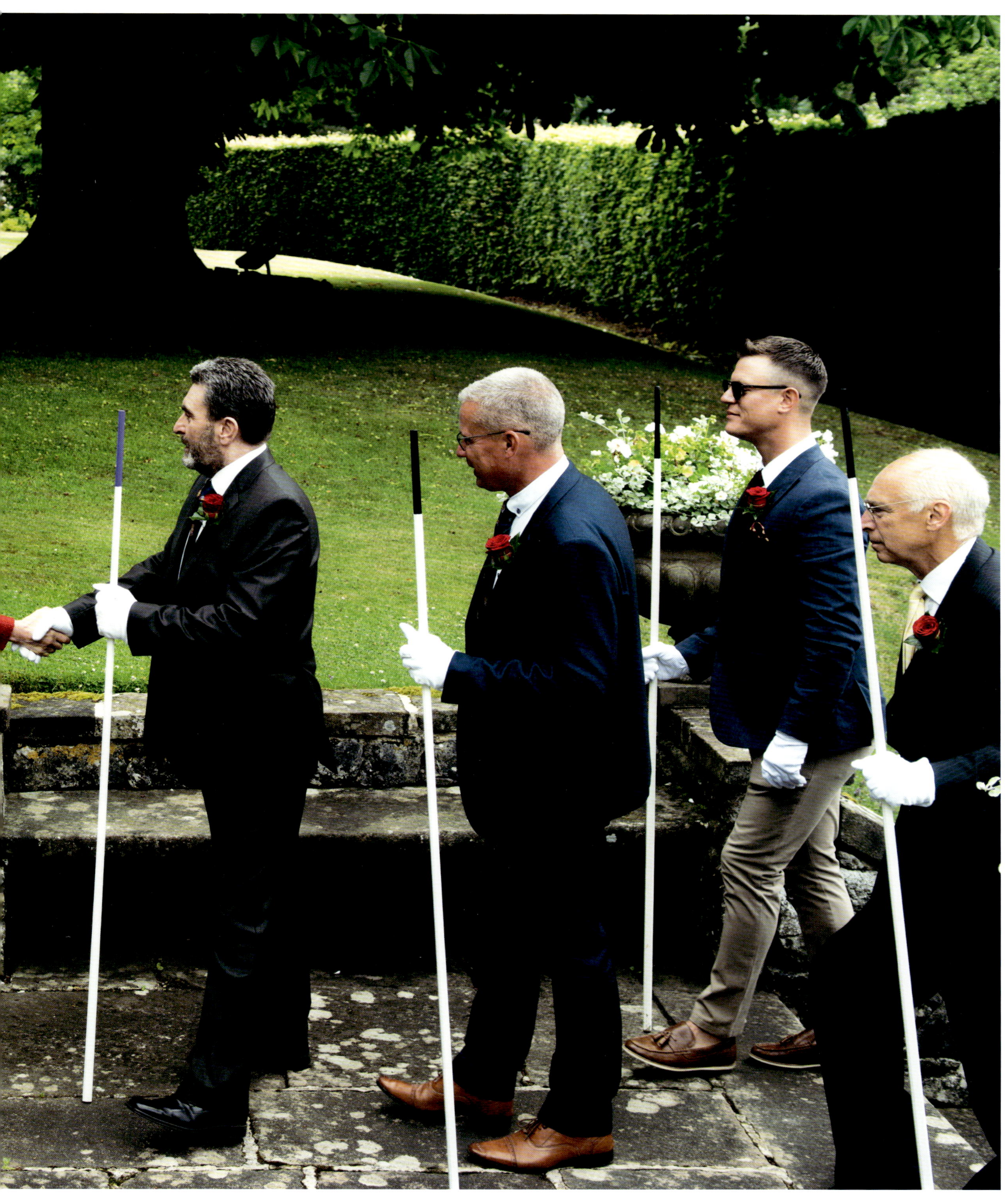

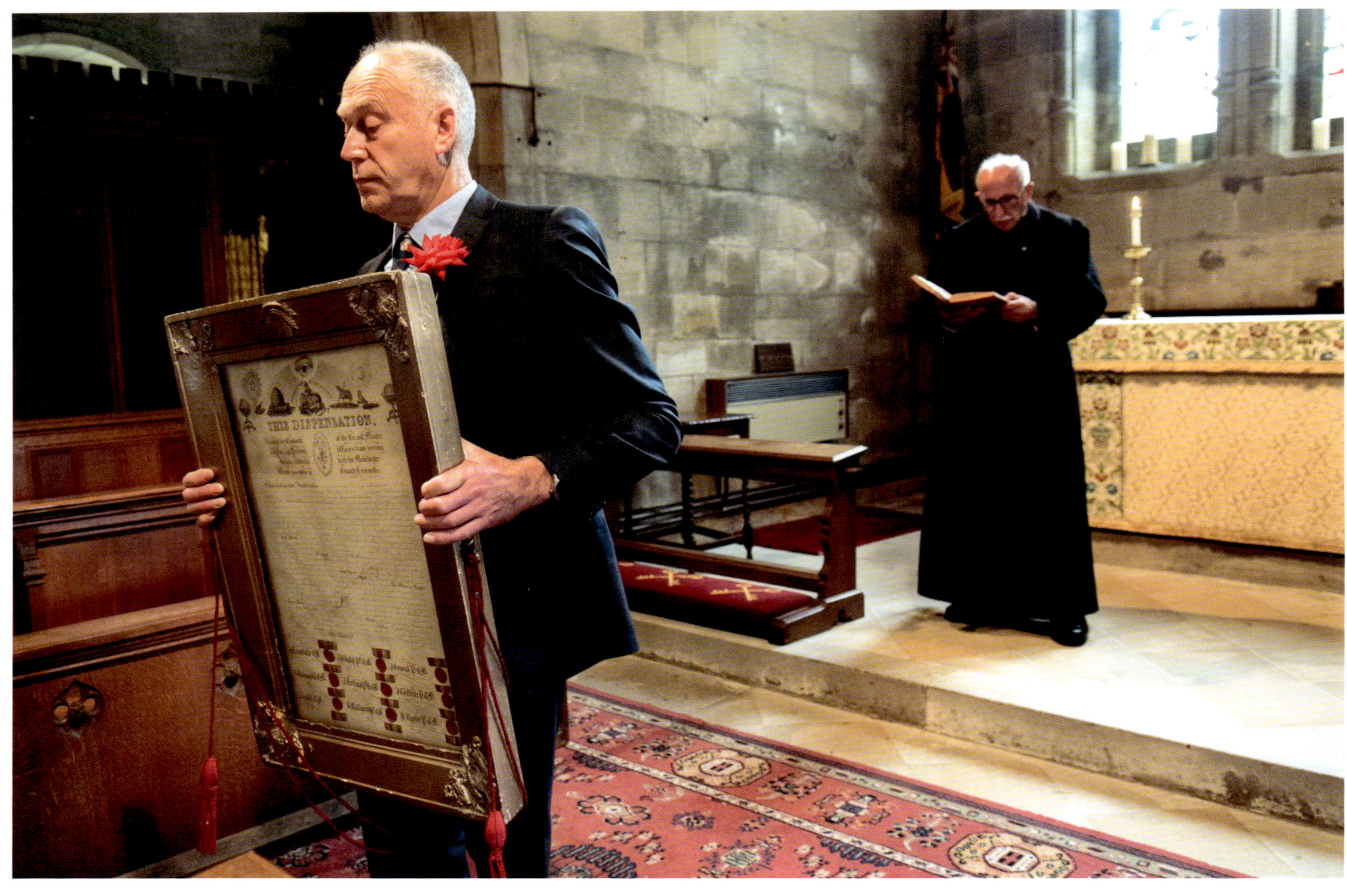

ODDFELLOWS: THE LOYAL LAUREL AND CROWN LODGE
Parwich, Derbyshire
2023

The framed Dispensation is carried by Arnold Chadfield, it was placed on the altar table during the Oddfellows service at St Peter's Church.

Members parade around the village wearing white gloves and linking little fingers, they carry white sticks with coloured tops that denote their degrees within the Oddfellows.

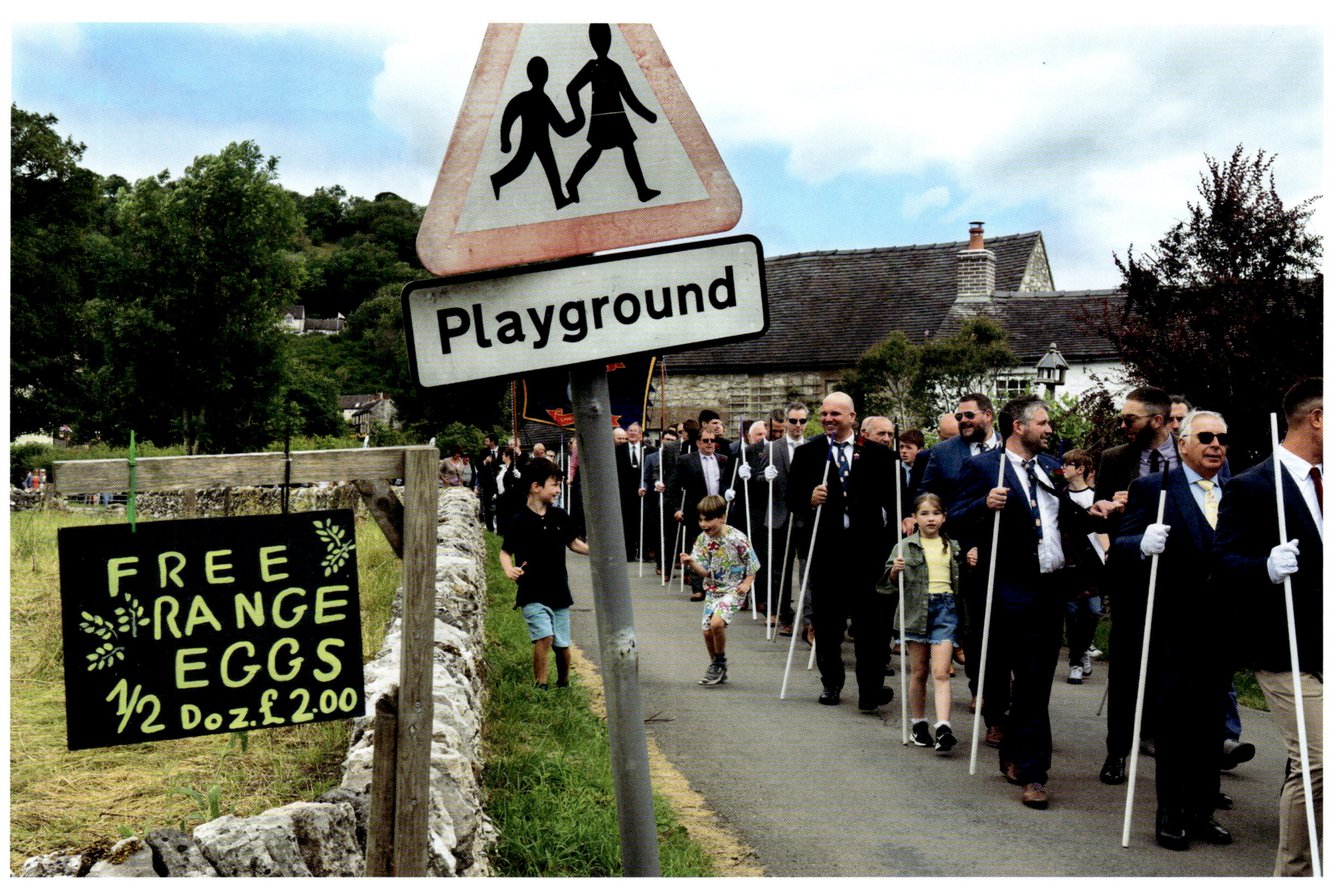
Playground
FREE
RANGE
EGGS
1/2 Doz.£2.00

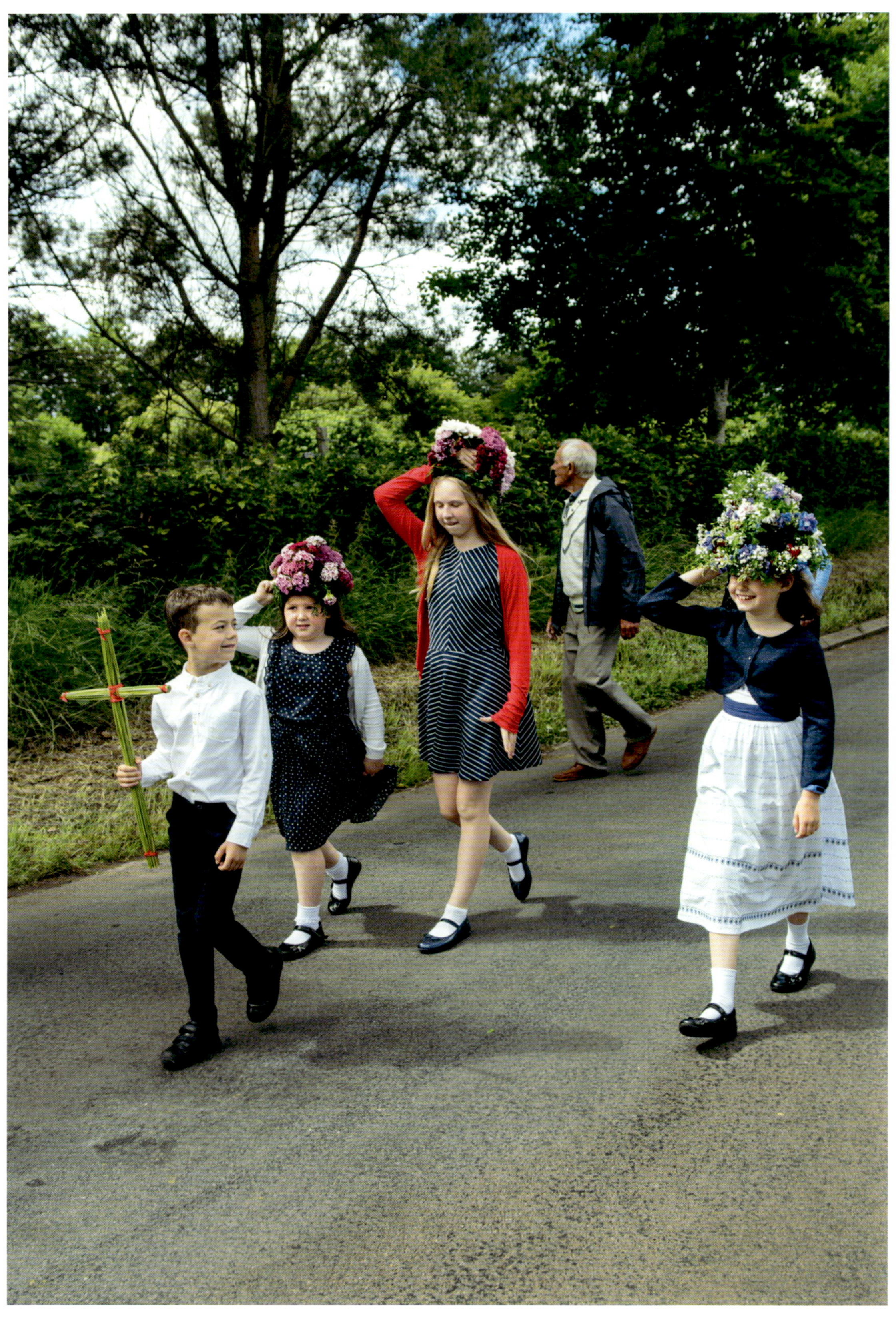

RUSHBEARING
Great Musgrave, Cumbria
2022

Children make their way from the village institute to St Theobald's Church; the boys carry rush crosses and the girls are wearing their floral crowns.

At the end of the day's events the floral crowns and crosses are placed above and around the door of the church, where they will remain until replaced the following year.

Following the service, everyone walks back to the village where a cream tea is held in the Union Jack decorated village institute.

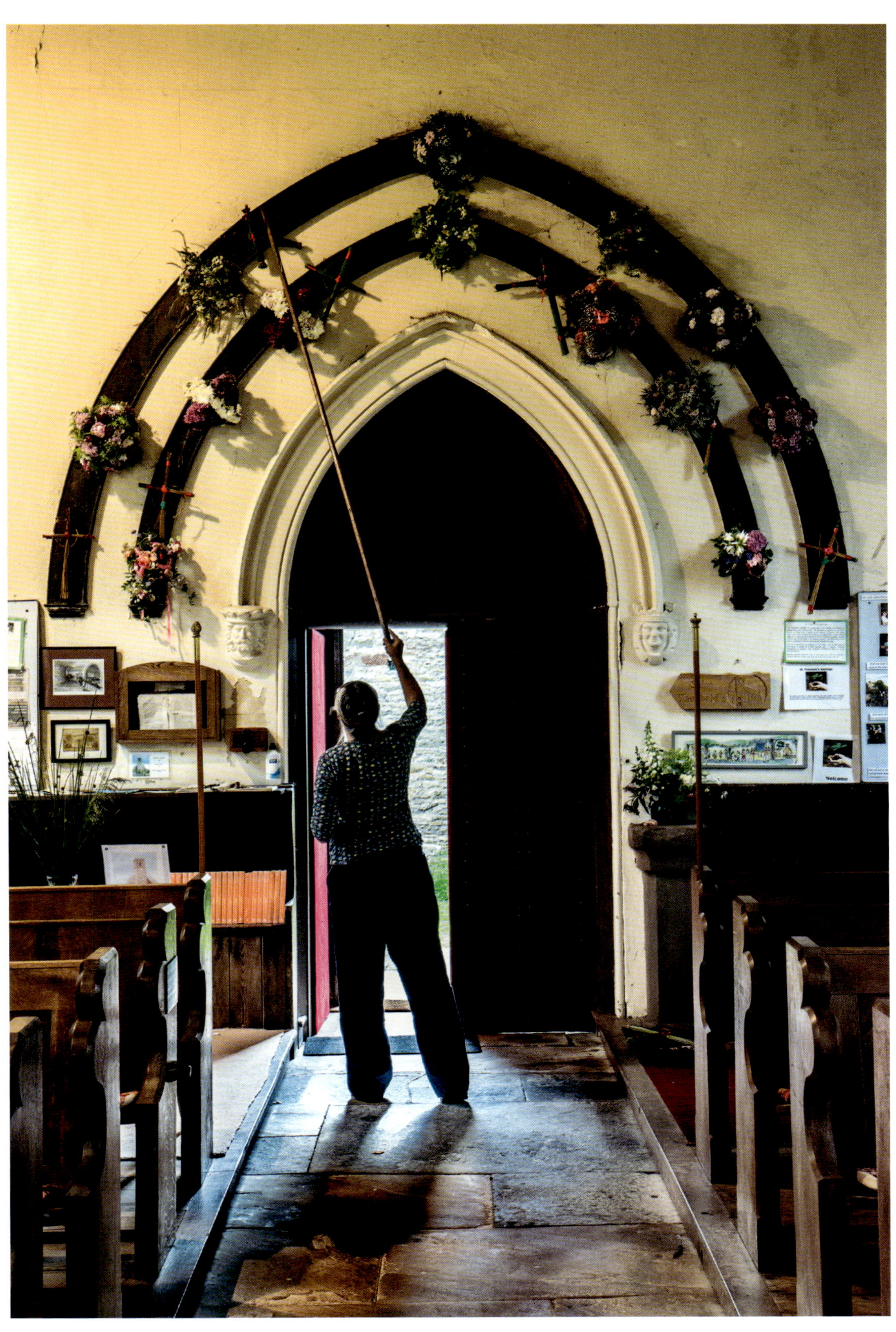

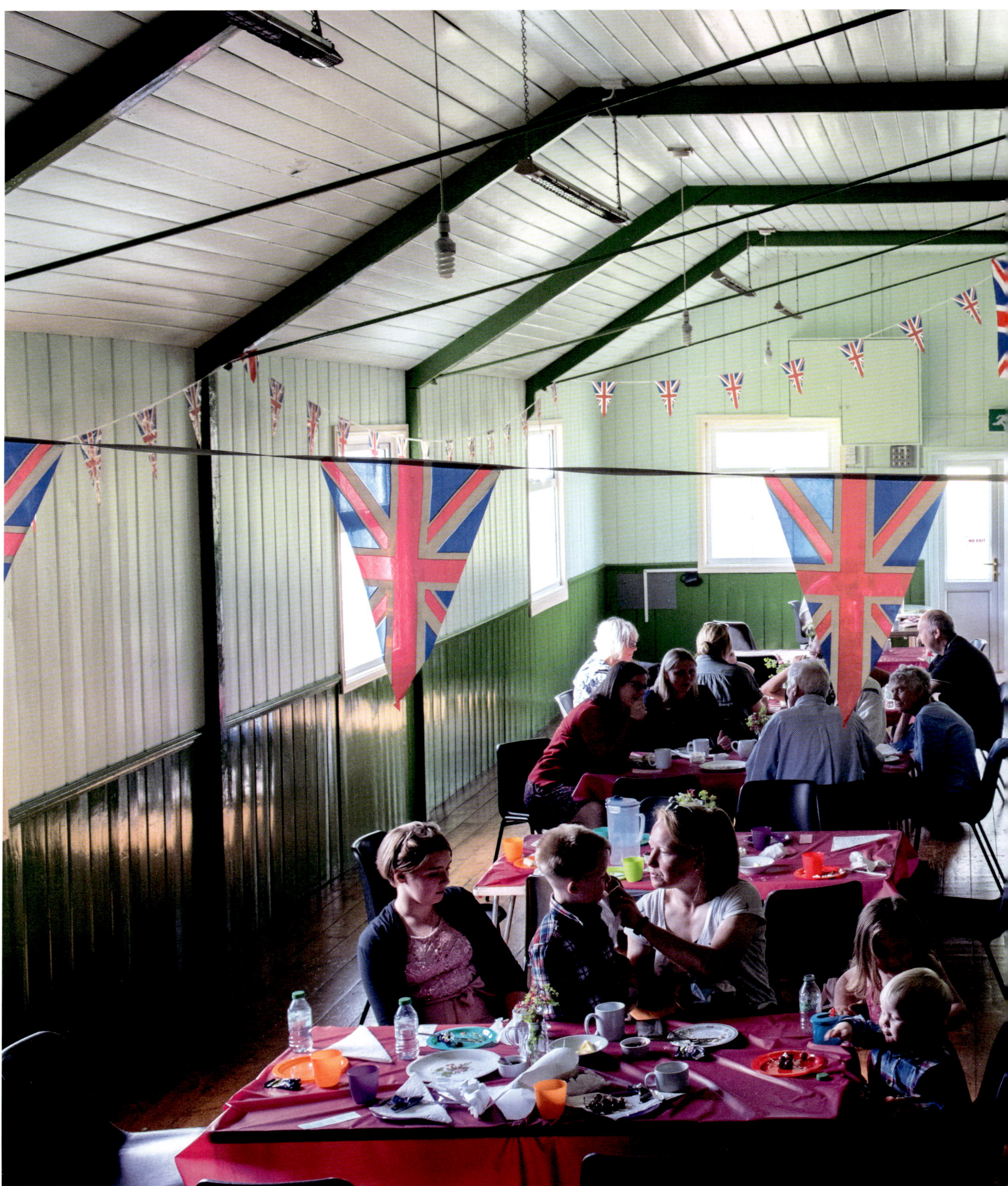

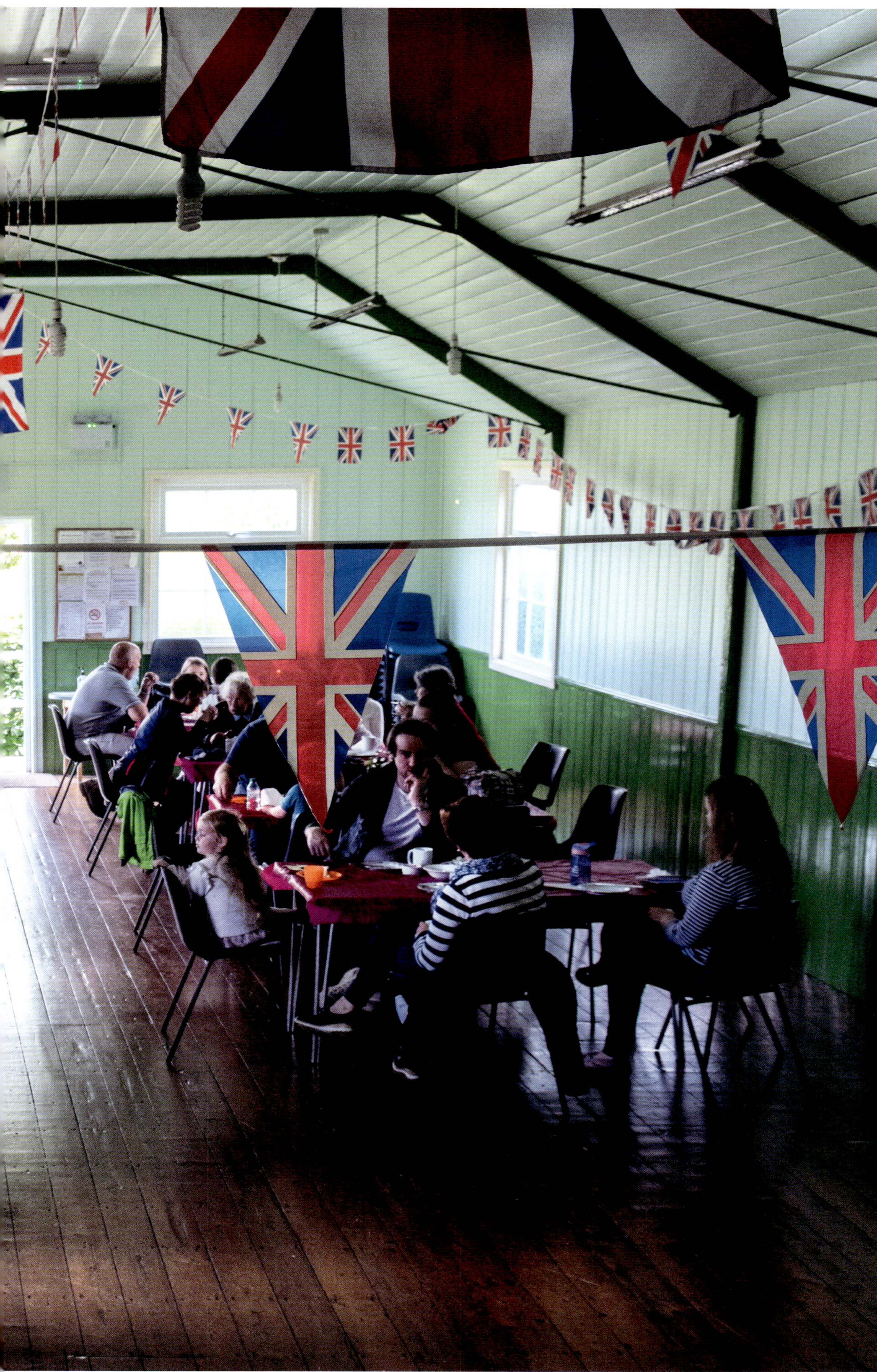

RUSHBEARING
Great Musgrave, Cumbria
2022

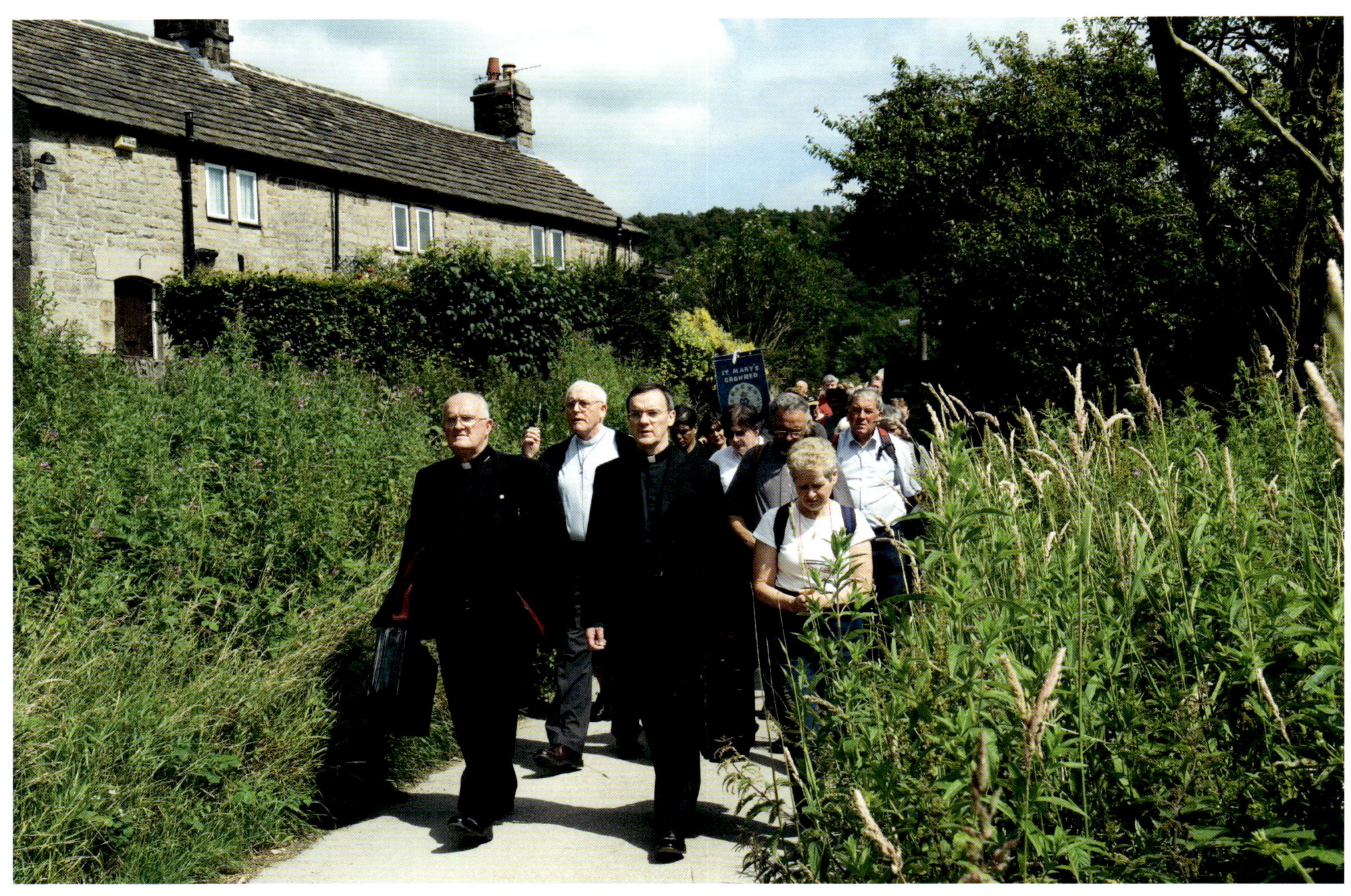

PADLEY MARTYRS PILGRIMAGE
Grindleford, Derbyshire
2008

Pilgrims walk from Grindleford train station to Padley Chapel where there is a Mass of the Martyrs to commemorate three brave Catholic priests who were hanged, drawn and quartered in 1588 for their faith.

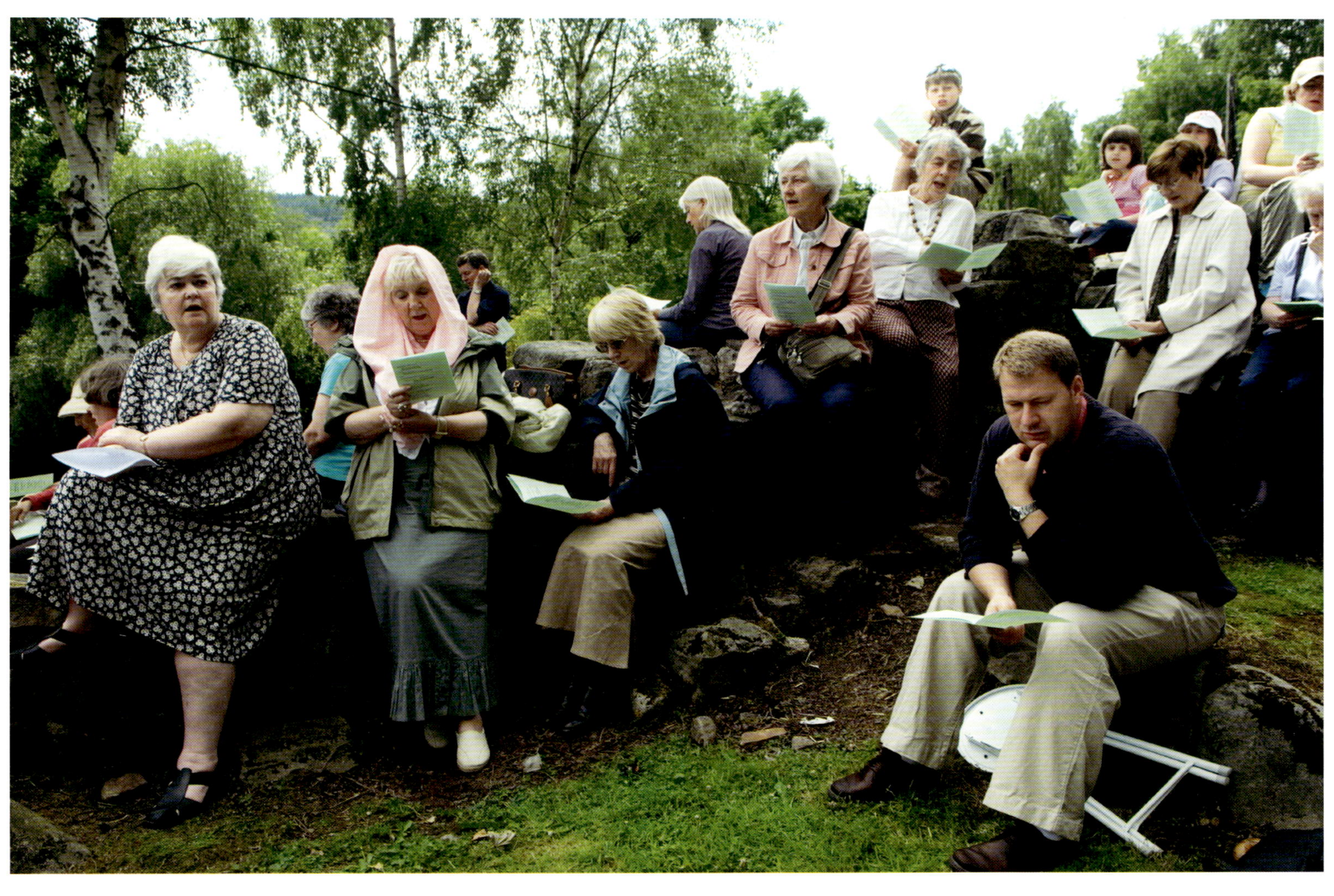

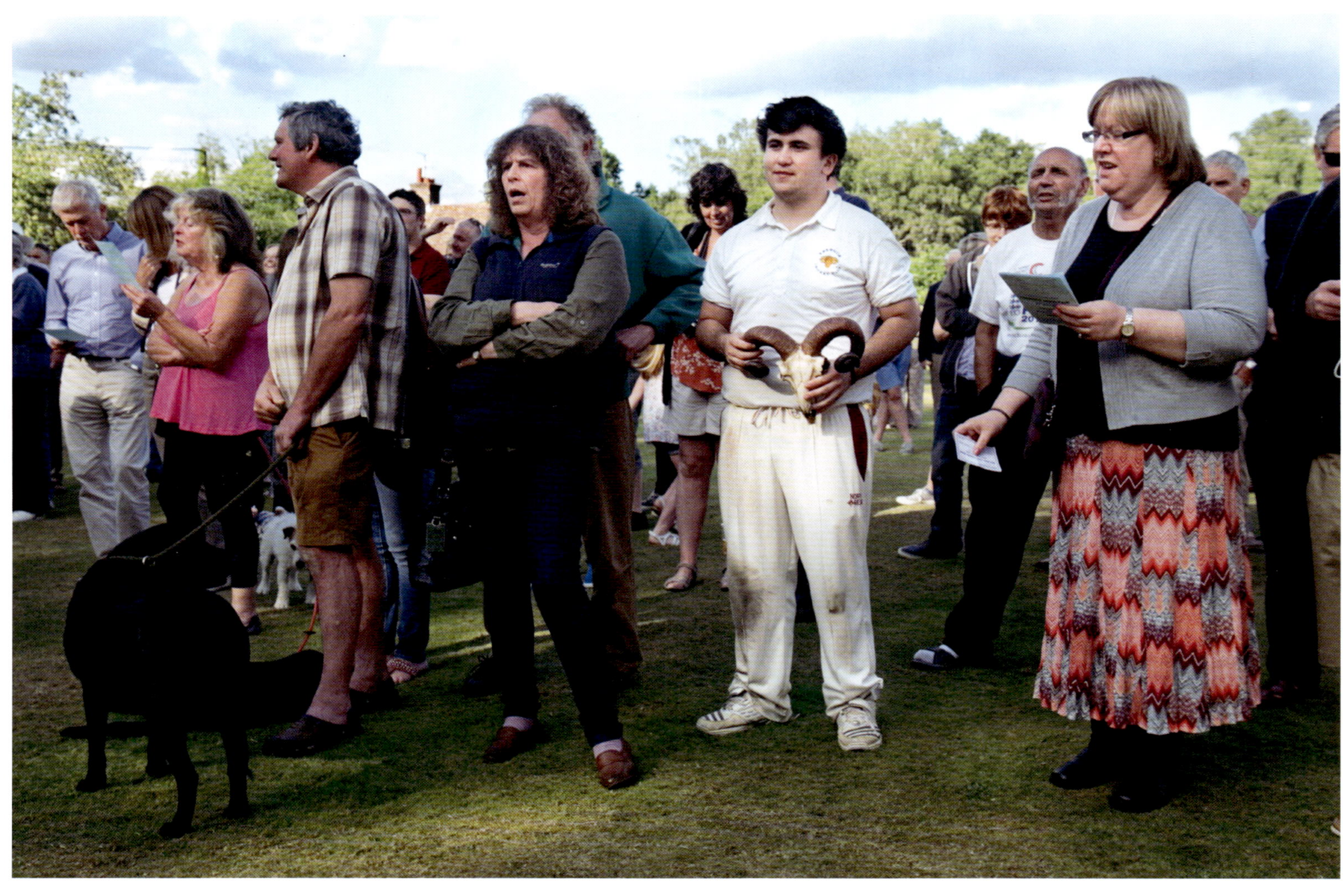

HORN FAIR
Ebernoe, West Sussex
2015

Oli Rose won the Horns Trophy with the highest score of 42 runs for Ebernoe Cricket Club; along with spectators they sing the traditional Horn Fair song.

'Caution Cricket in Progress' spectators with their ice creams at the annual Horn Fair cricket match.

After the team lunch of roasted lamb, tea and cake is provided for spectators; and of course the washing up has to be done.

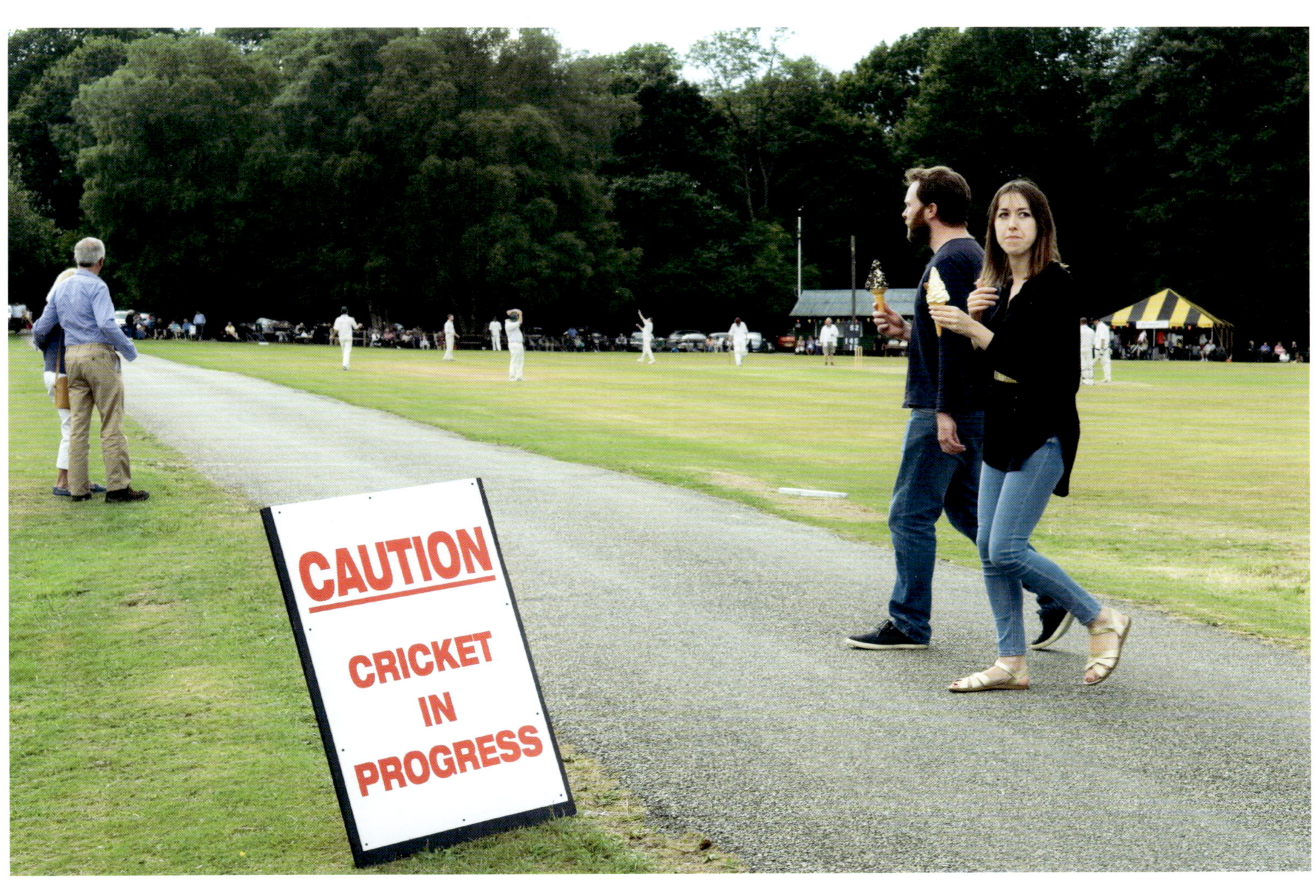
CAUTION
CRICKET
IN
PROGRESS

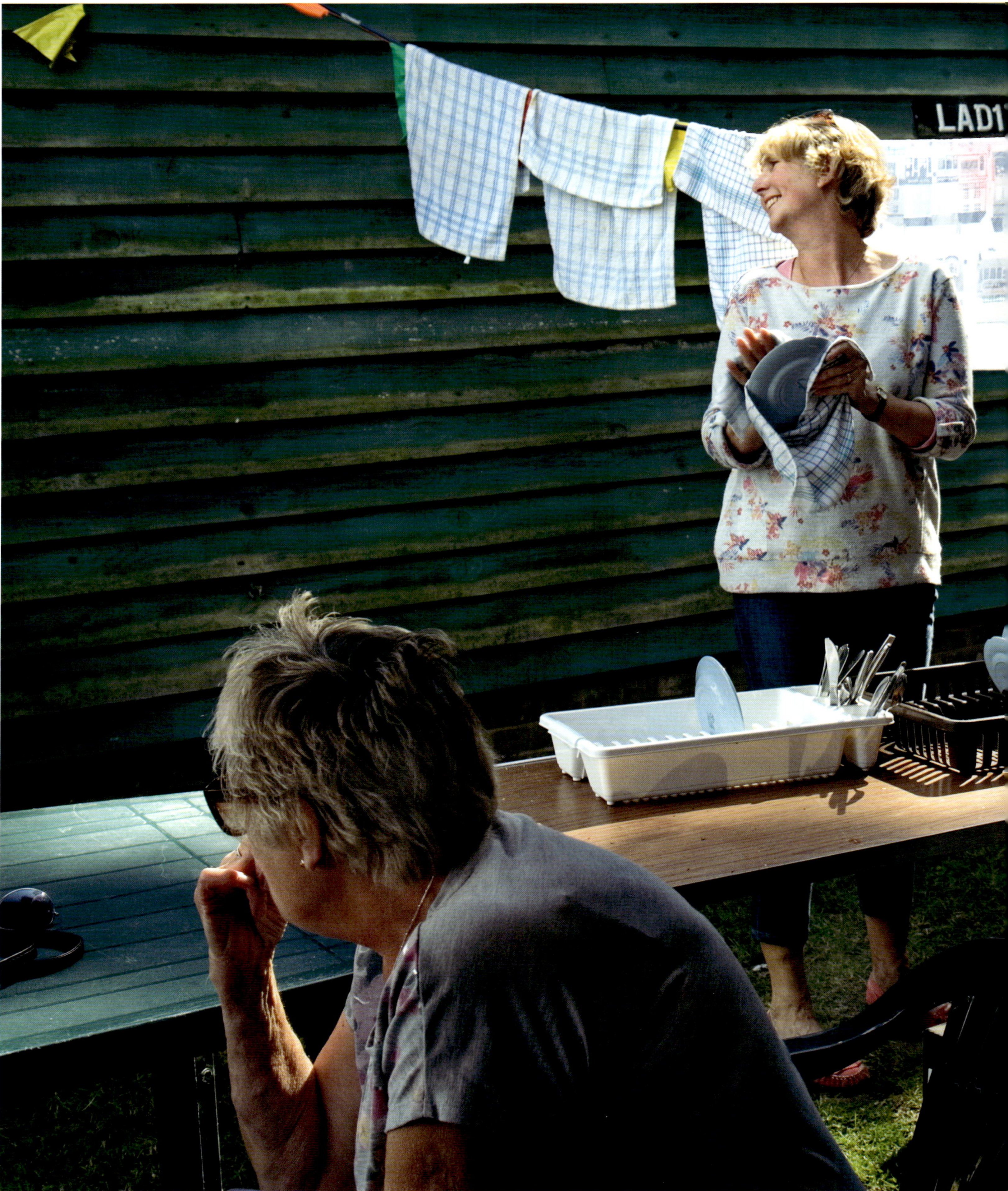
LAD1

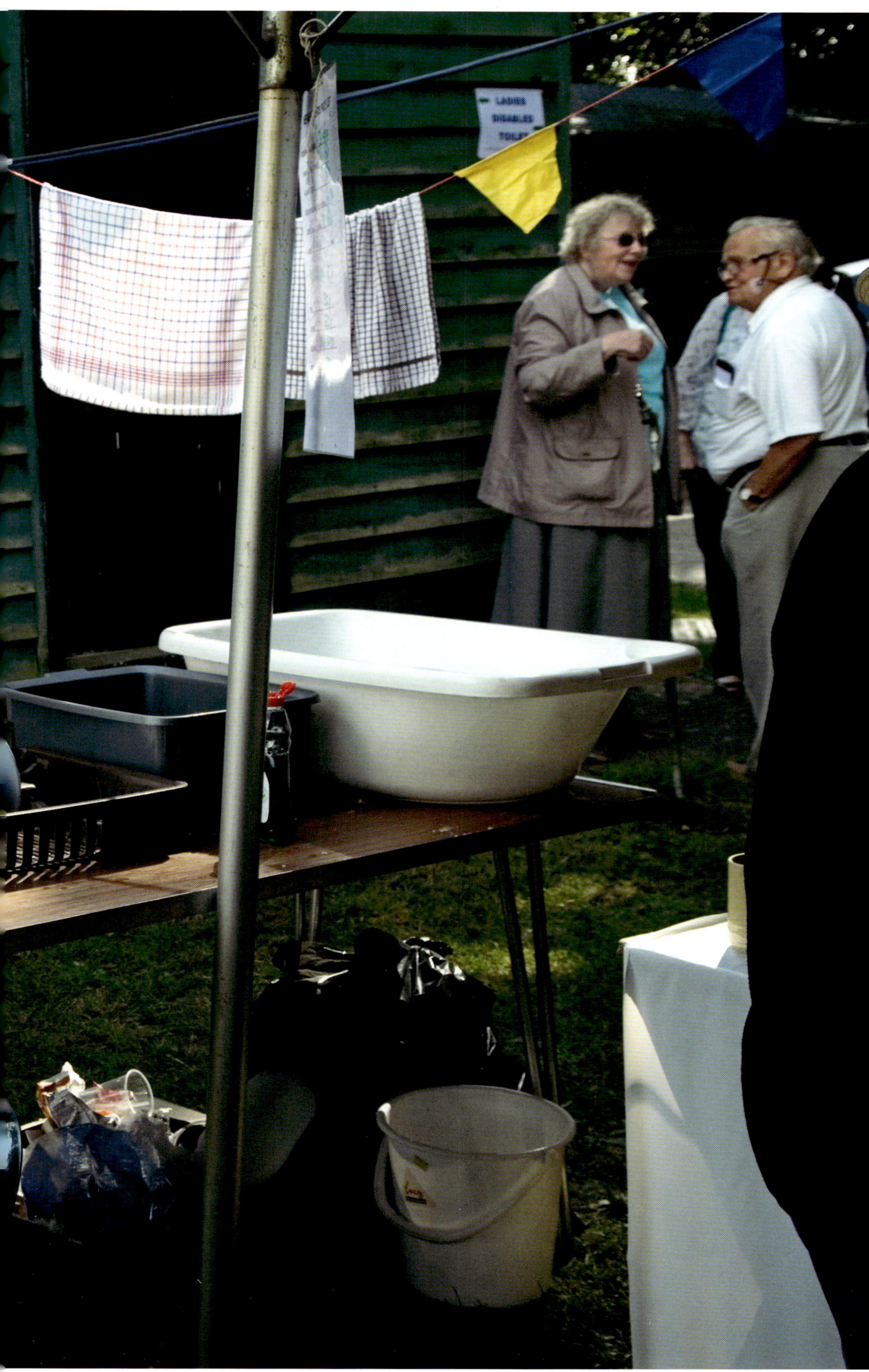

HORN FAIR
Ebernoe, West Sussex
2015

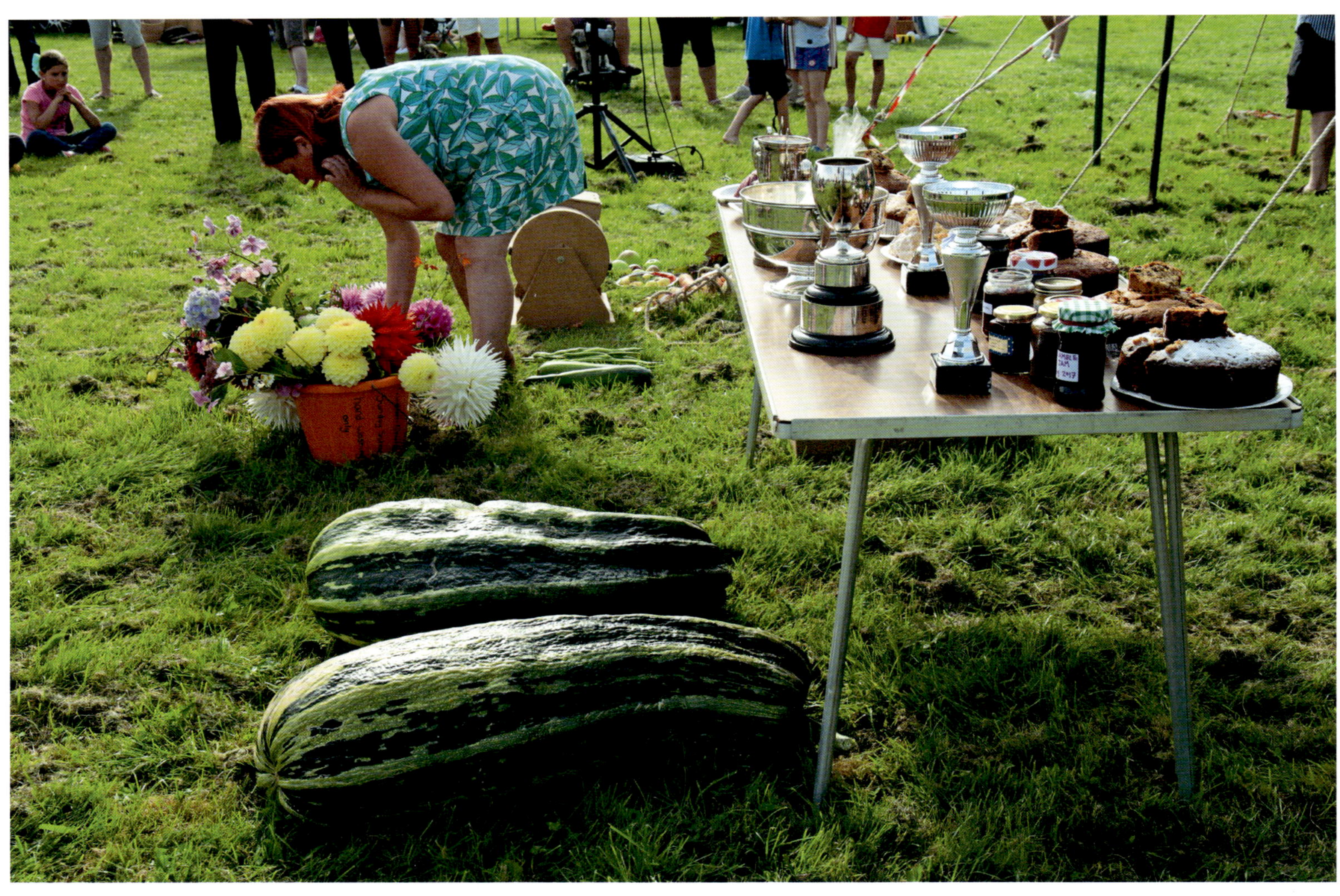

VILLAGE SHOW AND FETE
Cudham, Kent
2017

A committee member checks the winning entries before prize giving. Cakes, jams and pickles jostle for a space amongst the silver trophies about to be presented.

The Mayor of Bromley, Cllr Kathy Bance MBE, with purchases she made at the auction of home grown produce. Carrying an over-sized onion and homemade cake, her driver leads the way back to her official car.

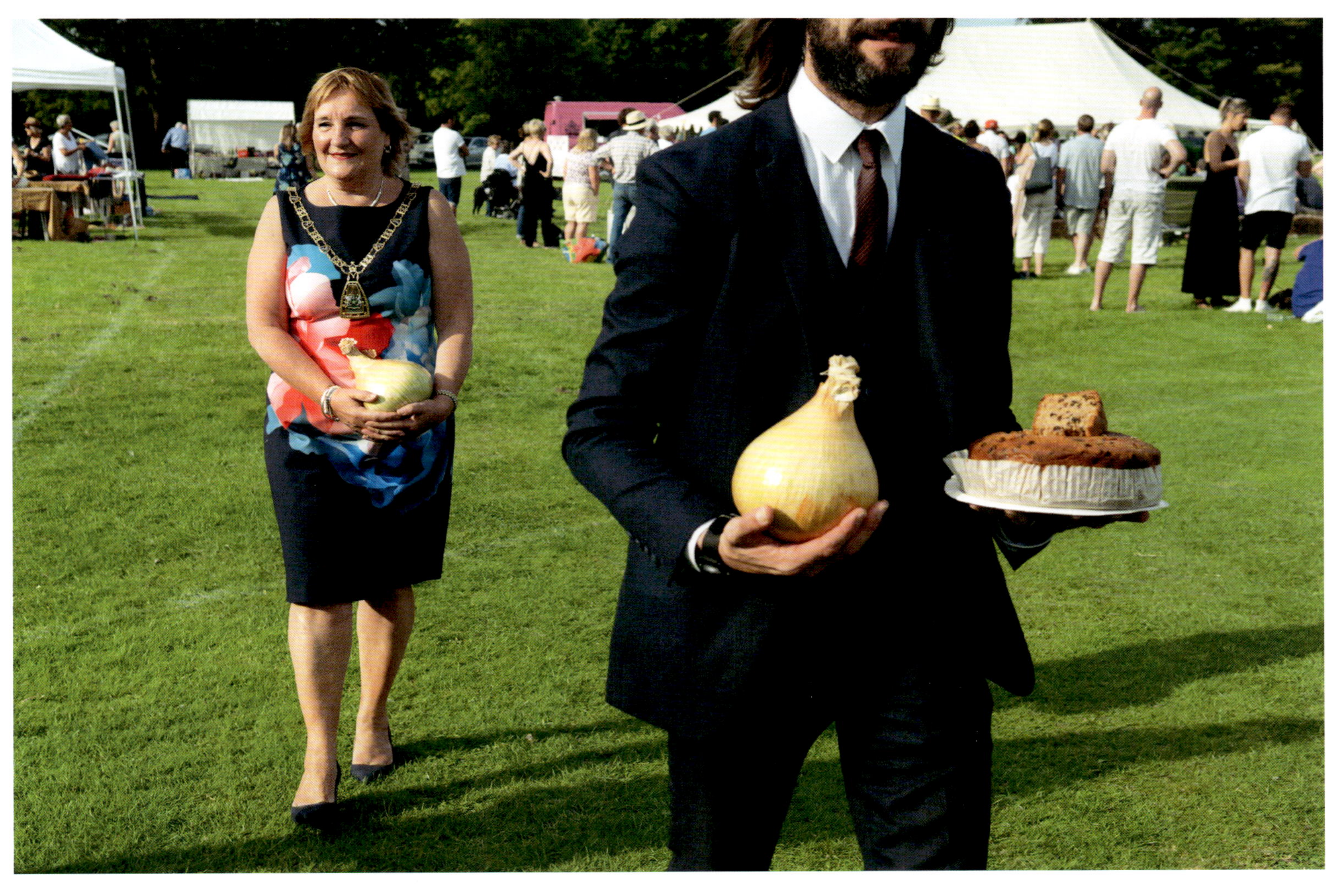

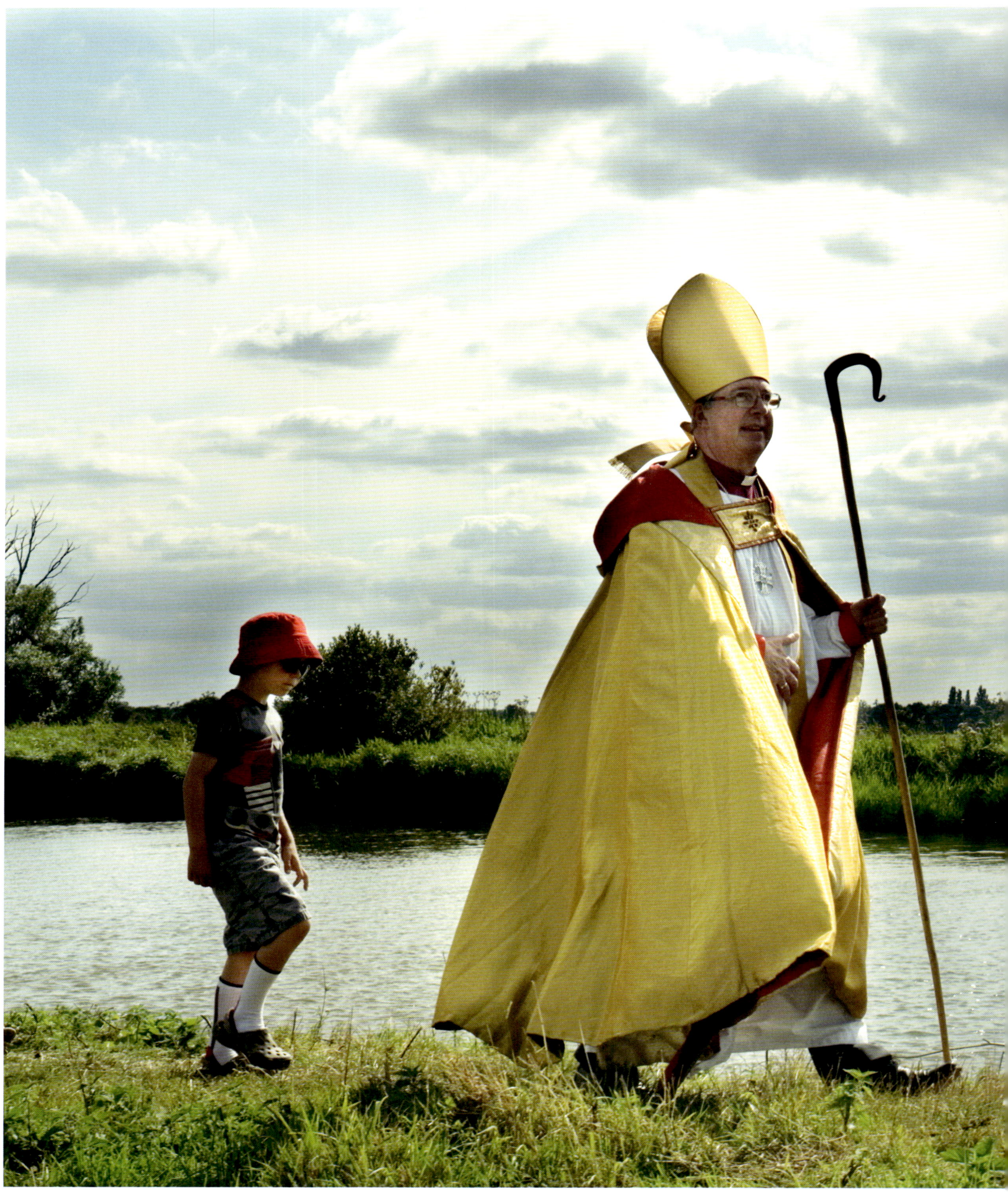

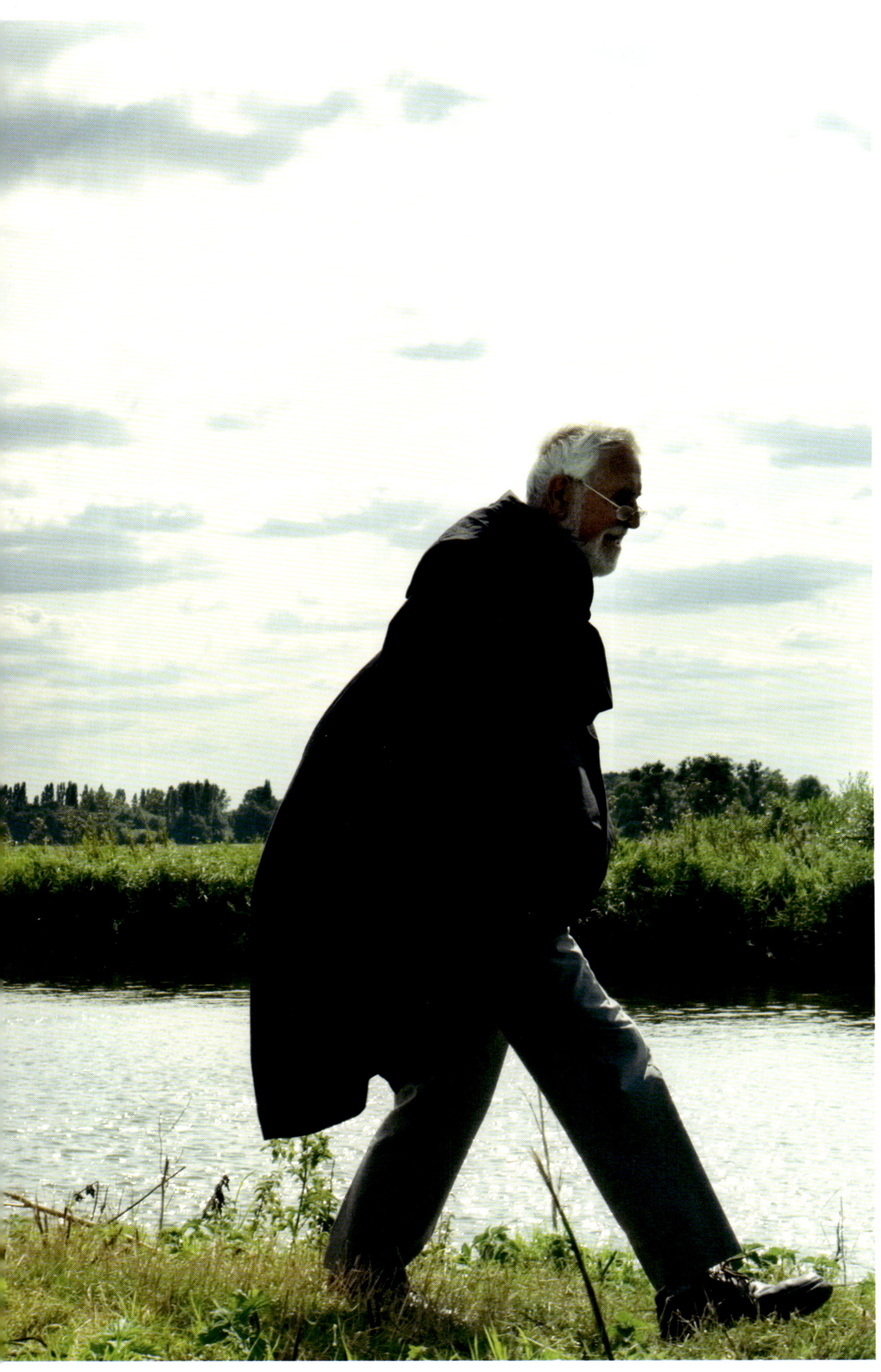

ST BENET'S ABBEY PILGRIMAGE
Ludham, Norfolk
2014

The Bishop of Norwich, the Rt Revd. Graham James, arrives in the grounds of St Benet's Abbey. A brother of St Benet's leads the Bishop towards the ruined Abbey where he will conduct an interdenominational service.

WALSINGHAM PILGRIMAGE
Houghton Saint Giles, Norfolk
2006

Roman Catholic pilgrims, some barefooted, walk in procession from The Basilica of Our Lady of Walsingham, informally known as the Slipper Chapel, behind a statue of Our Lady of Walsingham into the village where they hold mass in the grounds of the ruined Abbey and old Priory.

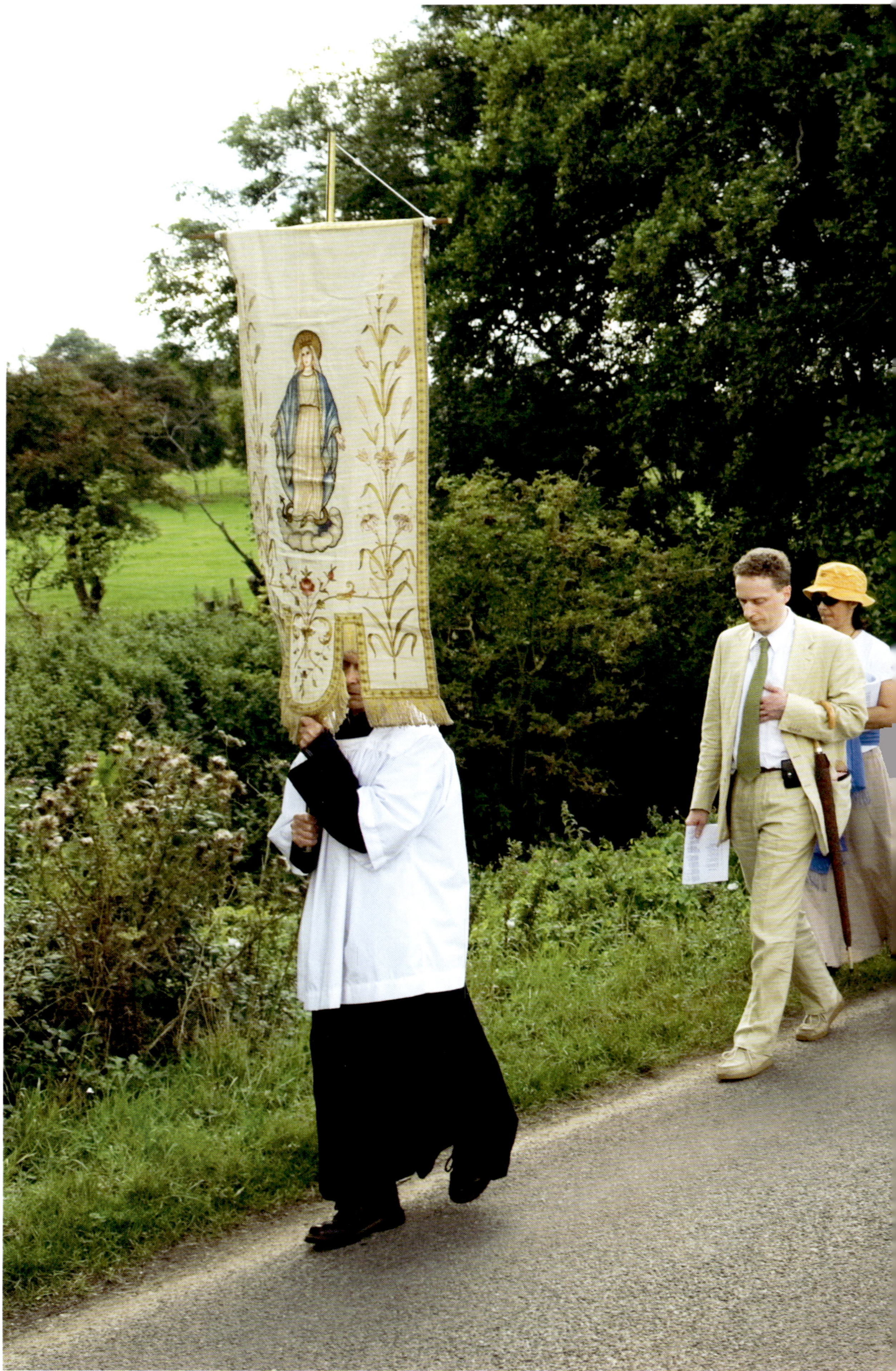

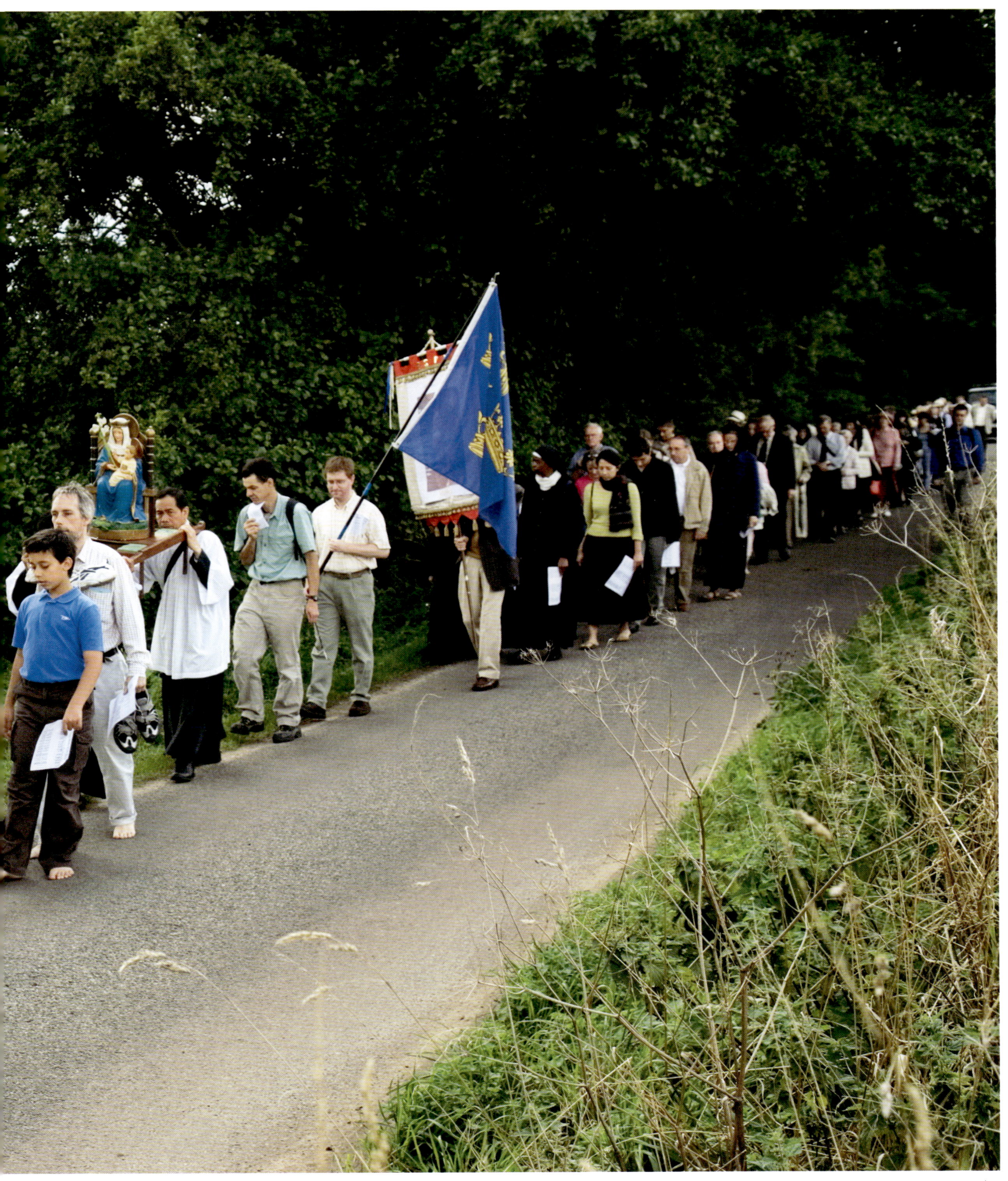

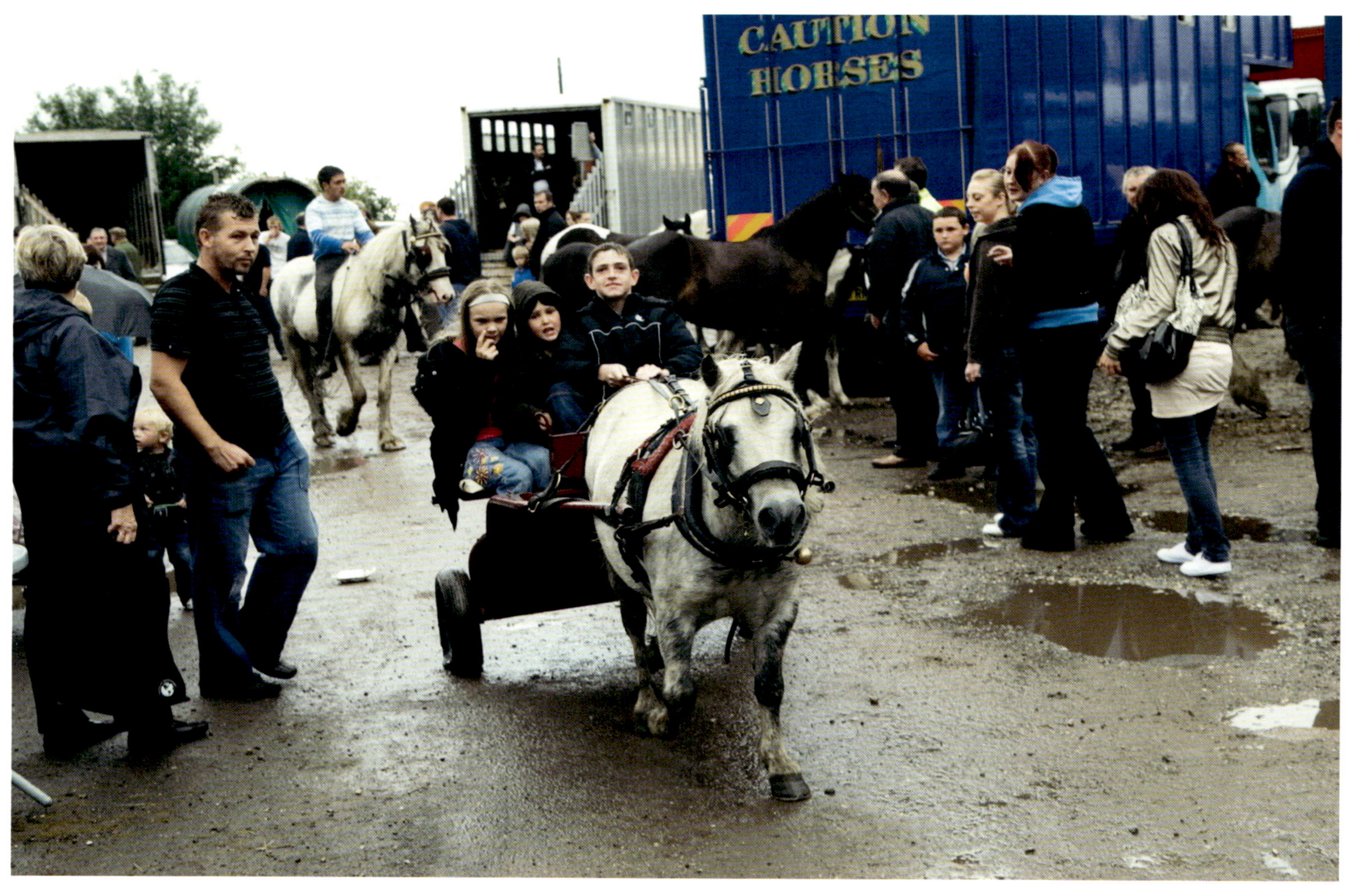

BRIGG HORSE FAIR
Brigg, Lincolnshire
2009

Children in a pony and trap amongst the gypsy travellers and horse dealers.

A gypsy showman dances continuously, performing a jig on a board. He is collecting for the World Cancer Research Fund.

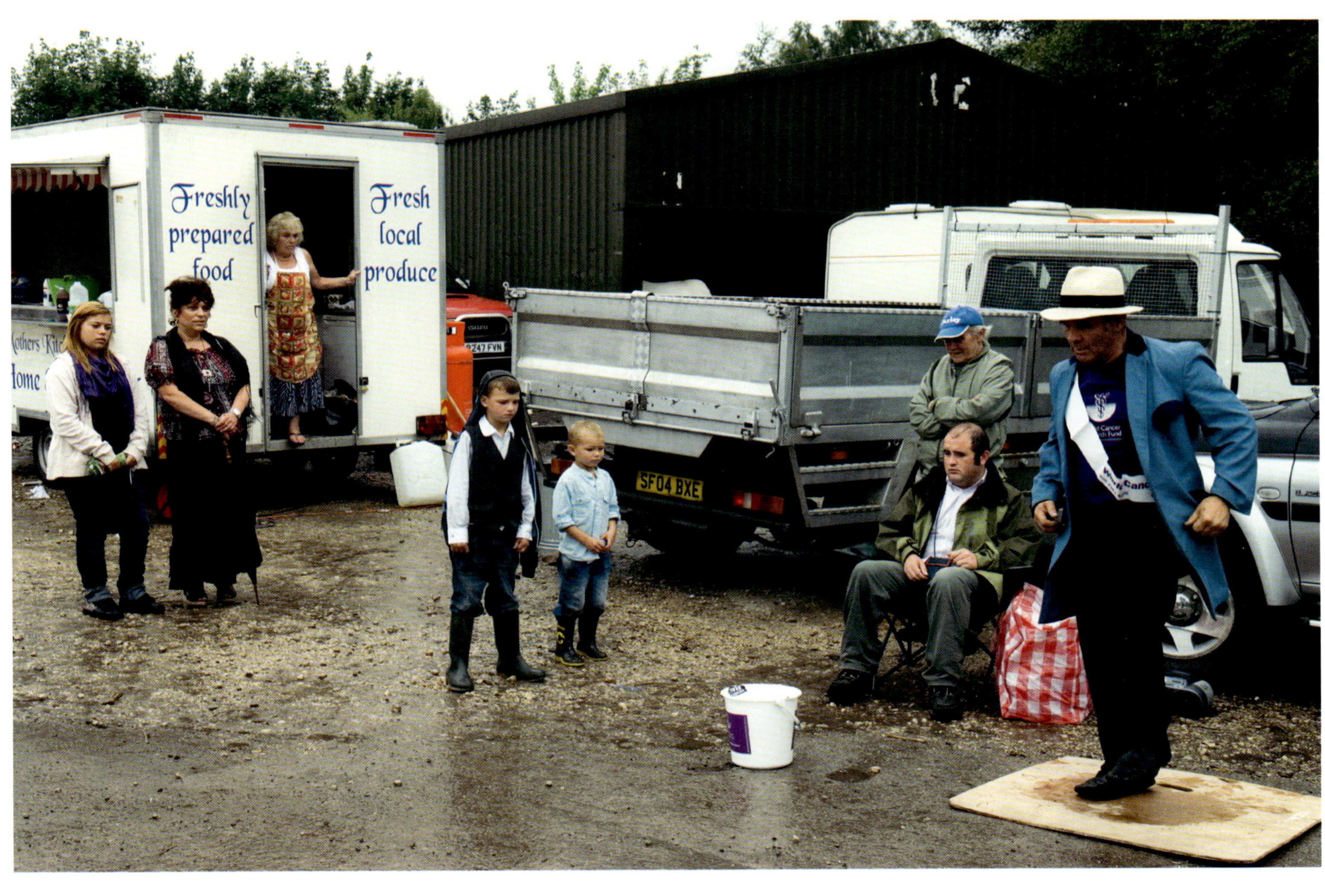
Freshly
prepared
food
Fresh
local
produce
SF04 BXE

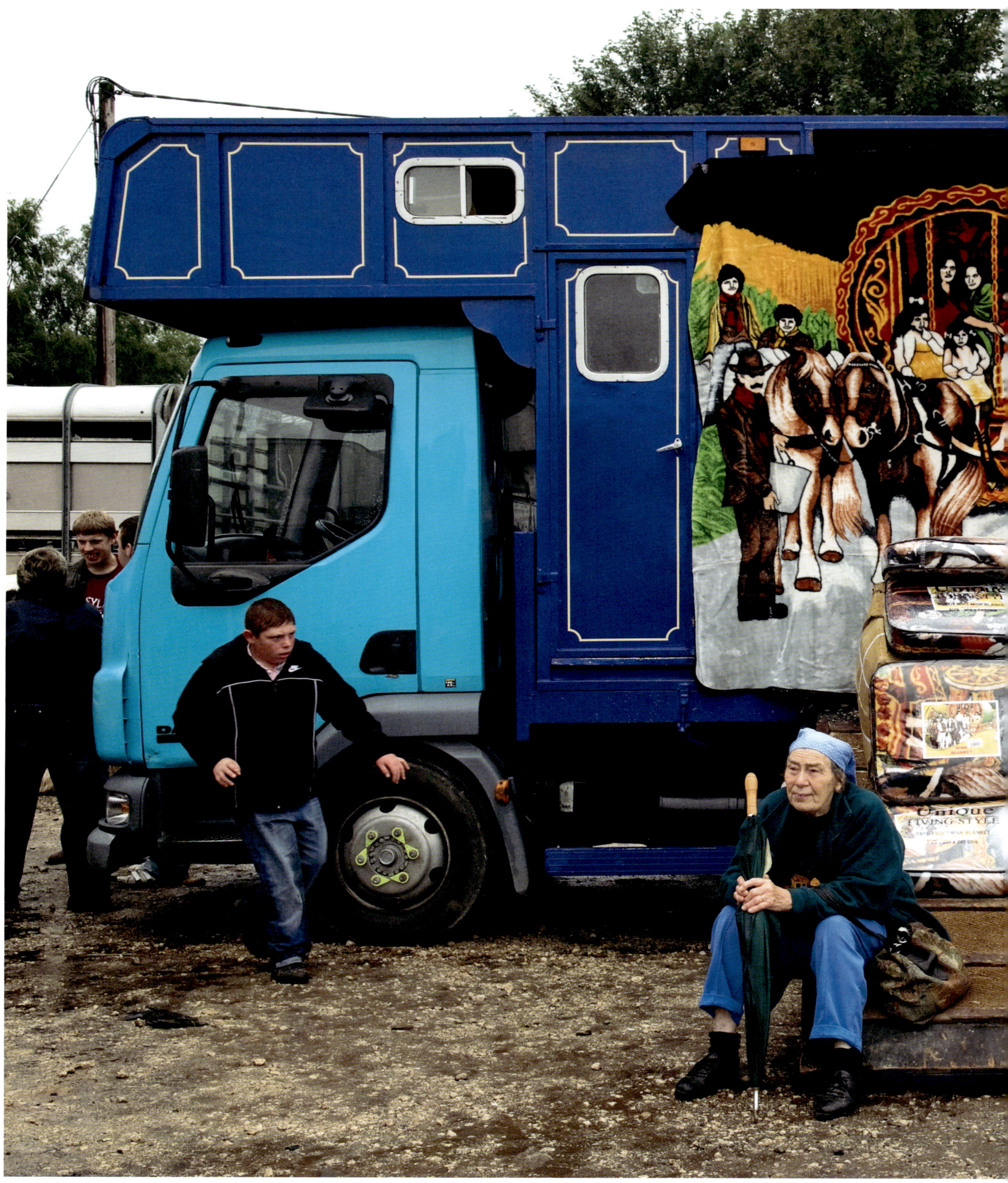
Unique
LIVING-STYLE

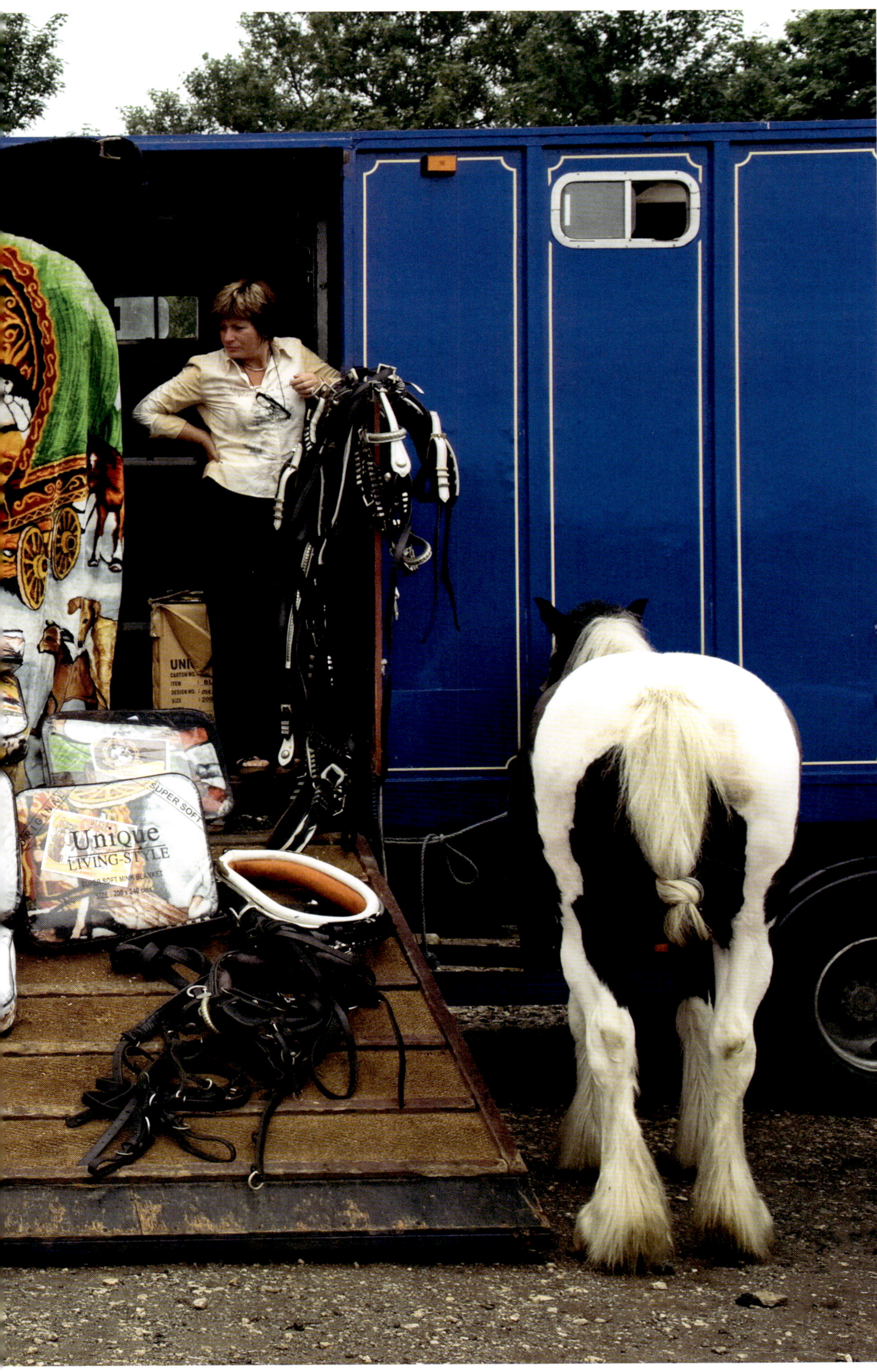

BRIGG HORSE FAIR
Brigg, Lincolnshire
2009

A market trader stands in her horse lorry; she is selling large blankets depicting a traditional gypsy family and their horse drawn bow top wagon.

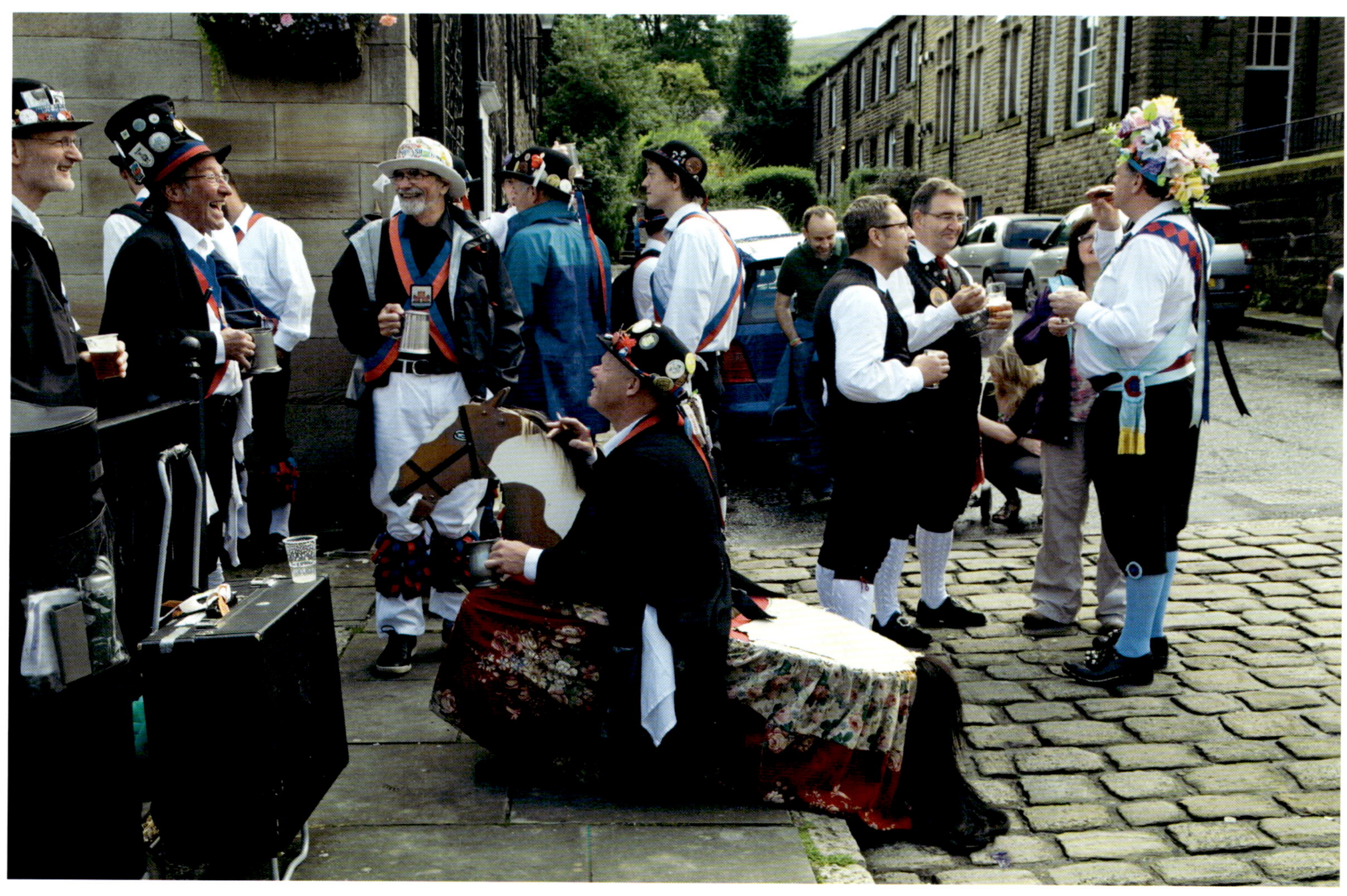

SADDLEWORTH RUSHCART
Uppermill, Saddleworth,
Greater Manchester

Morris Men at the Saddleworth Rushcart weekend enjoy a pint or two.

Tea and cakes are served in the rain while Morris Men dance on the final day as the Rushcart makes its way home to St Chad's Church in Uppermill, Saddleworth.

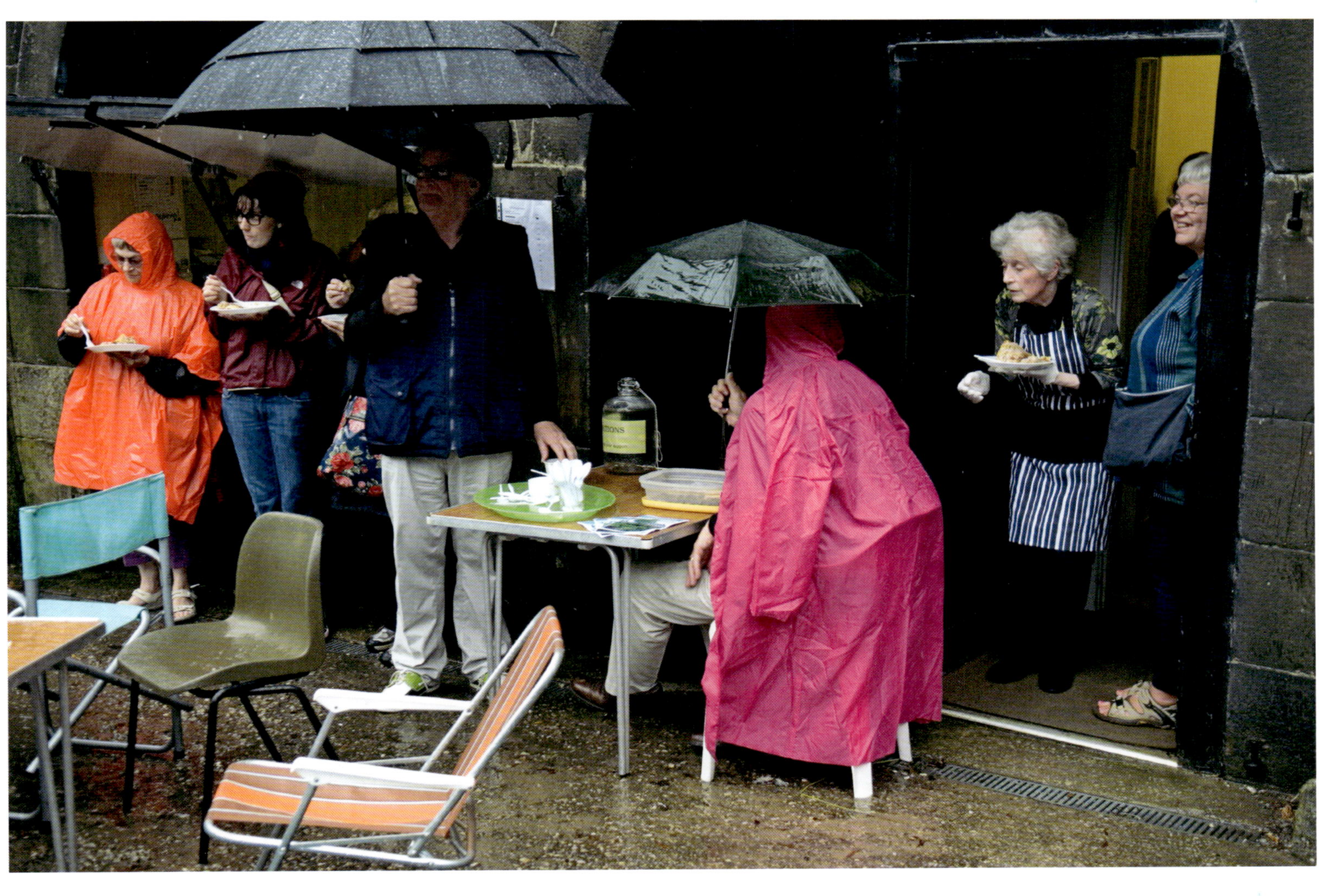

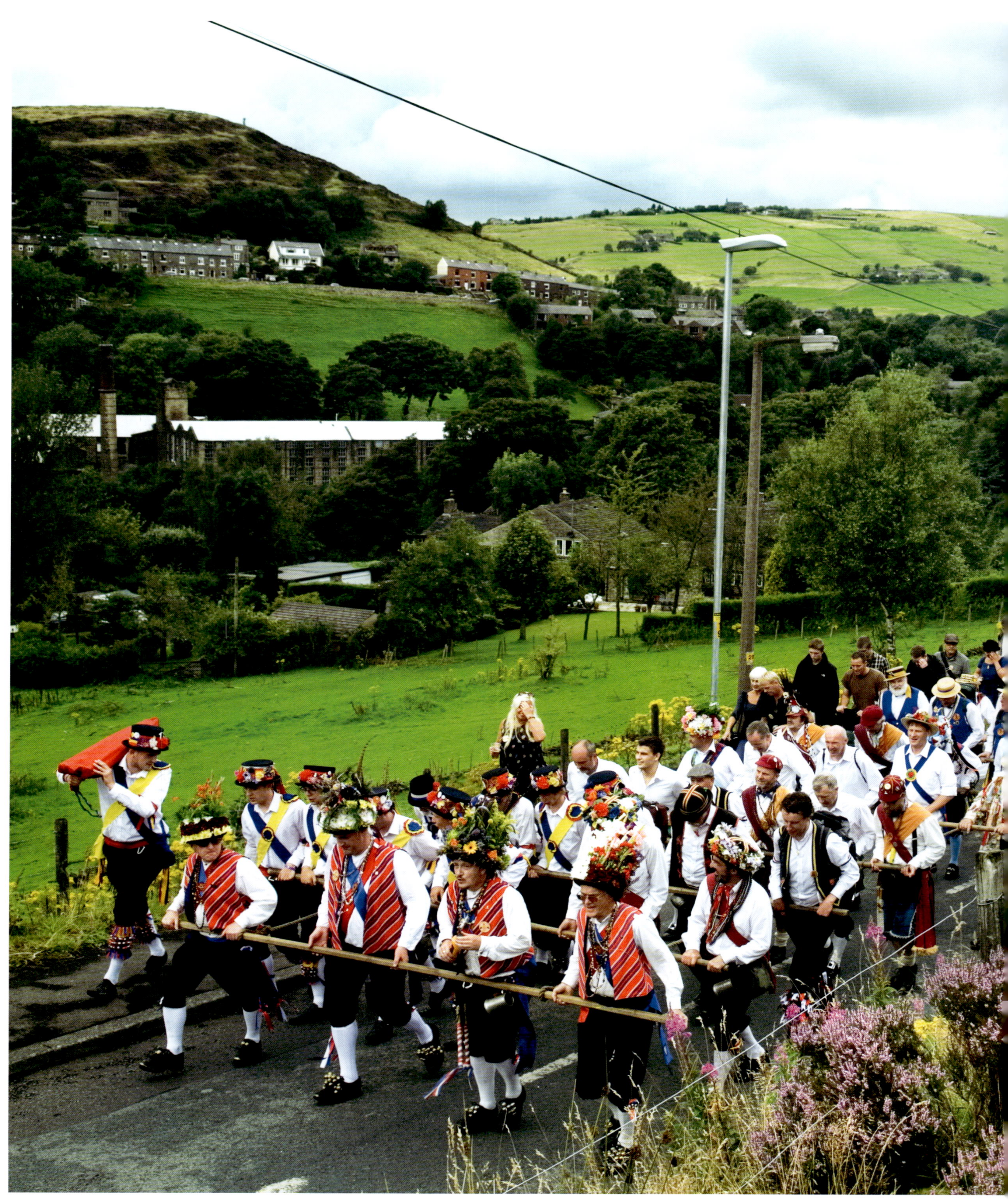

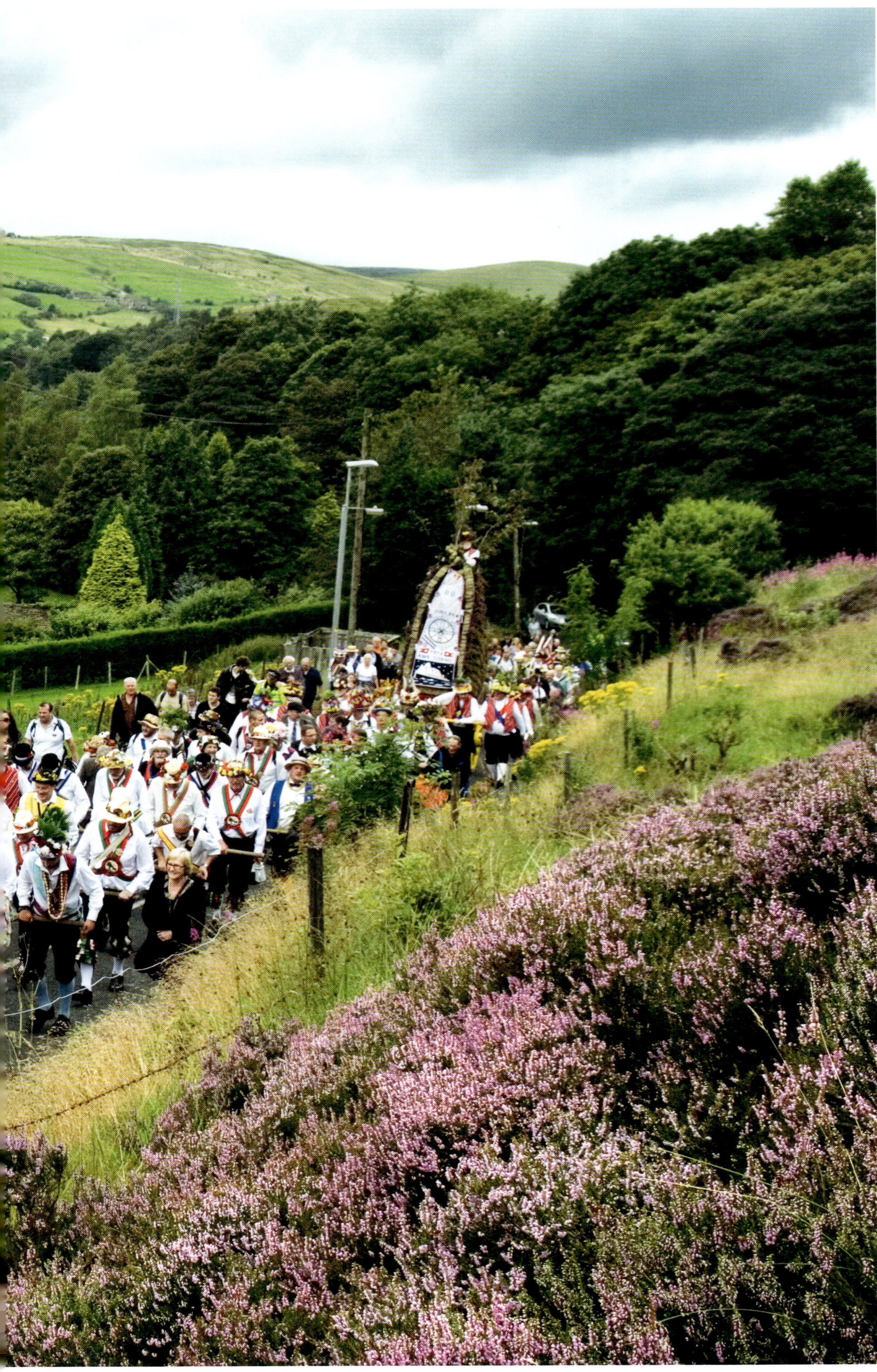

SADDLEWORTH RUSHCART
Uppermill, Saddleworth,
Greater Manchester

The Rushcart on its way to the village of Dobcross is pulled up a steep hill as it tours Saddleworth villages.

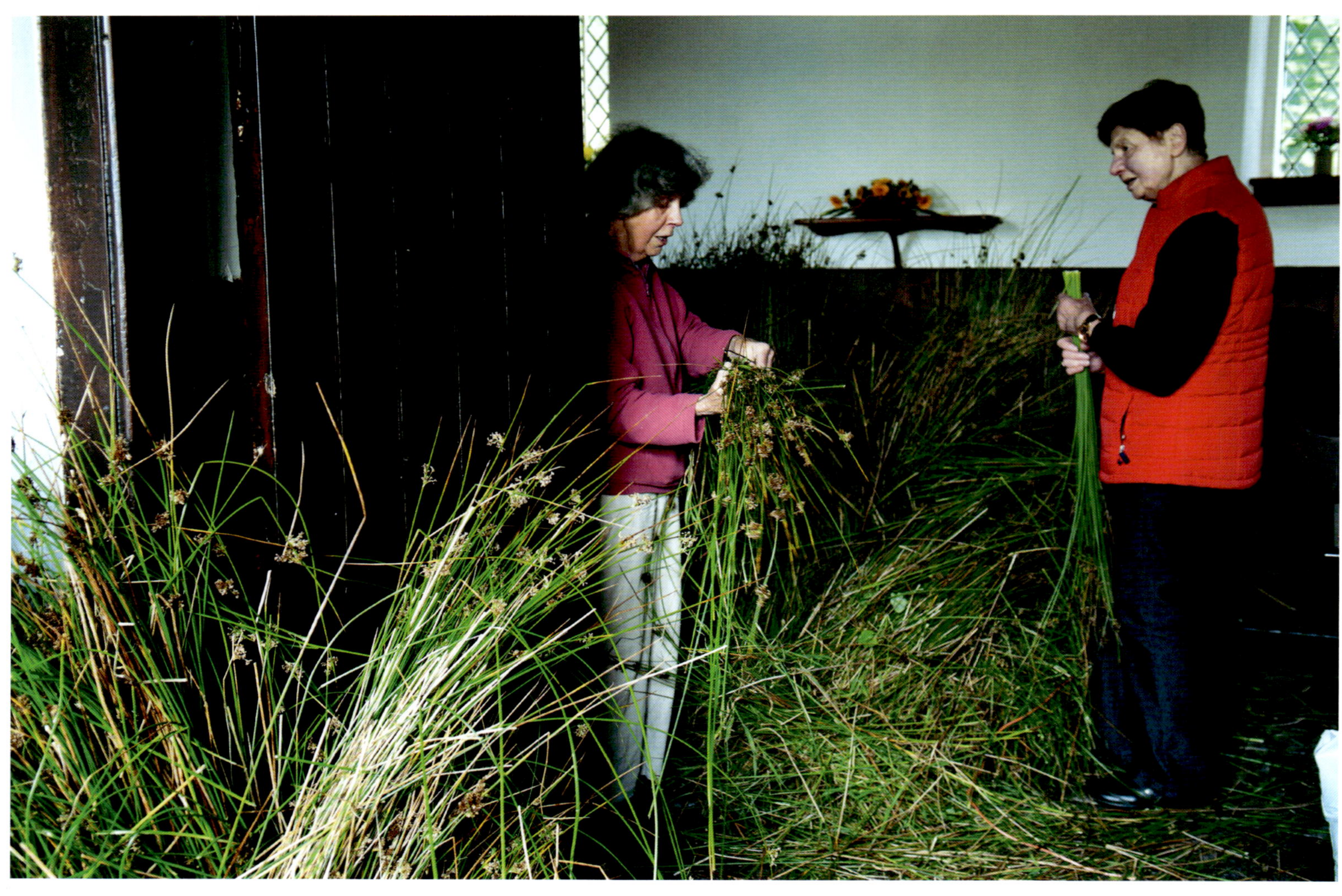

RUSHBEARING CHURCH SERVICE
Macclesfield Forest, Cheshire
2017

Ladies of the parish preparing to decorate St Stephen's Church, more commonly known as the Forest Chapel, ready for the annual open air Rushbearing church service.

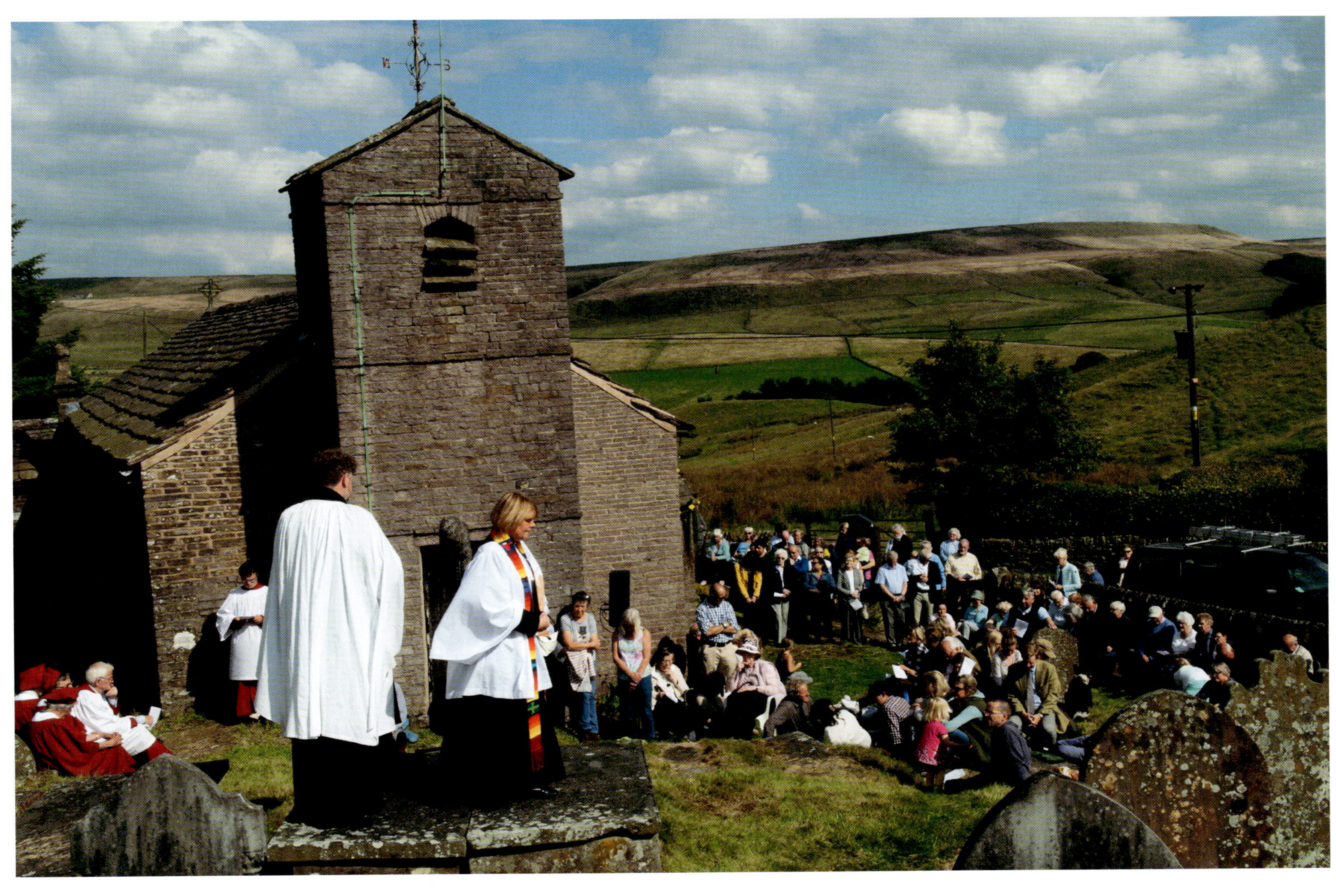

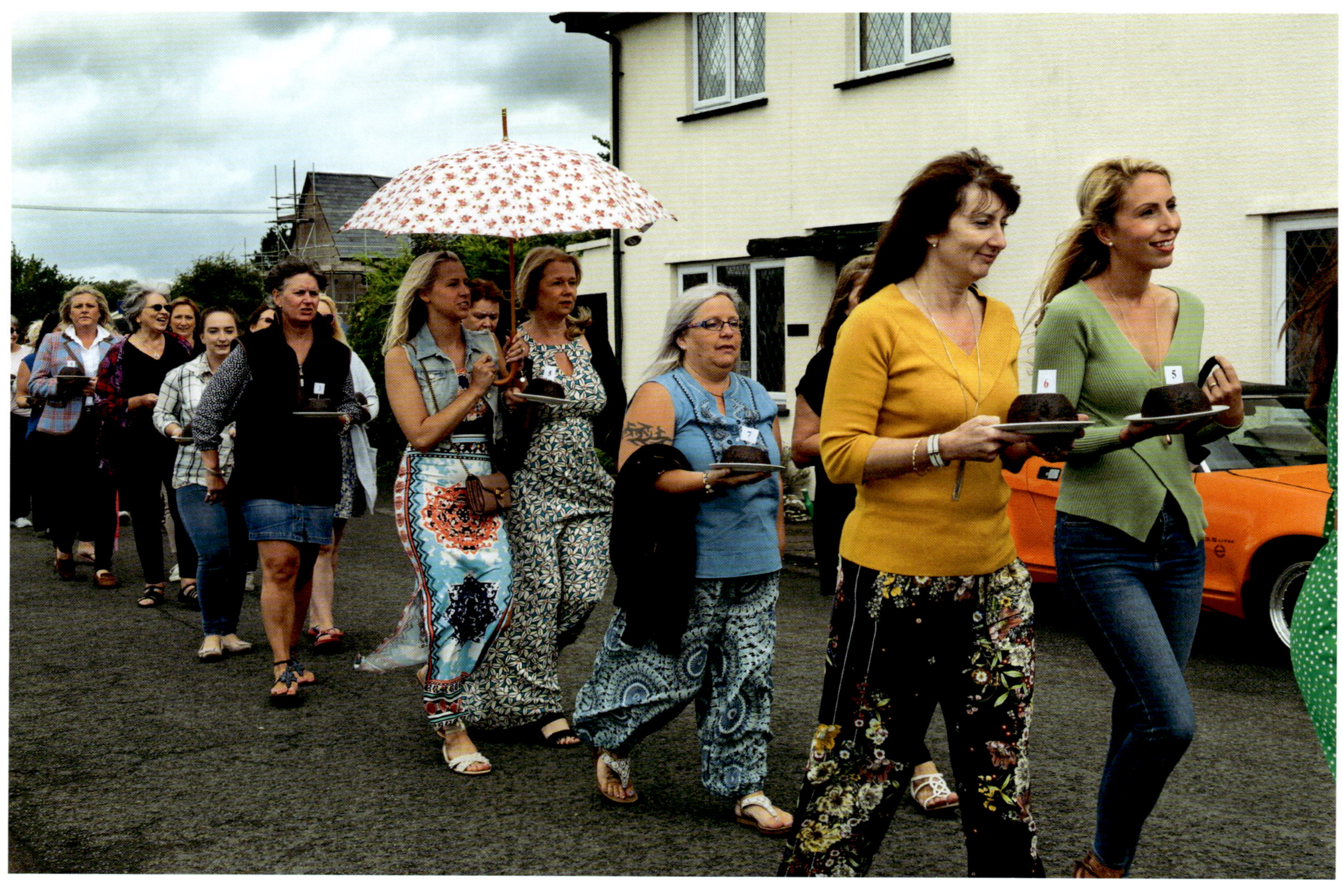

HARVEST HOME
East Brent, Somerset
2018

Ladies of the village and their guests take part in the Parade of Christmas Puddings from the village hall to the marquee, while men carry a 120lbs Harvest Cheddar Cheese and a 6ft loaf of Harvest Bread. All will be shared at the communal meal.

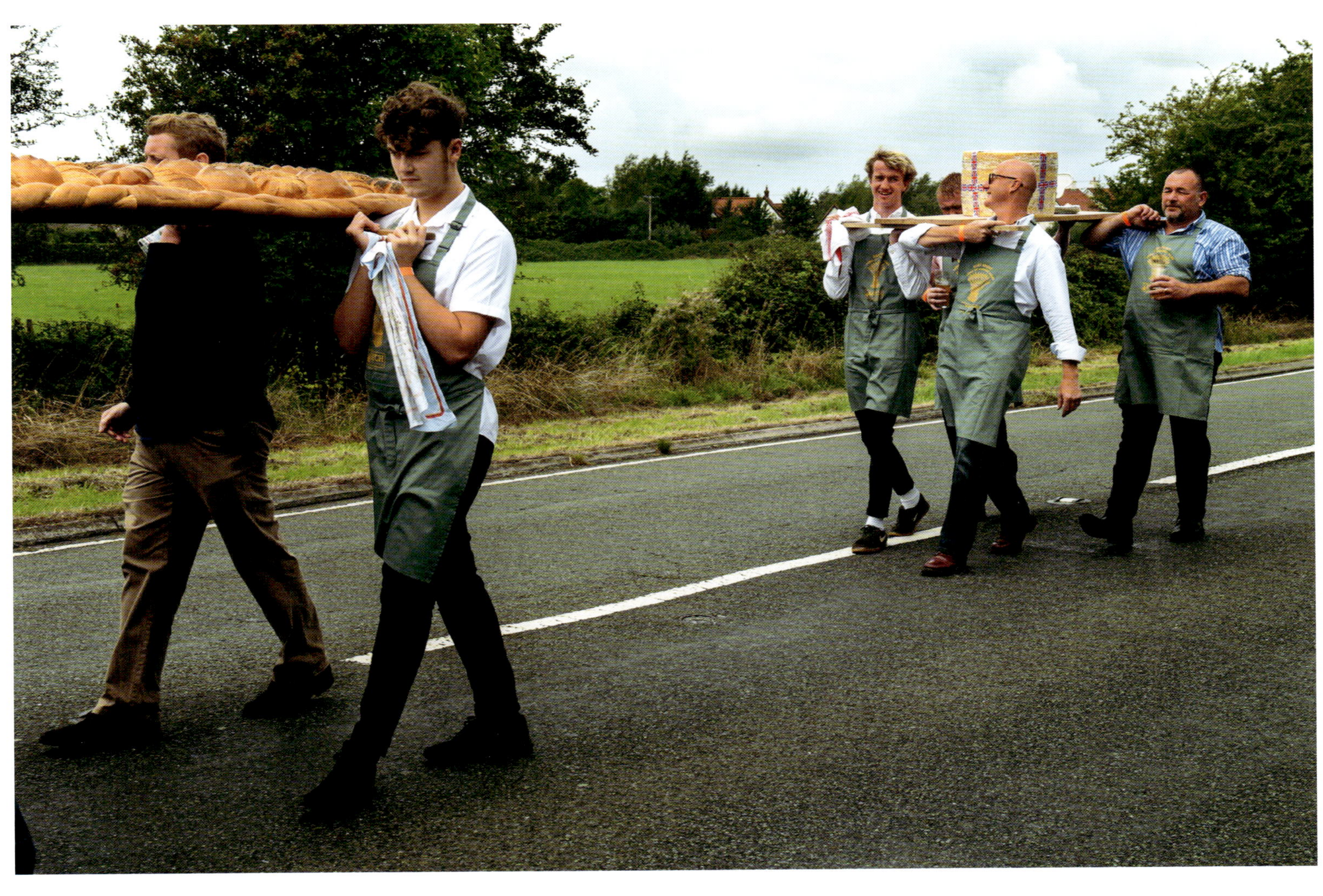

HARVEST HOME
East Brent, Somerset
2018

Tim Hawkings who is Vicar of St John the Baptist, the Parish Church in Axbridge, takes Grace before the commencement of the Harvest Home meal.

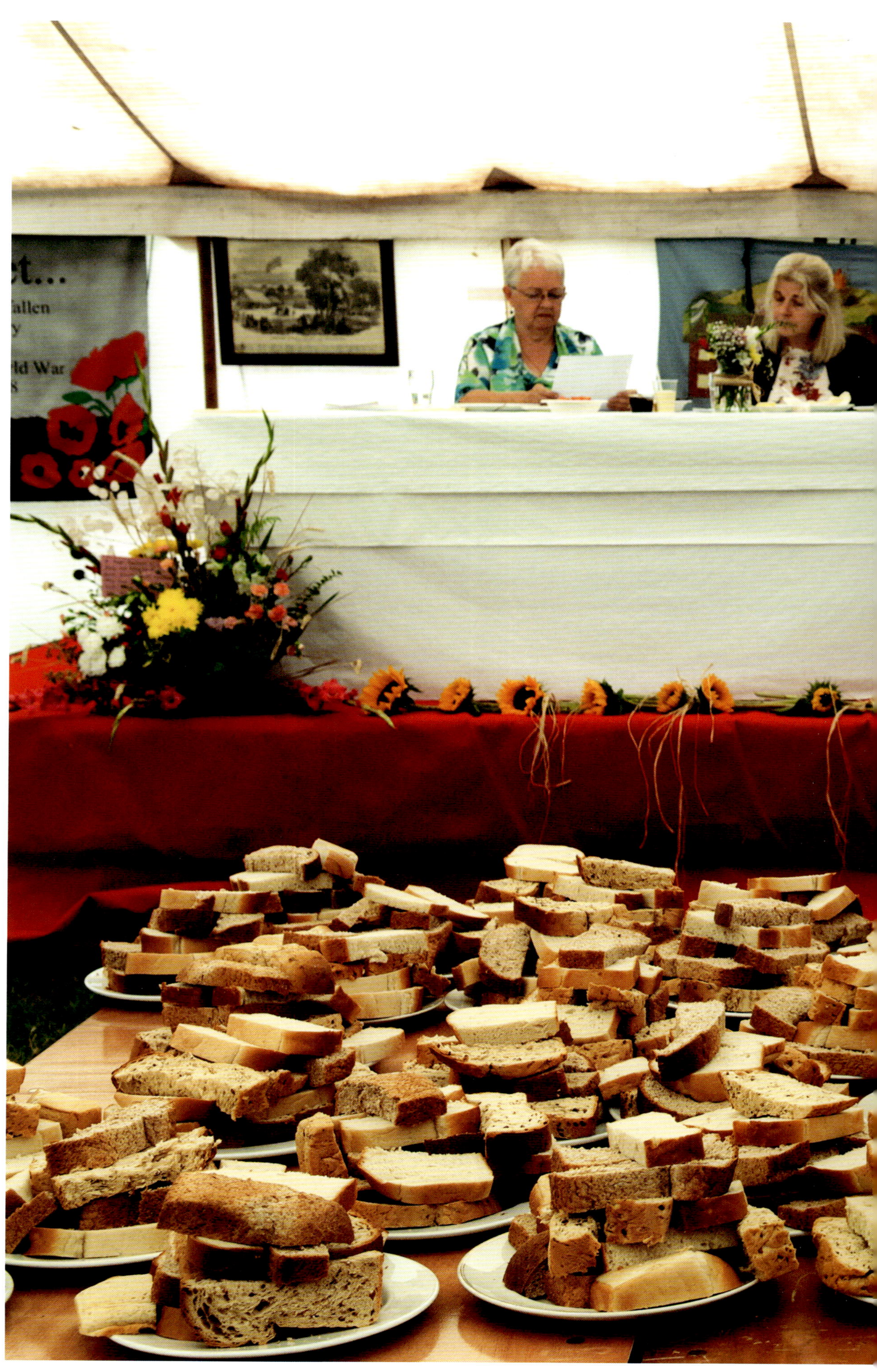

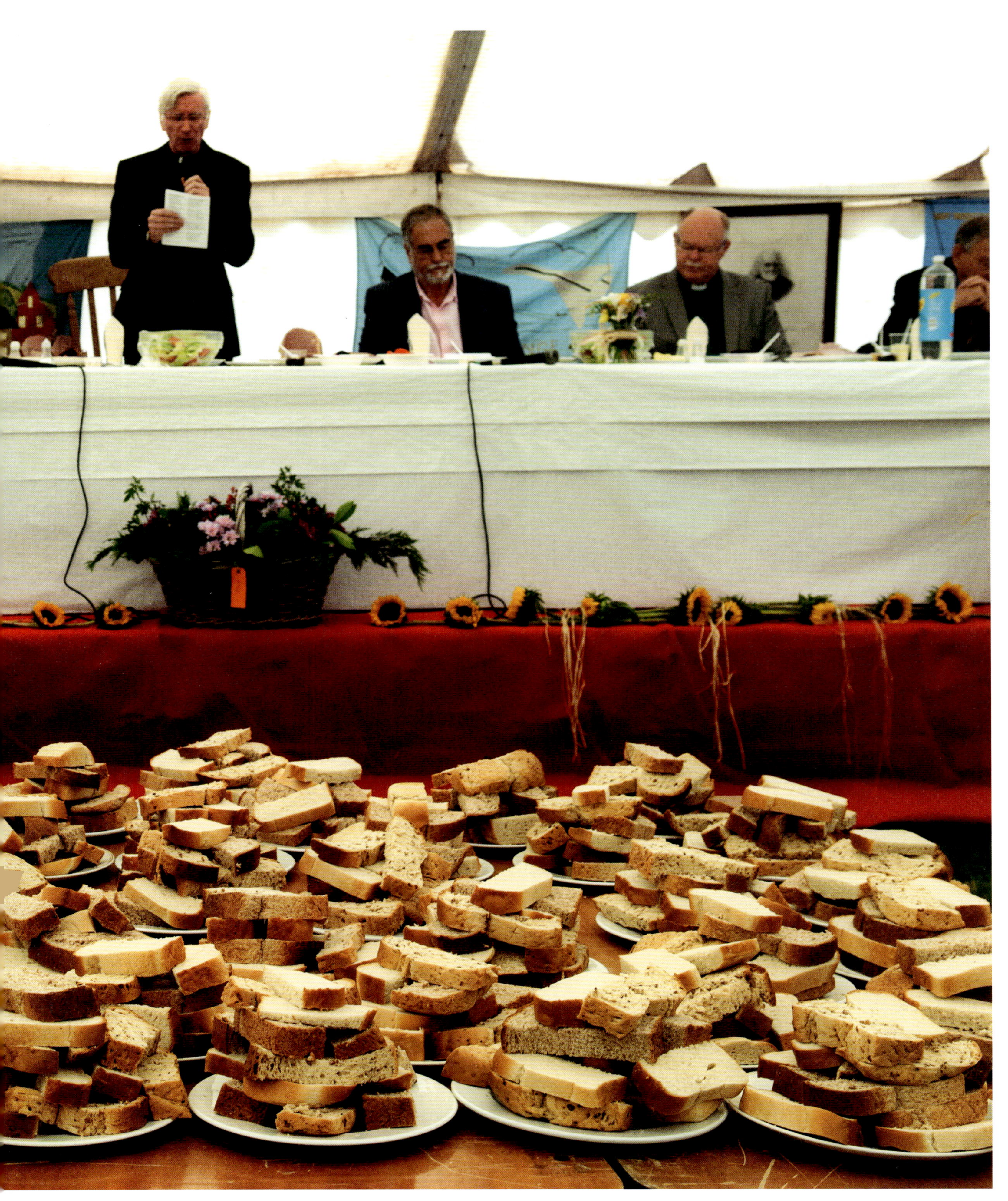

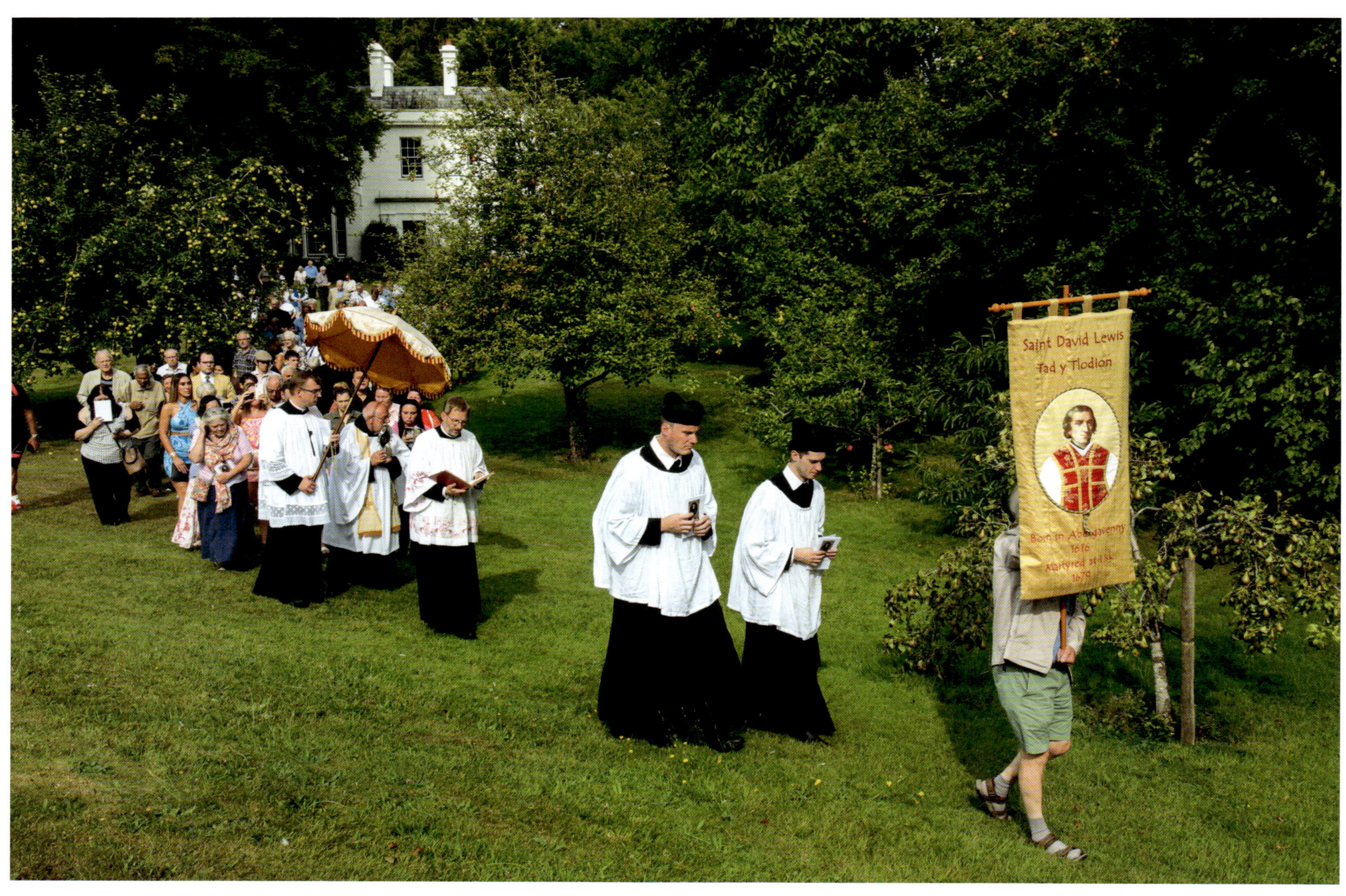

SAINT DAVID LEWIS PILGRIMAGE
Usk, Monmouthshire
2022

David Lewis was a Jesuit Catholic priest and martyr, he was the last Welsh Catholic priest executed for his faith during the Protestant Reformation.

At the Priory Church of St Mary a child, accompanied by her sister and mother, venerates his relic by kissing it.

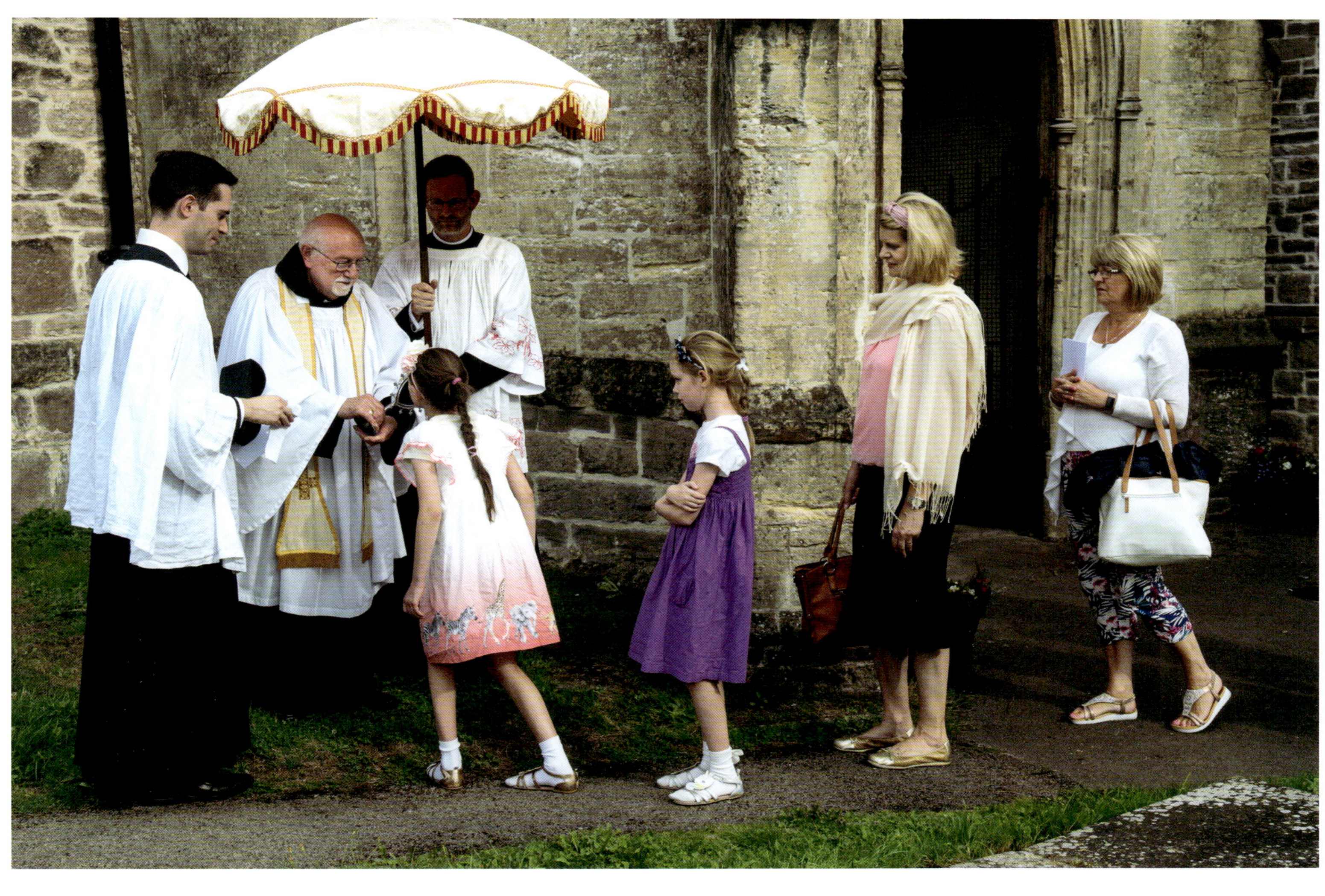

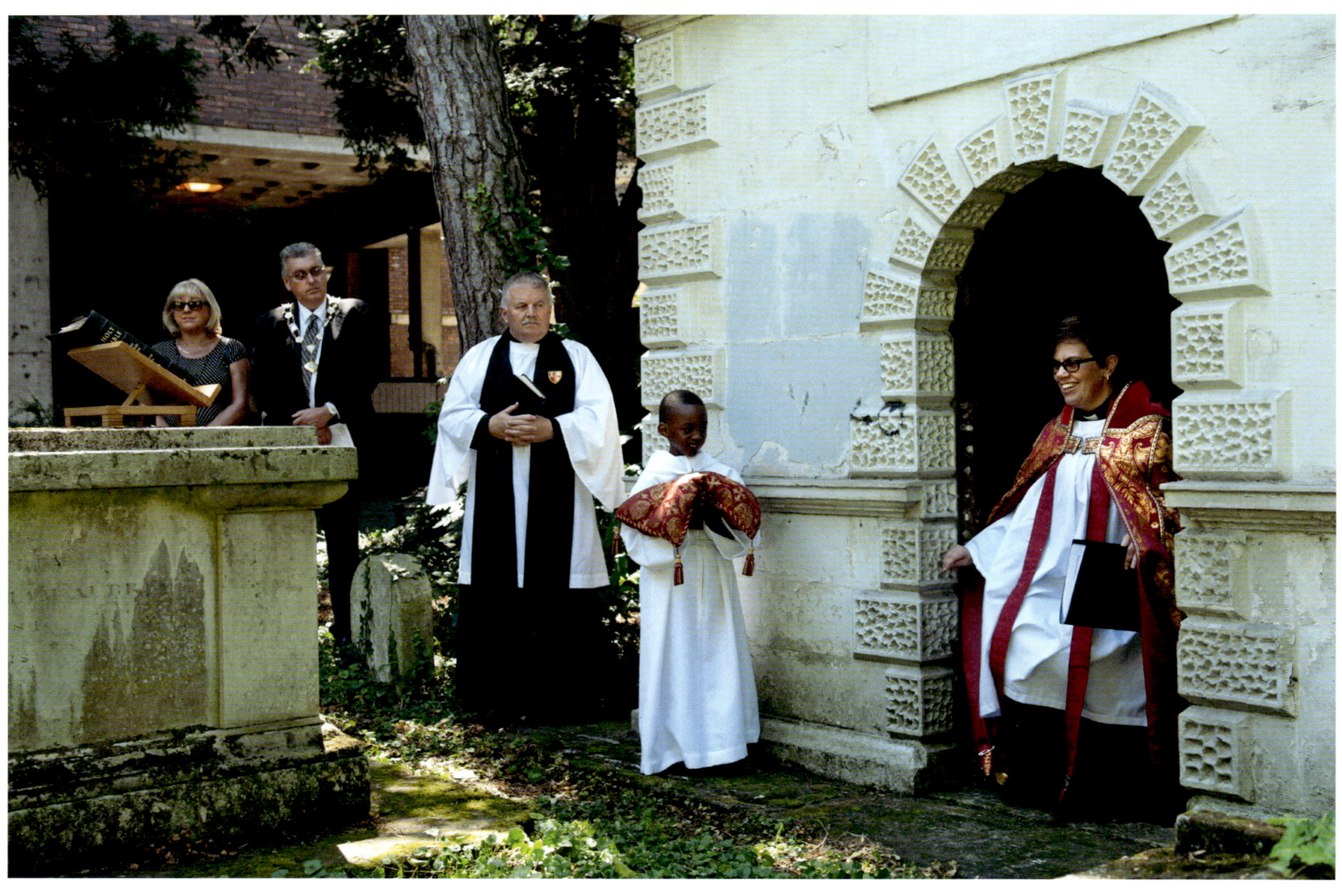

THE INSPECTION OF THE GIBSON TOMB
Sutton, London
2016

In St Nicholas' Church graveyard the Revd. Justine Middlemiss exits the Gibson family vault.

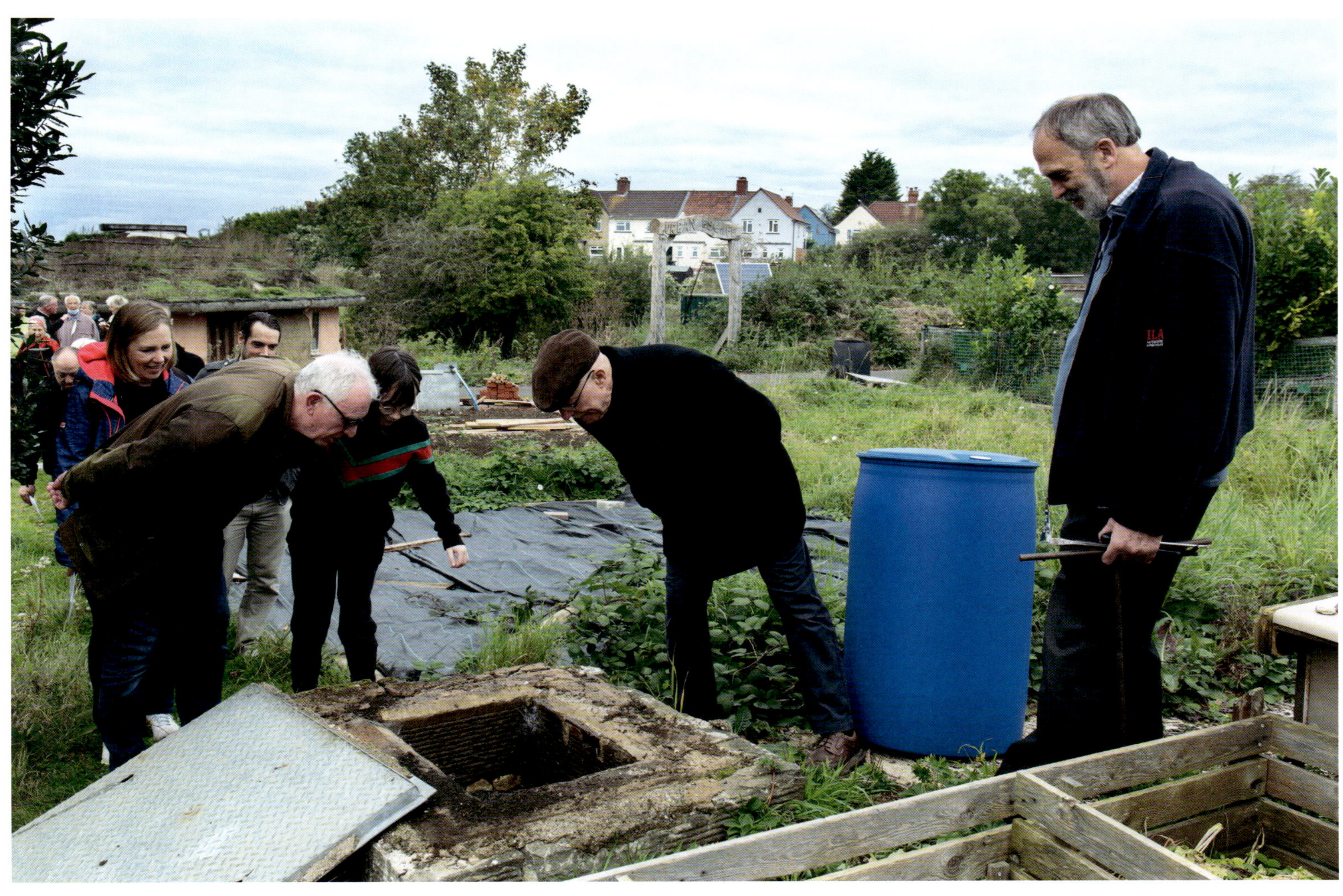

WATER PIPE WALK
Bristol, Avon
2021

Parishioners from the Church of St Mary the Virgin, Redcliffe, walk two miles along the route of a water pipe that may have been made of wood when it was first laid down in 1190 to provide fresh water to the parish. A manhole cover is lifted so that a Victorian cast iron replacement can be inspected.

THE DRUID ORDER
London
2012

At the start of the Druid Order's year the Autumn Equinox is celebrated at the top of Primrose Hill.

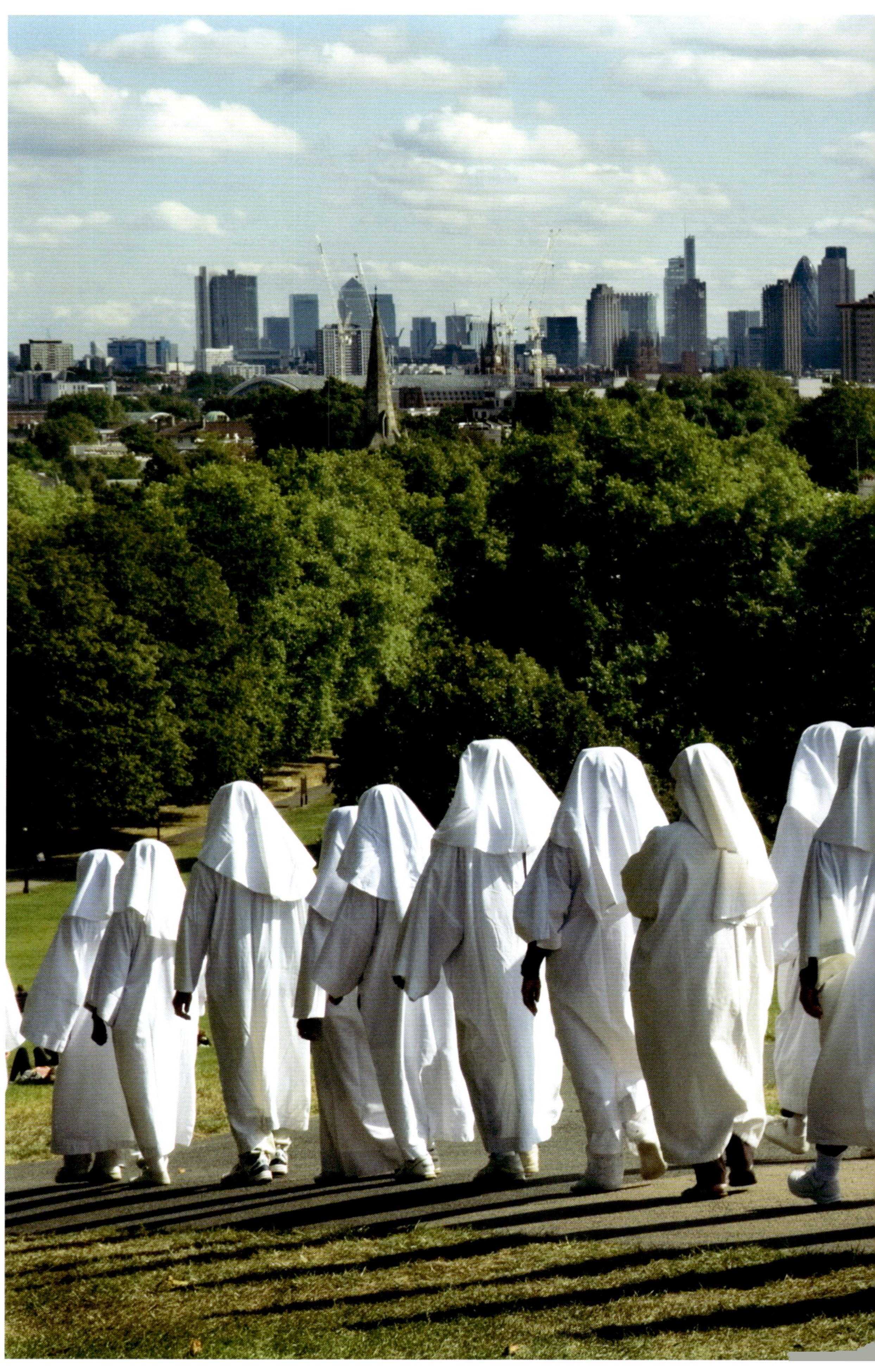

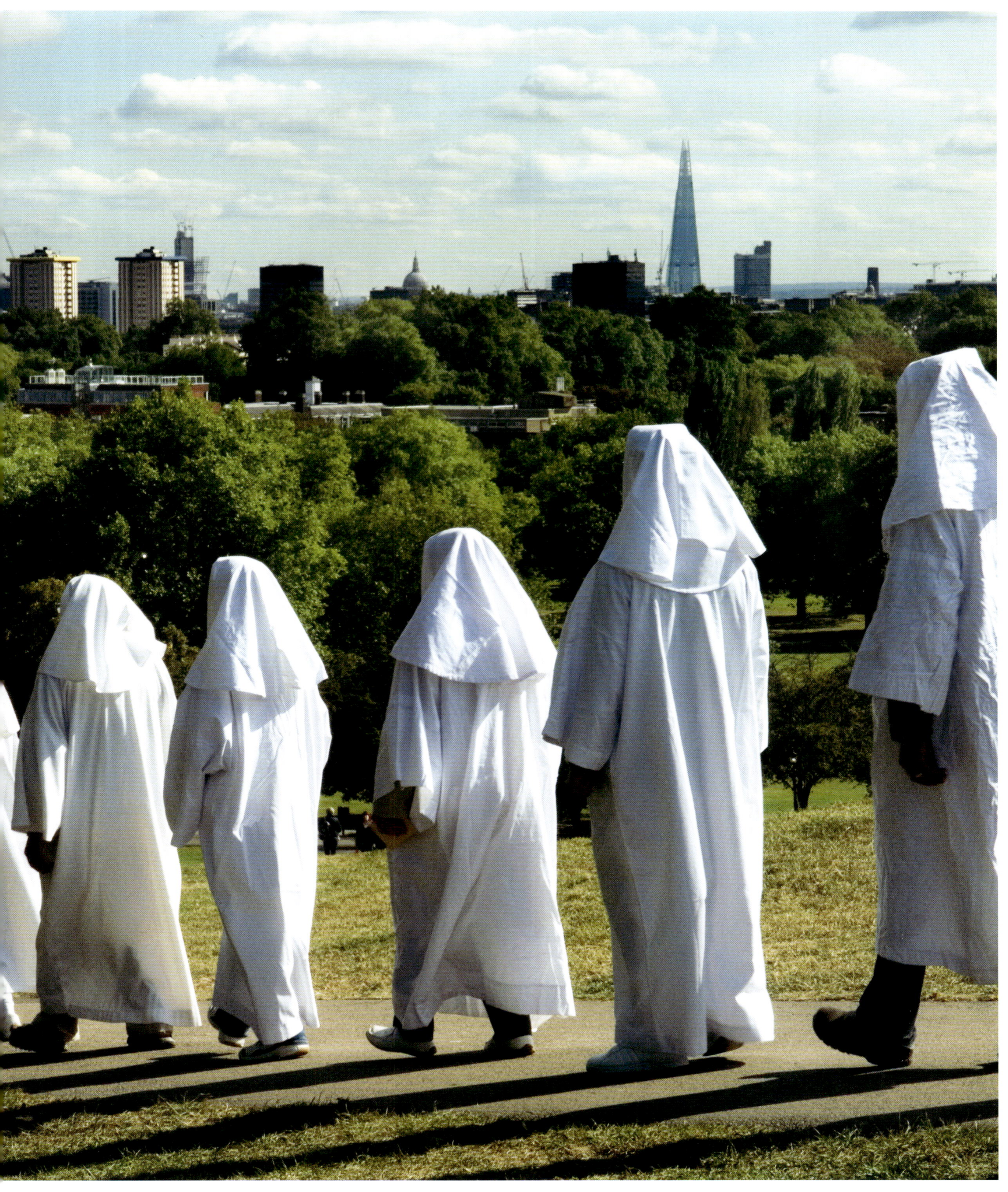

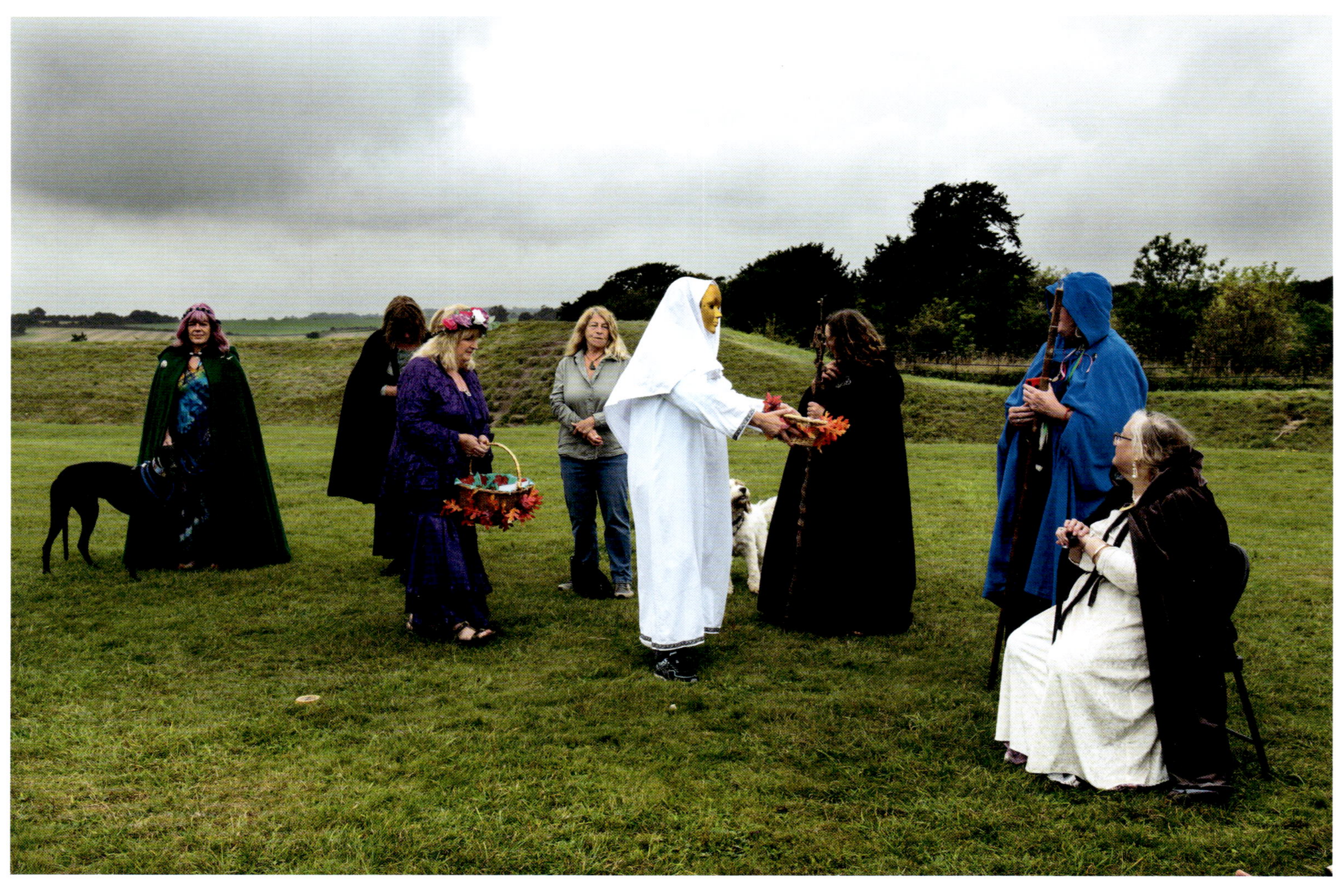

DORSET DRUID GROVE
Knowlton, Dorset
2021

Members of the Dorset Druid Grove celebrate the Autumn Equinox amongst the ruins of Knowlton church, built in the 12th century, it stands within a Neolithic henge, symbolising the transition from pagan to Christian worship.

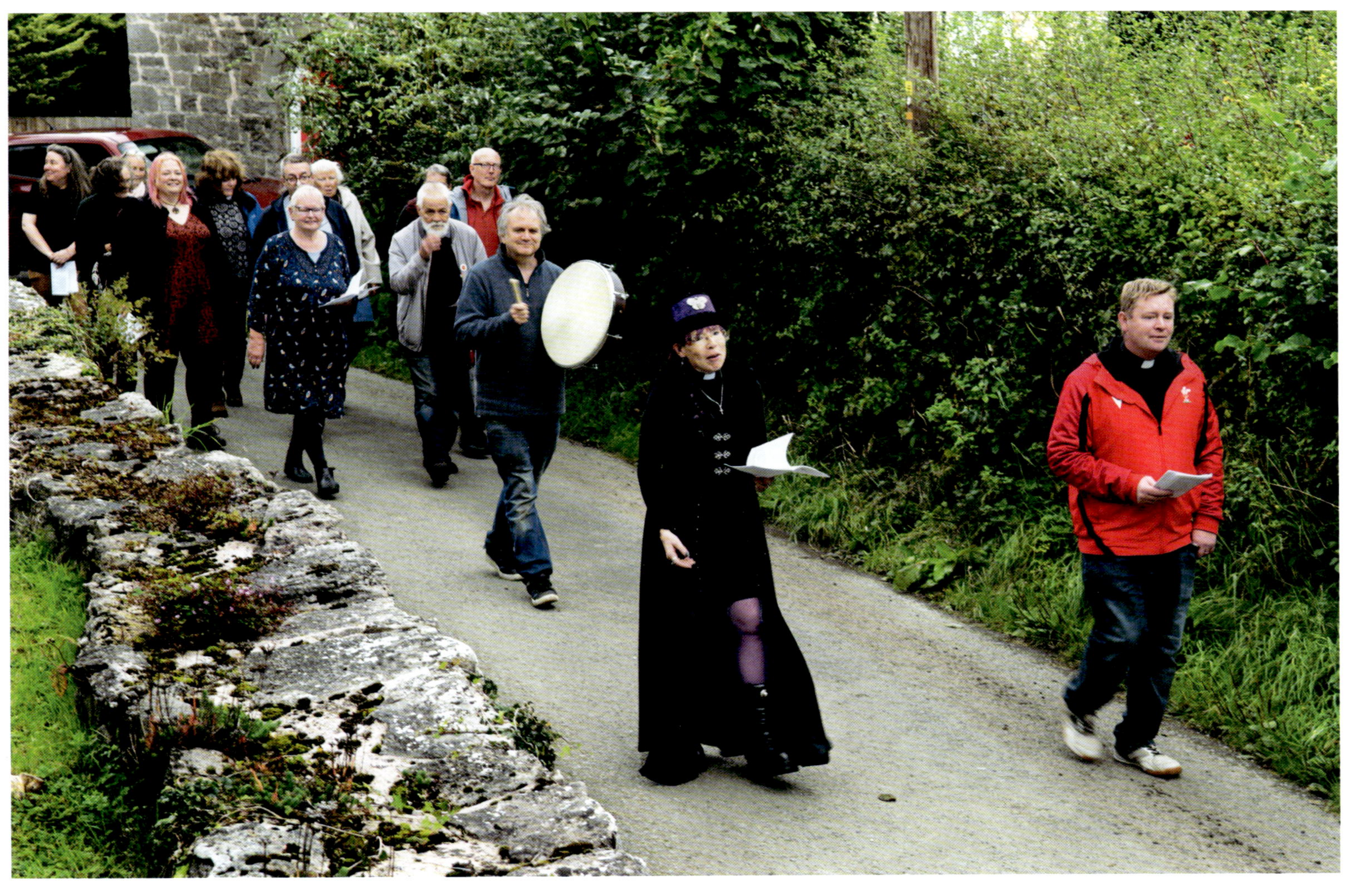

FEAT STONE
Efenechtyd, Denbighshire
2023

The Revd. Diana Greenfield leads parishioners around the circular church site prior to the church clypping ceremony that takes place after the Patronal Service.

FEAT STONE
Efenechtyd, Denbighshire
2023

As part of the day's festivities village strong men traditionally attempted to throw the Feat Stone, a 101 pounds smooth oval stone backwards over their heads. Ellis Hughes who lives in the village, turns sharply to see how far he has managed.

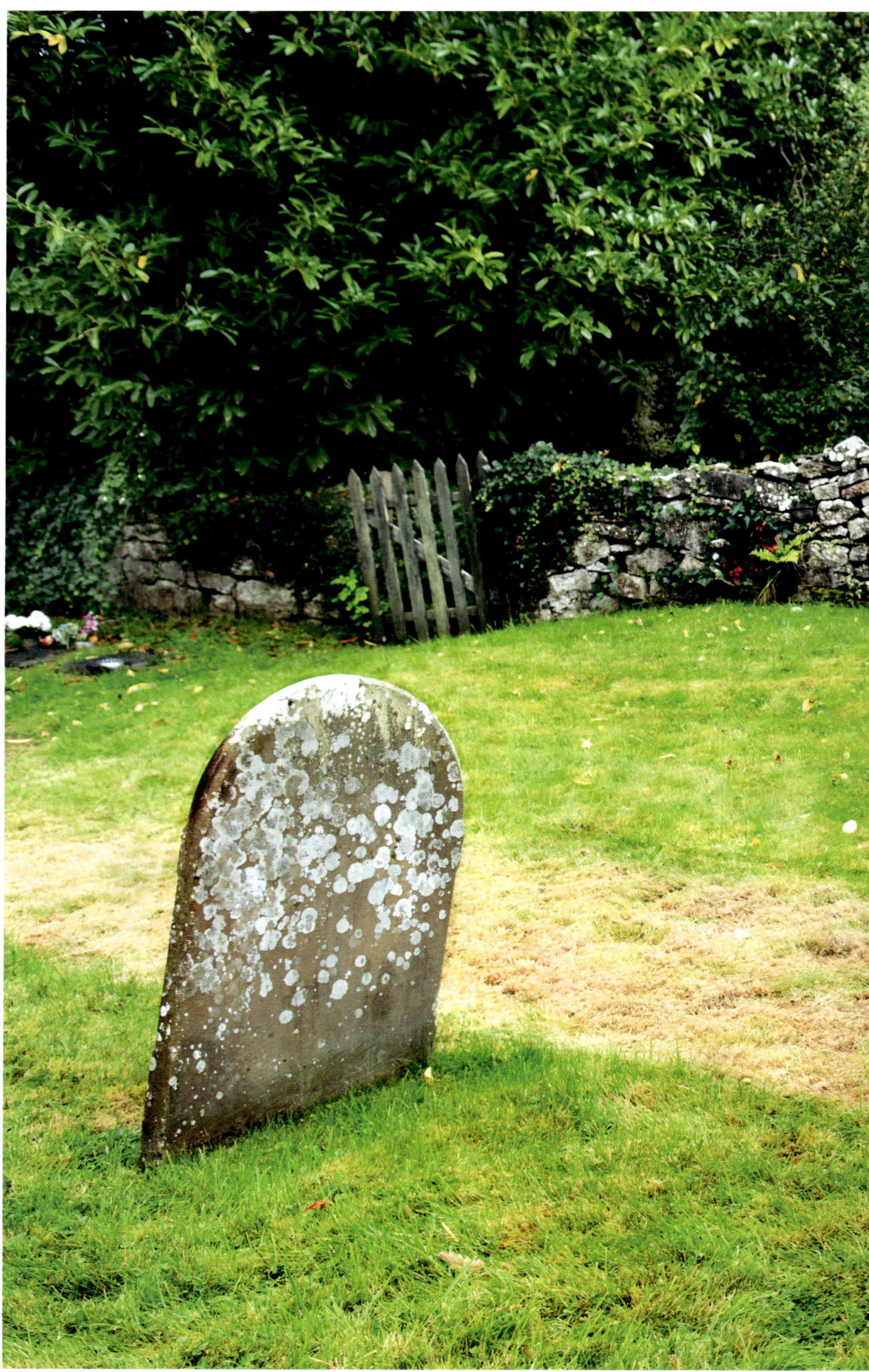

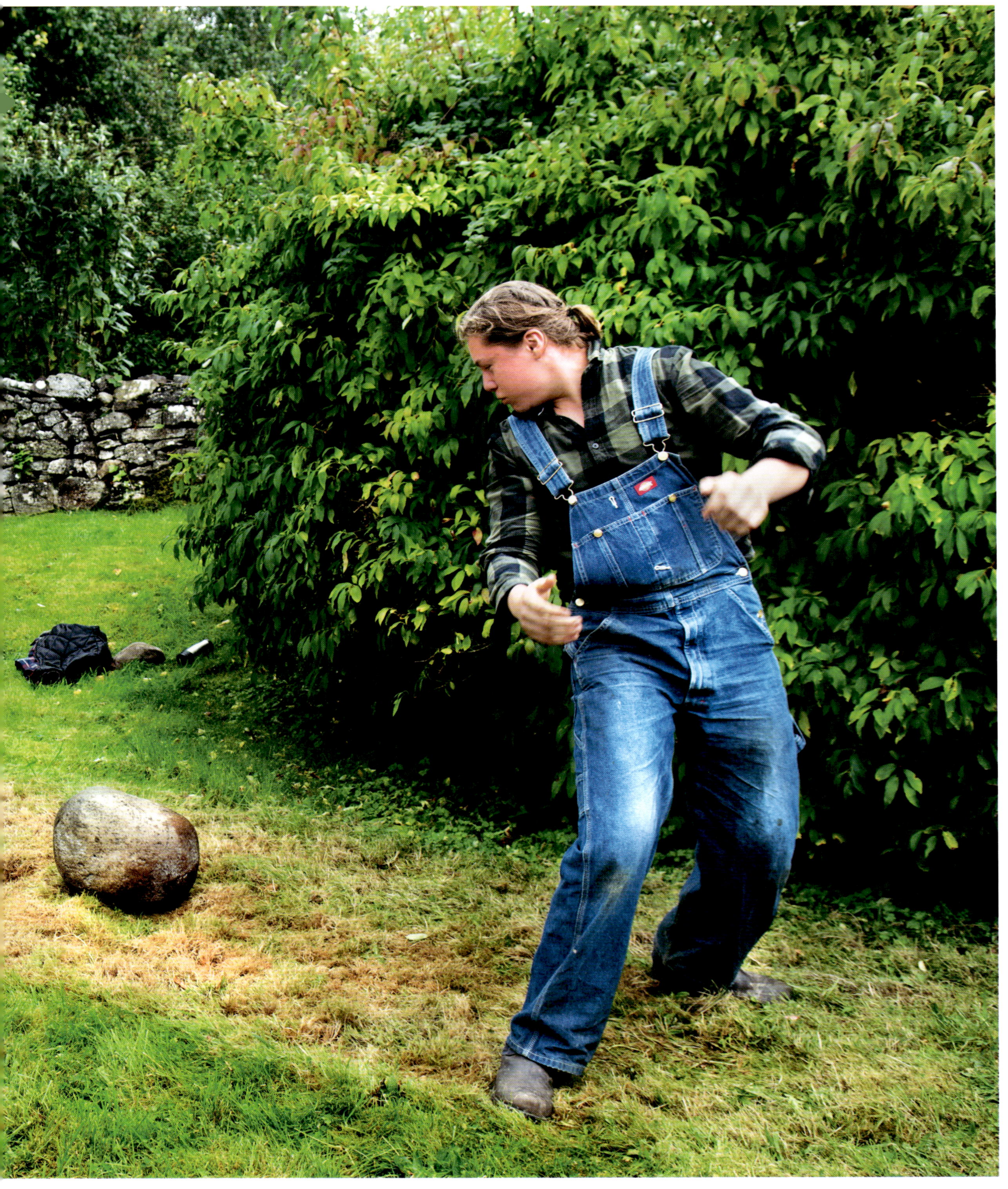

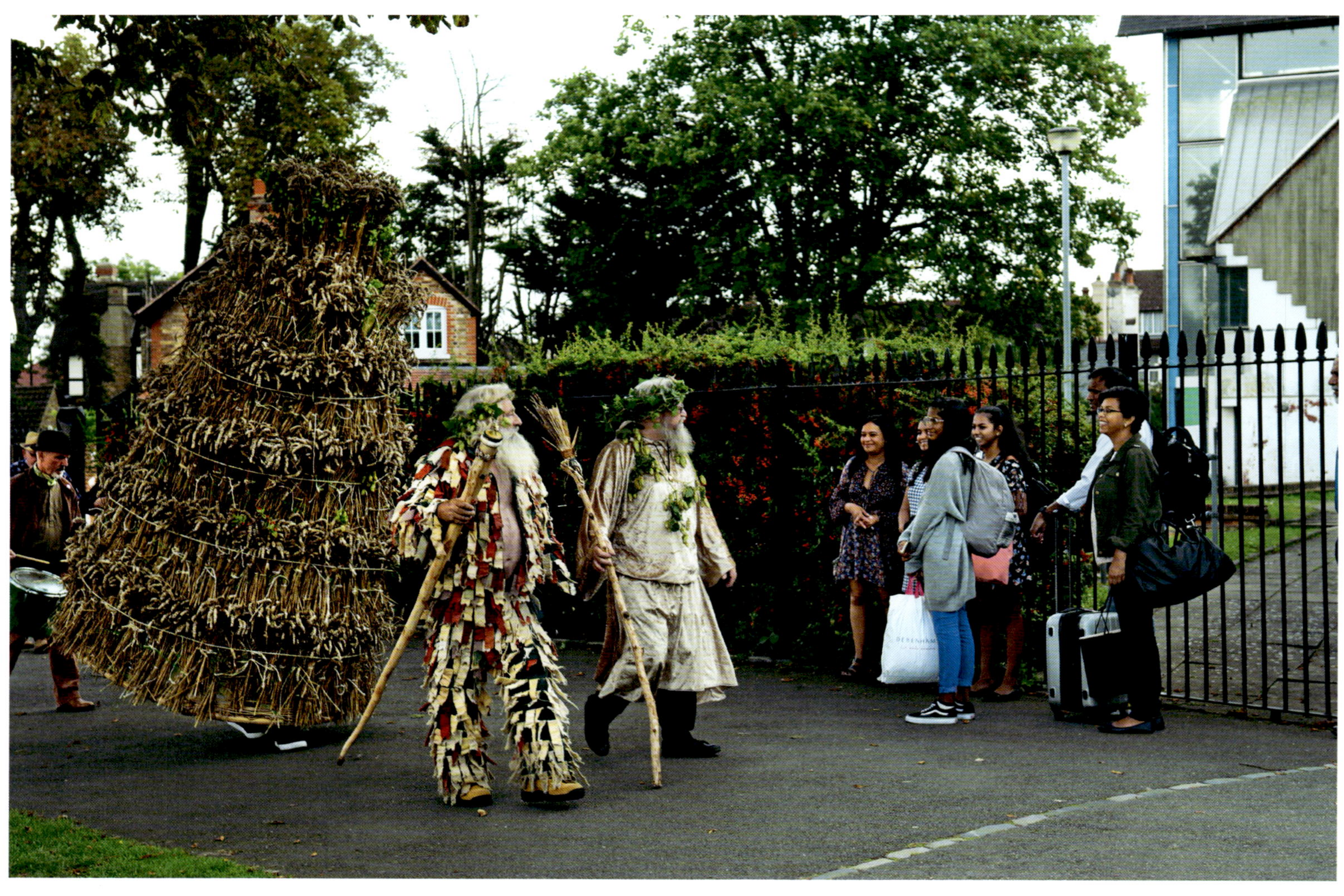

STRAW JACK
Carshalton, Sutton, Surrey
2017

Two white bearded 1970s latter day hippies, crowned in laurels and carrying their staffs of office, lead Straw Jack around the sleepy south London commuter suburb.

As the day turns to night, Straw Jack is slowly dismantled, cremated on a brazier in the garden of The Hope pub.

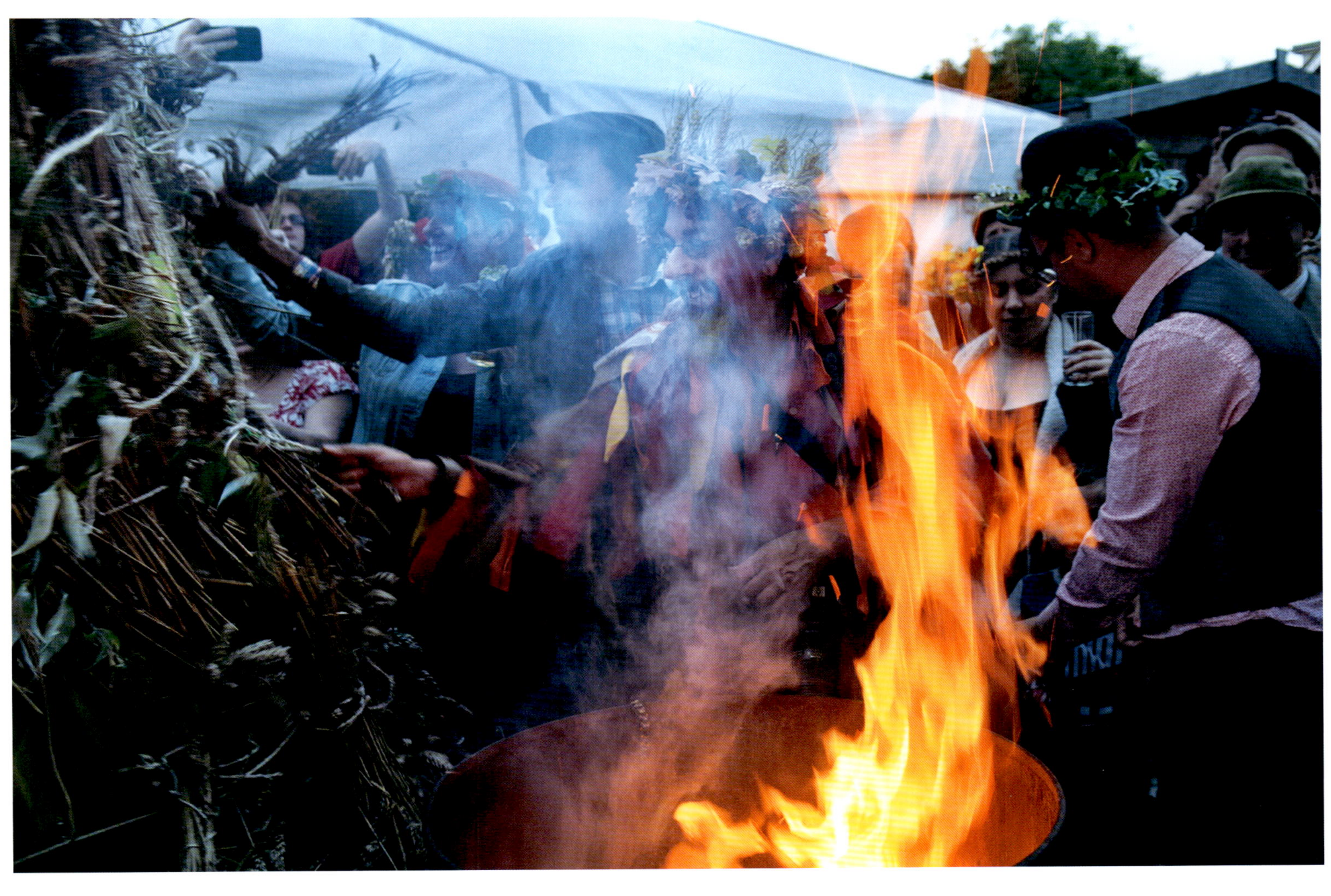

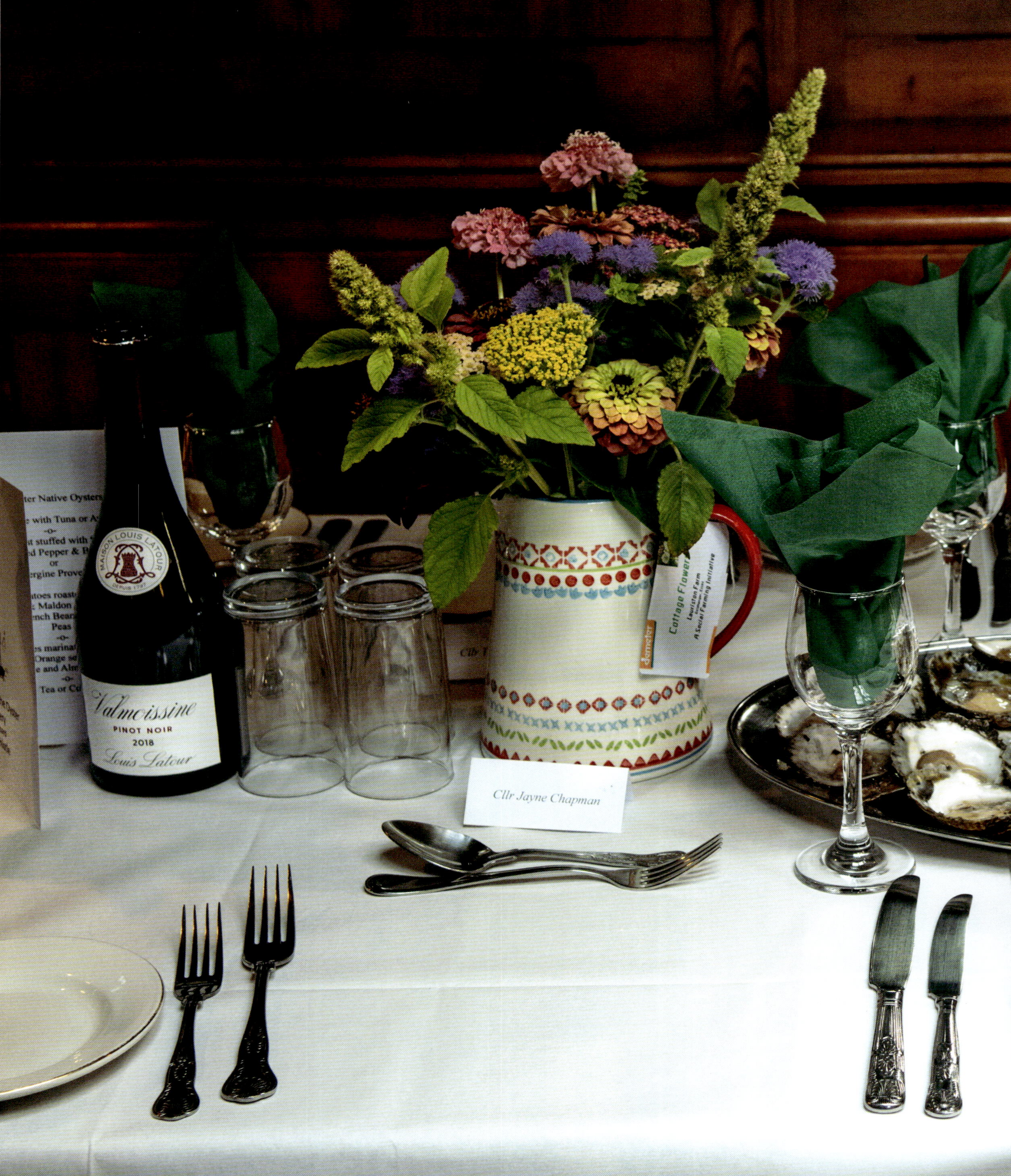
MAISON LOUIS LATOUR
Valmoissine
PINOT NOIR
2018
Louis Latour
Cllr Jayne Chapman
Cottage Flowers
Lauriston Farm
A Social Farming Initiative

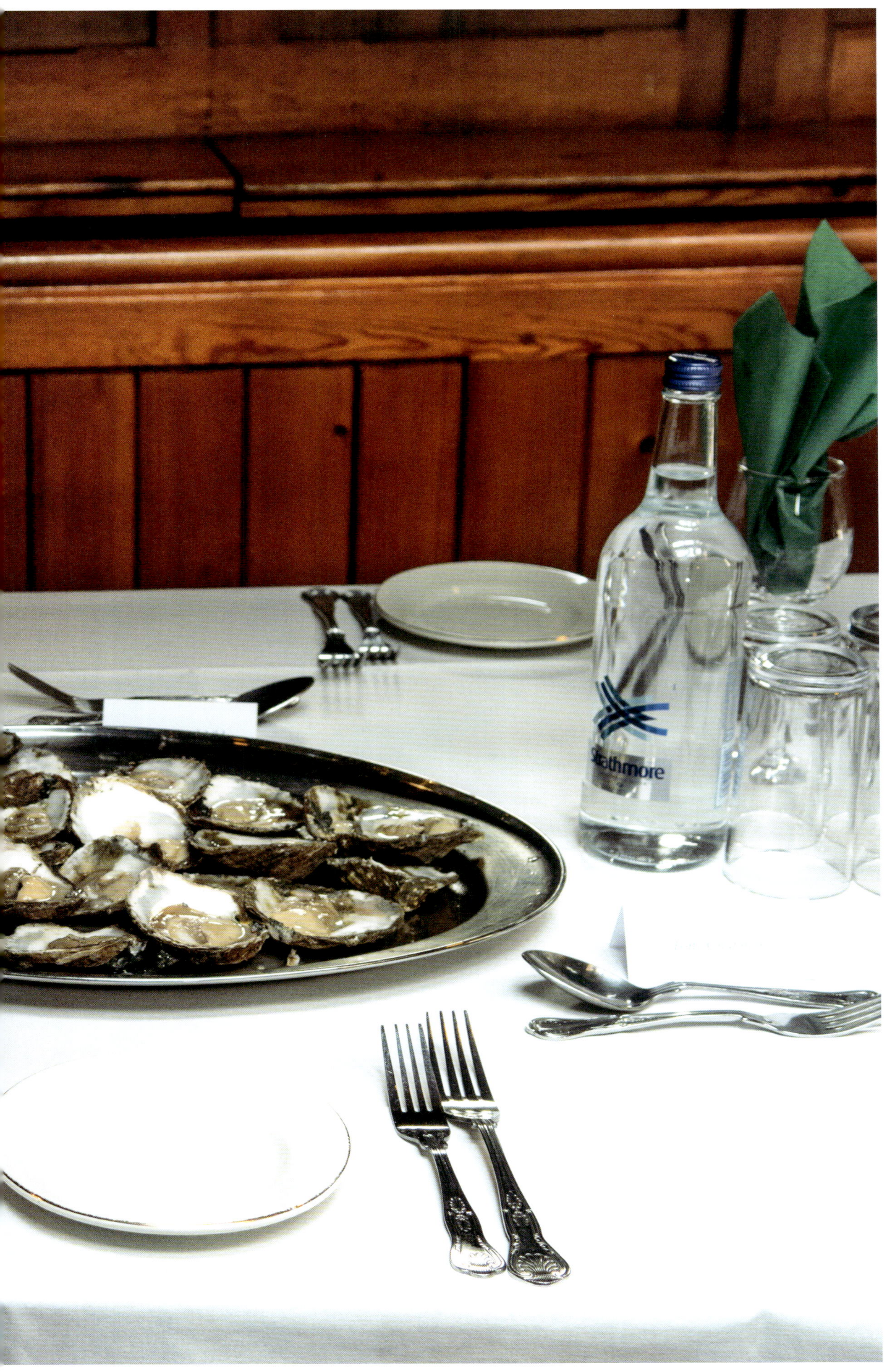

THE OPENING OF THE COLNE OYSTER FISHERY
Brightlingsea, Essex
2021

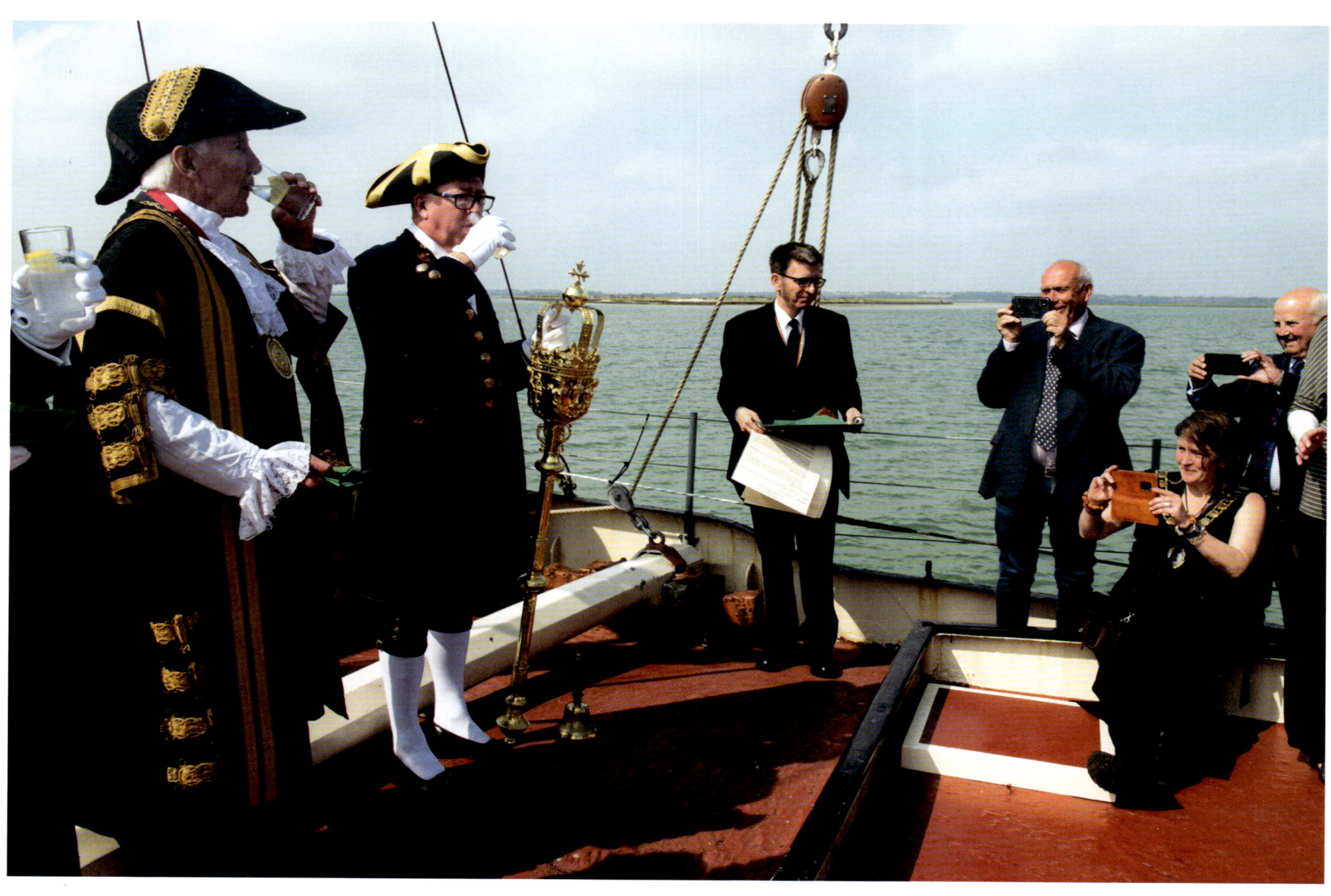

THE OPENING OF THE COLNE OYSTER FISHERY
Brightlingsea, Essex
2021

The Opening of the Colne Oyster Fisheries takes place on the first Friday in September aboard the Thistle, a Thames Barge.

Below deck, oysters are on the luncheon menu. As the meal ends Mayor Cllr Robert Davidson and guests raise a glass to Queen and Country.

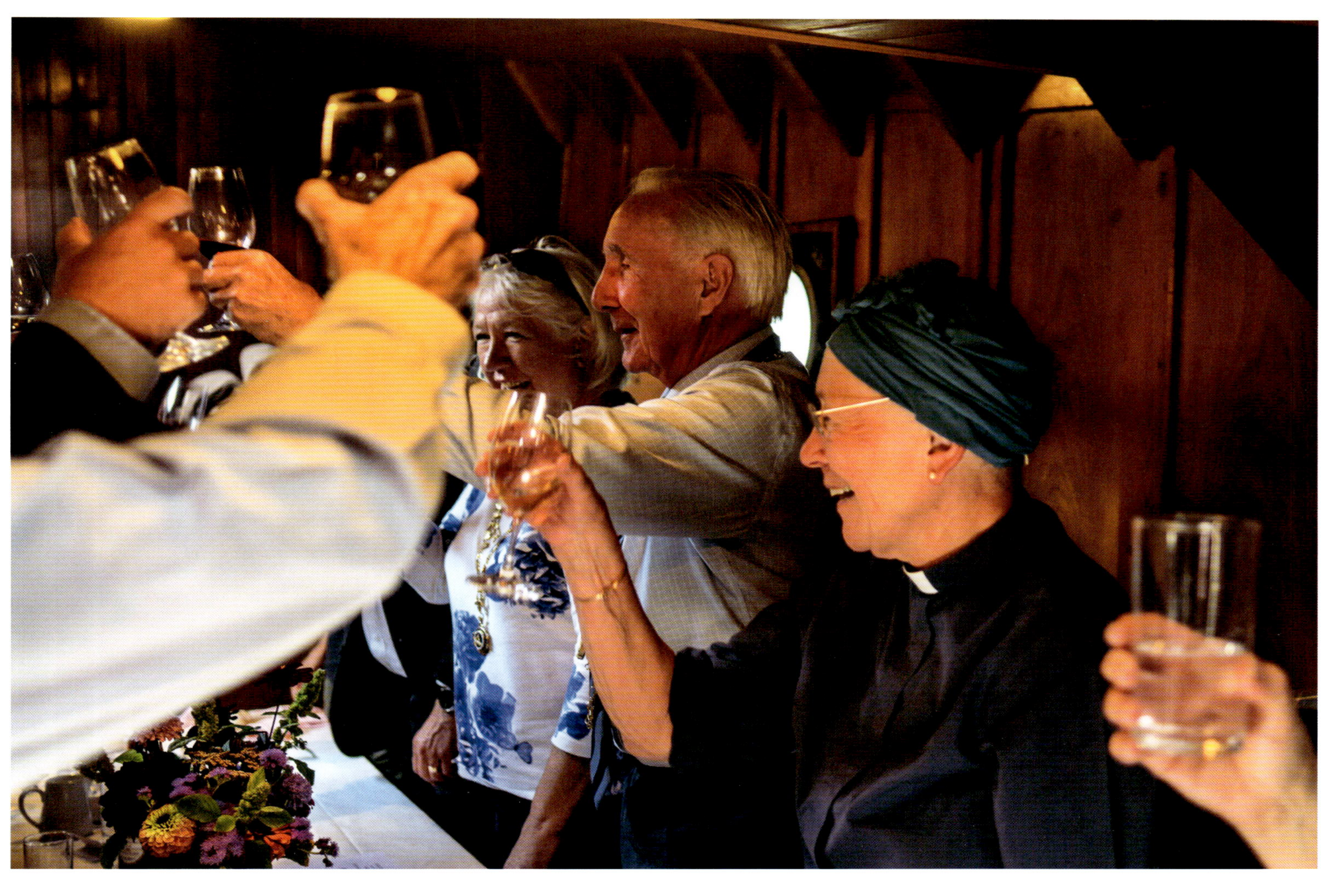

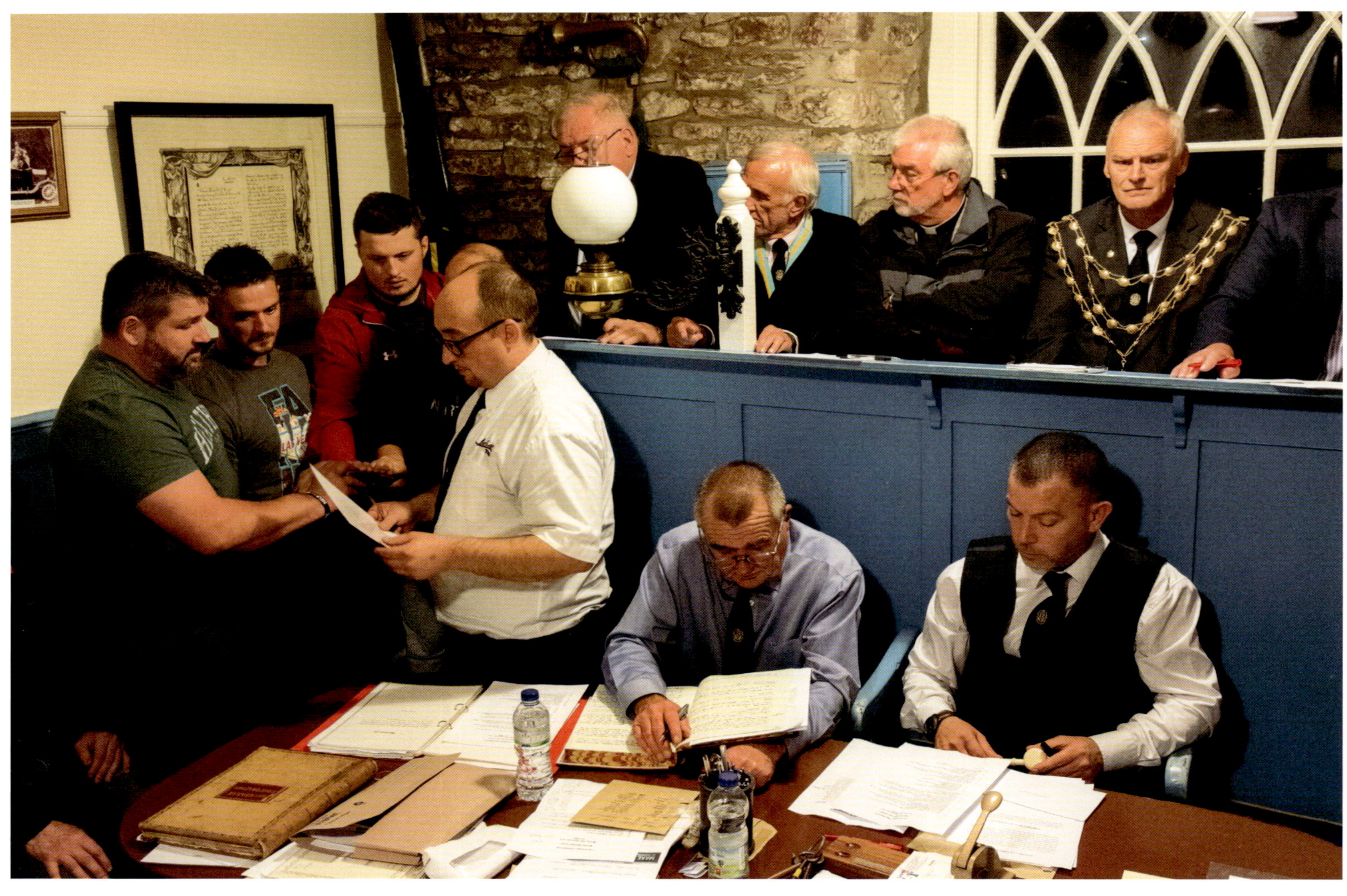

ELECTION OF THE NEW PORTREEVE
Laugharne, Carmarthen
2019

David Lynn Jones the newly elected portreeve presides over the Corporation in the Big Court of the town hall. Members of the jury are being sworn in. Afterwards he is chaired three times around the town hall. He wears the chain of office consisting of solid gold miniature cockleshells. One added by each new portreeve, with their name and date of tenure on the reverse.

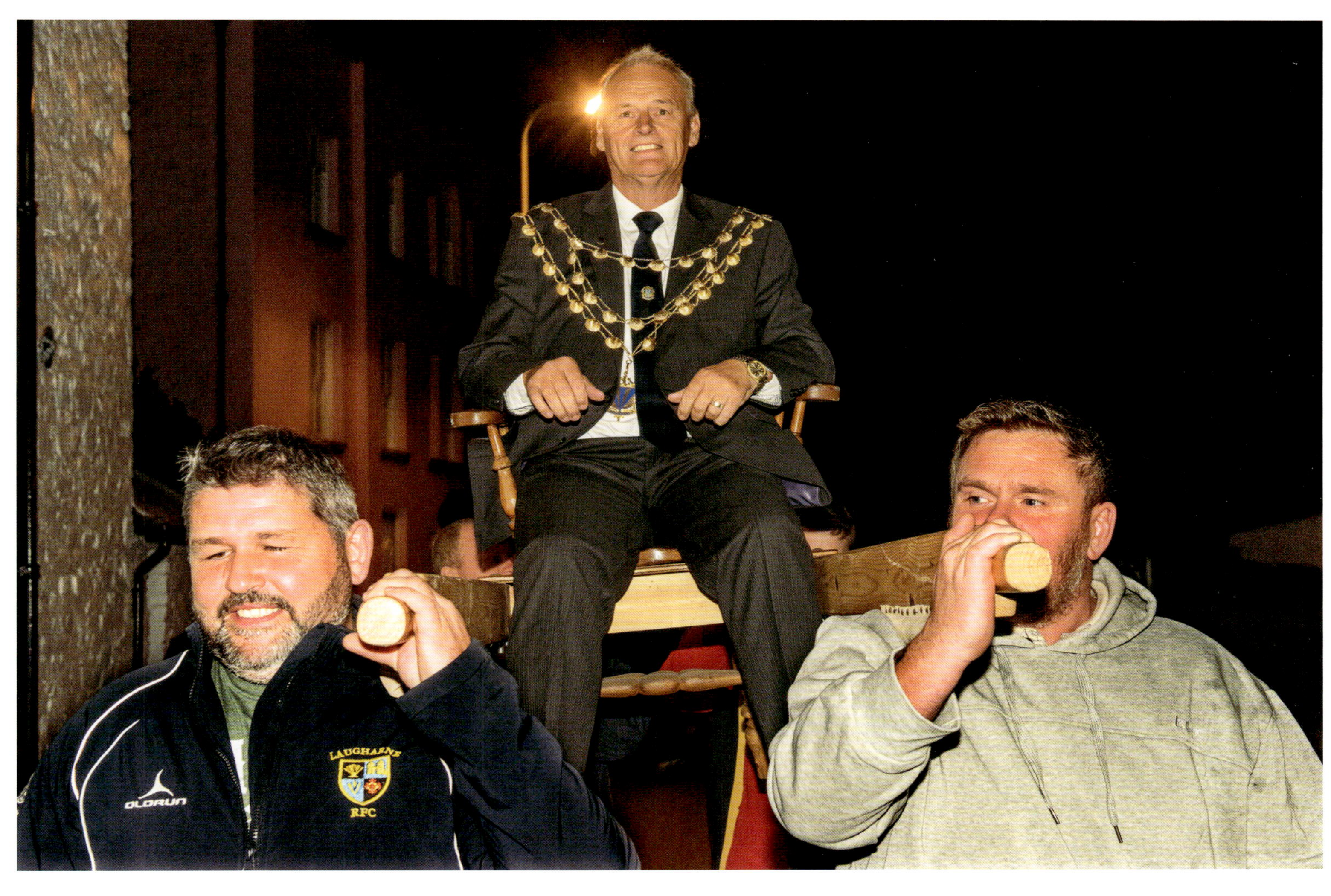
LAUGHARNE
RFC
OLDRUN

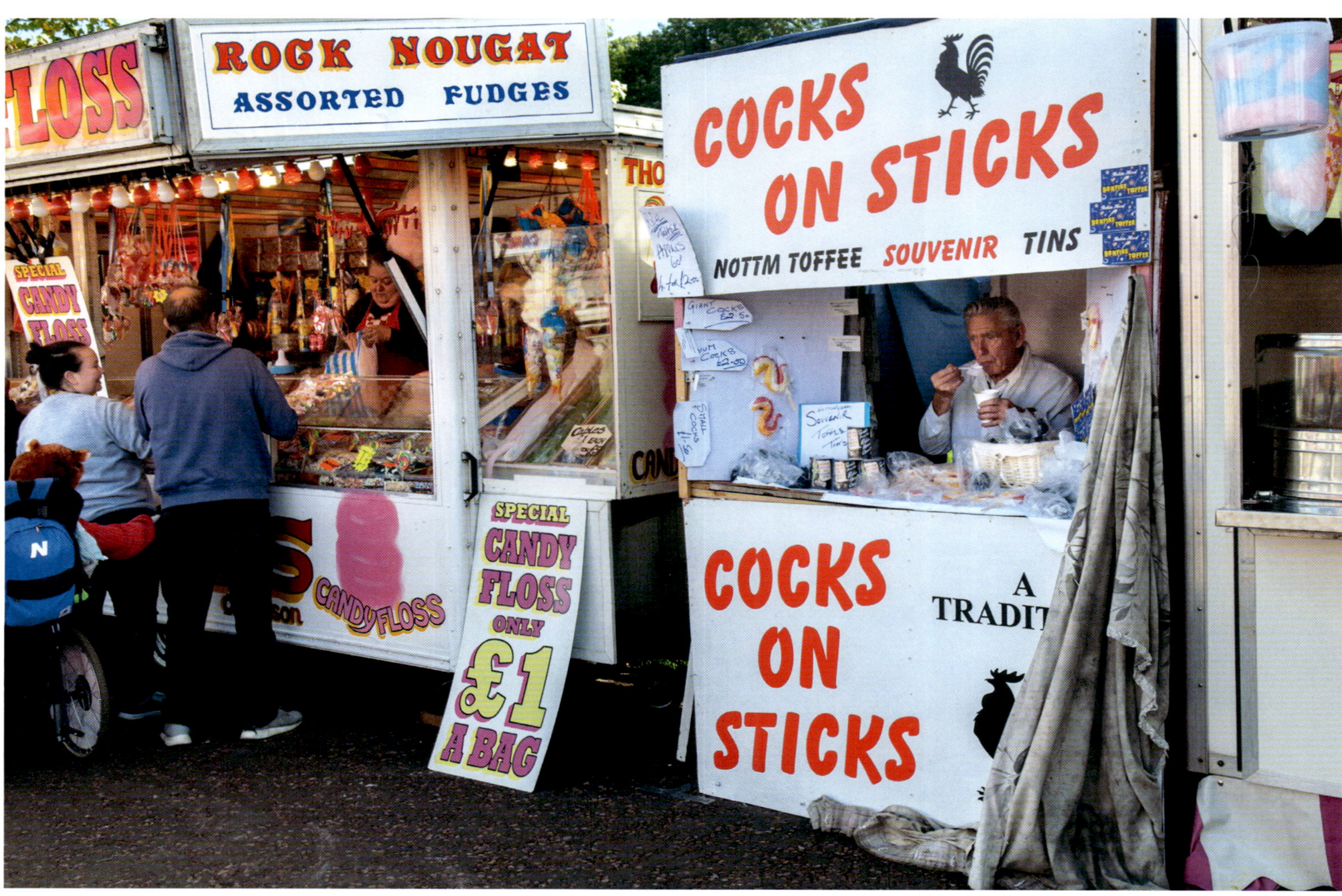

COCKS ON STICKS
Nottingham, Nottinghamshire
2017

Ray Brooks sits in his booth at the Nottingham Goose Fair; his family have made Cocks on Sticks, the traditional Goose Fair sweet since the 1890s.

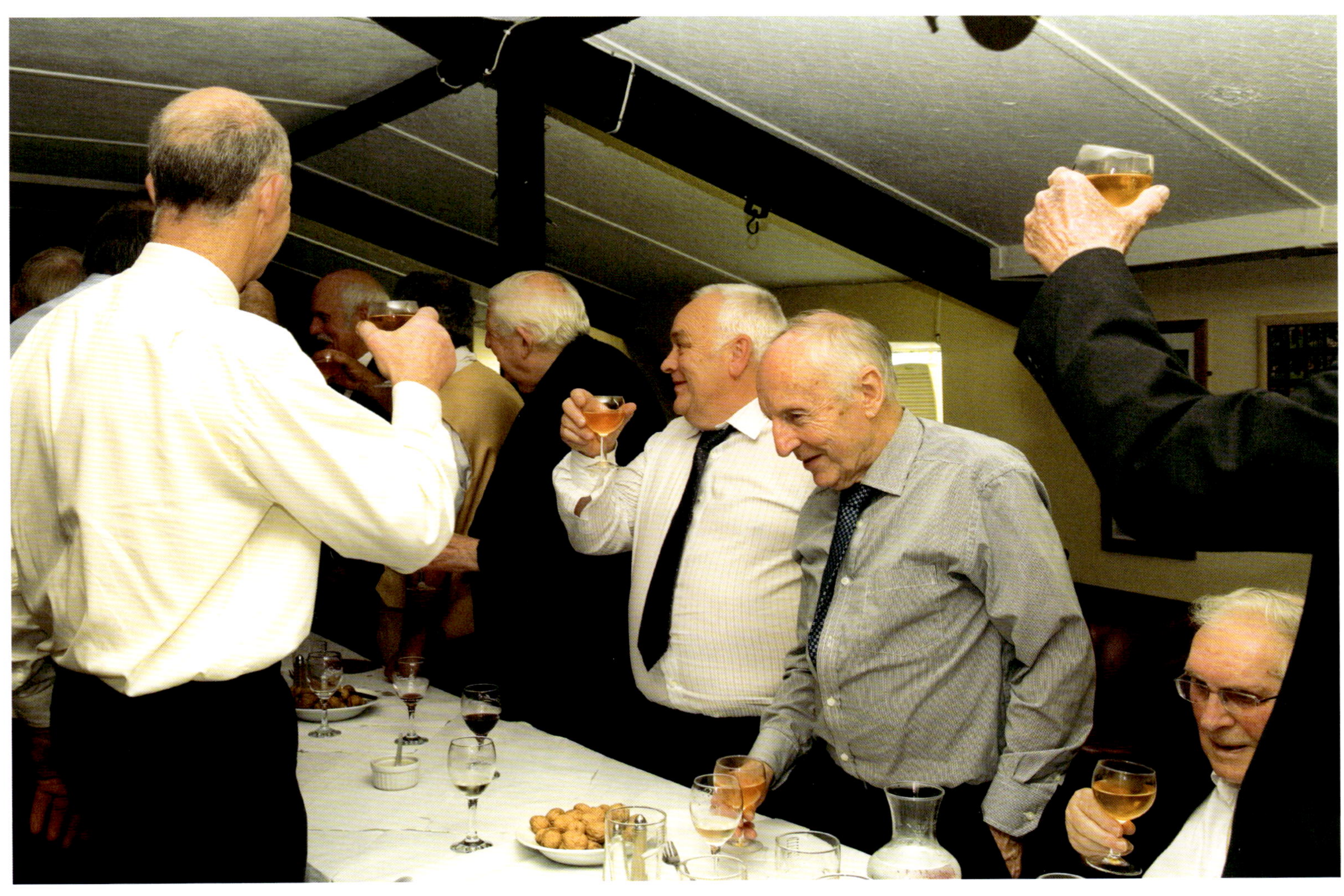

COURT LEET
Watchet, Somerset
2014

On the last Thursday in October, at the Bell Inn, the annual Court Leet is held. After the business of the day there is a lunch and a loyal toast is drunk, made from a secret punch recipe and served with bowls of walnuts.

BACK END DAY
Battersea, London
2010

London Cob Horse dealers 'back end day' sale outside the Flanagans Arms pub. It's the last day of trading in the year.

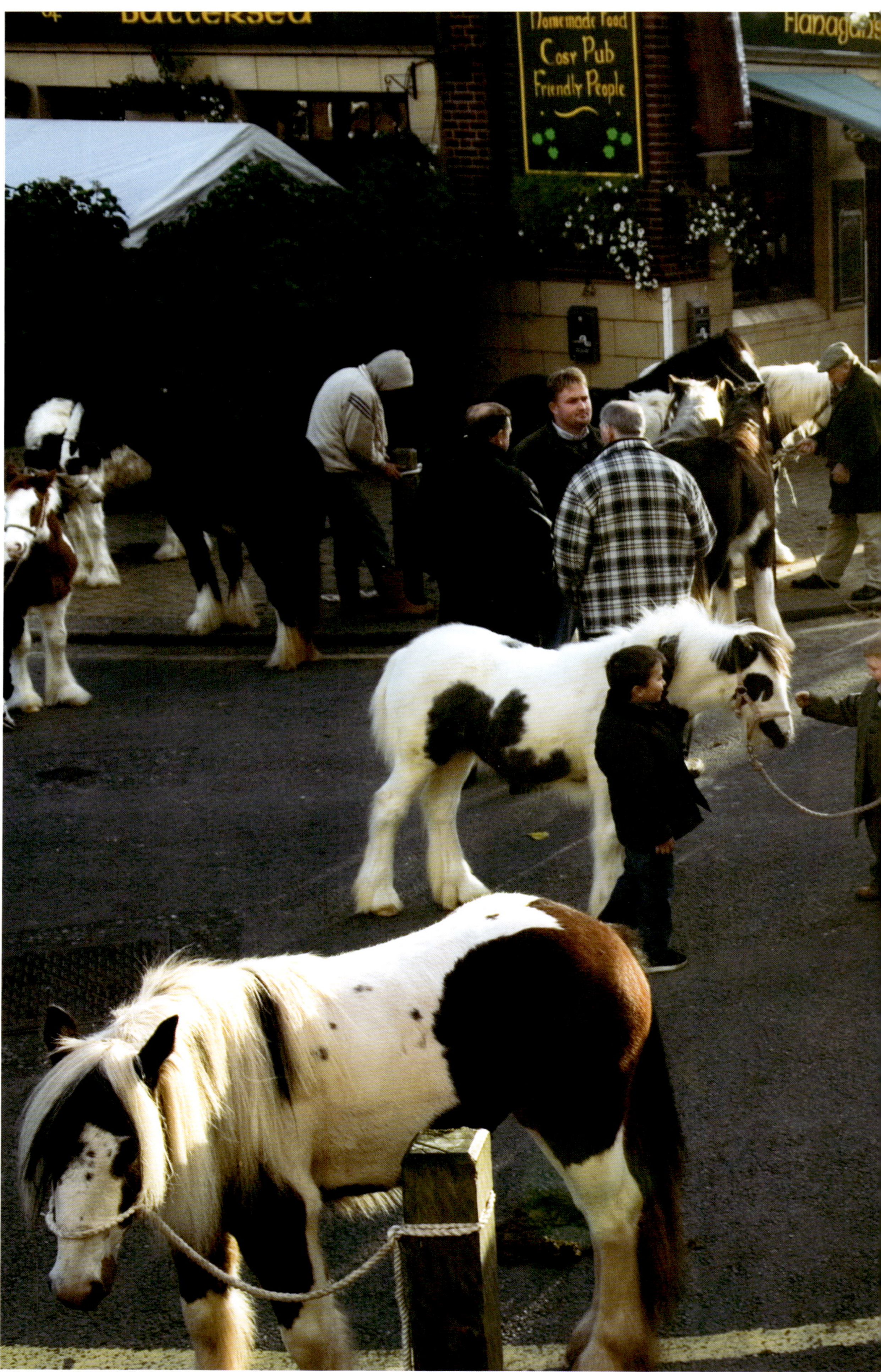

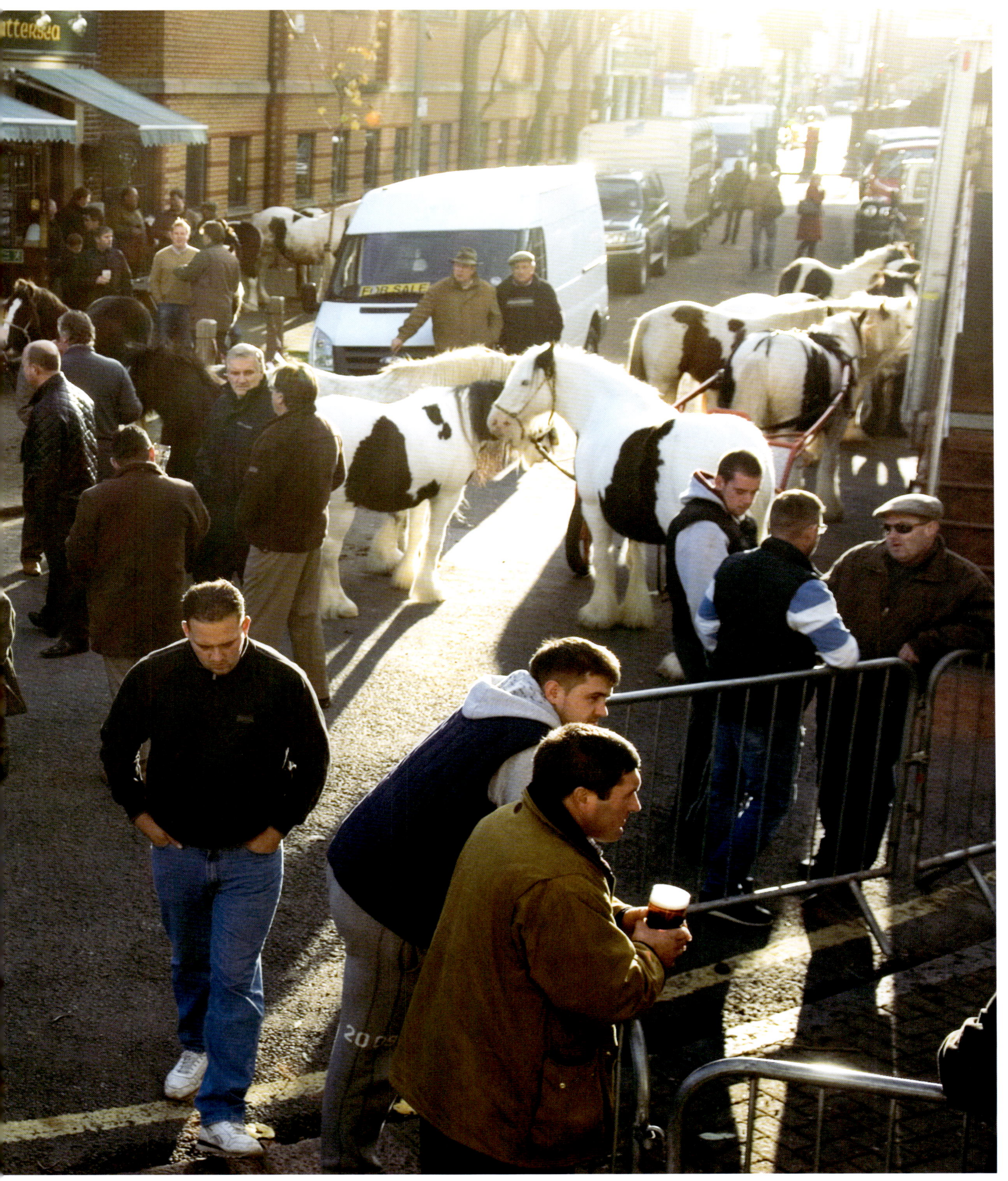
FOR SALE

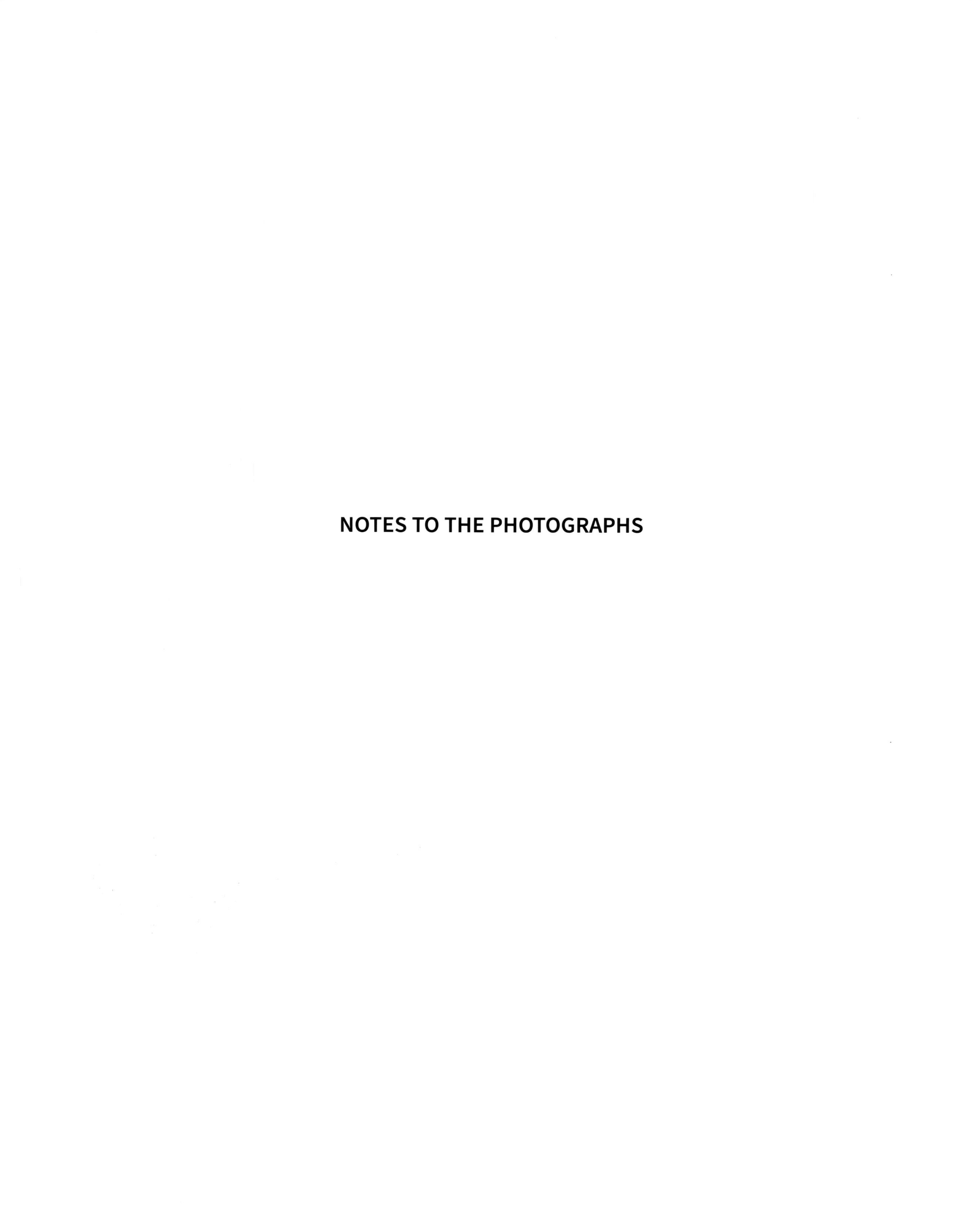

NOTES TO THE PHOTOGRAPHS

KEEPING OPEN AN ANCIENT RIGHT OF WAY

Bucks Green, Sussex
25th December 2022

On Christmas Day each year a horse is ridden through the Fox Inn from the front garden to the back along a bricked path to keep open an ancient right of way. In 2022 Amelia Ward rode Freddy a 13 hand bay, Welsh Section C gelding through the pub for the third year. The pub was originally a mix of buildings separated by a bridleway, which is now inside the pub. Freddy stopped at the bar to greet the bar staff and then went through the back door and into a marque erected for the occasion to the delight of the many locals who were enjoying a pre-Christmas lunchtime drink.

BOARS HEAD CEREMONY

The City of London
9th December 2015

The Worshipful Company of Butchers' Boars Head Ceremony leaves the Pewterers Hall for the annual short walk to the Mansion House. These days, due to Health and Safety rules and regulations, a papier-mâché model of a boar's head is carried in procession and on arrival is presented to the Lord Mayor. A real boar's head has been sent ahead; to be consumed amongst much pomp and ceremony by City dignitaries. The Butchers are one of the oldest of the City's Livery Companies and their records stretch as far back as 975AD. The Boars Head Ceremony can be traced back to 1343 when John Hammond, a grocer, was the City's Lord Mayor. The Butchers of London needed a place to clean and dispose of offal or any 'beast entrails'. A parcel of land was provided and the Butchers were required, 'to pay for the repair and maintain a certain wharf, they and their successors, for ever, rendering yearly to the Mayor of London, at Christmas, a boar's head.' The cost of this annual stipend was to be met from the funds of the Butchers Guild. One of the earliest records to survive in their account books notes, 'Pd. For a boar to my Lord Mayor £1.4.0d.'

WILLIAM ROGERS BEQUEST

Nevern, Pembrokeshire
21st December 2014

The William Rogers bequest of beef and barley takes place on St Thomas' Day, 21st December and marks the feast of St Thomas the Apostle. It was a day that in the past saw the poor of a community asking for money and food, including going from door to door amongst the better off in the parish. Known as going 'a Thomassing' or going 'a gooding', people would seek money and food to help them through Christmas and the winter weeks that followed. William Rogers a native of Nevern was a wealthy businessman who owned a messuage, shop and premises in Kensington High Street, London. In his will dated 1806 amongst other bequests he left £800 of stock, at 3% interest. The dividend was to provide 'good beef and good barley' for the parishioners of Nevern. The Rector of St Brynach's church, the Revd. Neil Llewellyn, reads a short passage from the bible before blessing the brisket of beef to be distributed to eligible pensioners living in the village.

CHOOSING DAY

Brightlingsea, Essex
6th December 2021

Choosing Day takes place at All Saints Church, on the first Monday following St Andrew's Day. The Mayor of Sandwich has a Deputy at Brightlingsea and Choosing Day is when the Mayor's Deputy of the Cinque Port Liberty is elected. The Cinque Ports, in Kent and Sussex, are a confederation formed in the 14th Century to unite those in the front line against possible war with France. Brightlingsea became a 'Limb' to the port at Sandwich, and as such has its own Deputy who is the representative of the Mayor of Sandwich. Freemen of the town; those born there, or who have married into the place, do the choosing. For newcomers there is a fee to pay of eleven pence old money once residential qualification of a year and a day has been attained. Following a short service and speeches, the new Freemen of the Town are elected. Oaths of loyalty are sworn, the new Deputy is installed and the ceremony is over. The Mayor of Sandwich, Paul Graeme, and Sandwich's Town Serjeant, Kevin Cook, who carries the Hog Mace, leave with the Revd. Caroline Beckett for the Liberty Hall Community Centre annual lunch attended by several hundred Freemen, who all applaud each other and the top table guests.

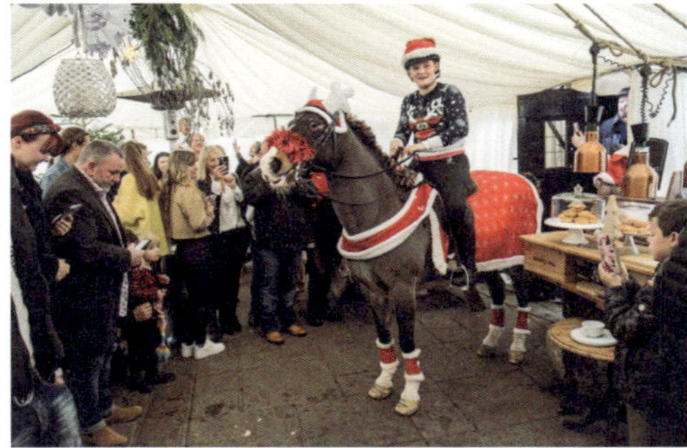

Keeping open an ancient right of way

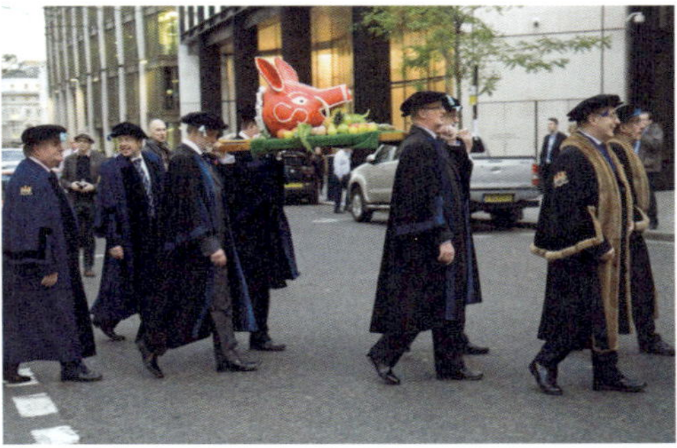

Boars Head ceremony

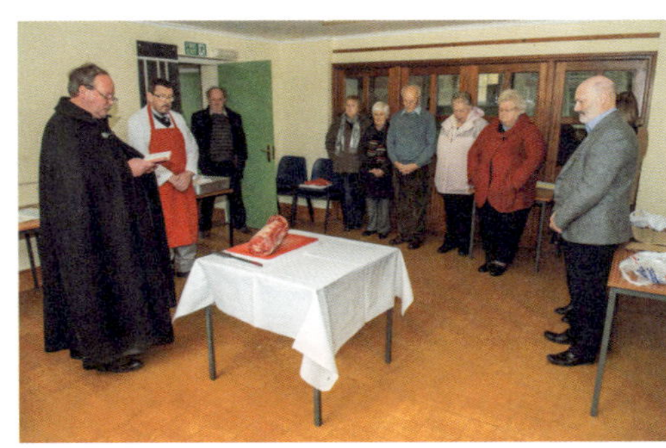

William Rogers bequest

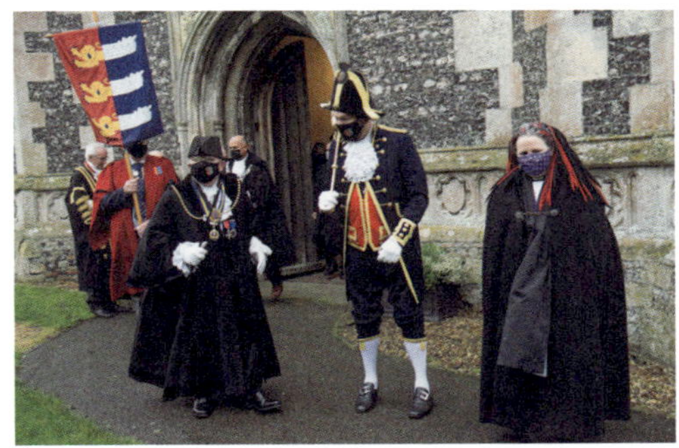

Choosing Day

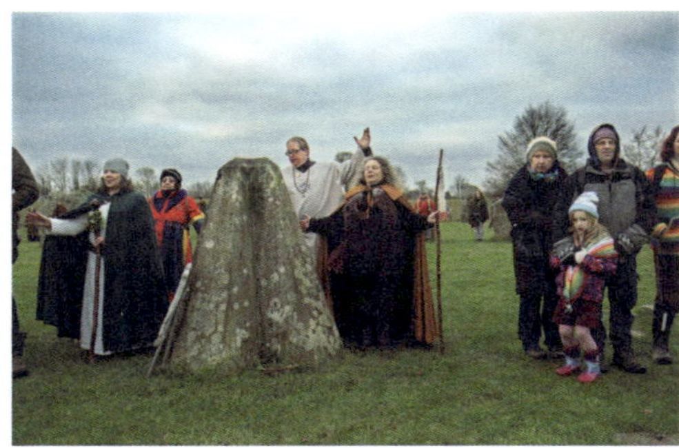

Winter Solstice

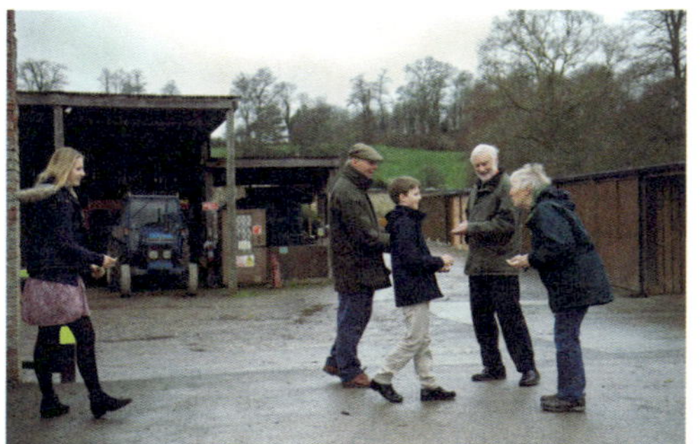

The Penny

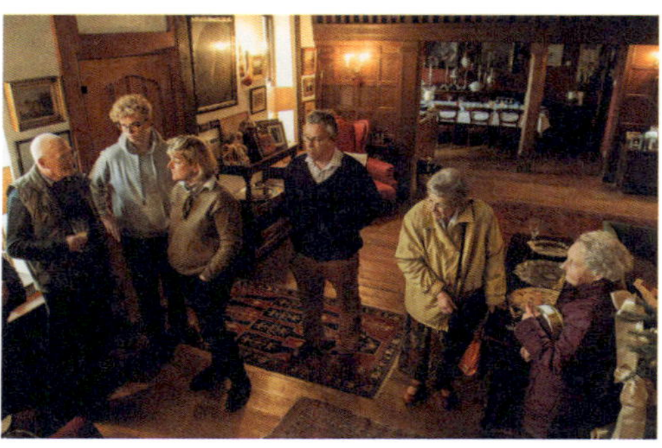

Flour

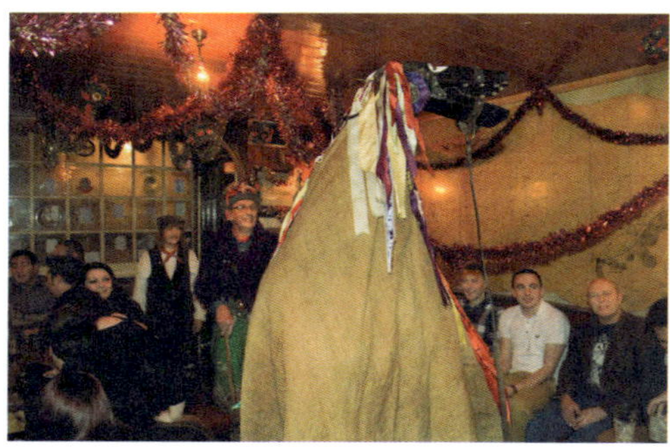

Sangate Hoodeners

WINTER SOLSTICE
Avebury, Wiltshire
21st December 2021

Druids and pagan pilgrims gather to celebrate the winter solstice, a time of death and rebirth, the shortest day of the year and the longest night, when the power of darkness is honoured, and the rising of the sun is celebrated. A loose double circle is formed at The Obelisk; Archdruid Henk Vis leads the small group through the druidic ritual, the cardinal directions are called, East, South, West and North; the elements too, Earth, Air, Fire and Water which are the building blocks of all life. The Avebury complex is one of the largest and most complex of Britain's surviving Neolithic henge monuments; consisting of a massive bank and ditch within which there is a huge stone circle, 1,300 feet in diameter, that contains within it two smaller circles. The Obelisk was the central stone of the Southern Inner Circle and survived, fallen long enough for William Stukeley (1687-1765) to describe it, "… obelisk of this temple is of circular form … a vast bulk, 21 feet long and 8 feet 9 inches in diameter; when standing, higher than the rest."

THE PENNY
Sherborne, Dorset
25th December 2015

The Wingfield Digby family, whose ancestral home is Sherborne Castle, have continually lived on the estate since 1617. Alice, Robby and their father Mr Kenelm Edward Wingfield Digby distribute The Penny annually on Christmas Day to all who attend at the Estate Yard. Since Victorian times with inflation The Penny has now become a newly minted one pound coin, with a 50p and 20p piece sealed within a dated Sherborne Castle Estates commemorative card, "Wishing you a Merry Christmas and a Happy New Year." In 2015 approximately 40 to 50 local residents, both young and old, collected the charitable dole money. Chocolate coins in gold foil are given to the children.

FLOUR
East Hendred, Oxfordshire
21st December 2016

The Flour distribution in 2016 was a tin of biscuits for the first time and was given to qualifying pensioners. For very many years a sack of wheat to mill for flour was distributed on St Thomas' Day; this was then superseded by two bags of flour. The Eyston family decided as not enough pensioners did all their own baking anymore, a tin of biscuits would be more useful. There are 24 eligible pensioners in the village; they were all written to and 13 came to the Great Hall for a Christmas drink and mince pies, which were handed around by Alexandra and Edward Eyston and their son Tom. In 'The Book', Edward records the names of all the pensioners who collected their gift. Hendred House has been continually occupied since 1265, first by the Arches family, then by the Eyston family, who are heirs of the Arches. The Eystons first acquired the property in the mid 15th century and remain lords of the manor to this day.

SANDGATE HOODENERS
Sandgate, Kent
21st December 2012

Hoodening is a tradition peculiar to the Isle of Thanet in Kent, though in recent years the tradition has spread further afield. It was first recorded in the eighteenth century. The traditional midwinter play was performed by groups of farm labourers when work was short and Christmas was approaching. The Hoodeners went around their neighbourhood performing a short humorous sketch, knocking on doors, especially of those more wealthy members of their community, hoping for some largesse. The teams of the Hoodeners varied slightly from village to village and often included a couple of musicians. At Sandgate, the hooden horse was traditionally accompanied by a Leader, the Lad and a Mollie – a man-woman figure who was past her prime. She carried a besom broom and swept the road in front of the hooden horse as it walked from one house to another. David Rivers who played Mollie, seen here wearing a top hat and green dress and carrying a traditional old-fashioned besom broom, kept the tradition alive for many years. The custom now no longer takes place.

SOUL CAKING
Antrobus, Cheshire
2nd November 2012

Soul caking is a traditional folk play once popular in north Cheshire; it can be traced back to the early 1800s. Soul caking or souling takes place in early November. It's believed that more than forty Cheshire villages once performed their own version of this play. The play is now performed on All Souls' Day evening, and again on several weekends in Antrobus and surrounding villages. The term 'soul caking' derives from former days when teams would tour their local territory and perform for wealthy households and receive for their efforts 'soul cakes', a rough type of baked parkin along with some beer. Nowadays they get more of the latter than the former as they tour pubs and clubs in the area. The cast of nine characters include the Letter-in, the Black Prince, King George, the Quack Doctor, Old Mary, Beelzebub, Dairy Doubts, the Driver and Dickie Tatton the wild three-legged horse. Here in the new village hall, Dickie Tatton and his Driver, played by Trevor Collins in Cheshire Hunt livery, entertain a very small group. The play is a traditional mumming hero-combat play, involving a sword fight with the Black Prince being slain, only to be revived by a magic potion administered by the Doctor. Dickie Tatton's head is a real pony or donkey's skull mounted on a pole and is believed to be over 150 years old, with its jaws wired so it can 'snap' its teeth at the audience.

ST NICHOLAS-AT-WADE HOODENERS

St Nicholas-at-Wade, Kent
17th December 2014

The history of the Hoodeners play goes back many centuries; it is performed over several days around the Winter Solstice in East Kent. It involves a hooden horse; a type of hobby-horse with a wooden head on a pole with the operator hidden by a sheet of sack cloth. In the past Hoodeners used to go from house to house in their community and perform plays in return for largesse; nowadays you're more likely to find them touring pubs and fund-raising for charity. Several modern revivals have taken place after the custom almost died out. The play is centred on the theme of death and resurrection, winter and the coming of spring. A new humorous play is written each year in rhyming couplets referencing recent local, national and international events although the setting is based on a ploughing team from the 19th Century. At St Nicholas-at-Wade the traditional cast of characters is: the Boy, played by Simon Gray, the Wagoner in top hat and frock coat played by Peter 'Budgie' Paul. Simon Lane is Dobbin the hooden horse, George, the musician, is Ben Jones. Sam, a farm labourer, is played by Roy Fairbrass and David Gray plays Molly, a man-woman figure. After each performance Christmas carols are sung and a collection is made. In 2014 the Hoodeners raised £1,553.48, which was split between two local charities.

CALEDONIAN FRIENDLY LODGE OF ODDFELLOWS

Newburgh, Fife
31st December 2016

The Caledonian Friendly Lodge of Oddfellows is the last remaining Oddfellows Lodge in Scotland and on New Year's Eve they parade along the town's High Street. Formed in 1827 as a society for working men; tradesmen who carried out unusual or miscellaneous trades – odd fellows. Larger trades such as the Masons, had guilds or syndicates to represent them. Subscriptions were paid monthly or quarterly and benefits paid out to members should they fall on hard times. Many of these groups disappeared with the foundation of the Welfare State. In Newburgh the first Hogmanay torchlight procession was held in 1885 and is now the only surviving parade in Scotland, gathering at 7 pm at The Steeple. Tom Wright, the Apprentice – the last person to join the Lodge – wears a Janiform mask, the All Seeing Eyes that look into the future and remember the past. He leads the torchlight procession on Neddy, a Clydesdale horse riding bareback and facing backwards. Behind are a group of Oddfellows in 21st century masks and fancy dress. The Keeper of the Keys, Neil Barlow and Mark Johnston follow, carrying the Lodge Box containing the Lodge Keys; the symbolic and sacred Tenets of the Oddfellows Lodge. They were granted to Newburgh when it was affiliated to the Caledonian Lodge of Oddfellows in 1827. The highest office in the organisation is held by Graeme Kirk, the Most Noble Grand Oddfellow, he wears a tall conical shaped blue and red crown and red robes and is accompanied by Bob Stewart, the Left Hand Supporter to the Most Noble Grand, they are amongst many other office bearers. The procession of Oddfellows make their way along the High Street and back again stopping three times, once at the nearest point on the walk to the Most Noble Grand Oddfellow's house, where they sing, *For he's a Jolly Good fellow*. Then at the Laing Museum where office bearers receive refreshments and finally at the door of Lodge Lindores 106, the Masons club where the Masons provide further New Years Eve refreshments. Nowadays the Lodge is a charitable organisation that raises money that is distributed to local old people's associations in the community.

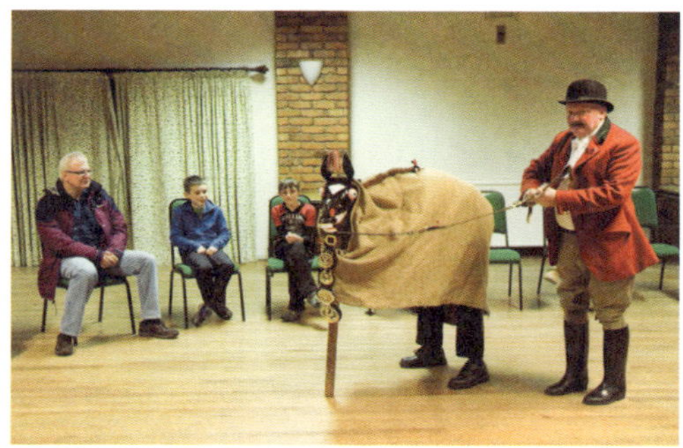

Soul Caking

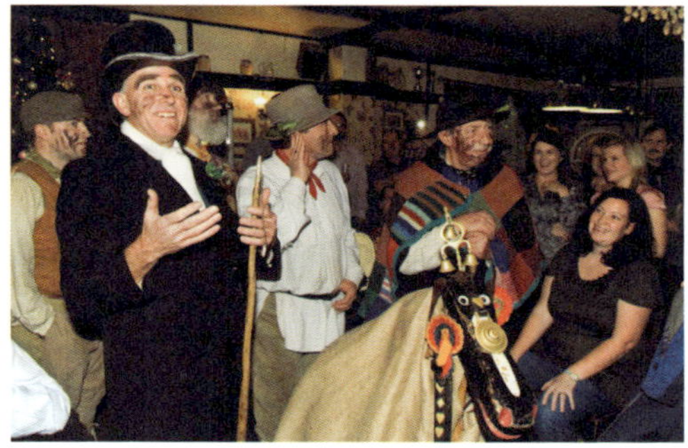

St Nicholas-at-Wade Hoodeners

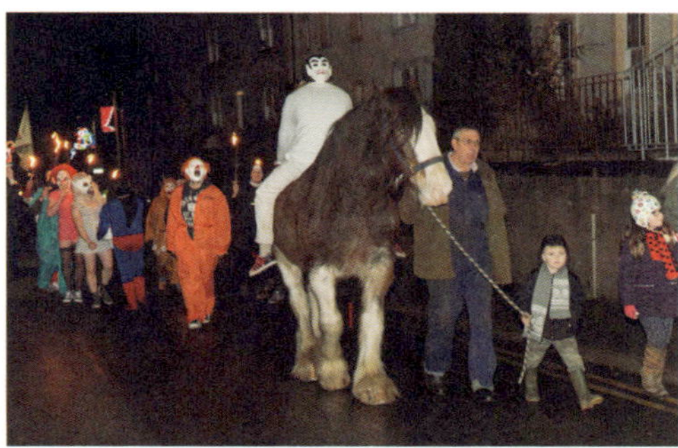

Caledonian Friendly Lodge of Oddfellows

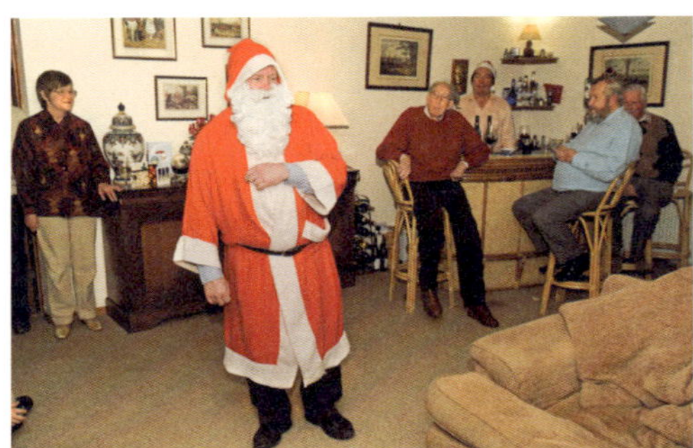
Bampton Mummers

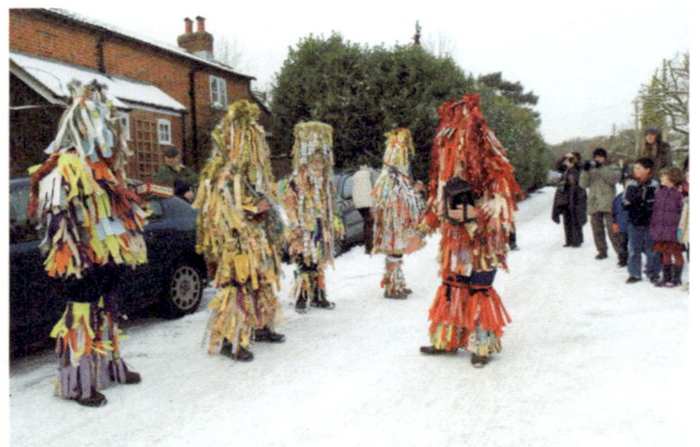
Otterbourne Mummers

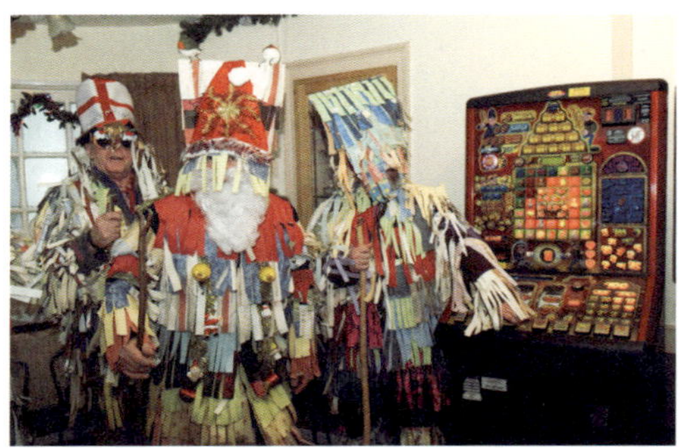
Overton Mummers

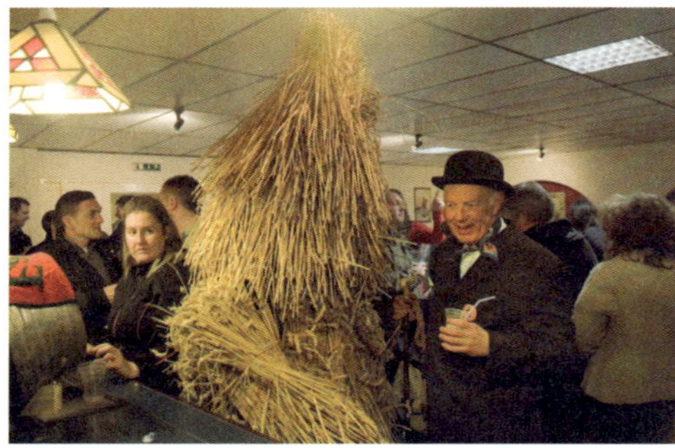
Straw Bear Festival

BAMPTON MUMMERS
Bampton, Oxfordshire
24th December 2008

Mumming plays differed from one village to another and have been popular since the 18th and 19th centuries when cheaply produced chapbooks with the play's script published for the first time became easily available. The Bampton play was revived in 1946 and they now perform in private homes and the village pubs on Christmas Eve. The play is one of death and revival, with much locally themed adlibbing. At Bampton, unlike elsewhere, the play is performed in two acts; death and resurrection occur twice. The characters are: Father Christmas, Saint George the Knight, The Turkish Knight, Doctor Good, Robin Hood, Bold Little John, The Royal Apprucia King, Soldier Bold, Jack Finney and Old Tom the Tinker. The play ends with the actors centre stage singing, "… Christmas has come so welcome us now and give us good cheer, for Christmas comes but once a year."

OTTERBOURNE MUMMERS
Otterbourne, Hampshire
19th December 2010

The Otterbourne Mummers traditional Christmas folk play was always performed on the last Sunday before Christmas. It was revived in 1975 by Paul Marsh whose great uncle, Tom Goodchild, had performed the play in the 1900s, and still remembered all the words when Paul wrote them down in 1972. The five performers look striking in their costumes made with strips of colourful wallpaper that have been sewn onto their undergarments. As in other mummers plays Old Father Christmas introduces the performance, there is then a sword fight symbolising good over evil; King George slays the Turkish Knight, only to be revived with a magic potion by Old Doctor Brown who then '… sends him on his way.' Finally Little Jolly Jack is introduced and topical references are inserted into the script to keep the performance fresh. The mummers finish with a rendition of "We Wish you a Merry Christmas and a Happy New Year … We'd all like a drop of whisky and a glass of good beer." The custom has now lapsed with the last performance being in 2019.

OVERTON MUMMERS
Overton, Hampshire
26th December 2014

The Overton Mummers play follows the traditional Christmas folk play format, one of death and resurrection. Once performed by groups of village labourers over the mid winter period, when work was short and money even shorter. The men would, as other mumming teams did, visit the big house and the wealthier residents in their community, have fun, perform a play and make a collection. The play, regularly performed up until 1939, was revived again for the 1951 Festival of Britain and lapsed once again, before finally being revived in 1971. Nowadays the play is traditionally performed on Boxing Day outside in the village and during the summer at the Sheepfair festival. The cast includes Father Christmas who introduces the play to the audience, King George, Rumour, Bold Slasher, Turkish Knight and the Doctor who administers a magic potion that restores those slain in a sword fight. Twing Twang then appears and another sword fight takes place, this time with Father Christmas. Finally the performance ends with the singing of the carol, *God Rest Ye Merry Gentleman*. A collection is made for the St Michaels Hospice, a local charity.

STRAW BEAR FESTIVAL
Whittlesea, Cambridgeshire
12th January 2008

The Straw Bear festival used to takes place on the Tuesday following Plough Monday – the first Monday after Twelfth Night – the traditional start of the English agricultural year. Over mid winter work would have been short at the start of the agricultural year, and those men still without work dressed up, blackened their faces to disguise themselves and pulled a plough around their community hoping for a little sustenance and, or, money. In 1882 the local newspaper reported that, "... he (the Straw Bear) was then taken around the town to entertain by his frantic and clumsy gestures the good folk who had on the previous day subscribed to the rustics, a spread of beer, tobacco and beef." The custom lapsed during the late 19th century, the Straw Bear appearing once more in 1909. Revived in 1980, the festival has expanded over the years. These days there is a concert on the Friday night, and on the Saturday folk festival acts from all over Britain perform around the town. However the Straw Bear appears only during the Saturday before the Sunday Bear Burning ceremony.

RIPON SWORD DANCE PLAY

Ripon, North Yorkshire
26th December 2008

Like other mummers Christmas plays, the theme is death then revival and the celebration of good over evil. The Ripon Sword Dance Play is performed on Boxing Day, starting at about 10 am in the Market Place. During the morning the Sword Dance Mummers perform to very few. At some performances there is no one there to watch at all, while at some pitches a single householder might stand in a doorway and watch. Nevertheless the show goes on. In the evening, starting at The Magdalens, the group perform at many of the pubs and clubs in the town, where they are warmly and noisily received. In 2008 there were just four performers St. George played by Geoff Hyde, Doctor & Beelzebub by Paul Freeman, Slasher & Little Wit by Simon McCudden and the Fool played by Jim Coulson. For many years members of the Hardcastle family performed the play, which was passed down from one generation to the next. That succession has now died out; there are now no direct descendants taking part.

MARI LWYD

Llangynwyd, Bridgend, Glamorgan
31st December 2012

The Mari Lwyd – the Grey Mare – is a pagan midwinter wassailing custom, traditional to South Wales. In the past the Mari Lwyd, a horse's skull mounted on a pole, toured the parish visiting different households. Doors were locked and a verse singing 'competition' took place between those inside the house and the Marie Lwyd team outside. When eventually the householders were unable to sing another verse, the Mari Lwyd was let it. These days the Mari Lwyd visits the local pubs and clubs in the Llynfi Valley conferring good luck for the coming year. Gwyn Evans, the ostler, keeps the tradition alive, passed down from his father Cynwyd. He wears a top hat and sings the Mari Lwyd song to gain entry to The Railway Inn that's crowded with New Year's Eve customers. Mike Smith carries the horse under a white sheet decorated with ribbons; his two attendants with collecting buckets are Graham Richards and Andrew John. In 2012 over £450 was collected for Air Ambulance Wales.

BODMIN WASSAILERS

Bodmin, Cornwall
6th January 2016

The Bodmin Wassailers gather at the Town Hall on Old New Year's Day. The first recorded evidence of the Bodmin Wassailers is in the will of Nicholas Sprey the Town Clerk dated 1624. He left 13 shillings 4 pence to provide an annual Wassailing Cup. The present Town Clerk, Stephen Facer, entertains the Bodmin Wassailers at his personal expense, £35.00, in the Mayor's Parlour. Wassailing songs are sung, and a toast is made to Nicholas Sprey. The Wassailers then walk around the town, often unannounced, visiting shops, pubs and the occasional private home where they sing wassailing songs and spread good tidings for the coming year. In 2016 the Wassailers raised £450 that was split between Bodmin Age Concern and Bodmin Hospital League of Friends.

BURNING THE ASHEN FAGGOT

Laymore, Dorset
6th January 2020

Once common in many West Country villages, on Old New Year's Eve, the custom of Burning the Ashen Faggot has now been largely forgotten. At the Squirrel Inn, local farmer Mike Turner, who makes the Ashen Faggot, revived the tradition about 50 years ago. Approximately 15 feet long the Ashen Faggot is bound into twelve sections with green lengths of hazel or 'beams' that hold it together, one section representing each day after Christmas. As a beam bursts into flame everyone is encouraged to 'sup up'. Two charred pieces from the previous year's Ashen Faggot are given to the youngest person in the pub, in 2020 that was 17 year-old bar girl Katie Winkler and the oldest Eddie Holman, a local who was 77 years old. They light the new Ashen Faggot with those remnants, as a symbolic 'everlasting flame'. The Ashen Faggot takes approximately five hours to be consumed pushed into the hearth from time to time by Mike Turner who keeps a watchful eye on it. According to legend a woman straddling the Ashen Faggot will fall pregnant before the following New Year.

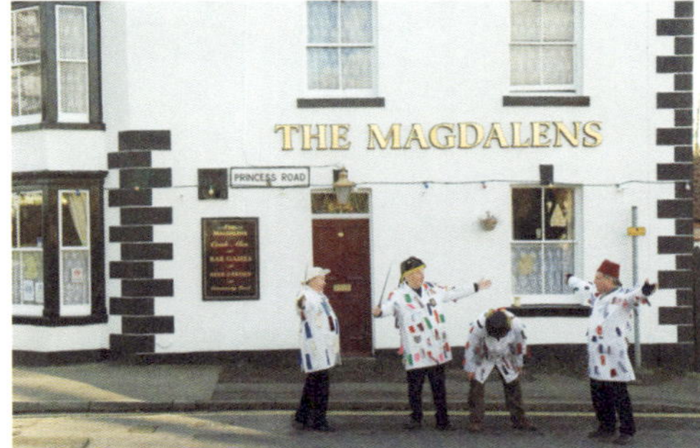

Ripon Sword Dance Play

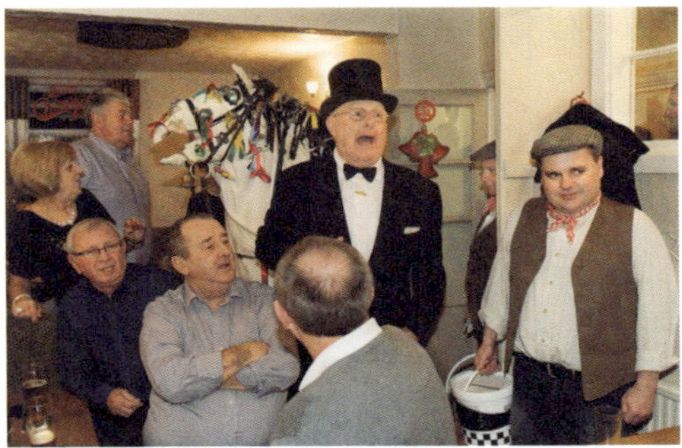
Mari Lwyd

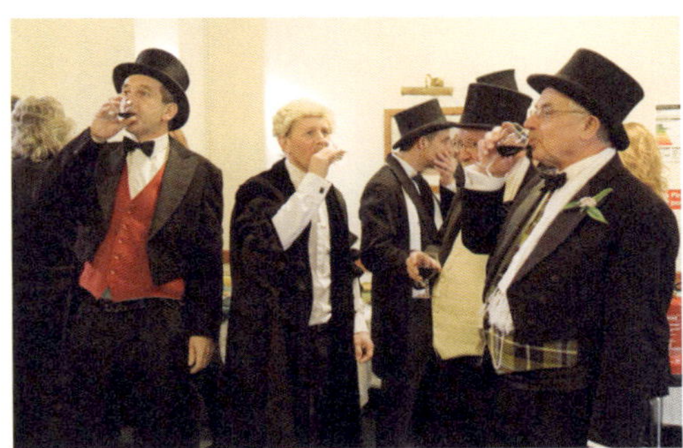
Bodmin Wassailers

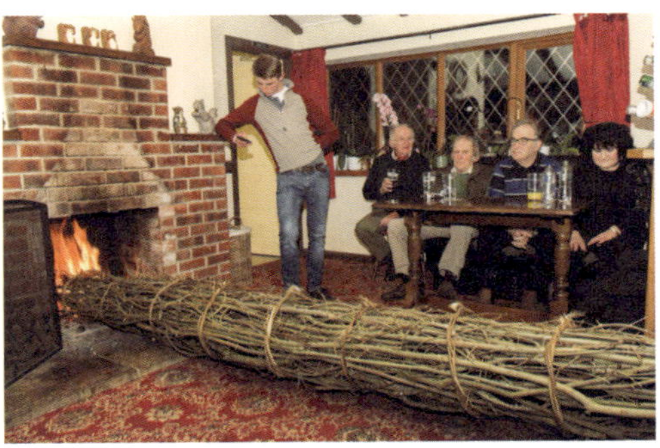
Burning the Ashen Faggot

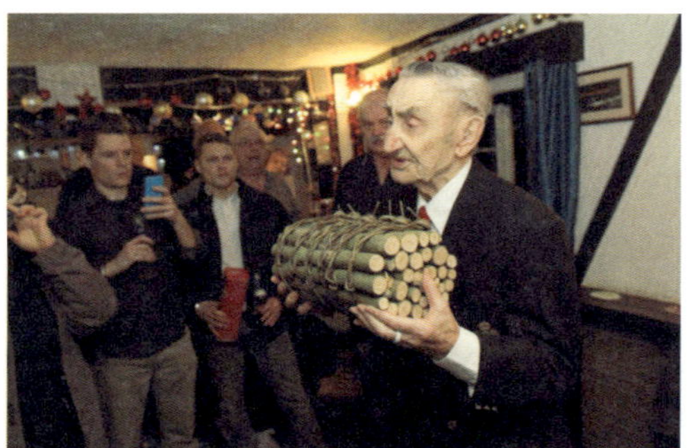

Wassailing

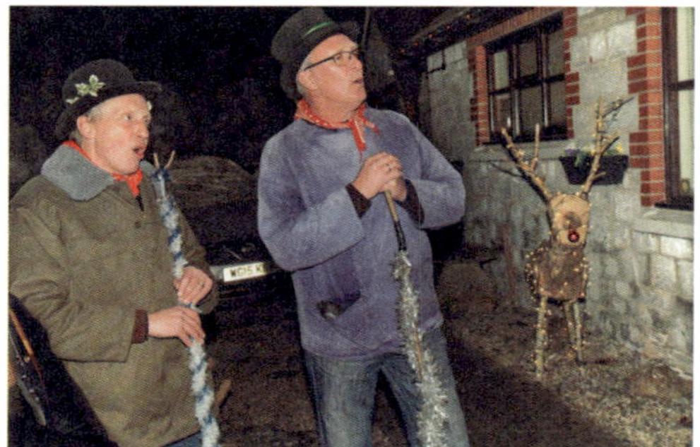

Drayton Wassail

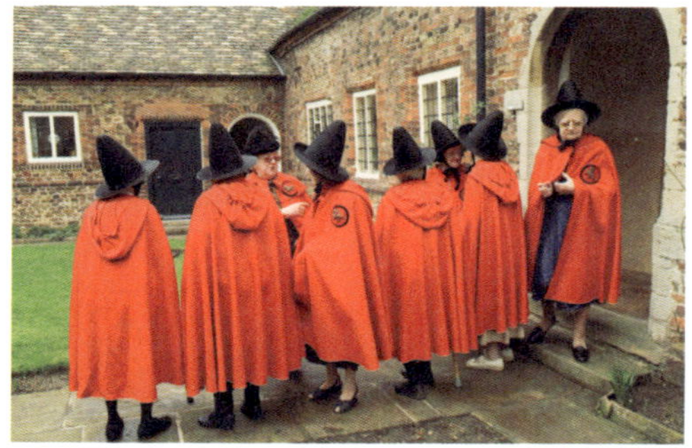

Old Ladies of Castle Rising

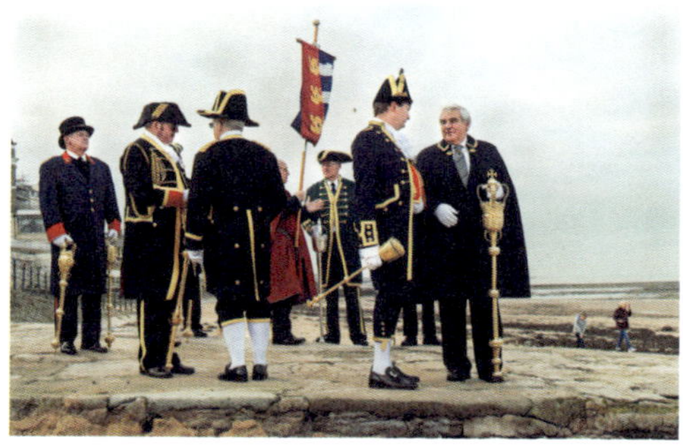

Blessing of the Sea

WASSAILING

Curry Rivel, Somerset
5th January 2016

Anglo-Saxon tradition dictated that at the beginning of each year, the lord of the manor would greet those assembled with the toast, 'waes hael', meaning 'be well' or 'be in good health', to which his followers would reply 'drink hael', or 'drink well'. From this, a tradition of house wassailing evolved where groups of men would go from home to home wassailing; bringing good cheer, wishing the householders a happy new year. In return they would be invited in for some sustenance. Bill Richards, 91 years old, is the senior Wassailer and can trace back his family's wassailing involvement in the village over 150 years. He leads the group of Wassailers around the village of Curry Rivel on Old New Year's Eve, singing the village traditional wassailing song, and bidding the house holders, "... and a happy New Year," before being invited in for refreshments. Paul Willey, Bill Richards and Garry 'Budgie' Eagle lead the singing by a group of about ten local men. In 2016, £271 was collected for St Margaret's Hospice. In the West Country, part of the Wassailing tradition was the burning of an Ashen Faggot or Ashten Fagot, which is similar to a Christmas Yule Log, from which the modern chocolate ones derive. The sticks are ash and the 'bonds' are made of willow withies tied in a willow rose knot. Traditionally the oldest person in the room places the Ashen Faggot onto the fire. Bill Richards makes a short speech before placing it onto the fire in the King William IV pub. In the past at Curry Rivel as each 'bond' burst, a toast would be drunk. Until recently the brewery provided a barrel of cider and beer for the Wassailers, but alas no longer.

DRAYTON WASSAIL

Drayton, Somerset
5th January 2017

In Anglo Saxon Britain the salutation "waes hael" meant 'be in good heath.' There has been a house visiting wassail tradition in Drayton for at least 250 years and most probably for much longer. In the past the Wassailers were working men in the village that would have had little work or none at all around Christmas time. On Old Christmas Eve they went from house to house around the village calling on the gentry and the better off collecting gifts of food and a little money that they then shared out amongst themselves. These days, according to tradition, the Wassailers, '... will not knock at the front door and it should not be opened until they sing the line, "Oh maid, maid, maid with your silver headed pin, pray open the door and let us in." Gathering outside to welcome the Wassailers, leaving windows open and your front door ajar is now acceptable. A small bite to eat, a drink or two is rarely refused.' The Wassail party visit about ten houses in the village, finishing up at the Drayton Crown. The Drayton wassailing carol was collected by Cecil Sharp in 1903 (an English collector of folk songs and dances) when visiting the village and has been handed down from one generation to another. Donations are collected that go towards good causes in the village.

OLD LADIES OF CASTLE RISING

Castle Rising, Norfolk
24th February 2007

The Almshouses,The Hospital of the Holy and Undivided Trinity, in Castle Rising was founded by Henry Howard, Earl of Northampton and built between 1609 and 1614. Henry Howard's will established a charity which provided sheltered accommodation for thirteen poor spinsters or widows from Castle Rising Parish, aged 50 or over, one of whom was to be their governess. On Founders Day each year the residents wear their traditional scarlet cloaks and pointed black hats to attend a memorial service in the 'Hospital' chapel. Gathering prior to the service in the central courtyard the governess checks that everyone looks in order.

BLESSING OF THE SEA

Margate, Kent
8th January 2017

In the Greek Orthodox Church's annual calendar, The Blessing of the Sea takes place on Epiphany, 6th January, marking the baptism of Jesus Christ in the River Jordan. The celebration is organised by the local Greek Orthodox Church whose Archbishop leads the devotions that begin at the church of St Michael the Archangel. After a short service a procession of many dignitaries in full regalia, both religious and civic, walk to the Marine Sands, where prayers and blessings are said and a white dove, a symbol of peace, is released. A small wooden cross is thrown into the sea; retrieved and given, in 2017, to Gregorios Theocharous the Greek Orthodox Archbishop of Thyateira and Great Britain, seen here as he embraces Trevor Willmott, the Bishop of Dover. The Very Revd.

Archimandrite Vissarion Kokliotis, Mr Michael Papadopoulos, president of Margate's Greek Community and Cllr. Robin Edwards the Mayor of Margate pause for a moment's reflection. The celebrations have been taking place in Margate since the 1960s. Margate was chosen for this celebration because of the large community of Greek Cypriots living in the town.

SHROVE TUESDAY FOOTBALL

Atherstone, Warwickshire
5th February 2008

This medieval football game has been played since at least 1199 between teams from Warwickshire and Leicestershire. According to legend the 'Match of Gold' was originally a bag of gold and the Warwickshire team won. Other theories speculate that the ball represents the head of a man executed in medieval times that was thrown to the baying crowd. These days the game often gets rough and there have been several attempts to end the tradition. There are few rules, two being that the game must be played in Long Street, the main street through the town and that no one is to be killed. Shops and buildings are boarded up; some local schools give their children the day off. The game starts at 3pm, the ball being thrown down from an upstairs window at the 'Connie', the Atherstone Conservative Club by a local celebrity. The winner is the person who is holding the oversized ball when the whistle blows at 5pm. There is a lot of very rough play as groups of players representing local pubs compete for possession of the giant ball over the two hours. Once they have it, that 'team' then tries to retain 'ownership' forming a huddle around the ball until the whistle blows.

WIDOWS BUN

Bromley-by-Bow, London
23rd March 2008

The Widows Bun celebration takes place annually on Good Friday at the Widows Son Inn. The pub was built in 1848 on the site of an old widow's cottage; according to legend a widow's son went to sea and drowned. But he had written to his mother to say he would be home for Easter and that he looked forward to one of her hot cross buns. She never gave up hope, and every year baked a bun, saving it for his return. After her death a large collection of hot cross buns was found in a net hanging from a rafter in her cottage. An apocryphal story; during the 18th and 19th century 'Good Friday bread', bread baked on Good Friday was thought to have medicinal properties, hardened over the months or years it would be grated into food to help digestive or bowel problems. The Inn known locally as the Bun House has continued with the tradition of a sailor from the Royal Navy placing a new bun in the net hanging above the bar each year. There was disco dancing, karaoke and a free feast for the locals after the ceremony in 2008.

HERCULES CLAY PENNY LOAF DAY

Newark-on-Trent, Nottinghamshire
7th March 2015

Hercules Clay was a wealthy cloth merchant and a former Newark businessman who in 1643 was Royalist Mayor of the town during the English Civil War. For three nights in a row he dreamt his house would be bombed in an attack by the besieging Parliamentary forces. He took this as an omen, moving his family out just before the house was indeed damaged by a mortar shell fired from Beacon Hill, intended for the Royalist HQ. He died in 1645. In his will he left two legacies, one to provide for an annual sermon with the 'Corporation to be in attendance', in which the preacher was to 'exhort the people not to set their affections on things of this world but by their good works to lay hold on eternal life', and another to provide Penny Loaves to be distributed to the poor of Newark. Today local dignitaries walk in procession from the Town Hall to St Mary Magdalene Church behind a white gloved local sea scout who carries Clay's bible, which is placed on the altar. Twelve Penny Loaves, along with other donations, are given to the local food bank. Afterwards, back at the Town Hall, the Penny Loaf reception is held for the Corporation and local dignitaries.

LANE SETTING GRAZING RIGHTS

Ratcliffe Culey, Leicestershire
31st March 2016

The Lane Setting Grazing Rights in Ratcliffe Culey have been auctioned annually since 1786, 20 years after the Enclosure Act. The auction takes place at the Gate Inn on the first Thursday after Easter. Following the auction those present, mainly local farmers, traditionally sing the once hugely popular 1903 musical hall song *Little Yellow Bird*, also known as *Goodbye, Little Yellow Bird*. The song is a sentimental tale of the decision to choose freedom over love and is considered a commentary on the social classes in Britain of the time. Afterwards a buffet supper is

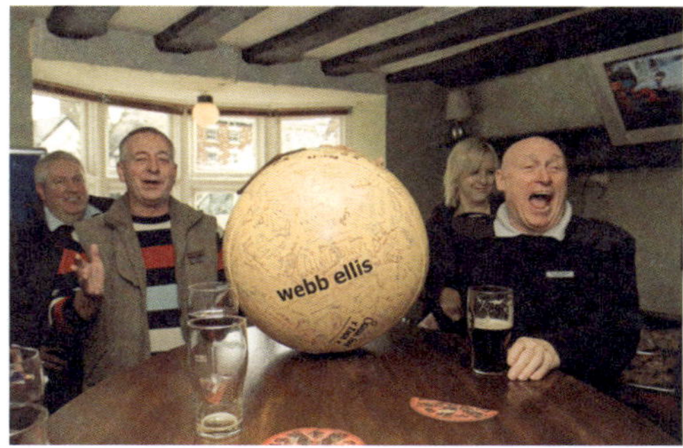

Shrove Tuesday Football

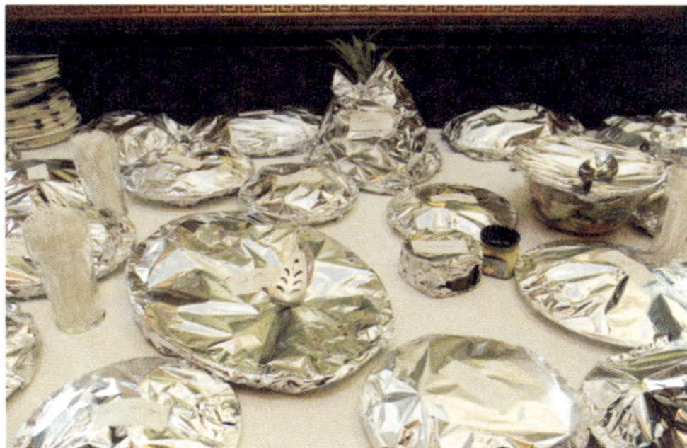
Widow's Bun

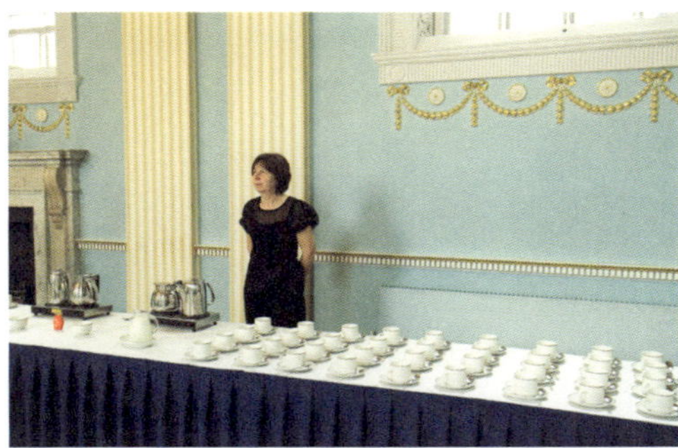
Hercules Clay Penny Loaf Day

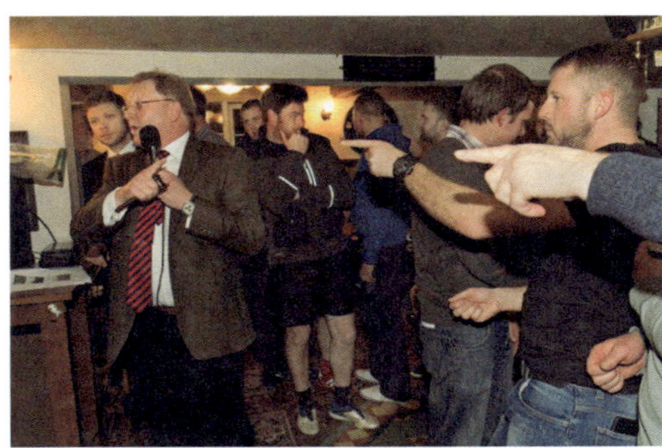
Lane Setting Grazing Rights

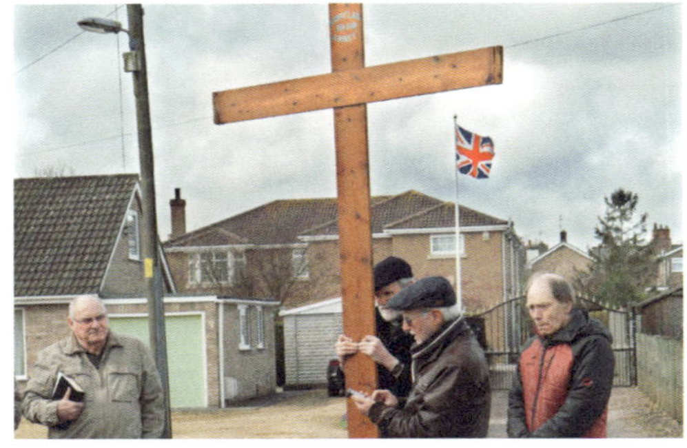
Good Friday Walk Of Witness

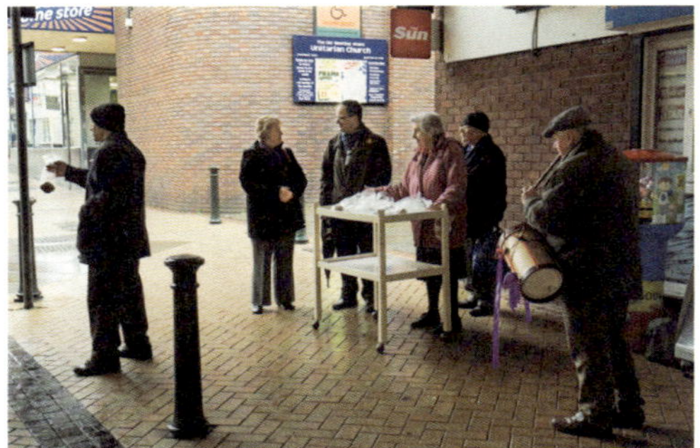
Mary Mallatratt Hot Cross Bun Legacy

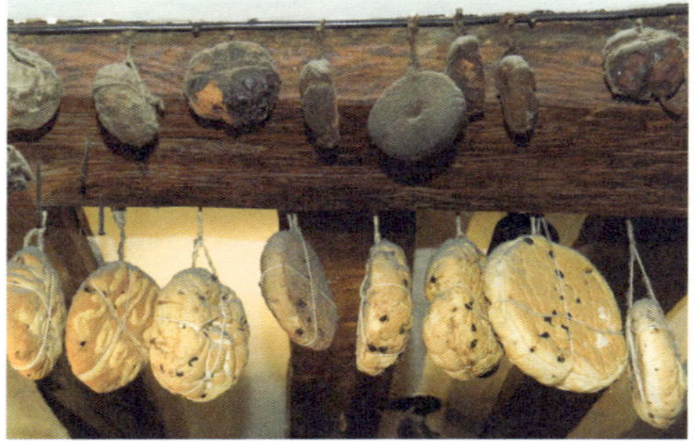
Good Friday Hot Cross Buns

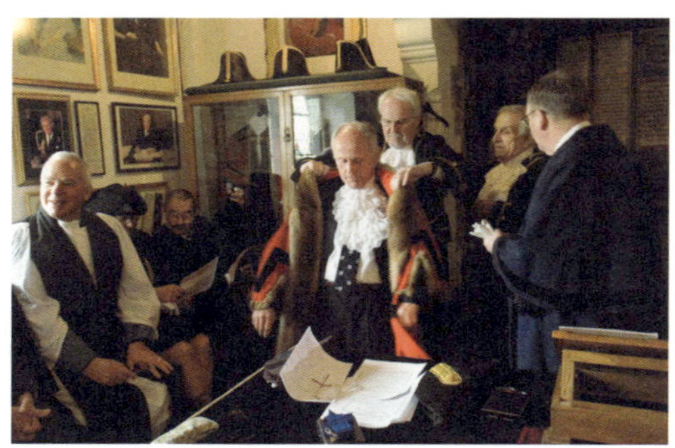
Mayoring Ceremony

served. In 2016 over £525 was made from the auction, those funds going to the Parish Council. The auctioneer was Keith Parsley assisted by son James.

GOOD FRIDAY WALK OF WITNESS

Crowland, Lincolnshire
30th March 2018

The Good Friday Walk of Witness is an annual interdenominational service that takes place around the world. It sees Christians of different denominations imitate the journey that Jesus Christ took carrying his cross through the streets of Jerusalem. In Crowland the walk starts at the Abbey and ends at Trinity Bridge. The Walk of Witness was sponsored by Christians Together in Crowland and led by Revd. Charles Brown who was the Priest-in-charge and Mick Goodman from the Methodist Chapel, along with Father Jim Burke from the Roman Catholic community in Spalding.

MARY MALLATRATT HOT CROSS BUN LEGACY

Mansfield, Nottinghamshire
2nd April 2015

The Mary Mallatratt Hot Cross Bun legacy takes place on Good Friday. Unitarian Church members distribute 48 hot cross buns to children in the Four Seasons shopping centre around the corner from their church. These are now distributed in clear plastic bags as required by Heath and Safety standards. After the death of her 7 month old son from brain damage in 1876, Mary became increasingly involved with the affairs of the Unitarian Church Meeting House. In her will of 1894 she bequeathed monies for schoolbooks for the Meeting House and for a stained glass window. She also left £100 to the trustees to provide buns annually on Good Friday.

GOOD FRIDAY HOT CROSS BUNS

Horndon on the Hill, Essex
25th March 2016

In 1906 Jack Turnell took over the 15th century pubic house, the Bell Inn, on Good Friday and hung a celebratory Hot Cross Bun from a ceiling rafter to mark the occasion. A new hot cross has been added each year since. During the Second World War a concrete bun was hung due to food rationing. These days a prominent local from the village is asked to hang the bun. In 2016 that was Mr McNally. Afterwards the Head Chef, Stuart Fay, and his children served Hot Cross Buns to all the pub's customers.

MAYORING CEREMONY

Winchelsea, East Sussex
5th April 2015

Winchelsea, is one of seven Cinque Ports, the name is Old French, meaning 'five harbours', an alliance of Sussex and Kent ports that was formed in Saxon times. Its primary objective was to provide ships and men to the Crown in times of war, up to 56 ships and men for 15 days, at any time of the year. Winchelsea joined those 'five harbours' in 1190. King Edward I, in about 1292, granted the town the right to have a Mayor and Corporation. Records of the Mayors exist from 1295. The Mayoring Ceremony now takes place annually on Easter Monday and since 1665 has been held in the Upper Court Hall. In 2015 Dr John Spencer became the newly elected Mayor chosen from amongst the Freemen, along with twelve Jurats of the Town, who are assisted by their Town Clerk, Chamberlain and Sergeant-at-Mace. The ceremony recognises the continuing existence of one of the last surviving unreformed Corporations of England and Wales. This is thanks to a former Mayor, Frederick Inderwick, who was also a member of the House of Commons. and able to persuade his colleagues that to strip Winchelsea Corporation of its powers would make it impossible for the town to remain a head port of the Confederation of the Cinque Ports; they agreed to exclude Winchelsea from the Municipal Corporations Act of 1833, established to look at abuses in local government. The Corporation's role is now largely ceremonial, though there are responsibilities for the on-going care and maintenance of the main listed ancient monuments in the town and of Winchelsea museum. Following the ceremony guests attend the Mayor's Reception, a traditional lunch in the New Hall.

THE GREAT BARMOTE COURT

Wirksworth, Derbyshire
15th April 2015

The Great Barmote Court takes place in the Moot Hall. It exists to uphold the laws relating to lead mining in the Derbyshire ore field, laws which have existed in one form or another for the past 13 centuries. Prior to the court sitting a bread, beer and cheese lunch is served. The Grand Jury is formed of twelve members resident within the jurisdiction of the Court in the High Peak or working within Wirksworth. They sit before a miners' standard dish made in the reign of Henry VIII and originally used for testing the miners' wooden dishes against the regulation model. The main duties of the Steward are ceremonial but not exclusively, the courts' jurisdiction still exists, and in 2013 the Low Peak Barmote Court was called upon to rule on lead mining rights in a cavern in Castleton, Derbyshire.

IDDESLEIGH MEN'S FRIENDLY SOCIETY

Iddesleigh, Devon
2nd May 2022

The Iddesleigh Men's Friendly Society was founded on 20th August 1838 as a means of providing sick pay and funeral benefits for its members. The Society's Club Day is now held annually on the early May Bank Holiday Monday. The day starts with the ringing of the church bells, followed by a roll call held outside the Duke of York Inn, then a march through the village behind the society's banner to St James' Church, where a service takes place conducted by the Revd. Susan Oldham. Afterwards it's back to the pub; which is open all day. As 12.30 approaches society members line up behind the Hatherleigh Silver Band, plates of hot mashed potatoes are carried at the front of the procession to the Northcote village hall for the annual Club Day Feast. Ham salad, and hot mashed potatoes are washed down with copious jugs of locally brewed cider, beer and wine. There is a raffle, speeches and finally the 'day's business'. These days the annual subscription of £25 covers a death benefit of £800 paid out to full members who have paid into the mutual fund since they were about 45 years of age. In addition there is a £3 per week sickness benefit, but it has not been claimed for a very long time. Back at the Duke of York Inn, the Hatherleigh Silver Band entertain, there are more raffles and prizes, and in the evening a pub band.

ASCENSION DAY CAROL

Cambridge, Cambridgeshire
9th May 2013

On Ascension Day the St John's College choir, made up of boys from the St John's College School (the choir school) and 'Gentlemen' from the University student body, sing the Ascension Day Carol at 12 noon from the top of the College Chapel, the tallest building in Cambridge. This tradition started in 1902 after a discussion between Cyril Rootham the college organist and Sir Joseph Larmor, a Fellow at the College. Larmor was insistent that a choir would not be heard in the College's First Court, if they were to sing from the top of the College Chapel. Rootham decided that Ascension Day, which celebrates the Christian belief in the Ascension of Jesus into Heaven 40 days after his resurrection at Easter, would be the perfect time to see who was correct. So without telling anyone he ascended the 163 feet high tower along with the choir and at 12 noon they sang an Ascension Day motet. Rootham was delighted to prove Larmor wrong when he was seen to open his ground floor window to check where the music was coming from. A small crowd had gathered, the singing proved hugely popular and has been repeated every year since.

SAINT GEORGE'S DAY

Dartford, Kent
23rd April 2019

Saint George's Day is the feast day of Saint George the patron Saint of England. It is celebrated on 23rd April, believed to be the date of his death in AD 303 by beheading in Palestine; ordered by Roman Emperor Diocletian for refusing to renounce his Christian faith. Born in Cappadocia – now Turkey – in AD 270, over time he became an early Christian martyr. George became known in England during the 7th-8th centuries and was later venerated as a warrior saint, a crusader Knight (1189-1192), often depicted as a dragon-slayer clad in chain mail armour and mounted on a rearing horse. He had become idealised for his valour and selflessness in battle, but it was Henry V who invoked George as England's patron in 1415 – after the battle of Agincourt. England's flag, a red cross on a white background had been introduced as part of the uniform of English soldiers by Edward I (1272-1307) so his men would be recognised in battle. Edward I was to make this red cross a symbol of England. Though not a national holiday, many towns and villages celebrate Saint George's Day, with parades, flag waving and an opportunity to be proud and English. In the Saint George's Day parade through the Priory shopping centre Councillor Mayor David Mote, Saint George and town hall dignitaries promote Dartford and being English. Sitting in their coin-operated ladybird Car Kiddie Ride, and looking surprised, the cartoon characters are the fairy Princess Holly and her best friend Ben Elf from the magical Kingdom of Elves and Fairies, a pre-school animated television series.

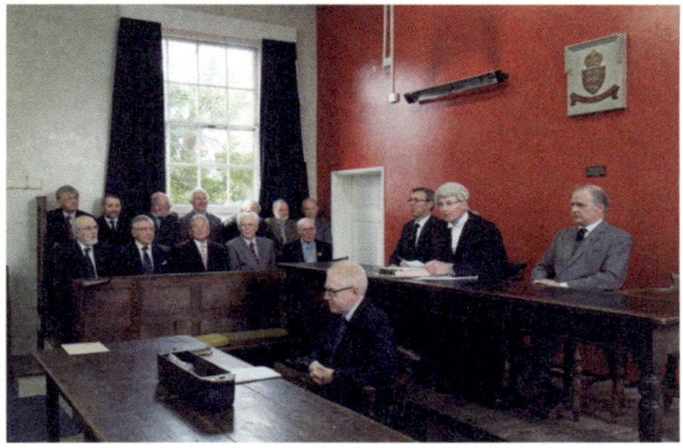
The Great Barmote Court

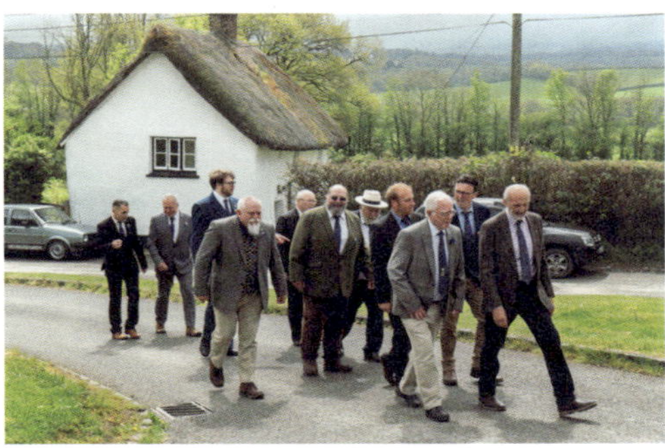
Iddesleigh Men's Friendly Society

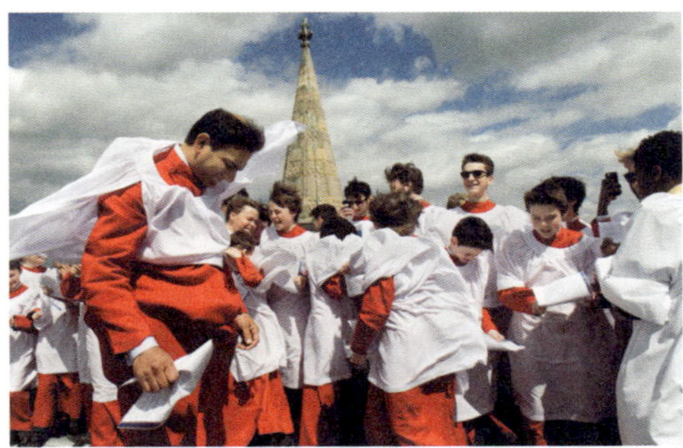
Ascension Day Carol

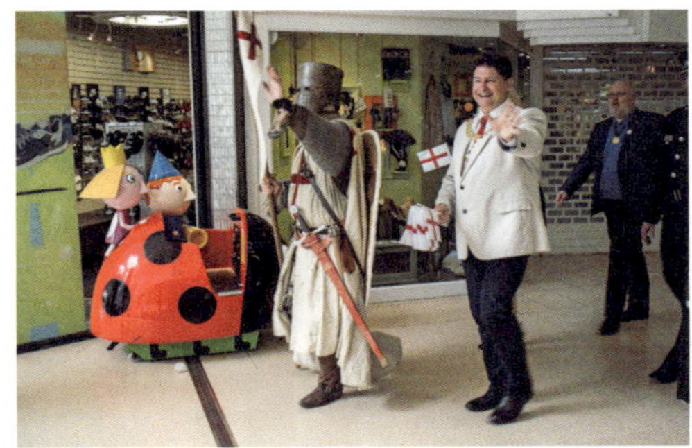
Saint George's Day

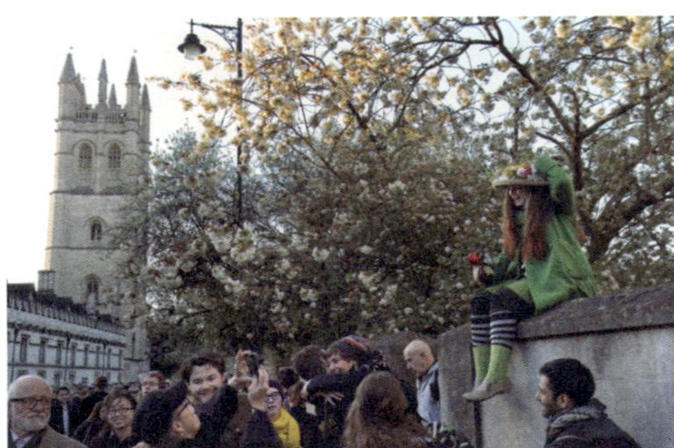
May Day

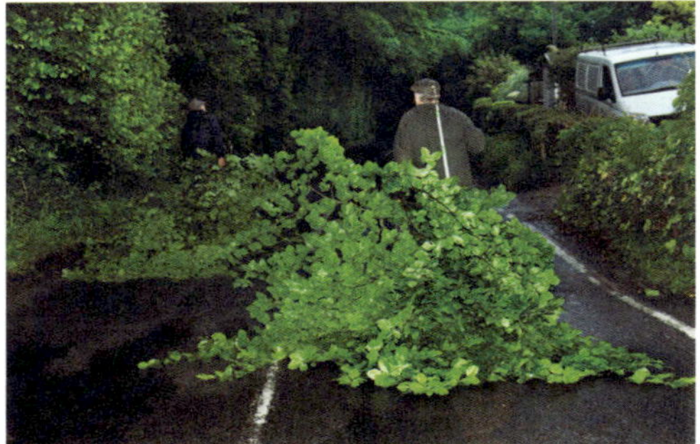
The Harting Old Club

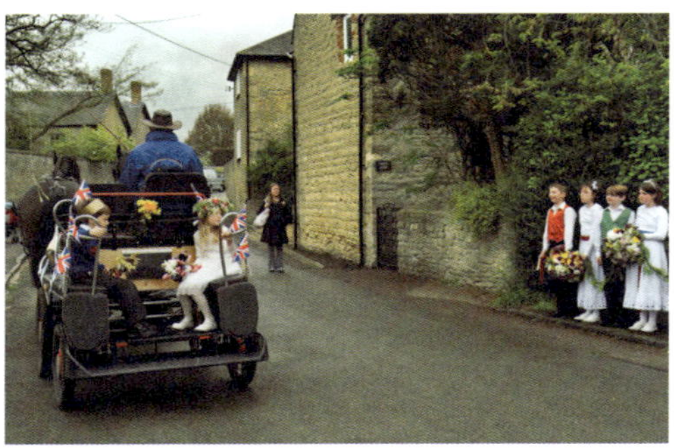
Garland Day

MAY DAY
Oxford, Oxfordshire
1st May 2013

The May Day tradition, the celebration of spring with the singing from the top of Magdalen College Great Tower stretches back over 500 years. The event now starts at 6am with Magdalen College Choir welcoming the rising sun by singing a variety of suitable madrigals and the Latin, *Hymnus Eucharisticus* composed in the 17th century by a Fellow of Magdalen College. It has been sung every year ever since. The Choir is made up of choristers who are part of the College Foundation and attend Magdalen College School, and Academical Clerks and Organ Scholars who are undergraduates at Magdalen College. With modern amplification, the thousands of students and visitors that crowd the streets below can hear the singing and prayers led by the Dean of Divinity. The Great Tower's bells ring out over the city for around 20 minutes. Many revellers have been up all night partying and, now slightly worse for wear, follow the Morris dancing, the May morning revelry across the town. Others head for breakfast. By 9 am the party is winding down; gown and town drift back into their habitual rush hour daily routines.

THE HARTING OLD CLUB
South Harting, West Sussex
25th May 2014

Harting Old Club is a Friendly Society that can trace its history back to 1800, though village records first mention the club in 1738. The society was formed to help the poor and unemployed men of the parish and is perhaps one of the oldest or the oldest Friendly Society in Britain. Club Day now takes place on Spring Bank Holiday Monday. At dawn committee members collect green beech tree boughs from the Warren Wood and drag them back into the village to decorate the entrance to St Mary's and St Gabriel, the parish church, and the White Hart pub, which used to be the 'home' of the Old Club. They also 'plant' a green bough in The Square at the bottom of the village. At 11am the Old Club roll call is read from the steps of St Mary's and St Gabriel Church, then the Horndean silver band lead a procession of Old Club members each carrying a newly peeled Hazel stick, and wearing a red, white and blue rosette behind two large red, white and blue flags. They process down The Street to The Square and walk around the 'planted' green beech tree bough, a throwback perhaps to pagan tree worship; then back up through the village to the church for a short service of thanksgiving followed by a feast for members and male guests in Harting Community Hall. Any healthy male between 15 and 45 years of age can join the Old Club; the subscription is £5 per year. The main rule has always been "… that the intent and purpose of its establishment is for raising a common stock or fund for the support and maintenance of its members in old age, sickness or infirmity, and for their decent burial…" Sickness benefits of £1.20 per week are paid when a member is ill, for a continuous period of up to nine months. After that, or if it is considered the member is unable to work for his living, he is superannuated and receives £12 per year for the rest of his life. When a member dies, £60 is paid towards his funeral expenses and it is an unwritten rule that a member receives £20 if his wife dies.

GARLAND DAY
Charlton-on-Otmoor, Oxfordshire
30th April 2014

May garlands were once synonymous with May Day, which in many villagers was known as Garland Day – villagers went garlanding. At Charlton-on-Otmoor the children from the Church of England, St Mary the Virgin Primary School elected a May Queen and King. Their parents and school teachers have been busy all morning and much of the day before making elaborate May Day garlands and incorporating small crosses in bouquets of flowers that will be carried in procession to the church. Along with their teachers the older children – the girls wearing long white dresses and the boys in white shirts, brightly coloured waistcoats and grey trousers – carry a long rope covered in greenery that the seven May garlands are attached too. On route to the church the May Day carol is sung with the Queen and King of May travelling in style in a horse drawn trap. During the May Garland service, the bouquets are blessed; the seven May garlands are attached to the 16th century rood screen and the May Day carol is sung once more. Some of the girls are garlanded, and afterwards Maypole dancing takes place in the Crown Inn car park.

HUNTING THE EARL OF RONE

Combe Martin, Devon
30th May 2011

Known once as the Combe Martin Revels, Hunting the Earl of Rone was banned in 1837 for licentiousness and drunken behaviour, but revived and re-invented in 1970. The village festivities take place over four days during the Spring Bank Holiday weekend. The village production includes Grenadier guards, a Hobby Horse, the Fool, numerous locals dressed in period costume, drummers, many musicians and a donkey. According to the Earl of Rone Council, "visitors can dress for the occasion, and should look like 19th century peasants; no jeans or hoodies please." The Earl of Rone wears sackcloth from head to foot and a hideous mask, the emblem of the festival. He is hunted each day but to no avail. Eventually captured on the Monday by the Grenadier guards he is mounted facing backwards on a donkey and paraded through the village. At various prearranged spots he is shot by the Grenadiers only to be revived by the Fool and Hobby Horse. The party make its way to the beach, where the Earl of Rone is finally dispatched execution style and thrown into to the sea. But who is the Earl of Rone? According to the Combe Martin tradition he was the Irish rebel and aristocrat Hugh O'Neill, Earl of Tyrone who was forced to flee from Ireland in 1607. Shipwrecked he managed to make it ashore in Raparee Cove near Ilfracombe. However history recalls that he made it to France, from there found his way to Rome and ended his days in Spain.

WELL DRESSING

Bisley, Gloucestershire
14th May 2015

The origins of the Well Dressing in Bisley are obscure. It takes place on Ascension Day and could date to pagan times as an offering to the gods for a reliable water supply. Others suggest the village celebrates the purity of their water supply after surviving the Black Death in 1348. While still others date the custom to 1863 when Revd. Thomas Keble established the tradition shortly after he had 'tidied up' and formalised the village's main water supply bringing together fresh water from seven wells in a Victorian ornate stone water-head in Wells Road. Today after a short service in All Saints Church, pupils from Bisley Blue Coat Church of England Primary School form a procession through the streets with members of the clergy and the silver band playing *Onward Christian Soldiers*. They carry 22 floral garlands of fresh summer flowers; at the wellhead, prayers are said and hymns are sung. Everyone is then welcome to a tea provided by the Women's Institute at the village hall.

OAK APPLE DAY

St Neot, Cornwall
29th May 2016

Oak Apple Day, the 29th of May, celebrates the restoration of King Charles II to the throne of England, Scotland and Ireland. In 1651 the 21-year-old Charles Stuart, son of the recently executed King Charles I famously hid with Major William Careless in an oak tree after defeat by Oliver Cromwell's men at the Battle of Worcester – capture would have been certain death. Eventually escaping he was able to reach France and safety. In Paris he was re-united with his mother, staying for over eight years until the English Parliament invited him back as King Charles II. (Oliver Cromwell had died in 1658.) He entered London on his 30th birthday, 29th May 1660. The English Parliament passed into law "An Act for a Perpetual Anniversary Thanksgiving on the Nine and Twentieth Day of May" declaring 29th May a public holiday. Known as Oak Apple Day and sometimes Restoration Day the public holiday was one of the very few days that working men and women could have off from the continual grind of everyday life. The national holiday lasted from 1660 to 1859. The day is still celebrated in St Neot with the carrying of the Oak Bough through the village by the Tower Captain; in 2016 the procession was led by the Revd. Phillip Biggs. After a short speech and blessing, villagers hoist the bough to the top of the tower where it remains for the year. Afterwards, a barbeque with refreshments and folk singing takes place in the church. Many participants wear an oak apple and a sprig of oak in their buttonhole or pinned to their dress.

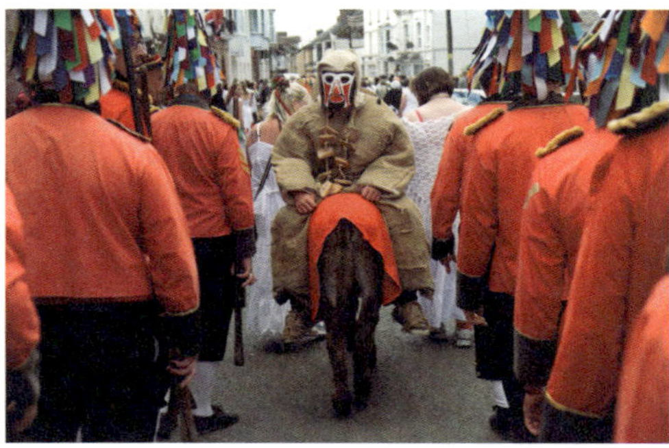

Hunting The Earl Of Rone

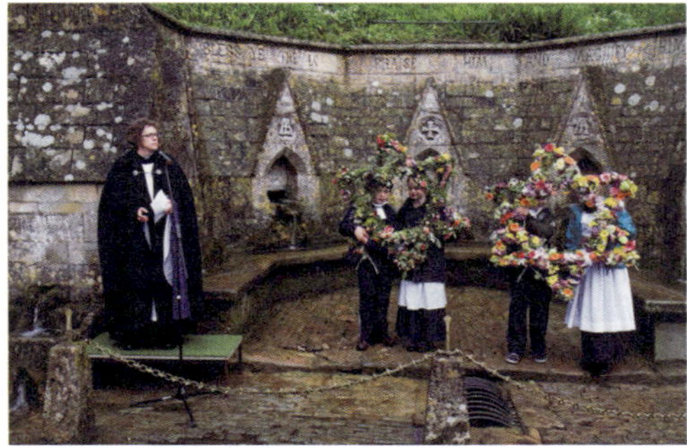

Well Dressing

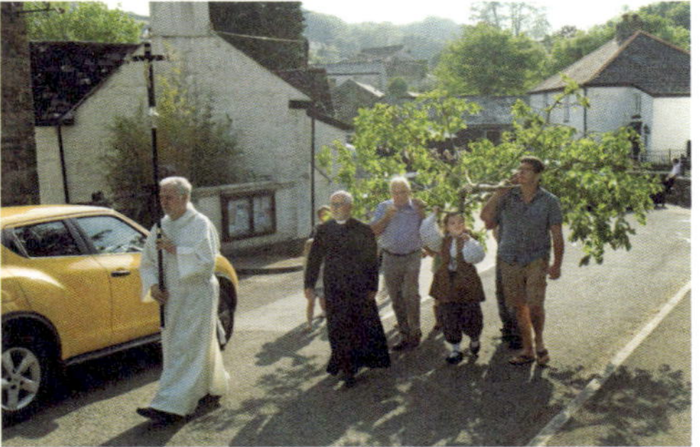

Oak Apple Day

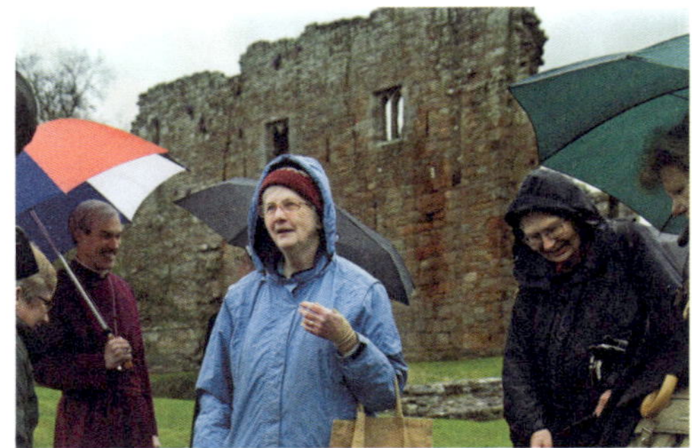
Lady Anne Clifford Dole

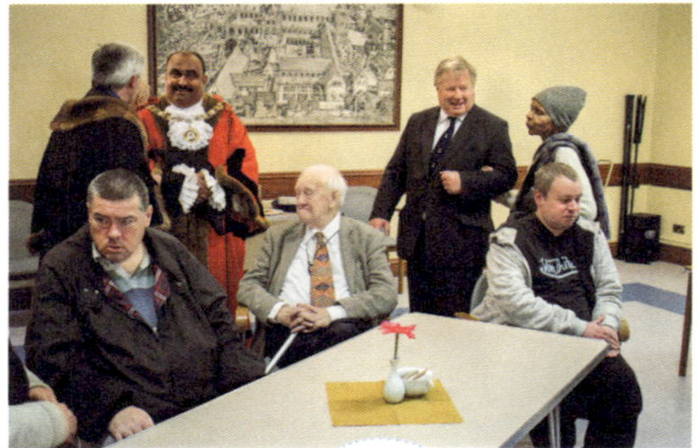
Nepton Distribution

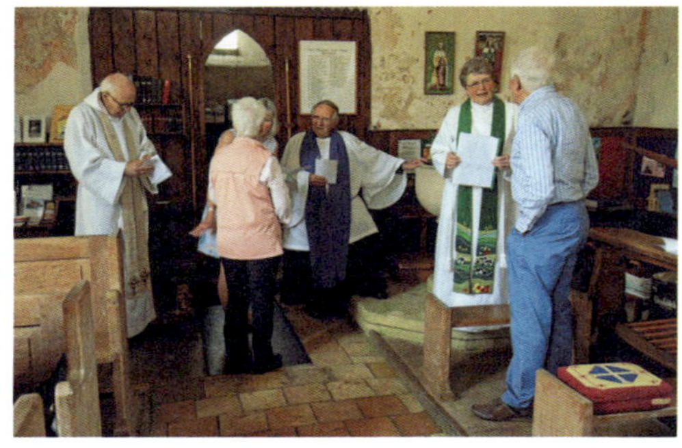
Saint Walstan's Day

LADY ANNE CLIFFORD DOLE

Brougham, Cumbria
2nd April 2016

The Lady Anne Clifford Dole (1590-1676) took place in the ruins of Brougham Castle; it was the four hundredth anniversary of Lady Anne's mother's death, Margaret Clifford Countess of Cumberland, on 24 May 1616. Lady Anne was the daughter of George Clifford, 3rd Earl of Cumberland, whose family owned vast estates in the north of England. Her two older brothers died as children and following the death of her father, Anne, his sole heir, had expected to inherit her family's five castles and vast estates across Cumbria and Yorkshire. Instead her father left his estates to his brother – though this was normal – Anne's uncle and his son, her cousin Henry. Anne spent four decades in a legal dispute with them and refused to accept any compromise. The only way she could have the estates restored to her family was if her uncle died and her cousin Henry died without issue, which Henry did in 1643. The inheritance was hers; Anne was 56. Because of the English Civil War she stayed in London for a further six years, eventually leaving court and returning to the North, where she found the family estates in very bad repair. She was a devout Christian and over the next 27 years, she rotated with her household between the various Clifford family castles in Appleby, Brough, Brougham, Pendragon and Skipton, restoring and rebuilding all that had fallen into disrepair. She also restored churches, built almshouses and provided for the poor. She exercised her influence and authority and was actively involved with her tenants. She died at Brougham Castle on 22 March 1676, in the room where her father had been born and her mother had died. An annual collection is made, referencing a bequest in memory of her mother Margaret that provided for the poor of the parish of Brougham.

NEPTON DISTRIBUTION

Barking, Essex
21st May 2019

The Nepton Distribution takes place annually in May or early June at St Margaret's Church Centre. It is the longest continually observed monetary charity in the country after the King's Maundy Money. Ann Nepton, the wife of the deceased poulter Thomas Nepton, provided in her will of 1728 a trust using a property in Dunning's Alley, London which after the death of her son Joseph Green, would pass to the Company of Poulters, a London Livery Company, to pay £40 per annum in perpetuity to the "poor people of Barking in the county of Essex". The distribution takes place in the Church Centre, during a 'tea and biscuits' gathering. The names of the recipients are read out, they raise a hand and a member of the Company of Poulters hands out the payment of £50 in a small brown sealed envelope. The Company of Poulters has been adding to the legacy for many years from one of its charitable funds. The Mayor of Barking, Councillor Abdul Aziz, the Rt. Revd. Trevor Mwamba, Reg Beer JP, and the Upper Warden of the Worshipful Company of Poulters along with other local dignitaries attended the distribution. Afterwards the beneficiaries and dignitaries make their way to the Nepton Tomb in the churchyard where prayers are said and a wreath is laid.

SAINT WALSTAN'S DAY

Bawburgh, Norfolk
27th May 2018

Saint Walstan was an Anglo-Saxon prince who at the age of 12 with his parents' permission dedicated himself to a life of prayer, but not as a monk. He became a serf to a man at Taverham devoting his life to farming; he is a patron saint of farm animals and agricultural workers. Walstan died on the 30th May 1016 while at work in a meadow. He is remembered for miracles that occurred during and after his life. He was buried at Bawburgh where his hearse, pulled by two oxen, stopped; a spring, which was later discovered to have curative properties sprung forth. Through the Middle Ages agricultural workers visited his shrine, he had become a local cult figure and by 1309 the revenues generated at Bawburgh by pilgrims provided an income for six priests and the church vicar. After the Dissolution of the Monasteries (1536 -1541) the church fell into disrepair. However during the 19th century the village church regained its prosperity when miracles became associated with the water obtained from the well. In 1913 the Eastern Daily Press named Bawburgh the 'Lourdes of Norfolk'. Saint Walstan's life is still celebrated each year when a special Patronal Service takes place on the nearest Sunday to 30th May. After church, the congregation walk the short distance to Saint Walstan's Healing Well, prayers and hymns are sung and his life remembered. Afterwards a simple meal is held in his memory in the village hall.

WILKES WALK
Leighton Buzzard, Bedfordshire
9th May 2015

Wilkes Walk is an annual procession to the Almshouses in North Street on Rogation Sunday in memory of John Wilkes, the father of William Wilkes the founder of ten almshouses in the seventeenth century. His son, Matthew left funds to be devoted to this annual commemoration. The Town Crier leads the way, a garland bearer, clergy, Almshouse officials, the choir of All Saints Church and parishioners follow. At the Almshouses the choir sings a short anthem, prayers are read in thanksgiving for the Wilkes family and a reading of part of the 1646 will takes place. While this is read a member of the choir must be "upended" – stood upon their head as stipulated in Matthew's will. The tradition was once part of the annual beating of the parish boundaries, where it was the traditional for youngsters to be bumped, beaten or upended at boundary parish points to help them remember the location of those landmarks. Each member of the almshouses also receives a small remuneration to celebrate the day. In the past refreshments were provided at the Market Cross, originally this took the form of buns and free ale, but at times this became very unruly when the ale ran out. Buns, soft drinks and tea are now provided back at the church instead. Young members of the choir are given a £1 and the Vicar gets £50, which is then passed onto a local charity.

VISITATION COURT DAY
Greenwich, London
17th June 2019

Shortly before his death in 1614 Henry Howard, Earl of Northampton, founded the Trinity Hospital almshouses for the poor men of Greenwich. Though not a member of the Mercer Company, he entrusted the management of the Trinity Hospital to the City of London Mercer Company. On Visitation Day some members wear their traditional frock coats and top hats, they greet members of the Mercer Company, and attend a service in the chapel, followed by a champagne reception. Mercer Company members then attend a secret court meeting in upstairs rooms. A sumptuous lunch is provided in the private garden for residents and their guests.

JANKYN SMYTH CAKE AND ALE CEREMONY
Bury St Edmunds, Suffolk
26th June 2015

Jankyn Smyth was a merchant and great benefactor to Bury St Edmunds, leaving many important bequests to the town. In 1473 he left his estate at Rougham, his house and more land to provide funds with which the citizens of the town could pay the taxes due, as required upon the election of each new Abbot of Bury St Edmunds. In his will of 1481 he made provision for the College of Sweet Man Jesus, his chantry in College Street where prayers could be said for the dead for a period of years upon payment of the appropriate fee or donation. Henry Herdeman, a priest, was granted a royal licence, whose sole purpose was to say prayers, a daily mass for the King, Queen, and Royal Family; and for the soul of the great benefactor Jankyn Smyth. Funds were also left for a Mass to be held annually, on 2nd February and another on 28th June, the anniversary of his death. This included money to provide cakes and ale for the residents of the five Guildhall Feoffment Almshouses along with their guests and trustees. The Jankyn Smyth Cake and Ale Ceremony continues, and takes place on the third Thursday in June in the Guildhall. It is believed to be the oldest endowed charity in the country still in existence.

FRIENDLY SOCIETY CLUB WALK DAY
Long Sutton, Somerset
1st June 2019

The Long Sutton Friendly Society was formed in 1818 to provide insurance in the form of welfare benefits for its members, who were in the main agricultural workers, should they fall on hard times becoming ill and unable to work or were made unemployed. Today there are approximately 80 members of the all male society; the annual subscription is £35. A bereavement benefit of £100 is still paid upon the death of a member or a member's wife. The day starts with the church bells being rung at 6.00am and is followed by the Roll Call of Members outside the village hall. There is no official dress code but members are expected to be, "booted and suited and everyone has been persuaded to buy a club tie," navy blue with horizontal red and white narrows stripes; "red, white and blue rosettes are worn too." After the Roll Call of Members there is a procession headed by the Banner Bearer, Secretary, Chairman and President of the society followed by the Sherborne Town Band and then the members. They parade

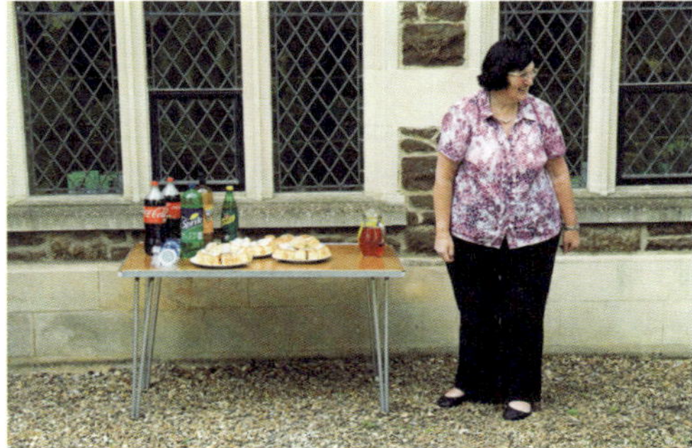
Wilkes Walk

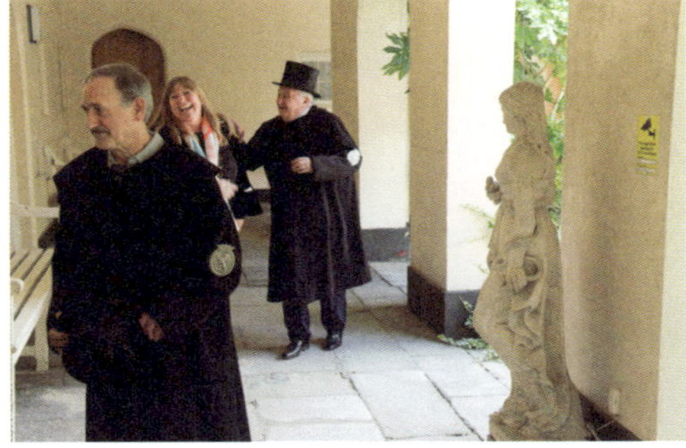
Visitation Court Day

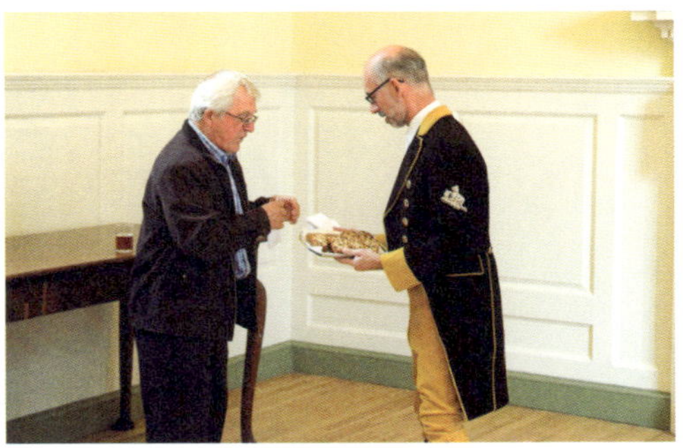
Jankyn Smith Cake and Ale Ceremony

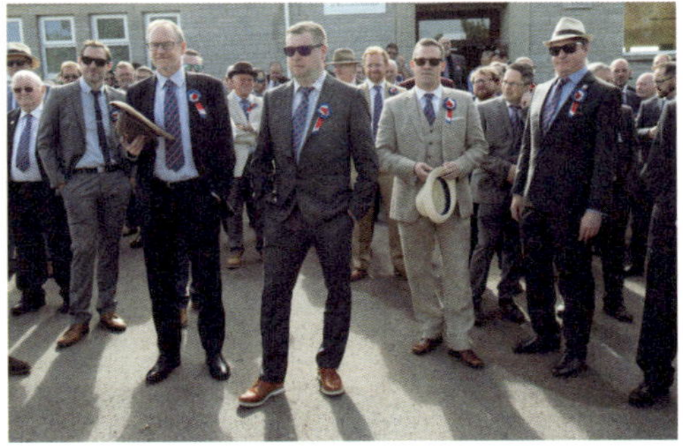
Friendly Society Walk Day

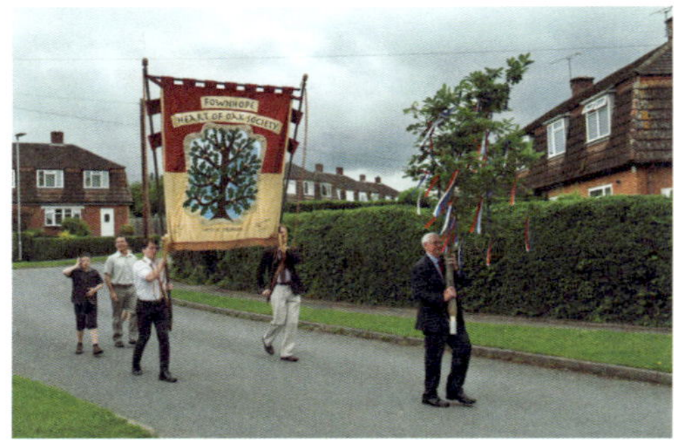

Fownhope Heart of Oak Society

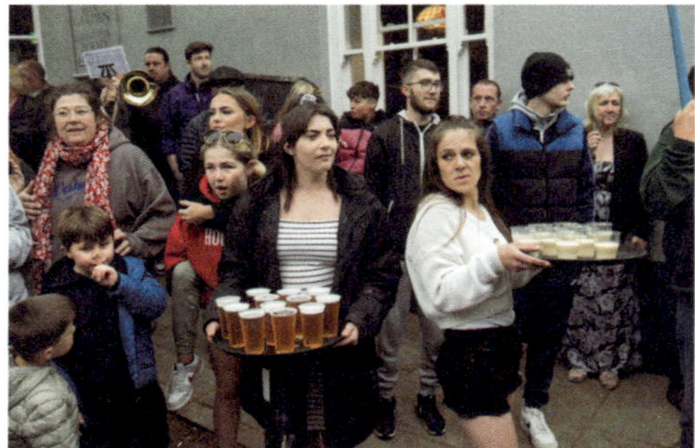

Rowell Charter Fair

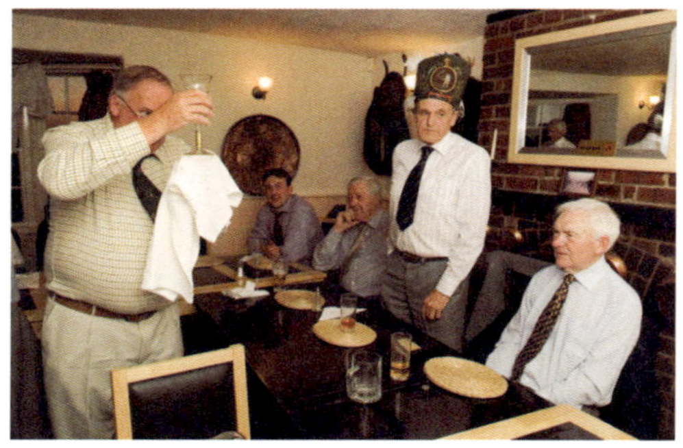

Duck Feast

from the village hall to the Holy Trinity Church for their annual service, stopping outside the West Door for the National Anthem. The banner, with its motto 'United We Stand, Divided We Fall' surrounding a pair of clasped hands, is draped across the altar during the service. Afterwards the parade reforms and sets off on the Club Walk, calling at five private homes or farms for refreshments. This is followed by the annual luncheon in the golf club for members and guests. Nearly £1,500 was collected in 2019 and was divided amongst local charities and the parish.

FOWNHOPE HEART OF OAK SOCIETY
Fownhope, Herefordshire
3rd June 2018

The Fownhope Heart of Oak Friendly Society was established in 1876. Their purpose was to help the rural workforce with insurance should members suffer hardship, whether through illness, bereavement or loss of work. Changes to the Financial Services Act 1989 made it too onerous to continue as a Friendly Society, the 'friendly' status (in the context of insurance) was no longer acceptable and so was dropped. But the Club Walk Day tradition continues, the members forming a social group, enabling fund raising for local causes. The Club Walk Day was originally held on 29th May, Oak Apple Day, one of the few days in the years that agricultural workers had a day off work. The holiday can be traced back to the restoration of King Charles II in 1660 and Parliament declaring 29th May a public holiday in his honour. Club Walk Day now takes place on the nearest Saturday to 29th May. At dawn an oak tree bough is cut and dressed with red, white and blue ribbons. At 10.30am it's carried at the front of the parade, followed by the club banner, then the Drybrook band playing suitable marching music. Membership is open to all, once a small joining fee has been paid. Many members carry flower sticks that are unique to Fownhope. Taking up the rear are the Leominster Morris dancers. The procession leaves the New Inn and makes its way to St Mary's Church for a short service of thanksgiving, then tours the village stopping at various 'big' houses where refreshments are provided and the flower sticks are judged: finally finishing up at the Whiterdine Field for competitive village sports and a barbeque pig roast.

ROWELL CHARTER FAIR
Rothwell, Northamptonshire
5th June 2023

The first reference to a market is from 1154 when Roger, the Earl of Clare, acquitted the monks and canons of Sulby Abbey from paying any tolls for articles bought or sold at Rowell Fair. The Clares, a powerful Norman family, owned estates across England and Wales. In 1204 Roger's son Richard the Earl of Clare was granted a Charter for the fair by King John. And in 1614, when William Cockayne became Lord of the Manor having purchased the estates, King James I granted the Royal Charter of today's Proclamation. The manorial rights have remained in the Cockayne family and descendants ever since. Over the centuries the fair has evolved from a busy livestock market to the fun fair that it is today. In 1968 the Rowell Fair Society was formed to "… preserve and maintain the traditions of the ancient Charter Fair". This had become necessary as by the 1960s the tradition had almost died out. The Charter Fair takes place on Proclamation Monday, the day after Trinity Sunday. At 6am Frank York, Bailiff to the Lord of the Manor, on horse back accompanied by John Newman, Chief Halberdier, and various local civic dignitaries gather outside the west door of The Holy Trinity Church, the national anthem is sung, the Charter Proclamation is read and the fair is opened. The procession moves to the War Memorial to pay its respects and then to the eight locations – pubs or sites of former pubs in the town. At each the Charter Proclamation is read and the Rowell Fair traditional tipple, a rum and milk beverage, along with a pint or two is served to the bailiff, halberdiers and dignitaries. At each of the stops after the reading of the Charter and when the dignitaries have moved on, a very rough but goodhearted scuffle takes place between the townsfolk and halberdiers. The townsfolk trying to capture a halberdier's two-handed polearm. By 7am breakfast is served in Tresall hall above the Conservative Club. The Charter having been proclaimed throughout the town.

DUCK FEAST
Charlton St Peter, Wiltshire
1st June 2009

The Duck Feast takes place annually on June 1st, or the nearest Monday, at the The Charlton Cat public house. The feast celebrates the poet Stephen Duck (1705-1756) and has been taking place since 1734. In that year Lord Palmerston (Henry Temple, 1st Viscount

Palmerston (1673-1757) gifted the rent from a piece of land, now know as Duck's Acre, to the village in perpetuity. The rent at first paying for a yearly feast in the local pub attended by 12 of Duck's fellow threshers and the poet himself, then later all the adult males of the village. A toast is made, "In remembrance to Lord Palmerston and the Reverend Stephen Duck" by drinking 2/3 pint of ale from a special glass and downing it in one. The Chief Duck sits at the top table wearing a tall green leather hat, decorated with duck feathers and an image of a thresher working with a scythe. After the feast and toast by the Chief Duck there is a reading from *The Thresher's Labour*. The Duck family were very poor, he attended a charity school, leaving aged 13 and going to work in the fields as a farm labourer. Once married he became determined to better himself to escape the grinding poverty; he started to read widely and write poetry encouraged by the village squire, schoolmaster and rector. He was 'discovered' by the prebendary of Winchester Cathedral, who promoted Duck as sincerely pious man of sober wit. In 1730 he combined many of the poetic pieces into *The Thresher's Labour*. The epic poem is a description of the struggles faced, and is a representation of the working class of that time. The work became celebrated throughout London society. On Friday the 11th September 1730 the Right Honourable the Earl of Macclesfield read the poem to Queen Caroline and her Court in the Drawing Room at Windsor Castle. Duck was later taken to meet her; Queen Caroline was impressed and became his patron. He was a candidate for the Laureate, though did not succeed. He eventually became a pastor at Byfleet in Surrey and committed suicide in 1756 by drowning.

BEATING THE BOUNDS

All-Hallows-by-the-Tower, City of London
2nd June 2011

Beating the Bounds, establishing the parish boundaries by beating the ground at designated points, takes place annually on Ascension Day at All-Hallows-by-the-Tower church, which is the oldest church in the City of London. St Dunstan's College students return from Catford, South London to their roots in the parish of St Dunstan-in-the-East to take part. City grandee Sir Paul Judge, Alderman of Tower Ward in the City of London and Chairman of the Governors of St Dunstan's College and former student explains the meaning of this ancient custom outside a Pret A Manger café, before the boundary is beaten. "When maps were rare and most people illiterate, the geographic boundaries of each parish needed to be handed down, so that such matters as liability to contribute to the repair of the church or the right to be buried within the churchyard were not disputed. In the past hymns would be sung and prayers said for God's blessing."

BEATING THE BOUNDS

St Botolph without Aldgate, City of London
13th June 2011

The annual Beating of the Bounds of St Botolph without Aldgate, a Church of England parish church in the City of London takes place annually on Ascension Day or the nearest suitable date. The Lord Mayor of the City of London, Alderman Michael Bear, wearing a scarlet robe that's furred and bordered in black velvet, his chain of office and a very large brimmed tricorne velvet feathered hat, walks with the Portsoken Volunteers and various City of London dignitaries around the parish boundary of the ward of Portsoken. This is one of the 25 ancient wards that are still used in local elections. Children follow from the Sir John Cass Foundation Primary School, who at various boundary points are given a short history lesson by the Rector of St Botolph, Laura Burgess, before they vigorously Beat the Bounds with long garden canes.

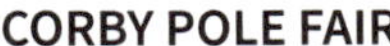

CORBY POLE FAIR

Corby Old Village, Northamptonshire
3rd June 2022

Once every twenty years Corby Pole Fair takes place in the Old Village. In 1585 Queen Elizabeth I granted the village a Charter Fair; traditionally any stranger to the village on fair day had to pay a toll to enter. This was with reference to the Charter excusing residents from paying road tolls. Non-residents who refused to pay were carried on a pole and locked in the stocks. These days the fair starts with the church bells being rung at 6 am and a reading of the Charter at the St John the Baptist Church by the vicar, the Revd. Paul Frost, who is then 'chaired' along with the Mayor Cllr Tafadzwa Chikoto and the village's oldest resident Mrs June Thompson to the two other old village entrances where the Charter is read once again. Hymns are sung after each reading of the Charter, and *God Save the Queen* sung after the final reading. A free breakfast is then served in the Charter Field. Throughout the day there are a variety of events at key points around the village celebrating Corby's history. The Corby Silver Band leads a procession featuring Queen Elizabeth I, along with giant papier-mâché

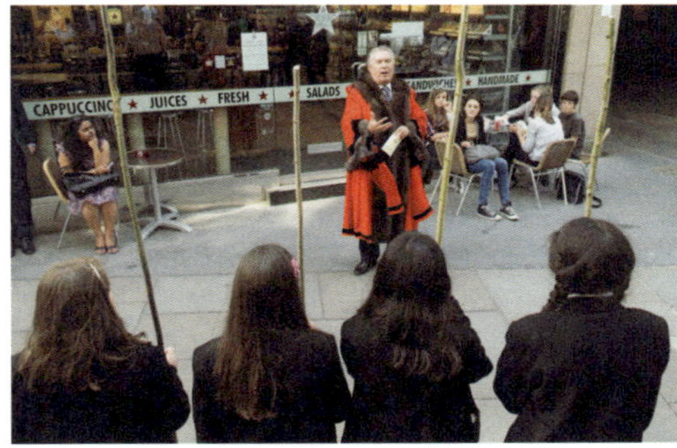

Beating The Boujnds, All-Hallows-by-the-Tower

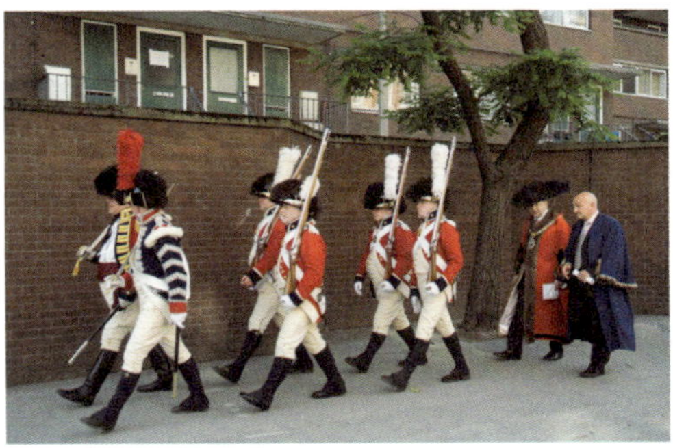
Beating the Bounds, St Botolph without Aldgate

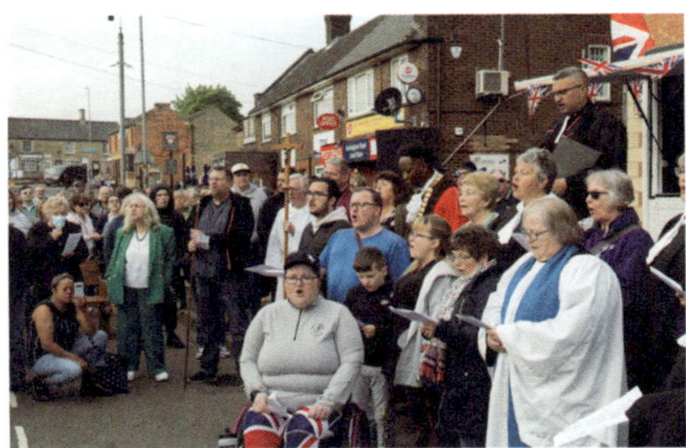
Corby Pole Fair

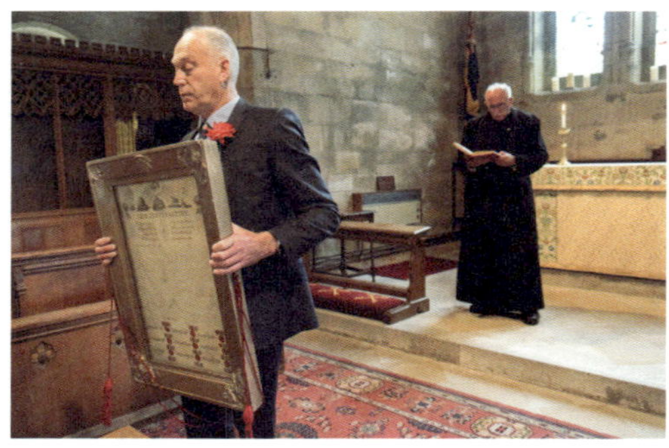
Oddfellows: The Loyal Laurel and Crown Lodge

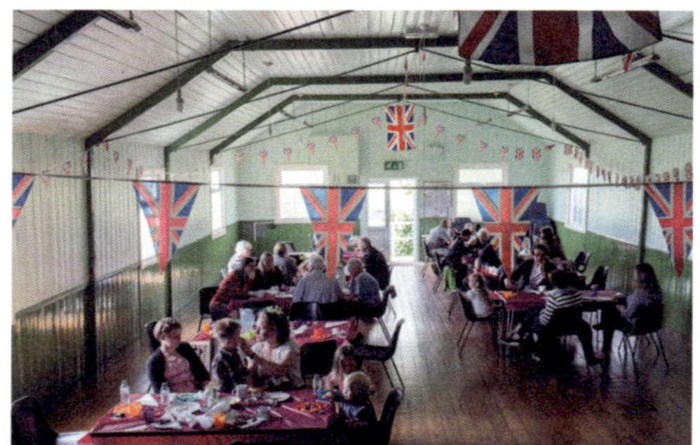
Rushbearing, Great Musgrave

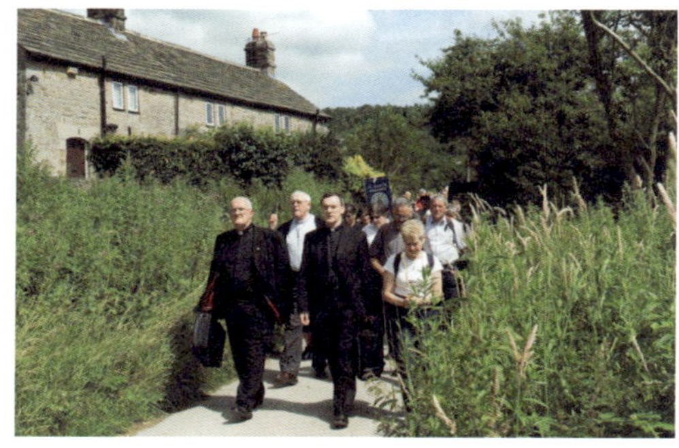
Padley Martyrs Pilgrimage

puppets, figures from local history. There is Morris dancing, an Ox Roast, a Viking encampment, and many other activities involving the village community that go on into the night.

ODDFELLOWS: THE LOYAL LAUREL AND CROWN LODGE
Parwich, Derbyshire
1st July 2023

The Parwich Oddfellows, The Loyal Laurel and Crown Lodge, gather in the village on first day of the Wakes Week. The day starts outside the Sycamore Inn with members singing the Opening Ode to the Stuttgart hymn tune, "Brethen of our friendly Order, Honour here asserts her sway; All within her sacred border, Must her high command obey…". Members are smartly dressed in dark business suits, with a red rose buttonhole. They carry white sticks also know as wands. There are five minor degrees within the Oddfellows starting with the white up to purple sticks; the coloured tops denote the level of a member's degree. White gloves are worn so that no man can be identified as either a working man with rough hands nor an office man with softer hands. They link little fingers to symbolise the strength of a linked chain as they walk in procession around the village behind the framed Dispensation that is dated 1836; this originally allowed the Oddfellows to gather and walk in procession behind the lodge banner – *Let Brotherly Love Continue*. The parade visits various 'big' and members' houses where refreshments are taken. At St Peter's Church, the Dispensation is placed upon the altar during the service. The day finishes with the Oddfellows Dinner in the Memorial Hall followed by a Fancy Dress and Carnival parade, live music, children's entertainments and sporting events that continue all week. The Oddfellows are a friendly society rooted in the 1730s with neither political nor religious affiliations. As a not-for-profit mutual society they believe in a community bonded by friendship, care and charitable support.

RUSHBEARING
Great Musgrave, Cumbria
2nd July 2022

The annual Rushbearing tradition takes place on the first Saturday in July, when a procession of children and their parents make their way from the village institute to St Theobald's Church. Behind the Musgrave Rush Bearing banner, the boys carry rush crosses and the girls wear their floral crowns. At the church after a short service, and the symbolic strewing of rushes, the crowns and rush crosses are placed on the altar. The tradition dates back to when church floors were earth and rushes were strewn annually over them to form a fresh green carpet. After the service everyone walks back to the Village Institute for a cream tea. Jackie Featherstone later hangs the crowns of flowers and rush crosses above and around the door of the church where they remain until replaced the following year. Great Musgrave in the Eden Valley is one of very few villages that still keeps this tradition alive. The tradition is a celebration of the village as a community, combining spiritual and social elements of life. In 2022, 16 children took part along with parents and village friends.

PADLEY MARTYRS PILGRIMAGE
Grindleford, Derbyshire
13th July 2008

On the 12th July 1588 two Catholic travelling priests, Nicholas Garlick and Robert Ludlam were discovered at Padley Hall along with members of the Fitzherberts, a prominent Catholic family. All were arrested. Both men had trained in France to become Catholic priests and had returned to England. Recusants – people who refused to recognise the supreme religious authority of Queen Elizabeth I were considered traitors. The two priests were imprisoned in Derby jail. While there they met a third Catholic priest Richard Simpson who had never been to Padley, but was a local man. The three priests were tried and found guilty; two weeks later they were hanged, drawn and quartered, their bodies being displayed on poles at St Mary's Bridge in Derby. The three became known as the Padley Martyrs. Nicholas Garlick was the first to die, and was hanged wearing his doublet. After being cut down, the doublet needed to be removed to make ready for the quartering. While this was happening he came to his senses and before being disembowelled was heard to speak to the executioners and those around him. Richard Simpson went next, dying with 'cheerfulness'. Robert Ludlam, who had witnessed his friends' deaths stepped forward, and after praying for England, for a bystander, for his enemies and lastly, having commended his soul into the hands of his Creator and Saviour, he delivered himself to the executioner. John Fitzherbert who had sheltered Garlick and Ludlam died in prison in 1590. His father Sir Thomas Fitzherbert died a Catholic in the Tower of London in

1591 after having been imprisoned more than 30 years for his faith. The annual pilgrimage and Mass of the Martyrs at Padley is in their honour, it began in 1898.

HORN FAIR

Ebernoe, West Sussex
25th July 2015

The highlight of the Horn Fair is the annual cricket match held on St James' Day between Ebernoe Cricket Club and a team from a nearby village. The Horns Trophy is presented to the batsman with the highest score. In 2015, Oli Rose for Ebernoe won the trophy scoring 42, beating Matt Hollier of the Wessex Pilgrims who scored 40. The horns used to come from the lamb roasted on a spit at one end of the cricket field for the player's lunch. After the presentation of the Horns Trophy the two teams and spectators gather to sing the Horn Fair Song. The Horn Fair is centuries old and was revived in 1864 having lapsed for a long time. Horn Fairs were noted for being unruly, licentious occasions where cuckoldry and seduction may well have taken place. The practice of dressing up with horns is alluded to in the traditional Horn Fair Song, and the old saying All's fair at Horn Fair may well originate from such events. Today there is a small funfair, an ice cream van and refreshments for the fairgoers and cricket followers.

VILLAGE SHOW AND FETE

Cudham, Kent
28th August 2017

The village of Cudham holds one of the oldest village shows and fetes in Kent dating back to Victorian times. It's held annually on August Bank Holiday Monday. The show of home grown produce is displayed in Saint Peter's & St. Paul's Church and is judged while the fete takes place. Winning entries are displayed in the recreation ground. Cudham Village Club's motto is "Fostering the spirit of friendship and citizenship in the community and promoting activities in the village." About 2,500 people attend and the money raised is used to fund the increasing costs of the event, and any profits are donated to local good causes.

ST BENET'S ABBEY PILGRIMAGE

Ludham, Norfolk
3rd August 2014

St Benet's Abbey was a medieval monastery of the Order of Saint Benedict, also known as St Benet's at Holme. The history of the Abbey is uncertain; St Benet's may have been founded on the site of a 9th century monastery where the Danes martyred the hermit Suneman. At about the end of the 10th century Wulfric an Anglo-Saxon nobleman rebuilt the monastery and by the 12th century St Benet's Abbey was flourishing. During the Dissolution of the Monasteries in the reign of Henry VIII, St Benet's was not officially dissolved – the only Abbey that was saved. Yet it fell into disrepair and then ruin very quickly. Henry appointed the Abbot as the Bishop of Norwich and to this day the Bishop of Norwich is still the Bishop-Abbot and the vicar of nearby Horning, which is the Priory of St Benet's. Since 1939 on the first Sunday in August, the Bishop with officiating clergy and the Brothers of St Benet's arrives at this remote ruined Abbey site in the Norfolk Broads. They arrive on a wherry coming up the River Bure to conduct an open-air interdenominational service. This sacred site has been a place of pilgrimage for over a thousand years.

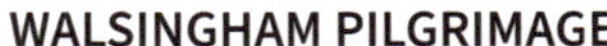

WALSINGHAM PILGRIMAGE

Houghton Saint Giles, Norfolk
19th August 2006

According to the Walsingham legend, in 1061 an Anglo-Saxon noblewoman, Richeldis de Faverches had a vision of the Virgin Mary, she was instructed to build a replica of the house of the Holy Family in Nazareth. It was to contain a statue of the enthroned Virgin Mary with the child Jesus seated on her lap. Among the relics was a phial reputedly of the Virgin's milk. Over the centuries the statue has become associated with childless couples and motherhood. Walsingham became one of the great centres of pilgrimage during the Middle Ages for people from all over northern Europe. The Abbey was destroyed during the reign of Henry VIII and the land sold. During the 20th century there was a revival and today over 250,000 pilgrims visit Walsingham each year, as individuals or as parish groups accompanied by their priest.

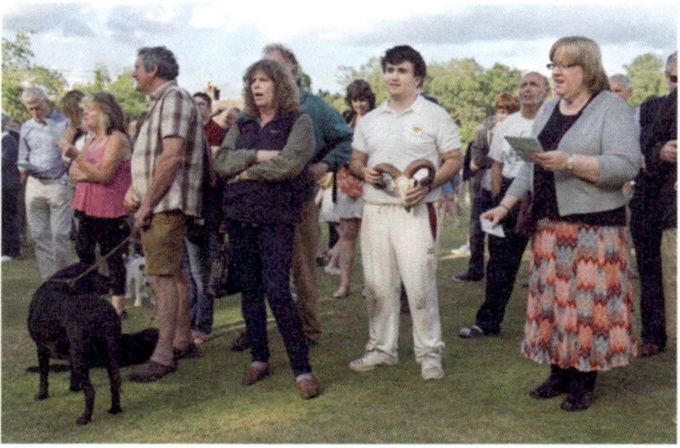

Horn Fair

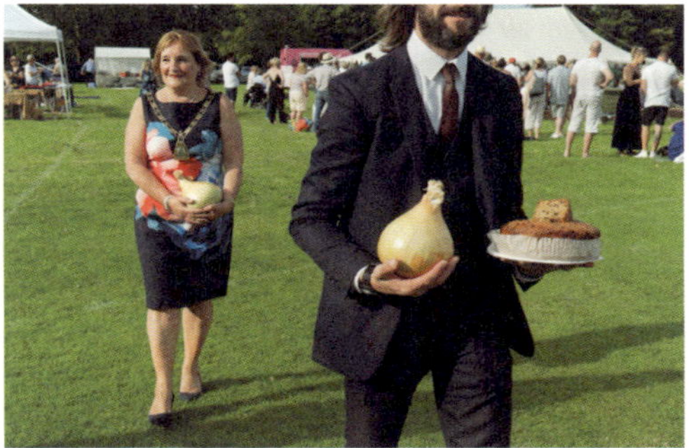

Village Show and Fete, Cudham

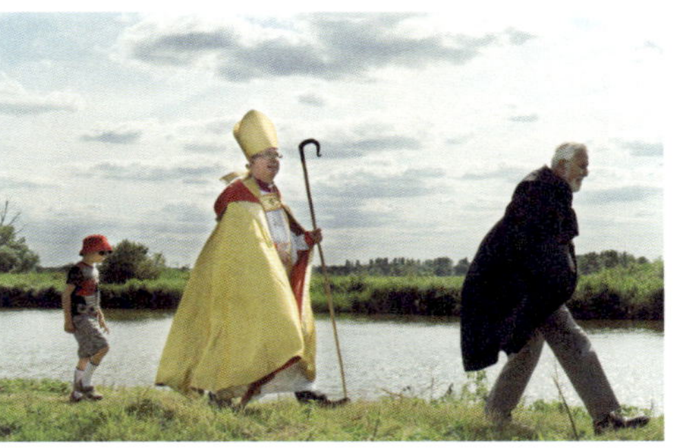

St. Benet's Abbey Pilgrimage

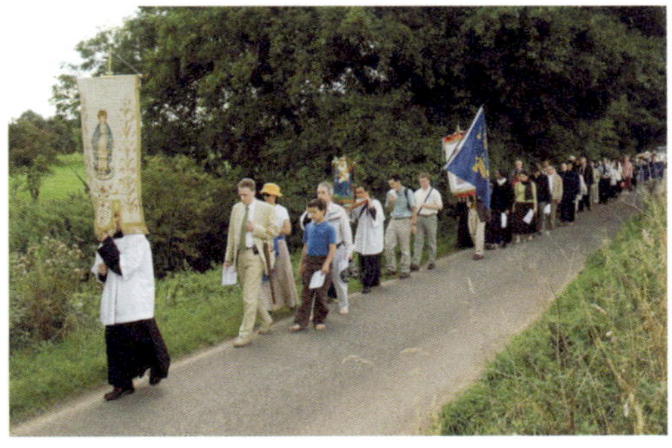

Walsingham Pilgrimage

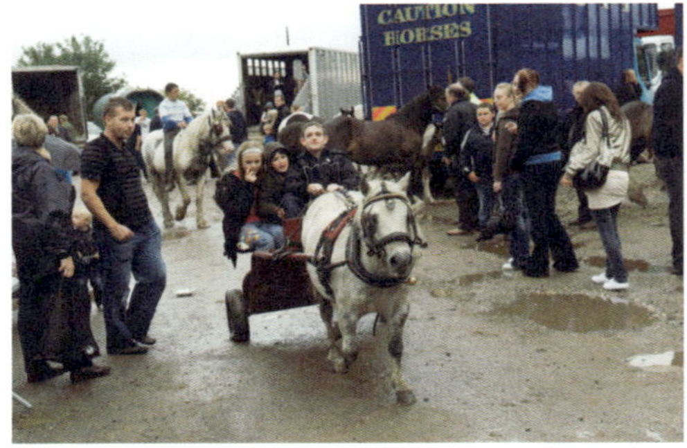
Brigg Horse Fair

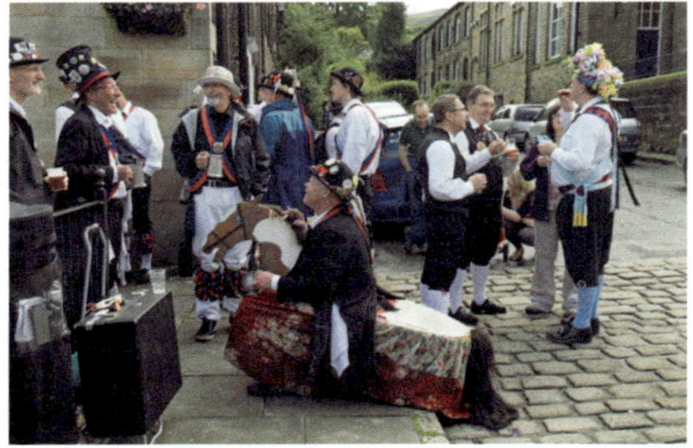
Saddleworth Rushcart

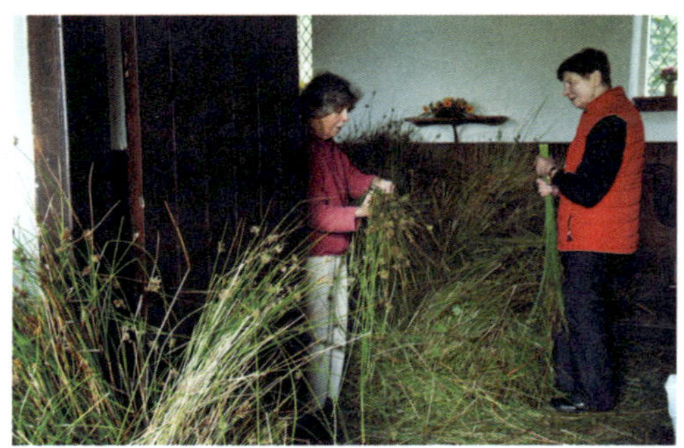
Rushbearing Church Service

BRIGG HORSE FAIR
Brigg, Lincolnshire
5th August 2009

There has been a Royal Charter fair held on the 5th of August since 1205 in Brigg, then a very small Lincolnshire settlement on the tidal River Ancholme. There was no bridge but a ford allowed people to cross back and forth. The yearly market took place and horses could have been traded from time to time. Sheep were traded, but it was not until Queen Victoria's reign that the Brigg Horse Fair gained prominence, with horse trading taking place in the centre of town up until the 1960s. The horse fair's location has been moved several times by the council since then, and declined almost to extinction. Today, however, the fair is celebrated primarily for historic and traditional reasons, and is primarily organised by horse dealers and the gypsy travelling community.

SADDLEWORTH RUSHCART
Uppermill, Saddleworth,
Greater Manchester
24th - 26th August 2012

The Saddleworth Rushcart origins are obscure, but it may derive from Rogationtide when parish boundaries were walked once a year with parishioners bearing freshly cut rushes that would then be spread over the earthen floor of the parish church. Before the Reformation churches served for many secular as well as religious purposes, seating was not usual until the early years of the 16th century. Renewal of the floor covering was usually carried out before major festivals such as Easter and the patronal festival. These were among the few times in the year that working men could take time off from labourers' toil. Merrymaking ceremonies grew up and were handed down the generations. Wakes Week, the mills traditional holiday period, would be one such time. By the early 20th century the tradition had all but died out, as local people were able to get away on their annual holiday often travelling by train to the seaside. Revived in the mid 1970s, The Saddleworth Rushcart tradition now takes place on the August Bank Holiday weekend. The cart is constructed over a period of several days, rushes are collected from the surrounding moors and built onto a two-wheeled cart, thirteen feet tall and slightly conical in shape. It weights over two tons and is pulled over the weekend through local Saddleworth villages; Delph, Dobcross, Greenfield and Diggle by the Saddleworth Morris Men, and other Morris teams invited from all over Britain. About 150 men pull on 'stangs' fixed to a strong rope, which in turn is fixed to the cart. Sitting on the top of the Rushcart, is the 'jockey', a chosen member the Saddleworth Morris team. On Sunday the Rushcart goes to the parish church of St Chad, Saddleworth in Uppermill where during the service rushes are strewn across the floor. Dancing takes place outside; tea and cake is served to spectators. The Rushcart remains at its home, in the church, until the following year.

RUSHBEARING CHURCH SERVICE
Macclesfield Forest, Cheshire
13th August 2017

The Rushbearing service takes place on the first Sunday after 12th August to celebrate the changing of the rushes on the church's earthen floor. The tradition dates back to the Middle Ages, when churches didn't have paved floors and they were covered with rushes to keep the dust and dirt at bay, and to add warmth in winter. Once a year the rushes were swept out and new, sweet smelling rushes re-laid. At St Stephen's Church, Forest Chapel, the custom is first mentioned in the church accounts of 1848, stating that a sum of five shillings was paid to 'William Smith for repairing the windows at the chapel and school broken at Rushbearing.' The annual rushbearing tradition, particularly in the North of England, has evolved often into quite elaborate festive occasions, with processions, food, drink, Morris dancing and merry making. At Forest Chapel, centre of a very small isolated community, it's quite different. Members of the congregation decorate the church but the service takes place outside in almost all weathers. In 2017 it was taken standing on a Table Tomb by the Revds, Steve Rathbone and Norma Robinson, Associate Vicar of St John's Macclesfield, who was the guest preacher. She is wearing a multi-coloured rainbow-striped pride scarf in support of the LGBTQ+ community's fight for acceptance.

HARVEST HOME
East Brent, Somerset
24th August 2018

Harvest Home traditionally celebrates the end of the harvest with a village communal meal. In East Brent it has been taking place annually since 1857. The celebration was started by Archdeacon George Denison, vicar for 51 years of the parish church, St Mary the Blessed Virgin, together with Churchwarden

John Higgs. Prior to this each farm in the village would have held a feast after harvest, resulting in not much work being done in the community for many days. They decided that after the harvest, the 3rd of September should be a holiday for the agricultural workers in their community. It is the longest running Harvest Home in Somerset. The day starts with a church service at St Marys, followed by the ladies of the village and their female guests taking part in the Parade of Christmas Puddings from the village hall to the marquee, a short walk down the A370. In 2018, 60 Christmas puddings had been bought from Asda for the occasion. Nominated men from the village carry a 120lbs Harvest Cheese made by the Cheddar Gorge Cheese Company Ltd, and a 6ft loaf of Harvest Bread created by Maisey's Bakery in Highbridge, that will be shared at the communal meal. The Burtle Silver Band led the procession while children carrying banners follow. Once at the marquee the Christmas puddings, and the 6ft loaf of bread and huge cheese are paraded around the marquee to much clapping while the Burtle Silver Band plays rousing marching music. The Harvest Cheese is placed on the top table. Tim Hawkings, Vicar of St John the Baptist, the Parish Church in Axbridge, cuts the first slice, which is tossed for the waiting waiters to scramble for, there is a £2 prize and much prestige! An act of Worship follows, Grace is said and luncheon commences, typically consisting of a cold roast, salt beef, ham, bread and salads served with beer, cider and soft drinks. Desert follows, uniquely in East Brent with a slice of Christmas pudding. Over 500 people attend, and provision is made for about 100 helpers. Tickets cost £25 per adult and £10 for under 14 year olds. In the afternoon, there are children's sports, a tug of war and afternoon tea and a pay bar.

SAINT DAVID LEWIS PILGRIMAGE

Usk, Monmouthshire
28th August 2022

Saint David Lewis (1616-1679) was a Jesuit Catholic priest and martyr, remembered as *Tad y Tlodion* – Father of the Poor. Born in Abergavenny, he was brought up as Protestant but after the death of both his parents in 1638 he set off for Rome to become a Catholic priest. Eventually returning to Wales in 1648 he joined the Jesuit Mission of St. Francis Xavier at 'The Cwm'. He was to work there for the next thirty years. Father David Lewis was arrested in 1678 at Llantarnam as he was preparing to say Mass. At his trial he was condemned as a Roman Catholic priest. Taking Mass was high treason and for this he was executed at Usk on Wednesday 27th August 1679. He was the last Welsh Catholic priest executed for his faith during the Protestant Reformation. Today, pilgrims walk from St. David Lewis and St. Francis Xavier Catholic Church to the place of execution, now in the grounds of a large private home. As they walk they recite the Litany of Loreto. Abbott Paul Stonham of Belmont carries his relic through the town to Saint Mary's Priory Church, where prayers are said at his grave and his relic can be venerated. Pope Paul VI canonised Father David Lewis in 1970.

THE INSPECTION OF THE GIBSON TOMB

Sutton, London
12th August 2016

Mary Gibson died 10th October 1793 aged 64. In her last will she bequested to the Minister and Churchwardens, £500 at 3% consolidated Bank Annuities on trust, to be applied amongst other ways as follows. '£5 to the Minister forever for preaching a sermon on the 12th August. £5 to be distributed that day by the Churchwardens to the poor. £4 to be divided between the Churchwardens on that day in every year for surveying and examining the Gibson's family vault.' This bequest has now been amalgamated with others left to the church, the revenues being used in the community. There is a short procession from St Nicholas' Church, the two keys to the family vault being carried on a red and gold tasselled cushion. The Mayor, his wife and a small crowd gather for the service of thanksgiving in the churchyard. Above the entrance to the family vault is the inscription "Within this Tomb lyes the Remains of James Gibson Esq and family Late Merchant and Citizen of London To whose Memory this Tomb was Erected 1777." The door to the tomb is unlocked, the Team Rector of Sutton, the Revd. Justine Middlemiss, walks in and remains for a few minutes before re-emerging. The small group on onlookers then gather and also inspect the content of the tomb; it contains six coffins.

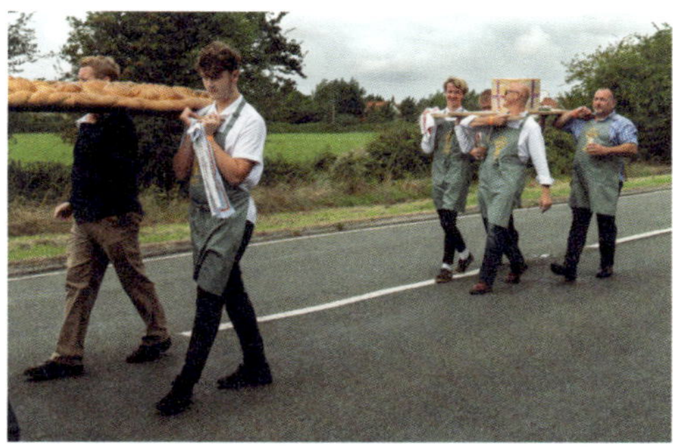

Harvest Home

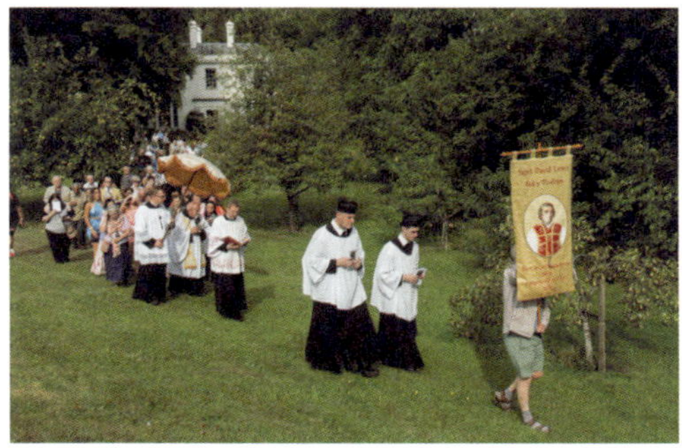

Saint David Lewis Pilgrimage

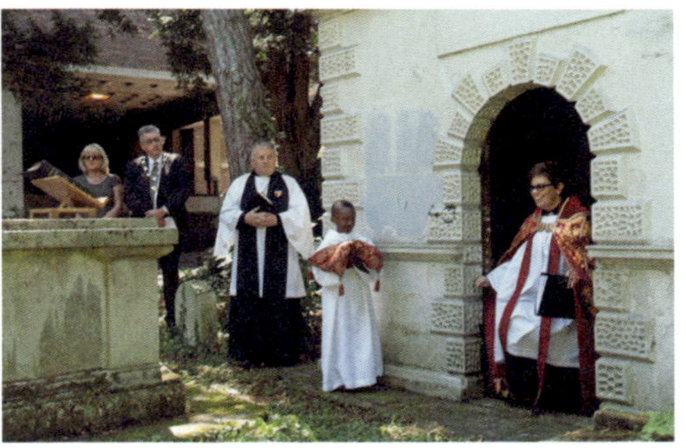

The Inspection of the Gibson Tomb

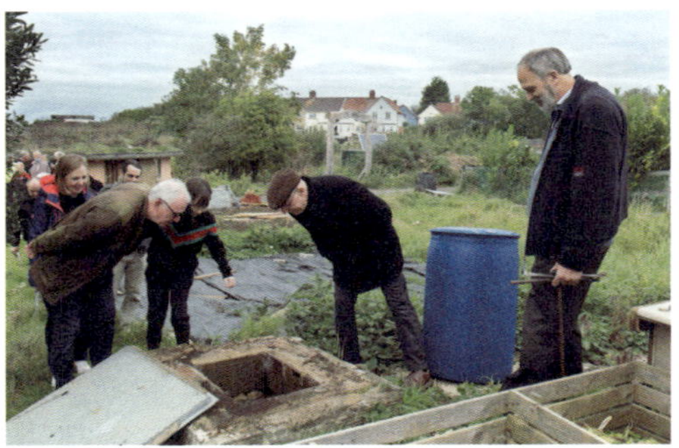
Water Pipe Walk

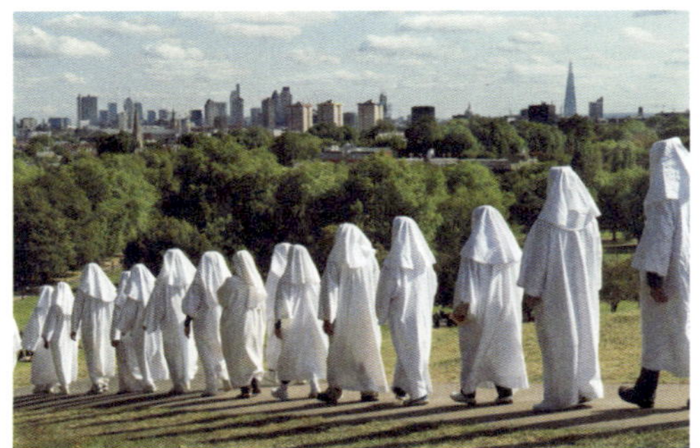
The Druid Order

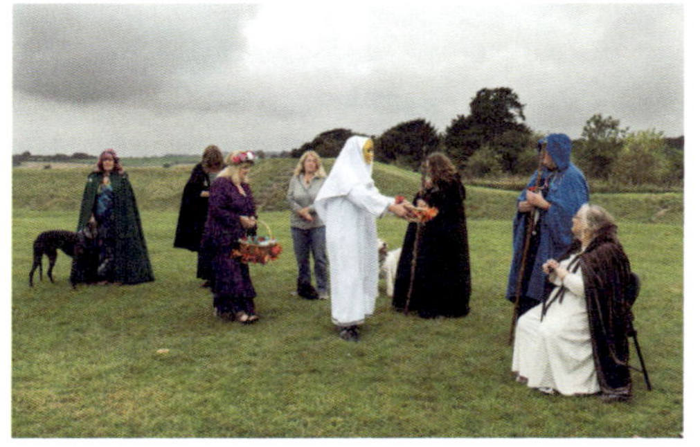
Dorset Druid Grove

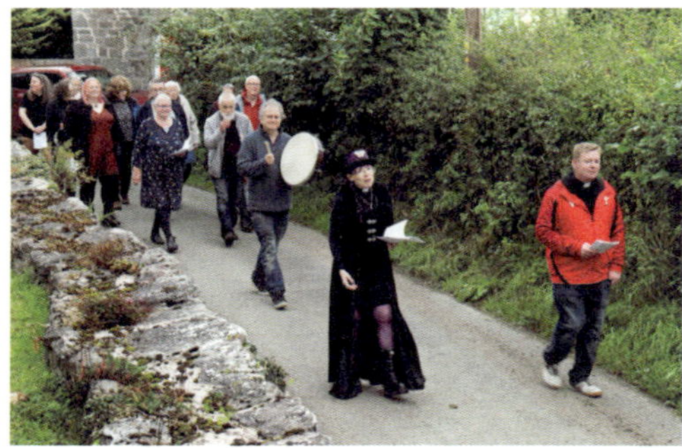
Feat Stone

WATER PIPE WALK
Bristol, Avon
23rd October 2021

Parishioners and clergy from the Church of St Mary the Virgin, Redcliffe, walk approximately two miles from the source of fresh water at Knowl Hill along the route of a water pipe that originally may have been wooden when first laid down by Robert de Berkeley in 1190. He donated the water to the people of the parish. In Victorian times the pipe was replaced with a four inch cast iron pipe. The inspection and walking of the pipe's route allows the church to claim the endowments and maintain the right of way. A manhole cover is lifted so the pipe can be inspected.

THE DRUID ORDER
Camden, London
22nd September 2012

Ancient druidism and Christian mysticism both taught the concept of the God within, that is, the inner union of God and man through the mind and soul of each person, not through the priest or pope of a cult or religion. The Druid Order believes in universalism and was founded in 1909 by George Watson MacGregor Reid, who has been described as 'the founding father of modern Druidry' and who put 'Druidry at the heart of the Stonehenge summer solstice'. They hold four public ceremonies, the first of their year is at Primrose Hill, dressed in white robes that represent purity, the ceremony marks the end of summer and the start of autumn. This is the start of the Druid year when day and night are equal.

DORSET DRUID GROVE
Knowlton, Dorset
25th September 2021

Ian Temple, who remains Archdruid, founded the Dorset Druid Grove in 2007. There are about 40 members of the Order, of whom half have been initiated as Druids into the Grove. Initiates practice the more magical and mystical elements of the Druid way. People of all faiths and paths are encouraged to attend and to take as large or small part in the Grove as they feel comfortable with. At the Autumn Equinox, Rita Andrew enacts Nerthus, sometimes known as the Earth Mother or Terra Mater, she is followed by the Handmaiden to Nerthus. They are distributing bread and fruits of the earth (apples), which represent the bounty of nature to members of the Grove; who have formed a circle within the prehistoric henge circle. Not all is taken, some is always returned to the Earth. Dennis Andrew, Grandmaster of the 'Knights of the Yew' the Inner Order of the Grove, explains. "Druidry has nothing at all to do with new-age spirituality or searching for answers to life's questions. We do not worship nature, we worship the Divine in nature, many Druids are animistic and we believe everything has its own individual God. Druidry is a philosophy and a faith, everybody's path is a unique connection to the Divine in nature, there is no 'corporate identity' that you find in organised religions. Every Druidic path has a follower of one, as we all have our own perception of what the Divine is. Because of this we have a policy within the Dorset Grove: instead of criticising our differences we celebrate the diversity."

FEAT STONE
Efenechtyd, Denbighshire
24th September 2023

The tiny church of St Michael and All Angels in the hamlet of Efenechtyd, Denbighshire was first documented in 1253, when the Bishop of Norwich was given charge to collect a tax to part fund an expedition to the Holy Land. Clearly much older, the church site is circular and probably covers an early Celtic pagan settlement. The Patronal Service, *Gwyl Mabsant* in Welsh, takes place on the nearest Sunday to the Saint's day, 29th September. Kept within the church and lying at the base of the rare wooden font, there is a large rounded oval Feat Stone or *Maen Camp*, it weighs 101 pounds. Prior to the Service, as part of the village festival, local strong men try to lift the stone and throw it backyards over their heads. Traditionally this was part of the sports and general festivities that took place in the hamlet over several days. In the past the winner would act as the local authority, an arbiter of disputes in the village during the coming year. The custom was revived some twenty years ago, and these days, strong men come from further afield to test their strength. There are now also smaller stones that can be rolled out by children or thrown by those strong enough to do so. After the Patronal Service parishioners led by the Revd. Diana Greenfield, the Dyffryn Clwyd team priest, leads members around the church's circular site, then with hands held and arms linked, the clypping of the church ceremony commences.

STRAW JACK

Carshalton, Sutton, Surrey
2nd September 2017

Straw Jack is a 21st century semi-pagan harvest celebration born in 2004, it takes place annually at the beginning of September. The enormous Straw Jack, 10 metres tall, is led around the town's boundaries by two white bearded 1970s latter day hippies crowned in laurels and carrying their staffs of office. Conveniently, Carshalton has numerous hostelries en route as a retinue of musicians, dancers, fire-eaters, painted ladies and tree huggers follow behind Jack to the surprise and astonishment of the residents of this sleepy prosperous south London suburb. As the day turns to night, Jack is slowly dismantled, cremated on a brazier to the accompaniment of local folk musicians in garden of The Hope pub in West Street.

THE OPENING OF THE COLNE OYSTER FISHERY

Brightlingsea, Essex
3rd September 2021

The Opening takes place on the first Friday in September aboard the Thistle, a Thames Barge in the River Colne off Mersea Island. The tradition, in various forms, dates from 1540 and sees the Mayor of Colchester along with the Town Serjeant, various civic dignitaries and representatives of the Cinque Port Liberty of Brightlingsea, all in full regalia, witness the symbolic lifting of the first oysters of the season. The Deputy Chief Executive reads the ancient proclamation declaring the fisheries opened. A traditional glass of gin is raised; there is a loyal toast to Her Majesty The Queen, which is accompanied by eating slices of gingerbread, witnessed by invited guests, who all go on to enjoy a Richard Haward Oysters three-course luncheon. Fine wines are plentiful and Her Majesty is once again saluted before the party sails back to Brightlingsea. It is traditional that before the ceremony, a letter is sent to HM The Queen, which states: "According to ancient Custom and Charter dating back to Norman times, the mayor and councillors of the Colchester City Council will formally proclaim the Opening of the Colne Oyster Fishery for the coming season and will drink to your Majesty's long life and health and request respectfully to offer to your Majesty their expressions of dutiful loyalty and devotion."

ELECTION OF THE NEW PORTREEVE

Laugharne, Carmarthen
30th September 2019

The Laugharne Corporation's annual election of the new portreeve takes place on the first Monday following Michaelmas in the Big Court of the town hall. The Corporation was established in 1291 by Sir Guy de Brian, a Marcher Lord and is one of the last surviving medieval corporations in the United Kingdom. It is presided over by the portreeve, aldermen, and the body of burgesses. The Corporation used to hold a Court Leet half-yearly that dealt with criminal cases, and a Court Baron every fortnight, that attended to civil suits within the lordship, especially in matters related to property and the administration of the common fields. The Laugharne open field system is one of only two surviving that is still in use in Britain today. Upon election the most senior 76 burgesses receives a strang of land on Hugden for life. The strang was once part of mediaeval strip farming practised within the community. Nowadays the land is grazed. Court meetings are held every two weeks and concern the administration of the strictly controlled grazing on Hugden, as well as other parcels of land and property owned in the town. Originally the local magistrates' body, it now acts as a registered charity, whose aims are to further the good of the people of Laugharne and in particular their health, education and welfare.

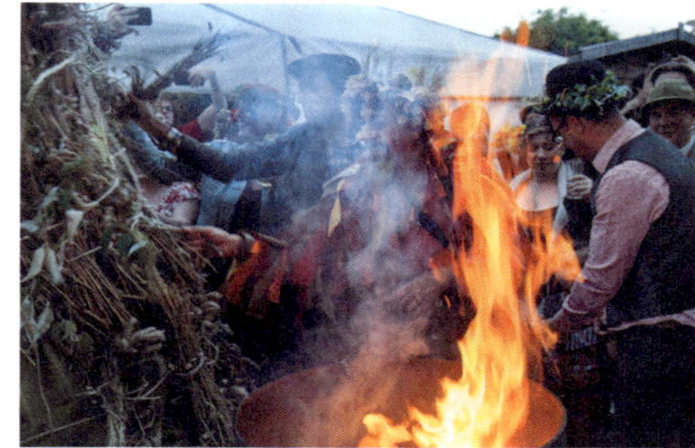

Straw Jack

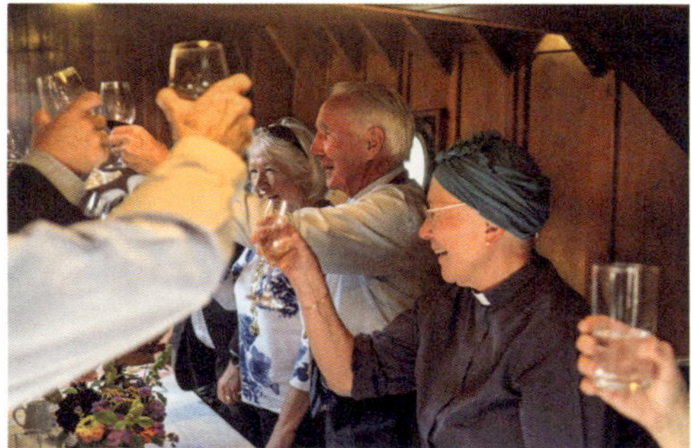

The Opening of the Colne Oyster Fishery

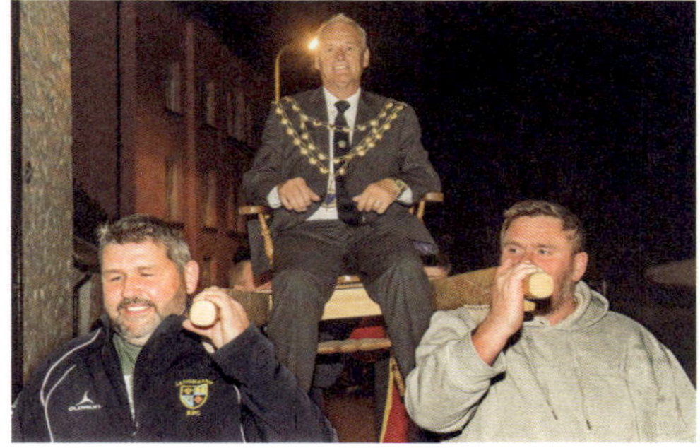

Election of the new Portreeve

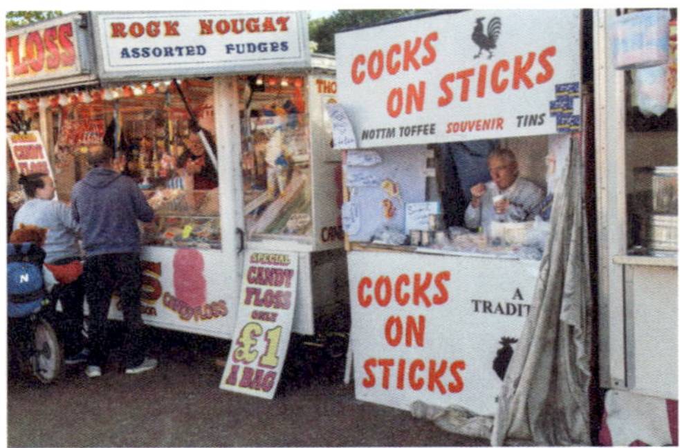

Cocks on Sticks

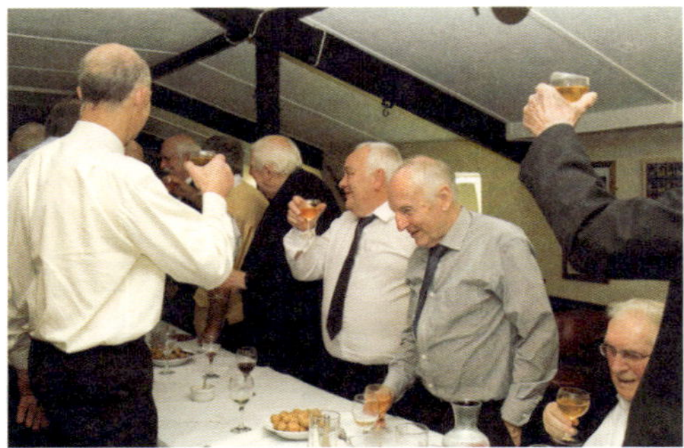
Court Leet

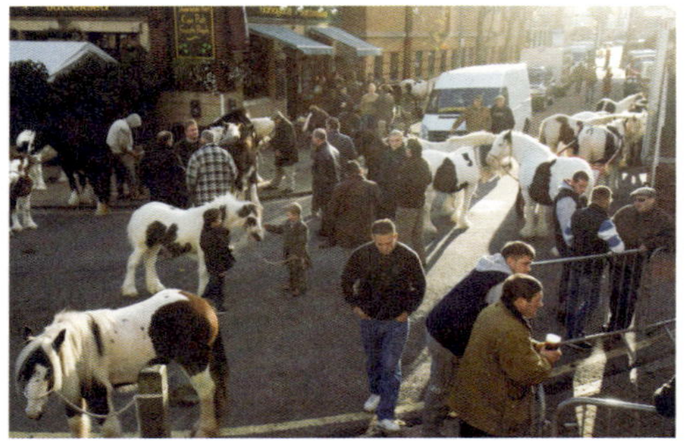
Back End Day

COCKS ON STICKS

Nottingham, Nottinghamshire
5th October 2017

87 year old Ray Brooks sits in his booth eating traditional mushy peas out of a polystyrene cup at the annual Nottingham Goose Fair, that can be traced back to a royal charter granted to Nottingham in 1284 by King Edwards I. Ray makes the handmade Cocks on Sticks, sweets that are unique to the Goose Fair. Whiteheads of Nottingham Ltd, founded by Ray's grandfather started the tradition in the 1890s. The company went into liquidation many years ago and Ray kept the tradition alive by making the sweets at home. Cocks on Sticks sell for £1.50 and £2.00 depending on size. The serpent reversed 'S' shaped sweets hang on the board-wall of his fairground booth. He waits for a few more customers before returning home and making more sweets for tomorrow's fair day. The fair takes its name from the huge number of geese that in the past were driven from the fens of East Anglia to Nottingham each year to be sold in the livestock market.

COURT LEET

Watchet, Somerset
30th October 2014

Watchet Court Leet meets annually on the last Thursday in October at the Bell Inn. First recorded in 1273 the court was originally responsible for administering law and order in the town. Today it is purely ceremonial. Jurors received a summons prepared by the court bailiff, bearing the Wyndham Family coat of arms, requiring that they attend at 12 noon to serve our sovereign lady the Queen and the lord of the said leet and frankpledge the Wyndham family. New jurors are sworn in, and officers of the court are appointed. Traditionally these have included along with the bailiff and deputy portreeve, ale tasters, inspectors of weights and measures, stock drivers, pig drivers, and scavengers, foreman of the jury, bellman and court constables. After the business of the day, a traditional goose dinner is provided for members of the court and local dignitaries. A loyal toast is drunk with a secret punch recipe served with bowls of walnuts.

BACK END DAY

Battersea, London
7th November 2010

London Cob Horse dealers met at least twice a year at the Flanagan Arms, an Irish pub in Battersea, that is opposite the old coal-fired power station. Once in the spring and finally in November, for their Back End Day sale, this was the last trading day of the year. A cob is traditionally a draft type pony. Typically of a stout build, with strong bones, large joints, and steady disposition, it is a body type of horse rather than a specific horse. Often used for everyday riding, they were in the past used for driving carts or pulling wagons – a typical working horse. Dealers sell, and then sell on. Of those horses not sold, many would have ended up in France at the boucheries chevalines, traditional horsemeat butcher shops. This informal gathering of cob horse dealers ceased around 2015, due partly because of the redevelopment of the area.

ACKNOWLEDGEMENTS

This fourth volume taken from My British Archive would not have been possible without the support of Caroline Warhurst and Dewi Lewis. Once again many many thanks.

Once a Year:
Some Traditional British Customs

My British Archive:
The Way We Were: 1968-1983

Colour Works:
The 1980s and 90s

An Annual Affair:
Some Traditional British Calendar Customs

An awful lot of background information and historical facts had to be looked up and checked. Checked with the participants, with contacts that I found through village websites and listing pages. Checked with Wikipedia, local newspapers and online blogs. *An Annual Affair* has been about 15 years in the making and, of course, to start with I had no idea that this project would form a substantial book. So inevitably, sadly I will have missed some people's names out of this acknowledgement who I made contact with very early on in this search for annual events. Some online sources too, will not have been credited. I am sorry.

Denise Andrew, Mike Andrews, David Barnard, Jennifer Batt, Sally Bell, Beth Bluck, Steven Burrows, Joanne Butler, Patricia Cantwell, Robert Clark, Trevor Collins, Tom & Gill Corbett, David and Maureen Crossman, Mayor Cllr Robert Davidson, Dorset Druid Grove, Andrew Edwards, Gwyn Evans, Edward and Alexandra Eyston, Stephen Facer, Jackie Featherstone, Paul Freeman, Janice and Andrew Gist, Keith Glenny, Tom Hanley, Geoff Hardwick, Charles & Marion Henshaw, Dr James Hyman, Maureen Jarvis, Ben Jones, David Jones, Brian & Christine Kell, Mike Kennett, Allen Kirkbridge, Sue Knigh, Colin P. Loader, Paul Marlow, Pete Marlow, Will Marlow, Paddie Marsh, Revd. Canon Charles Masheder, Councillor Mayor David Mote, Revd. Stephen Morris, Andrew Nethsingha, Revd. Susan Oldham, Sarah Oliver, Ross Parish, Bob Patten, Robin Peers, Melvyn Pett, Frank Pomroy, Malcolm Pratt, Jacqui Price, Sarah Rayfield, Steve Rathbone, Graham Richards, David Rivers, Don Rouse, Revd. Andrew Rycraft, Jayne Saunders, Paul Scoble, Dr Grant Scott, Averil & John Shepherd, Fr Bernard Sixtus, Humphrey Sladden, Robert & Alice Shields, Dr John & Ann Spencer, Katherine Spencer, Graham Strachan, Nigel Swinburne, Paul Taplin, Eddy Tennant, Edward Thompson, Jo Turner, Mike Turner, Bill Walker, Julie Watson, Amelia Ward, Albert Wilkins, Val Williams, Kenelm Edward Wingfield Digby, Jim Wheatley, Bill Whitfield.

SOURCES

Atherstone Ball Game Official, Bampton Archive, Calendar Customs, City of London Mercer Company, Corby Town, Drayton Village, Druid Network, Druids Order of Avebury, Earl of Rone, English Heritage, Nigel Fisher Brigg Blog, Folk Play Research, FolkWales Online Magazine, Fownhope Village, Friends of Saint David Lewis, Harting Parish Council, Long Sutton Parish, Liqui Search, Ministry of History, Open Sandwich Kent, Ortho Christianity, Pride Magazine Rutland, Religious Writings Padley Martyrs, Ripon Sword Dancers by Chas Marshall, St John's College University of Cambridge, St. Neot Church, Traditional Drama Research Group, You Tube, Wales Online, West Somerset Free Press, Worshipful Company of Butchers, Wikipedia, Richard Willcock, Upper Eden History Society, Writers Inspire.

A Church Near You, A Collection of Old English Customs: And Curious Bequests and Charities, John Bowyer Nichols and Son, London, U.K., 1842

I*n Search of Holy Wells and Healing Springs*, Pixyled Publications

In Search of Traditional Customs and Ceremonies, Pixyled Publications

The Hooden Horse of East Kent, Ozaru Books

Homer Sykes and Dewi Lewis would like to thank the following for their help in enabling this book to be published.

Adam Fallows
Aidan Brockel
Alan Gignoux
Alex Burt
Alexandra Hubbard
Allan Leonard Harris
Allyce Hibbert
Alvaro Soriano Pastor
Andrew Duke
Andrew Knightly Brown
Andrew Spackman
Andrew Summersgill
Andy Murfitt
Annabel Stacey
Averil Shepherd
Ben Jones
Berris Conolly
Bill Brooks
Bob Frith
Bob Pegg
Brenda Croskery Longlands
Brian Harris
Callum Gray
Carlo Chinca
Carrie Hoggan
Catherine Scrivener
Chengwang Liu
Cheryl
Chloe Davey
Chris Jepson
Chris Mammone
Chris Rodmell
Christophe Le Toquin
Colin Wilkinson
Conrad Birch
Dafydd Jones
Dan Germain
Dan Shiel
Dario Mitidieri
David Foy
David Lumb
David Oliver
David Sladek
David Suff
David Thornton
Dennis Oakley
Derek Medhurst
Doc Rowe
Donata Rogozik
Dr Claus Ramthun
Edmund Slater
Elizabeth Bluck
Elizabeth Orcutt
Emma Kate Spencer
Emma Thimbleby
Eric Fennesseey
Erica Toogood
Erik Kenward
Ethel Wolvovitz
Foraboschi Gianni
Fosse Meadows
Frederika Adam
Gareth Jones
Geoff Burton
Geoff Howard
George Bennett
Gerallt Pennant
Gerry Grimstone
Graham Wilson
Hana Bassett
Harry Steer
Heather Blackburn
Hugh Miller
Ian ED Cater
Isaiah Whisner
Jackie Slater
Jacky Chapman
James Dale
James TD Smith
Jamie Giles
Jarvis Cocker
Jess Moore
Jessica Hall
Jill Brown
JJ Waller
Joanna Walker
John Cole
John McMahon
John Mitchinson
John Myers
John Wilson
Jonathan Davies
Jonathan Dayman
Jonathan Reynolds
Josh Allen
Juanita Spooner
Karen Knorr
Kate Cheng
Kate Schermerhorn
Keith Harris
Knight of Words
Lally MacBeth
Leigh Cranston
Lindsey Stewart
Liz Thompson
Lloyd Jenkins
Lucy Wood
Lyndon Fright
Marcus Lyon
Mark Duncan
Mark Joyce
Mark Lewis
Martin Beddall
Martin Stein
Mary-Alice
Matt Staggs
Max Gowar
Michael Paley
Michal Kosakowski
Mick Taylor
Mick Williamson
Moira Bracknall
Niall Barton
Nicholas Mackey
Nick Bowman
Nick Foot
Nigel Dickinson
Norina Weiler
Omar El-Khairy
Owen Tromans
Pace Willisson
Pascale Spall
Pat Ashe
Patricia Baker-Cassidy
Patrick Carragher
Patrick Daniel
Paul A Murphy
Paul Edison
Paul Hibbard
Paul Holman
Pete Richardson
Peter Dench
Phil Robinson
Philippe Achache
Phoebe Kaniewska
Rachel Adams
Rachel Challoner
Ray Mcneill
Rhys Cuff
Richard Angliss
Richard Bradley
Richard Derwent
Richard Pearson
Robert Cloke
Robert Kirkup
Robert Phillips
Robert Wells
Roy Vickery
Sally Fear
Scott Saxon
Shannon Leigh Broughton-Smith
Simon Costin
Simon Robinson
Simon Roth
Simon Tasker
Simon Unwin
Stacey Baumgarn
Stephen Leslie
Stephen Miller
Steve Colgan
Stewart Weir
Stuart Emmerson
Stuart Moller
Tash Daly
The Creative Fund by BackerKit
Theo Sykes
Tim Chipping
Tim Johnson
Tim Sandle
Todd Specht
Todd Gage
Zoe Strachan